T0340340

INSIDER COMPUTER FRAUD

AN IN-DEPTH FRAMEWORK FOR DETECTING AND DEFENDING AGAINST INSIDER IT ATTACKS

INSIDER COMPUTER FRAUD

AN IN-DEPTH FRAMEWORK
FOR DETECTING AND DEFENDING
AGAINST INSIDER IT ATTACKS

Kenneth C. Brancik

CRC Press
Taylor & Francis Group
Boca Raton London New York

CRC Press is an imprint of the
Taylor & Francis Group, an **informa** business

The fundamental research and writing of this book preceded my employment at VerizonBusiness. The opinions, analysis, and writings are my own and were based on my computer science research as a former Doctoral student at Pace University, New York.

CRC Press
Taylor & Francis Group
6000 Broken Sound Parkway NW, Suite 300
Boca Raton, FL 33487-2742

First issued in paperback 2019

© 2008 by Taylor & Francis Group, LLC
CRC Press is an imprint of Taylor & Francis Group, an Informa business

No claim to original U.S. Government works

ISBN-13: 978-1-4200-4659-5 (hbk)
ISBN-13: 978-0-367-38806-5 (pbk)

This book contains information obtained from authentic and highly regarded sources. Reasonable efforts have been made to publish reliable data and information, but the author and publisher cannot assume responsibility for the validity of all materials or the consequences of their use. The authors and publishers have attempted to trace the copyright holders of all material reproduced in this publication and apologize to copyright holders if permission to publish in this form has not been obtained. If any copyright material has not been acknowledged please write and let us know so we may rectify in any future reprint.

Except as permitted under U.S. Copyright Law, no part of this book may be reprinted, reproduced, transmitted, or utilized in any form by any electronic, mechanical, or other means, now known or hereafter invented, including photocopying, microfilming, and recording, or in any information storage or retrieval system, without written permission from the publishers.

For permission to photocopy or use material electronically from this work, please access www.copyright.com (http://www.copyright.com/) or contact the Copyright Clearance Center, Inc. (CCC), 222 Rosewood Drive, Danvers, MA 01923, 978-750-8400. CCC is a not-for-profit organization that provides licenses and registration for a variety of users. For organizations that have been granted a photocopy license by the CCC, a separate system of payment has been arranged.

Trademark Notice: Product or corporate names may be trademarks or registered trademarks, and are used only for identification and explanation without intent to infringe.

Library of Congress Cataloging-in-Publication Data

Brancik, Kenneth C.
    Insider computer fraud : an in-depth framework for detecting and defending against insider IT attacks / Kenneth Brancik.
        p. cm.
    Includes bibliographical references and index.
    ISBN 978-1-4200-4659-5 (alk. paper)
    1. Computer security . 2. Computer crimes. I. Title.

QA76.9.A25B725 2007
005.8--dc22   2007017696

Visit the Taylor & Francis Web site at
http://www.taylorandfrancis.com

and the CRC Press Web site at
http://www.crcpress.com

Dedication

This book is dedicated to my Mother, who took care of four young adults; when my Father passed away early in my life, she was suddenly forced to reenter the job market, while still providing her family the care and support we all needed during our growing years through adulthood. I owe my strong work ethic and dedication to my personal goals to her and the good example she has demonstrated over many years as a supportive parent.

Contents

Preface

The insider threat has for too long been overlooked by many organizations in conducting their risk assessments and threat analysis processes. The financial and reputation risks may be high for organizations who fall victim to nefarious activities of an insider involving current or former employees, contractors, or perhaps trusted clients who are afforded similar access rights to applications, systems, and data as an employee; and the cost of ignoring preventative security solutions could become comparatively even higher in the long-term.

Information security concerns do not typically evaporate over time, but rather can evolve from what appears to be an isolated problem, to a systemic risk that has enterprise-wide implications. The enterprise-wide information security risks can be created by both external and internal threats; however, the latter risk is typically overlooked by many organizations. In an organization, the absence of evaluating the risks posed by the insider threat can have a deleterious effect on the information security governance process and can cause many negative consequences, including an increased level of risk to operations, finance, reputation, and strategy.

The absence of an effective information security governance process may lend itself to increased regulatory oversight, particularly when the risk involves the need for ensuring the safeguarding of sensitive nonpublic private information (NPPI) data. The need to safeguard NPPI data from both internal and external threats is also the focus of numerous states imposing breach notification laws and the pending federal legislation (Data Accountability and Trust Act [DATA]), which will mandate customer breach notification involving unauthorized access to NPPI data.

All roads within *Insider Computer Fraud: An In-Depth Framework for Detecting and Defending against Insider IT Attacks* point to the importance of maintaining strong security controls first. Then, using completed comprehensive and integrated data flow diagrams, the transactions transmission and storage life cycle (critical path) will be traced. The critical path will show the transmission and ultimate storage of NPPI and critical core transaction data elements, which will be useful for determining the assigned control points throughout the critical path where access controls, data origination and input, processing, and output controls exist.

Kenneth C. Brancik, PhD, CISA, CISSP, ITIL

Key Features

The primary goal of this book is to introduce the reader to the topic and problem of insider computer fraud (ICF), and to suggest a practical framework or methodology that can be used by any private-sector organization or government agency for identifying, measuring, monitoring, and controlling the risks associated with the insider threat. This book is not intended to offer a prescriptive process that requires a series of steps, which absolutely must be performed in order to benefit from any one step or process that is discussed in the ICF framework. The layers within the "Defense in Depth Model" used to mitigate ICF risks will be management's decision based on the results of their risk and privacy assessment; threat modeling; and decision to accept, transfer, or mitigate that risk. This book is not intended to provide exhaustive controls assessment for applications, systems, or any separate component of the information technology (IT) infrastructure of an organization. However, a horizontal analysis of application and system related risks is provided, and the interrelationships between an application and the IT infrastructure components it uses to transmit, process, and store the data will be demonstrated.

The book is process driven, to help in understanding both management and technical controls and how the two operating in concert have a positive synergistic impact in reducing ICF activity as well as reducing the risks over external threats. Although the primary thrust of the book focuses on the insider threat, many of the risks and controls apply equally to both internal and external threats in varying degrees. There is a symbiotic relationship that exists between the risks, controls, threats, and action plans that should be deployed to enhance overall information security governance processes.

The material presented will be beneficial to not only management, but the audit and compliance community as well. Where appropriate, the integrated risk assessment approach used to identify, measure, monitor, and control risks will aid auditors, compliance and privacy officers, regulatory examiners, and others who seek sound and best practices over the risk management process.

Based on the minimal amount of data available within the public domain on the insider threat and computer fraud, one of the primary goals of this book is to provide an orientation on an elusive topic for which the information is either not readily available or the data may lack the credibility to justify the development of a risk management strategy and action plans. The mitigation and prevention of financial losses associated with the insider threat can be mitigated or, hopefully, prevented if management deploys the appropriate safeguards based almost exclusively on deploying the *Defense in Depth* concept, with its foundation based on logic, cost effectiveness, and management's appetite or tolerance for risk.

The reader of this book will gain a familiarity with the following concepts that are all related to understanding the risks and controls surrounding ICF activity:

- *Strategic Planning Process*: The Insider Threat Strategic Planning Process is discussed in detail.
- *Risk Governance Process*: How an effective risk governance process for identifying ICF activity should be implemented is discussed.
- *Risk Categorization and Assessment*: The differences and similarities in determining inherent, residual, and net residual risk and how to integrate the threat assessment process into the risk assessment process are presented.
- *Risk and Threat Assessment Processes*: The interrelationship between the risk assessment and the threat assessment processes is covered.
- *The Defense in Depth Model and Security Efficiency Calculation*: Using Bayes' Theorem, the efficiency and effectiveness of each layer of protection in the Defense in Depth Model are quantified to assist management in their information security (InfoSec) strategic planning and risk reduction processes for both internal and external threats.
- *Application Security*: Industry sound and best practices are discussed in context with interrelated risks found within other IT infrastructure components and software (optimizers).
- *Penetration Testing*: Penetration testing criteria for Web-based applications, which could leave those applications vulnerable to both internal and external threats, are addressed.
- *Web Services Security*: Web services and supporting applications introduce security risks for internal and external threats. The knowledgeable insider can have greater access to and internal knowledge of the Service Oriented Architecture of an enterprise, which supports the use of Web services and the development activities of the applications and systems used to transmit data and messaging, leaving those applications and systems with an increased vulnerability.
- *Insider Computer Fraud Identification*: The importance of using various diagnostic tools for assessing ICF misuse detection using key risk indicators is discussed in detail. The key risk indicators include key fraud indicators (KFIs), key fraud metrics (KFMs), and key fraud signatures (KFSs), based on performing macro and micro taxonomies of a critical application.

■ *Control Point Identification and Forensic Foto Frames*: Based on the critical path of nonpublic private information (NPPI) and core data elements of transaction data of critical applications, control points (access controls, data origination and input, processing, and output) can be identified, measured, monitored, and controlled through data capture activity and other means. The data capture activity will be performed through the execution of the Forensic Foto Frame process that will collect key data by taking a "snapshot" of that data at stated control points. The snapshot of the data will be collected by the continuous Forensic Foto Frame process, and over time it will provide the necessary data to conduct an analysis of the normalcy of the captured data's behavior. The primary goal of the Forensic Foto Frame process is the profiling of the data versus the initial profiling of the behavioral characteristics of the insider. The behavioral characteristics or data profiling process will take the absolute values of each Forensic Foto Frame captured and begin the process of analyzing data normalcy in the context of a given set of variables. The variables may include but not be limited to the name of the insider who executed the transaction or processed the data. The metadata will also be analyzed for normalcy based on its description of various characteristics about the data, such as the time of day that the data was entered into the system and other relevant information. The data analysis can then assess the behavior of the captured data and metadata for negative patterns or trends (such as spikes) in absolute value changes and conclude on suspected insider misuse detection.

■ *Application Journaling*: The importance of application and IT infrastructure journaling is addressed in terms of its importance in the detection of ICF activity, the collection of computer forensics evidentiary data and metadata for event correlation purposes, root cause analysis, and strengthening the software engineering processes to "Bake" InfoSec journaling criteria and requirements within the software engineering and application development life cycle. In general, journaling is an important component of the eDiscovery process, which became law at the end of 2006.

■ *Privacy*: The increasing emphasis on regulatory compliance through the Sarbanes–Oxley Act, section 404 (SOX 404), Gramm–Leach–Bliley Act (GLB), Health Insurance Portability and Accountability Act (HIPAA), and other legislation and guidance have placed growing attention on ensuring the confidentiality, integrity, and availability of NPPI and core transaction data. A discussion of the importance of performing a privacy impact assessment, and data flow diagramming the critical path of NPPI and core transaction data between critical systems internally and externally is also examined.

■ *ICF Anomaly Detection*: The use of emerging technology through artificial intelligence, such as a novelty neural network that learns through neural associative memory (NAM), which can profile the behavior of data and metadata to flag anomalies in the behavior of data, which is instrumental in determining day zero insider threats involving data and metadata manipulation, is explored.

- *Information Security Pattern Analysis*: The use of security patterns has been gaining some level of traction in recent years. A discussion on how the use of these security software design and procedural patterns may assist in the identification and resolution of enterprise-wide high-risk threats is presented. The pattern development and analysis will be partly based on management's clear problem definition, context identification, forces determined, and finally a viable solution that can be used to mitigate both insider and external security threats.

Unfortunately, the insider threat topic, even though it is significant in terms of its impact on an organization's operational, financial, and reputation risk areas, has not yet reached critical mass in terms the public's awareness of insider risks and mitigating controls. Although there may be varying degrees of research into the insider threat problem, the absence of a large volume of credible writing on this topic and the general absence of a significant number of solution providers who offer a means for identifying, measuring, monitoring, and controlling risks associated with the insider threat remains a concern.

My goal in writing this book was to increase the awareness and importance of understanding the associated risks and controls involving the insider threat. By writing this book, I am confident that the volume of credible research and security solutions will occur in the near future and will incite an increased level of research, funding, and solution development activities. This book, together with other research available in the public domain, may serve as a stimulus for creating both public- and private-sector partnerships between corporations and state, local, and federal governments and the academic community. The INFOSEC Research Council (IRC) in their 2005 Hard Problems lists ranks the insider threat problem as number two, which I am hoping will spur an increased level of academic and professional research into this area. In 2007, I have observed a significant increase in interest for the topic of the insider threat. This year, I have been involved two workshops on the insider threat problem. The workshop participants include both the public and private sectors, along with academia involvement.

Organization of the Book

The following chapter summaries provide abstracts for each of the chapters within this book to allow the reader to focus on key chapters; however, it is highly recommended that the chapters be read in sequence, because the structure of the book is designed such that each chapter serves as a building block to each of the subsequent chapters in the book.

Chapter 1: Insider Computer Fraud

This introductory chapter provides an overview of insider computer fraud (ICF) and discusses the interrelationships between various chapters and related content contained throughout the book. There is discussion regarding the importance of developing and maintaining a robust risk assessment methodology, which serves as the prerequisite bedrock needed for developing *Insider Computer Fraud: An In-Depth Framework for Detecting and Defending against Insider IT Attacks*. The chapter provides a high-level synopsis of key chapters within the book which relates to and has a connection with an integrated risk assessment process. The Defense in Depth concept is a vital component within this book in context to its relevance and importance to other related topics discussed throughout the book.

Chapter 2: Related Research in Insider Computer Fraud and Information Security Controls

This chapter provides a high-level survey of key research and writing conducted on the topic of the insider threat. One of the more significant contributions to bringing increased attention to the insider threat was achieved in the Insider Threat Study prepared by the U.S. Secret Service and Carnegie Mellon's Software Engineering Institute. A previously unpublished article by Thomas Kellerman also provides insight into the insider threat problem and discusses authentication, privileges, physical security issues, and various warning signs.

Chapter 3: The Insider Threat Strategic Planning Process

This chapter provides a comprehensive review on a number of different areas related to the insider threat. The topic of strategic planning is broken down into a number of different processes and practices, which are woven together within this extensive chapter. The content provides the foundational knowledge needed to understand and apply the concepts presented within all the subsequent chapters. The sections of this chapter include, but are not limited to the following key areas: defining security objectives; understanding the security governance and risk management governance processes; the tailored risk integrated process (TRIP); application criticality determination and security; qualitative and quantitative risk ratings; inherent, residual, and net residual risk ratings; threat modeling; the Risk Assessment Heatmap and InfoSec Scorecard; industry sound and best security practices; data privacy legislation and the privacy impact assessment; data flow diagramming and determining the critical path of data; control point determination and key risk indicators (KRI); the Defense in Depth Efficiency Calculation; the strategic planning process for the insider threat; the Web-based application penetration testing process; utilizing software security design and procedural patterns for problem identification and solutions; determining the strategic, legal, and operational risk assessment; and developing strategies for implementing software engineering InfoSec process and product improvements.

Chapter 4: Information Technology Architecture and Insider Computer Fraud Prevention

This chapter focuses on the importance of a Risk-Based Information Technology Architecture for Threat Mitigation. An introduction to the components of a typical information technology infrastructure is also presented. Specifically, a high-level introductory discussion of typical IT infrastructure components include firewalls, packet filters, application gateways, routers, hosts, servers, PC workstations, and intrusion detection systems. The Zachman Architectural Framework is discussed in the context of preventing and detecting insider computer fraud activities. Also provided is an introduction to the types of systems and architectural designs for information processing, which includes Service Oriented Architecture (SOA) and Centralized Processing and Distributive Systems Architecture including Client–Server Architecture. Particular emphasis is placed on SOA, given its significance to illustrating how the Forensic Foto Frame concept works for ICF detection.

Chapter 5: Protection of Web Sites from Insider Abuse and the IT Infrastructure

This chapter describes insider attacks and the importance of developing an ICF taxonomy identifying the types of attacks that may exist. Based on the completed taxonomy, management can determine which category of attack would be most relevant to a particular organization. Also discussed are intrusion detection systems, vulnerability assessments, and other network testing. A comprehensive overview identifies the strengths and weaknesses of network intrusion detection systems (NIDS) and host-based intrusion detection systems (HIDS). A detailed discussion of the penetration testing process is provided. This chapter continues the discussion of firewalls and gateways introduced in Chapter 4, given their significant role in protecting Web sites from insider abuse.

Chapter 6: Web Services Security and Control Considerations for Reducing Transaction Risks

The goal of this chapter is to introduce the importance of Web services in conducting electronic commerce and its use internally within organizations as a means of facilitating interoperability between different applications, systems, and platforms. The chapter was included in this book because of the evolving and maturing nature of security risks and controls that could lead to heightened security risks for an enterprise. Specifically, a trusted insider who presumably has the greatest access to enterprise applications beyond the firewall in an organization, coupled with the greater potential to understand inside information about organizations and the IT infrastructure and business, could make Web services a prime target for potential insider abuse.

The chapter extends the discussion of the importance of architecture, particularly as it relates to SOA, as graphically illustrated in Chapter 4. The topic of Web services is featured in context of its growing importance and use within the financial services sector, major groups involved in establishing standards, current uses of Web services, and industry concerns relative to the surrounding security risks and controls. Security controls used within Web services and some of the problems associated with their use are also highlighted.

Chapter 7: Application Security and Methods for Reducing ICF

The discussion of application security in this chapter is significant. Overall, there is only a minimal amount of guidance in the marketplace for industry and government sound and best practices over application security. The current state of application security and the prevention and detection of the insider threat are provided. Application security is presented in the context of the Insider Threat Study that was introduced in Chapter 2.

In this chapter, a few of the key concepts discussed in Chapter 3 are reinforced. The importance of software engineering processing in ensuring application security is considered throughout the software development life cycle. The Threat Assessment Matrix and companion Threat Assessment Rating Reference Table that were developed in Chapter 3 can now be used to complete the insider computer fraud threat assessment (ICFTA), which is used for evaluating the level of net residual risk. Included within this chapter is a table that can be used to determine what application journaling could be captured and used for computer forensics purposes in providing some type of trace-back mechanism to determine the root cause of the insider threat. Finally, developing application-specific acceptable and unacceptable use policies are discussed with regard to their importance in preventing ICF activities.

Chapter 8: Insider Computer Fraud Taxonomy and the Art of the Key Fraud Indicator (KFI) Selection Process

The content of this chapter is significant because it introduces the concept of the KFI, which is really the nucleus of insider computer fraud identification and detection. The nexus between software vulnerabilities, application security, taxonomy, and insider computer fraud is explored. The trusted insider may have access to the source code of various programs used within an organization, which may introduce a point of risk. Application security and ICF are also addressed. For the first time in this book and discussed in detail are the problems surrounding the lack of secure authentication and access control features within applications and overreliance on the potential for organizations to place an overreliance on client-side validation.

Understanding the source of security problems is a fundamental first step toward achieving a viable solution, whether it involves insider computer fraud or other problems. As such, one of the primary goals of this chapter is to reinforce the importance of understanding the concept of ontology, which in the world of computer science is a data model that represents a domain and is used to reason about objects in that domain and the relationships between them. There is an obvious interrelationship between the results from performing an ontology and a taxonomy. The taxonomy, which classifies various components into various categories, aids in determining a KFI.

Upon completion of the ontology, taxonomy (macro and micro), the concept of *Forensic Foto Frame*, is introduced, which is a term used to symbolize a point within an organization's architecture where data are being collected at a defined control point (that is, access control, data origination or input, processing, and output). The Forensic Foto Frame takes a snapshot of the real-time data during transmission of the data and metadata within an application or system or in the transmission of data to another application. This chapter builds upon the topics discussed in previous chapters, most notably in Chapter 3, which discusses the topics of control point identification, KFI, and identifying and tracking the critical path of the transmission of data both internally within an enterprise and externally.

Chapter 9: Key Fraud Signature (KFS) Selection Process for Detecting ICF

One of the primary goals of this chapter is to inculcate the knowledge gained from previous chapters. A new concept of KFS builds upon the concepts discussed throughout the book, particularly as it relates to KFI, key fraud metrics (KFM), and finally the development of a KFS. The KFS is analogous to the intrusion detection system (IDS) signature that is commonly used within IDS for known network intrusion detection systems (NIDSs) and host-based intrusion detection system (HIDS) attacks. The concept of KFS is significant, because over time through system journaling of a KFI and perhaps other significant data elements, computer forensic analysis, the results of event correlation, and the results of the integrated risk assessment are important in understanding the threat vectors for known insider attacks.

The five phases of KFS selection are described, which include Phase I—Asset Risk Prioritization; Phase II—Data Criticality; Phase III—A Macro Taxonomy of ICF; Phase IV—A Micro Taxonomy of ICF; and Phase V—The Creation of Key Fraud Signature Association Rules (KFSAR). The concept of neural networks is introduced as a preview of what will be described in greater detail in Chapter 11. In the context of this chapter, there is a brief discussion on how the data collected and analyzed for developing a KFS can also be used for training and testing a neural network. The chapter continues into a discussion of KFSAR, which decomposes the topic down to its functional primitive state by describing the KFS format with associated examples.

In this chapter, a Data Definition Table is provided that presents realistic examples of how various data attributes (data and metadata) can be captured in a real-time manner using the concept of the *Forensic Foto Frame* given a particular business application (such as loans). A snapshot of one Forensic Foto Frame is used as an example to show the linkage between completing the ontology of information security concerns, the macro taxonomy of general categories of ICF, and the micro taxonomy of a business application (such as loans), showing each KFI that should be journaled, and finally how all this information can be used in developing a KFS.

Chapter 10: Application and System Journaling and the Software Engineering Process

This chapter discusses strategies for application and system journaling for the software engineering process using the SOA diagram, which was developed to illustrate how the Forensic Foto Frame can be used in capturing each KFI and other useful data, which might reflect the behavior of data within an application or transmission to other internal and external applications. Many of the data collection information that are being described in terms of the KFI and the development and analysis of each KFM and KFS may not necessarily be available within many internally developed applications or systems or commercially available third-party vendor software packages. Consequently, in order to collect the aforementioned information within applications and systems, the KFI will need to be identified and documented as described in detail in Chapters 8 and 9. Once the KFI selection process has been determined, the software development and engineering process needs to ensure that the journaling requirements are built into the applications and systems development. Consequently, if the journaling requirements for capturing KFIs are not identified within the business or user requirements and technical specifications phases of the software development life cycle (SDLC), the likelihood of that information being journaled is unlikely. Therefore, interrelationships exist between all phases of information security from the highest level of information security governance, the Defense in Depth Model and Efficiency Calculation, computer forensics, the KFI, KFM, and KFS, and finally to the software engineering process that emphasizes the importance of melding the journaling requirements of KFIs into an organization's SDLC processes.

Further described are various industry sound and best practices over journaling, which include but are not limited to the *National Industrial Security Program Operating Manual* (*NISPOM*). A cursory review is outlined for illustration purposes, the various components of an IT infrastructure that should include journaling and should be considered to better understand user activity. The illustrated IT infrastructure components included within the chapter to illustrate components that generate journaling activity, which could be captured and analyzed for ICF activity, involve Web servers, networks, the UNIX operating system, Windows NT, and mainframe computers using ACF2. Finally, a Journaling Risk/Controls Matrix for documenting KFI and KFM direct and indirect fraud scenarios is included. Direct risk scenarios are those situations where data and metadata elements can be directly attributed to fraud risks, versus indirect risks where monitoring the behavior of data is not indicative of potential ICF activity. Determining direct and indirect risk scenarios can only occur when the ICF framework has matured over time and when such distinctions can be made with some degree of accuracy.

Chapter 11: The Role of Neural Networks in the ICF Framework

This final chapter takes the next and last phase of the Defense in Depth Model, by moving beyond the misuse detection capabilities as provided and described in detail within the previous chapters. The last layer in the Defense in Depth Model involves considering the use of a neural network as potentially one layer in the Defense in Depth Model, to be used for anomaly detection. Until now, the discussion in the book has centered exclusively on identifying, measuring, monitoring, and controlling misuse detection involving trusted insiders, but it has not touched upon detecting day zero attacks or anomaly detection. The use of KFS is principally rule-based, and although the use of KFI is important, it has limited capability in detecting new ICF attack vectors perpetrated by the insider.

The use of neural networks for the purpose of fraud detection is relatively new and certainly not pervasive within the industry; however, its importance cannot be understated, and its benefits could someday be substantial, even though its use in the marketplace has not yet hit critical mass for fraud detection. The purpose of this chapter is to explore the possibilities and potential benefits for future use of neural network technology or some other type of artificial intelligence to explore methods and means of determining the holy grail of fraud detection, which is predicting the event in real-time or perhaps preventing the attack based on continuous monitoring of the behavior of data.

The basics of neural networks are discussed in terms of designing the neural network, learning the laws, supervised training, unsupervised training, neural associative memory, memory creation, the role of neurons, and the novelty neural network. The discussion of novelty detection is significant because abnormal or nonrandom behaviors are identified, and are the bedrock for ICF anomaly detection.

About the Author

Kenneth C. Brancik is considered one of the foremost thought leaders in INFOSEC, with more than a quarter of a century of IT and INFOSEC related work experience and advanced education. Dr. Brancik is a former federal bank regulator and for almost 15 years of his career he served as a corporate IT audit manager and consultant for some of the largest and most complex financial services and information security consulting firms in the world. He is a highly sought after speaker and consultant based on his many years serving both the public and private sectors.

Dr. Brancik earned his doctorate degree in computer science from Pace University in 2005, where he conducted the majority of his research and writing on this topic. He earned his master's from New York University and has received technical education from Columbia University in the analysis and design of information systems.

The opinions shared within his book are exclusively his.

Acknowledgments

I would like to thank the reviewers of the chapters in this book. The contents of this book have benefited greatly from their valued insights, comments, and suggestions.

Finally, I wish to thank the editor, Raymond O'Connell, and the entire production team at Taylor & Francis/Auerbach Group, for their assistance and guidance in the successful completion of this book.

Chapter 1

Insider Computer Fraud (ICF)

1.1 Introduction

The primary goal of this book is to introduce the reader to the topic of insider computer fraud (ICF) and to describe this emerging problem in terms that can be easily understood from both an academic and a practitioner's perspective. A second major objective of this research is to empower the reader with a comprehensive background on many different interrelated topics which provides context to the ICF problem. The third major objective is not to prescribe a solution to the complex problem of ICF, but rather to provide a framework to address the detection of ICF from a risk mitigation perspective. There are no definitive methods in existence today that can prevent ICF activities. However, through the use and integration of the ICF Defense in Depth Model as described and illustrated throughout this book, conceptual strategies will be introduced that will outline risk mitigation strategies.

1.2 The Primary Accomplishments of This Book

Given the absence of any significant published research on this topic, by default, any contributions made in this area will likely one day be considered as seminal work. This book will significantly raise the bar for those in the academic and professional communities who wish to extend this research further to address the risk mitigation process and solution.

Listed below are the primary accomplishments of this book, listed by its contributions to the discussion of specific topics:

1. *The Insider Threat Strategic Planning Process*:
   a. The development of the tailored risk integrated process (TRIP) used for identifying business and technology risks.
   b. An approach for completing a privacy impact assessment (PIA).
   c. Application criticality.
   d. Qualitative and quantitative risk ratings.
   e. Residual and net residual risk (NRR).
   f. The Defense in Depth Security Efficiency Calculation.
   g. An integrated internal and external threat modeling process.
   h. Developing data flow diagramming and the determination of a key risk indicator (KRI), the critical path.
   i. Calculation of the Defense in Depth Efficiency Calculation to assess the effectiveness of layered security.
   j. The use of security patterns in identifying and resolving InfoSec problems.
2. *Enterprise Architecture*:
   a. A high level of understanding of the various information technology (IT) infrastructure components as an important layer in the Defense in Depth Security Model.
   b. The Zachman Architectural Framework and its contribution to the identification of InfoSec risks and controls.
   c. The identification of systems architectural designs for information processing.
3. *Protection of Web Sites from Insider Abuse and the IT Infrastructure*:
   a. A macro and micro ICF taxonomy.
   b. The strengths and weaknesses of intrusion detection systems (IDSs).
   c. The importance of the penetration testing process.
4. *Web Services and Control Considerations for Reducing Transaction Risks*:
   a. The use of Web services to facilitate interoperability between different applications, systems, and platforms, both internally and externally.
   b. The importance of the Security Oriented Architecture and how the ICF framework can be used to identify, measure, monitor, and control these risks.
   c. The status of Web service risks and controls.
5. *Application Security and Methods for Reducing ICF*:
   a. The current state of application security and the prevention and detection of the insider threat.
   b. The importance of the software engineer process for defining the journaling criteria.
   c. The importance of the ICF threat assessment (ICFTA) in computing net residual risk.

6. *ICF Taxonomy and the Art of a Key Fraud Indicator (KFI) Selection Process*:
   a. The importance in the identification of a KFI.
   b. The nexus between software vulnerabilities detection, application security, developing a taxonomy, and determination of ICF activity.
   c. The importance of developing an ontology and taxonomy for ICF identification and prevention.
   d. The use of a Forensic Foto Frame within a Service Oriented Architecture (SOA) for journaling purposes and root cause analysis.

7. *Key Fraud Signature (KFS)*:
   a. The importance of identifying a KFI, a key fraud metric (KFM), and a KFS when identifying and monitoring ICF activities.
   b. The five phases of KFS selection.
   c. The creation and use of the data definition table for capturing data and metadata using the Forensic Foto Frame process.

8. *Application and System Journaling and the Software Engineering Process*:
   a. Understanding the importance of journaling and developing strategies for the use of key journaling within the software engineering and development processes.
   b. The importance of identifying a KFI and baking the journaling requirements of this information within the software engineering process and the KFI interrelationships with the KFM and the development of a KFS.
   c. Industry sound and best practices over application and IT infrastructure journaling.

9. *The Role of Neural Networks in the ICF Framework*:
   a. The importance of using the Defense in Depth Model for layered security protection.
   b. How neural networks can potentially enhance and advance the ICF detection and prevention capabilities through the use of anomaly detection for day zero attacks.
   c. The importance in the future advancement of understanding the behavior of data.

1.3 An Overview of Insider Computer Fraud

1.3.1 Insider Defined

Based on my definition, an insider is anyone who has the same or similar access rights into a network, system, or application. Therefore, a trusted insider can be a current or former employee, a contractor, consultant, service provider, software vendor, and so on. This more general definition will require organizations to expand their risk assessment and threat analysis to include all parties under this definition.

1.3.2 Fundamental Elements of Computer Fraud

The basic criteria that must be met for computer fraud to be considered include the following:

- Knowingly access or otherwise use a computer.
- Use or access of a computer without authorization or exceeding authorization.
- Use or access of a computer with intent to commit a fraudulent or other criminal act.

An important federal law governing fraud and related activity in connection with computers is Title 18 U.S. Code, Section 1030. This law was originally enacted in 1986 and is known as the Computer Abuse Amendments Act of 1994. Section 1030 punishes any intentional, unauthorized access to a protected computer for the purpose of:

- Obtaining restricted data regarding national security.
- Obtaining confidential financial information.
- Using a computer that is intended for use by the U.S. government.
- Committing a fraud.
- Damaging or destroying information contained in the computer.

A protected computer under this section is one that has the following characteristics:

- Is used exclusively by a financial institution or the U.S. government.
- If use affects a computer used by a financial institution or the federal government.
- Is used in interstate or foreign commerce or communication.

Additional elements of computer fraud include unauthorized access (or exceeding one's authority), an intent to defraud, and obtaining anything of value, including money and software.

1.4   Insider Threat Concepts and Concerns

The insider threat is an elusive and complex problem. To reduce the problem to its functional primitive state and develop a workable methodology for risk reduction is a large undertaking; however, this book will provide the educational foundation to understand this issue and potential resolution. Although the ICF taxonomy indicates that there are many types of ICF, data input manipulation appears to be one of the most pervasive, based on my research. In addition to being pervasive, it is the fraud category that I believe has the greatest potential for risk identification and mitigation.

There are two schools of thought in evaluating and analyzing ICF activities, including an evaluation of profiling the behavioral aspects of the insider, based on some type of empirical study, and the evaluation of what motivates people to do certain things given a set of variables (that is, actions based on a set of facts and circumstances). Ostensibly, in the first method of evaluating the insider threat, people and their behavioral characteristics and subsequent nefarious actions are profiled.

The second precept of the evaluation of the insider threat is largely predicated upon profiling data versus people, based on the previously described behavioral traits and circumstances. My research was predicated exclusively on profiling the behavior of data versus people, largely because it was a unique approach to addressing the ICF problem that has not been evaluated or analyzed in substance by anyone, at least in an academic research setting. Equally as important, I wanted to eliminate the objectivity of having to make judgments about people and what motivates them to act or react in a certain way based on a given set of circumstances. In brief, there seemed to be too many variables that I just could not control or feel comfortable in evaluating.

To validate my hypothesis that the insider threat can be identified, measured, monitored, and controlled, I needed to deploy a framework that was predicated upon the Defense in Depth Model concept. This model evaluates the insider threat from a holistic manner compared to a customized micro approach, which would assess risk based on a specific modus operandi, which details the specifics on how an insider computer fraud was perpetrated. The concept of layered security has to start from a robust InfoSec risk assessment process that includes a comprehensive threat assessment, which then surgically adds or removes additional layers of protection to an IT infrastructure, depending on the unique risk profile and culture of that organization. The concept of risk acceptance is very important in my framework, because of the potential for a high overhead for implementing the framework in the long term. Although the framework is extensible and scalable regardless of size or sophistication or complexity of the organization, you do not want to use a 100-pound hammer to nail a single nail. But again, the risk assessment process needs to evaluate the criticality of systems and data and the organization's culture and appetite for risk.

At the risk of oversimplifying my framework, I will introduce a number of concepts or tools that were integrated within the framework that can be used for identifying ICF relative to data manipulation:

1. Application of the risk assessment process.
2. Deployment of the Defense in Depth concept within the Enterprise Architecture.
3. Focus on application security, which is most vulnerable to the insider threat.
4. Consideration of application and system data and metadata journaling requirements that will significantly increase in importance from a computer forensic

and event correlation perspective—note the importance of implementing "surgical" application and system journaling of data and metadata for misuse detection of known ICF vulnerabilities and exploits.

5. Evolution of the software development methodologies in existence today to ensure software security is "baked" into the software development life cycle (SDLC) in both structured software development and Agile programming.

6. Consideration of Web services and a SOA as the future of all "E" data transmissions or transactions both internally and externally over the next decade within the financial services sector and perhaps in other sectors; focus of hacking attacks (external and internal) likely to be on eXtensible Markup Language (XML) source code and EXtensible Business Reporting Language (XBRL) to manipulate data.

7. Need for a macro and micro taxonomy of ICF activities in organizations so as to understand the types and probability of attacks impacting an industry or sector within the critical infrastructure and to identify KFIs, KFMs, and KFSs.

8. Growing role for artificial intelligence (AI) relative to risk governance and management processes for reducing ICF activities, particularly related to anomaly detection (day zero ICF activity). (My research in this area involved experimenting in training and testing a novelty neural network, which uses neural associative memory [NAM] similar to the way the human mind learns and functions. Although my experiment had mixed results from an academic perspective, it holds promise for increased success with additional research and testing to further this eventual science.)

1.5 Defense in Depth

The concept of defense in depth is a practical strategy for achieving information assurance. Presented in this section is a brief discussion of the concept of defense in depth in the context of malicious hacker activity and architectural solutions to either prevent or detect ICF activity (see Figure 1.1).

As defined by The World Bank's *Electronic Safety and Soundness* 2004 publication,

> Defense in Depth is a twofold approach to securing an information technology (IT) system: (1) layering security controls within a given IT asset and among assets, and (2) ensuring appropriate robustness of the solution as determined by the relative strength of the security controls and the confidence that the controls are implemented correctly, are effective in their application, and will perform as intended. This combination produces layers of technical and non-technical controls that ensures the confidentiality, integrity, and availability of the information and IT system resources.[1]

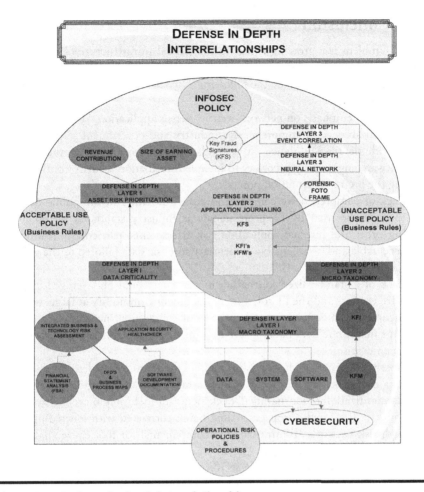

Figure 1.1   Defense in depth interrelationships.

In brief, the concept of defense in depth is important in that it represents a strategy that balances several factors involving protection capability and cost, performance, and operational considerations. It is a best practice strategy in that it relies on the intelligent application of techniques and technologies that exist today. Specifically, the strategy recommends a balance between the protection capability and cost, performance, and operational considerations.

One of the primary goals in the defense in depth concept is to prevent attacks against an enterprise's data and information systems. Threats to an enterprise's systems may originate from many different forms, which may include hackers, insiders, competition, and terrorists. Motivation by these groups and others may include intelligence gathering, theft of intellectual property, and identity theft; however, the primary focus of this discussion is on ICF activity, primarily centered on data input manipulation.

1.6 Conclusion

The ICF problem is a growing threat to the critical infrastructure of the United States, unless several fundamental root cause problems are addressed. The root cause problems for ICF include the following:

- Increased emphasis on network security versus application security.
- Overall absence of comprehensive industry and government standards that provide detailed guidance on methods and solutions for strengthening the software engineering processes to include information security controls during the preimplementation process.
- Lack of comprehensive computer forensic guidelines in the public domain that can be used by IT professionals as industry standards for conducting cyber and internal application risk assessments, particularly relating to acceptable and unacceptable evidentiary forensic data tailored to the specific insider E-crime.
- Lack of a standardized journaling format that could be leveraged by software vendors and the IT software development community at large, without incurring additional overhead and risk of conducting inconsistent and perhaps inaccurate data parsing activities for disparate applications throughout an enterprise.
- Absence of generic industry risk guidelines for defining and determining what data elements are typically at most risk for ICF and leveraging the eventual standardization of journaling data elements for inclusion in event correlation software (i.e., application journaling being correlated with journaling from high-risk network IT infrastructure components) for root cause analysis of potential ICF activities.
- Absence of public- and private-sector partnership for assessing processes and practices to encourage the development and implementation of emerging technologies for the detection and mitigation of ICF through the use of neural networks and other resources and technologies. (One of the specific goals and deliverables for such a partnership should be sanitized data that protect the anonymity of the parties involved in the crime, which could be used by the academic and professional IT community for conducting ICF research.)

Reference

1. Glaessner, Thomas C., Kellerman, Tom, and McNevin, Valerie. Electronic Safety and Soundness: Securing Finance in New Age (World Bank Working Papers). Washington, D.C.: The World Bank, 2004, pp. 159–160.

Chapter 2

Related Research in Insider Computer Fraud and Information Security Controls

2.1 Introduction

One of the most challenging aspects of researching and writing this book was obtaining well-researched and credible information on insider computer fraud (ICF) activities. More than 60 resources that I located as part of my research on this topic are noted at the end of this chapter; however, there were only a few academic dissertations or books that even remotely discuss actual solutions. This is an elusive topic. Many organizations might be reticent to speak about it due to reputation and other related concerns that may result in divulging the fact that a trusted insider was involved in perpetrating a fraud or some other financial, related crime. As such, there are only a handful of books that are dedicated to discussing insider threat as the broad category and even fewer, to my knowledge, that cover a subset of the topic, which involves perpetrating computer fraud through data input manipulation. Complicating matters further, obtaining any specific information from the government on closed insider fraud cases might be a challenge, given the Freedom of Information Act (FOIA) requests exemption status on many of these cases. Consequently, determining the specific modus operandi of how frauds were perpetrated was not obtainable.

As you will recall from Chapter 1, based on a taxonomy performed on ICF activities, several broad categories of potential insider fraud were identified, which include the following areas: manipulation of data input, billing schemes, data capture, errors, program altering schemes, check tampering, information privacy related fraud, and payroll schemes, to name a few. Outside of discussing the ICF taxonomy previously noted, none of the several other categories of fraud previously noted other than data input manipulation will be discussed in this book.

The selection of data input manipulation for discussion in this book was partly attributed to the pervasive nature of this type of crime based upon the cases I studied and the taxonomy I developed during this research. The selection of data input manipulation also mapped well into the driving concept behind this book, which primarily involves understanding the behavior of data which links closely with the risk assessment process and privacy impact analysis, performing macro and micro taxonomies of ICF threats in general and specific vulnerabilities within a particular application or system.

There are two schools of thought in understanding ICF activity. The first involves understanding the behavior of data; the second involves behavioral analysis of those involved in committing the ICF. The primary thrust of this book is to discuss how best to understand the behavior of data, which if performed correctly will lead to the insider who committed the fraud. Once the perpetrator is identified, then the behavior analysis would play a greater role in determining root cause and the identification process for isolating both internal and external information technology (IT) infrastructures or application or system weaknesses. Second, the use of behavioral analysis for determining the insider's motivation for committing the fraud can then be identified and analyzed so mitigating controls can be implemented.

A hybrid approach between the use of both approaches might entail analyzing the appropriateness of a user's behavior within an application or system and tracking negative patterns and practices that deviate from or violate an organization's acceptable use policy and other InfoSec policies, standards, and procedures.

No silver bullet exists to identify, measure, monitor, and control ICF activity, but introduced in this book is one approach that may have some value in reducing the risks associated with the insider threat. In reality and in the spirit of the Defense in Depth Model concept, layered protection might be the best strategy, through the effective implementation of both schools of thought. But again, for the purpose of this book's primary goal of identifying an ICF framework as one risk reduction strategy, the focus of discussion and presentation will be on analyzing the behavior of data. There are no claims being made within this book that analyzing the behavior of data is any more effective than performing a behavior analysis on the one who commits fraud. There are pros and cons in using both approaches, and their respective successes and failures is a good topic for further academic and professional research and writing; however, the focus of this book is almost exclusively on analyzing the behavior of data.

One of the goals of this book is to eventually create some science around ICF prevention and detection. The absence of solid credible data that is openly available in the public domain makes it challenging for researchers and information security professionals to advance the governance processes and practices within ICF. Perhaps one accomplishment of this book will be to encourage an increased level of public- and private-sector cooperation in the research and technological developments in this area. I would take great pleasure in seeing the maturity of my suggested ICF Framework extended to the maturity level of an ICF Model. The model would ideally include the testing of empirical data to simulate actual fraudulent activities, and the modus operandi of each known attack having a key fraud signature (KFS) assigned to the attack, and then the KFS data ported as a data flow into some event correlation engine for conducting an investigation, root cause analysis, and recommended solution.

2.2 Insider Threat Study: Illicit Cyber Activity in the Banking and Finance Sector

The most significant recent research conducted to date on the insider threat problem is captured within the joint report prepared by the U.S. Secret Service and Carnegie Mellon Software Engineering Institute.[1] In brief, the primary findings and implications of this research are as follows:

- Most incidents were not technically sophisticated or complex. They typically involved exploitation of nontechnical vulnerabilities such as business rules or organization policies (rather than vulnerabilities in an information system or network) by individuals who had little or no technical expertise.
- The majority of incidents were thought out and planned in advance. In most cases, others had knowledge of the insider's intentions, plans, or activities. Those who knew were often directly involved in the planning or stood to benefit from the activity.
- Most insiders were motivated by financial gain, rather than by a desire to harm the company or information system.
- A wide variety of individuals perpetrated insider incidents in the cases studied. Most of the insiders in the banking and finance sector did not hold a technical position within their organization, did not have a history of engaging in technical attacks or "hacking," and were not necessarily perceived as problem employees.

- Insider incidents were detected by a range of people (both internal to the organization and external), not just by security staff. Both manual and automated procedures played a role in detection.
- The impact of nearly all insider incidents in the banking and finance sector was financial loss for the victim organization. Many victim organizations incurred harm to multiple aspects of the organization.
- Most of the incidents were executed at the workplace during normal business hours.

2.3 A Framework for Understanding and Predicting Insider Attacks

An article written by E. Eugene Schultz in 2002 entitled, "A Framework for Understanding and Predicting Insider Attacks"[2] provides a high-level recap of what research has been conducted to date on this topic, albeit very limited. The term "Framework" in this title is somewhat a misnomer; however, a solid recap of efforts to date in addressing the ICF problem is provided. The highlights of this article state the following:

- An insider attack is considered to be a deliberate misuse by those who are authorized to use computers and networks. We know very little about insider attacks, and misconceptions concerning insider attacks abound.
- Considerations must be made when defining "insider attack":
  - Numerous definitions for the term "insider attack" have been proposed. Tugular and Spafford[2] assert that inside attackers are those who are able to use a given computer system with a level of authority granted to them and who in so doing violate their organization's security policy.
  - Insiders would usually be employees, contractors and consultants, temporary helpers, and even personnel from third-party business partners and their contractors, consultants, and so forth. It is becoming increasingly difficult to maintain a hard and fast distinction between insiders and outsiders.
  - Many "insider jobs" have turned out to be the result of complicity between an insider and an outsider.
- Myths and misconceptions include the following:
  - More attacks come from the inside than from anywhere else.
  - Insider attack patterns are generally similar to externally initiated attacks.
  - Responding to insider attacks is like responding to outside attacks.
- Tuglular and Spafford have proposed a little-known but nevertheless intriguing model of insider attacks. This model assumes that insider misuse is a

function of factors such as personal characteristics, motivation, knowledge, abilities, rights and obligations, authority and responsibility within the organization, and factors related to group support. The creators of this model have pointed out that insider attacks are more likely to occur under conditions such as breakdown of lines of authority within an organization.

■ Another model of perpetrators of computer crime and computer attacks is a psychodynamic-driven model by Shaw, Ruby, and Post. Based on research concerning the psychological makeup of convicted perpetrators of computer crime, Shaw et al. describe computer criminals in terms of traits such as introversion and depression. Unfortunately, however, Shaw et al.'s study focused exclusively on external attackers. This model is to some degree corroborated by a study conducted by psychologists at Political Psychology Associates Ltd., who discovered that the majority of insider abuse cases are linked to people who are introverted, poor at handling stress or conflict, and frustrated with work.

■ The 3DP (three-dimensional profiling) model is a criminological or profiling model developed by Gudatis. This model examines and applies the methodology of conventional criminal profiling to computer crime. Specifically, the model focuses on insider attacks and prescribes an organizationally based method for prevention. The utility of this model is twofold in that it allows for the assessment of an incident or attack using profiling in addition to the usual technical tools, and it provides organizations a way to evaluate and enhance their security processes and procedures from a human perspective as a preventative measure.

■ Research into insider attacks is, without question, in its infancy. The current state of the art does not, for all practical purposes, allow detection, let alone prediction, of insider attacks. Detection capability is desirable, but it is, unfortunately, post hoc in nature. Given the potential damage that can result from insider attacks, the state of the art for detecting insider attacks is not nearly as advanced as necessary to make a difference for most organizations. The most pressing need, therefore, is to develop the ability to predict insider attacks. If you can predict attacks or even impending attacks, we can intervene sooner and more effectively.

■ Einwechter proposed that a combination of intrusion detection systems (IDS)—network intrusion detection systems (NIDS), network node intrusion detection systems (NNIDS), host-based intrusion detection systems, and a distributed intrusion detection system (DIDS) be used to detect insider attacks. What Einwechter proposed is a giant step in the right direction because it attempts to capitalize on multiple indicators of insider attacks.

■ Collecting and analyzing data that is likely to yield multiple indicators are, in fact, the only viable directions given how subtle and different from conventional (external) attacks insider attack patterns often are.

■ Although IDS output can be useful in detecting insider attacks, relying on IDS output alone for insider attack detection is fundamentally risky. Second, as mentioned previously in this paper, many insider attacks are quite different from outsider attacks, and, as Einwechter concedes, today's IDSs are geared toward detecting externally initiated attacks. Again, heavy reliance on IDSs to detect insider attacks is unwise.

■ They indicate, for example, that many different potential indicators of internal attacks exist, and that no single indicator can normally provide conclusive indication of an insider attack. These potential indicators include the following:

- *Deliberate Markers*: As indicated in the previously cited study by Suler, attackers sometimes leave deliberate markers to make a "statement." Markers can vary in magnitude and obviousness. Finding the smaller, less obvious markers earlier—before the "big attack" occurs—should be a major goal of those faced with the task of detecting insider attacks.

- *Meaningful Errors*: Perpetrators, like anyone else, make mistakes in the process of preparing for and carrying out attacks. The perpetrator will then erase the relevant log files and the command history.

- *Preparatory Behavior*: The perpetrator may, for instance, attempt to gain as much information about the potential victim system as possible. The use of commands such as **ping**, **nslookup**, **finger**, **whois**, **rwho**, and others is only one of many potential types of preparatory behavior.

- *Correlated Usage Patterns*: Correlated usage patterns are patterns of computer usage that are consistent from one system to another. These patterns might not be noticeable on any one system, but the fact that they occur on multiple systems can reveal intention on the part of a potential perpetrator.

- *Verbal Behavior*: The previously cited works by Morahan-Martin and Collins showed how in the technical arena verbal behavior is linked to aggression, dominance, and other factors. Verbal behavior (either spoken or written) can, of course, also provide an indication that an attack is imminent.

- *Personality Traits*: In the previously cited study, Shaw et al. and others suggest that personality factors (particularly introversion) can be used in predicting insider attacks.

2.4 Methodology for the Optimization of Resources in the Detection of Computer Fraud

Although dated, a paper written by Thurman Stanley Dunn in 1982[3] offers a solid level of specificity in terms of the modus operandi that an insider fraudster could use to perpetrate a crime. The highlights of this paper are as follows:

■ There are surprisingly few common forms of computer fraud manipulation—in fact, just these three:
  • Input Transaction Manipulation Schemes
  • Unauthorized Program Modification Schemes
  • File Alteration and Substitution Schemes
■ **Input Transaction Manipulation Schemes**
  • *Extraneous Transactions*: Making up extra transactions and getting them processed by the system is a rather straightforward form of input manipulation. A perpetrator may either enter extraneous monetary transactions to benefit him- or herself, or he or she may enter file maintenance transactions that change the indicative data about a master file entity (customer, vendor, product, general ledger account, salesman, department, etc.) in some way that he or she will later exploit.
  • *Failure to Enter Transactions*: Perpetrators can obtain substantial benefits simply by failing to enter properly authorized transactions. One of the simplest examples involved action on the part of check-processing clerks who simply destroyed their own canceled checks before they were debited to their accounts. The same thing can happen in a customer billing system. File maintenance can also be excluded dishonestly with similar benefits.
  • *Modification of Transactions*: Fraudulent gains can be realized by altering the amount of a properly authorized monetary transaction. For example, a perpetrator may reduce the amount of charges against a particular account or increase payment into a particular account. Another scheme involves changing indicative data on file maintenance transactions. Examples are name, address, monthly closing date, account type and status, privileges, and so on. Because errors in indicative data are fairly common and controls over such transactions tend to be weak in many companies, this method is particularly promising to the perpetrator. The most insidious of all transaction modification methods involves "exploitation of blanket file maintenance transactions." More specifically, this is a transaction that instructs the system to change the corresponding master file data element for any and all corresponding fields filled out on the input form. (The best advice is to avoid the use of such transactions.)
  • *Misuse of Adjustment Transactions*: Misuse of adjustment transactions is a common ingredient in input manipulation schemes. Here the term "adjustment" refers to monetary corrections of past errors or inaccuracies that have come about in a system through physical loss or spoilage of materials. Often, perhaps out of concern to set things straight as quickly as possible, adjustment transactions are processed without adequate control. The result can be computer fraud of massive proportions.
  • *Misuse of Error—Correction Procedures*: Millions of dollars have been embezzled by perpetrators under the guise of error–corrections. Although

many of these abuses are special cases of previously mentioned methods of manipulating input, it is felt that error–corrections are often a problem and deserve special attention. Ways that perpetrators abuse error–correction procedures include entering extra error–corrections, failing to enter necessary corrections, and modifying properly authorized corrections.

■ **Unauthorized Program Modification Schemes**
  • *Difficulty in Detection*: Program modification schemes are the most insidious and difficult to detect. Even though the reported instances of such cases is fairly low, leading auditors and security consultants share a chilling view of reported statistics: reported incidence bears no relation to the actual enormity of the problem.
  • *Reasons for Enormity of Problem*: To explain this commonly held view, consider the following:
    ■ Some program modification schemes are untraceable.
    ■ All program modification schemes are difficult to detect.
    ■ Motivation for perpetrators is high because a single blitz can effect large benefits rapidly with little chance of detection or prosecution.
    ■ Larcenous strategies for modifying programs exist.
    ■ The siphoning off of small sums from numerous sources is commonly referred to as breakage. This method is particularly well suited to being implemented via program modification, because a few simple lines of code can bring about repeated theft of large amounts. Breakage can be employed whenever a computation is called for:
      • Computation of applicable service charge
      • Computation of discounts
      • Payroll withholding computations
      • Computation of retirement benefits
      • Computation of interest on savings
      • Computation of welfare, Medicare, social security, or unemployment benefits
    ■ In any of these situations, all the perpetrator has to do is instruct the computer to accumulate amounts resulting from rounding, and possibly small additional amounts, and to allocate the sum of all such amounts to a single account to which he or she has access. This activity will not be readily detected by systems controls because the total amount of money involved will agree with any predetermined control totals. The individuals involved are unlikely to notice a discrepancy in their accounts. Even if they do notice a discrepancy, they are unlikely to comment if the amounts involved are small.
  • *Undocumented Transaction Codes*: By programming the computer to accept undocumented types of transactions, perpetrators can arrange to receive substantial profits in a very short time. Once having made provisions for processing of the extra transaction type, there are several means to get the

necessary transactions into the system. The transactions may be computer generated, input by the programmer where controls (or lack of controls) allow it, input via the addition of an extra input file, and so forth.

- *Balance Manipulation*: Simple, undisguised balance manipulation is a method that involves assuming that processing results will not be properly reviewed. A dishonest programmer can modify appropriate programs so that all totals and balances appear to be correct for any given day. The work factor involved in modifying all programs involved is typically high, so the programmer will more often attack just one or two programs.

- *Deliberate Misreporting with Lapping*: A program that was manipulated to cause misreporting either fails to apply a charge to a perpetrator's account (the charge gets applied to another account) or credits a perpetrator's account with a payment (the account that should have been credited is not posted). Either way, certain problems are bound to arise. In the first case, complaints can be expected from those whose accounts now carry unauthorized charges. In the second case, complaints can be expected from those whose accounts were not credited. To avoid this process of deliberate misposting, correcting the deliberate misposting and creating another deliberate misposting called lapping is used to continue the fraud. All lapping schemes of any merit call for masterful time management and meticulous record keeping on the part of the perpetrator.

- *File Modification*: Altering programs to effect secret changes in account status is a fairly common programming technique for computer fraud. Examples of account status changes include opening an account for subsequent fraudulent manipulation in order to receive automatic payments (payroll, retirement, unemployment, welfare, etc.); destroying the record of a fraudulent account; inhibiting the printing of an account's past-due status; and increasing a credit limit on a credit account so that a greater charge will be authorized.

- *Fudging Control Totals*: This tactic is often combined with other programming schemes. The approach involves processing that occurs without being properly reflected in control totals.

■ **File Alteration and Substitution Schemes**
  - *Access to a Live Master File*: One fairly common form of fraudulent file alteration is to obtain "access to a live master file" and (using a program specially written for the purpose, a general retrieval program, or a utility) to make surreptitious changes to the file. Changes may include modification of monetary amounts or changes to other data.
  - *Substitution of a Dummied-Up Version for the Real File*: This scheme depends upon one of two possible sequences of events. In either case, the scheme begins with the perpetrator obtaining access to the master file, possibly under the guise of making a copy for use as test data. Then the file is run against a program, either in-house or at a service bureau. The program creates a similar

file, containing only a few modifications. The newly created file is then sub-
stituted for the live file and returned to the data library.

- *Access and Modification of Transaction Files Prior to Processing*: Possible
  fraudulent actions that may be involved in this type of scheme include
  addition, modification, and deletion of input transactions.

2.5 Managing the Insider Threat

According to Tom Kellerman, MA, CISM, and Vice President of Security Awareness at CoreSecurity[4]:

> Training and technology go together, hand in hand, to help prevent
> insider attacks. For example, if an employee is not properly trained and
> held accountable for password management their computer might eas-
> ily be broken into. First one must identify all of the authentication
> and business rules in order to make educated decisions per level of risk
> associated with the insider threat. Workflow rules grant people permis-
> sions only for what they are allowed access to within a system. Such
> role-based access controls with a workflow infrastructure will manage
> many of the risks associated with the Insider threat. Each user should
> only be granted access to data if the user has a valid need to know.

2.5.1 Authentication

The first step to thwarting the insider threat is to authenticate each user on his or
her physical characteristics rather than on something he or she knows. Biometrics
coupled with public key infrastructure establish the legitimacy of a node or user
before allowing access to requested information. During the process, the user enters
a name or account number (identification) and password (authentication). The first
line of defense is access control. Incorporate a multifactor authentication method
for sensitive internal or high-value systems. Biometric devices fulfill the nonrepudiation element of layered security by authenticating a user by his or her physical characteristics. Implementing biometric technologies virtually guarantees to a
system administrator that the person who initiates the communication or system
access is who he or she claims to be.

2.5.2 Privileges

Without proper security, desktops give insiders access to programs, files, and shares
they may not be authorized to access. This may result in a very costly insider attack.
Simply by securing the desktop against excessive privileges for each user type, many

insider attacks can be successfully mitigated. Furthermore, these privileges should be constantly checked, especially when human resources are restructured. Insider authentication "logging" provides an audit trail, which serves as a deterrent to attackers.

Although strong authentication and role-based access can be effective in identifying who the person is and what he or she can do, one fails to address the collusion issue. Take for example security team best practices. A typical practice is to rotate job functions and event log readings. That way no security team member can hide anything. Another practice is to send team members away on vacation without any connection to the bank. This way if anything unusual occurs, or if the member is trying to hide anything, it shows up while he or she is gone.

There must be a separation of authority within institutions per permissions and authorizations. In other words, permission and access are granted based upon a user's need to perform his or her job functions only, which adds another easily managed security access layer and allows for more accurate auditing.

2.5.3 Physical Security Issues

- Physical access to networked systems facilities made by employees, contract employees, vendors, and visitors should be restricted.
- Access to sensitive areas should be controlled by smart card or biometric authentication.
- Consoles or administrative workstations should not be placed near windows.
- Alarms to notify of suspicious intrusions into systems rooms and facilities should be periodically tested.
- The backgrounds of all employee candidates should be vetted. This is especially important for candidates requiring access to the most sensitive information and mission-critical systems.
- Rooms or areas containing mission-critical systems should be physically segregated from general work spaces, and entry to the former should be secured by access control systems.
- Employees should wear clearly visible, tamper-resistant access and identification badges, preferably color coded to signify levels, or extent, of their access to critical systems.
- All vendor default passwords should be changed.
- All unused ports should be turned off.
- All users must affirm that they are aware of policies on employee use of e-mail, Internet, Instant Messaging (IM), laptops, cellular phones, and remote access. Someone should be responsible for enforcing these policies.
- All servers should be placed in secured areas. Always make sure server keys are securely locked.
- Employees should consistently log off their accounts when they are absent from their workstations, and portable devices should be locked to workstations.

- All sensitive data stored on user hard drives must be encrypted.
- Technical documents and diagrams that contain sensitive information such as TCP/IP addresses, access control lists, and configuration settings should be stored in secure spaces.
- Passwords should never be issued over unsecured channels (for example, cell phones, IM, cordless phones, radios, etc.).

2.5.4 Warning Signs

Insider threats are never random and are always premeditated. Before an insider threat has materialized, certain patterns of behavior are evident. A few of these red flags include:

1. The existence of rogue access points can indicate a system menace. Remote users can either be an insider threat or provide an internal access point for an external adversary. Due to the explosion in wireless usage, chief information security officers (CISOs) and systems administrators need to be aware of all wireless access points and remote users. All remote user access should be managed through a centralized access point. Given the size of the bank network, it is evident that identifying all boxes on a network is oftentimes difficult. A tool exists that identifies all Windows boxes and what they are connected to (go to: http://winfingerprint.com). This tool is very useful when attempting to discern how many remote users are utilizing an institution's network.
2. Disgruntled employees whose morale, evidenced by either conversations or e-mails, has noticeably slipped in past days should be monitored.
3. A user accesses a database or area of the network they have never accessed before.
4. Download spikes are noticed—Is a user downloading more information than usual?

2.5.5 HTTP Tunneling

Due to security considerations taken by systems administrators, Hypertext Transfer Protocol (HTTP) has become the universal entry mechanism to the corporate network. Of grave concern to most CISOs, there is no practical way to prevent covert communications of an insider user to the outside world. One can minimize the risk of a rogue HTTP tunnel by monitoring everyone's activity 24/7, but this is still not a 100 percent guarantee.

To block HTTP tunneling, an organization needs to do the following:

1. Check access log statistics to identify the presence and endpoints of the tunnel. Typically this can be accomplished by looking for extended sessions and related data.
2. Implement an application-level proxy and block HTTP CONNECT.
3. Require outbound authentication on the firewall for http, https, and Secure Sockets Layer (SSL).

Unarguably the best method is to have a strong policy of use agreement with your users and take corrective action against policy violators with suitable penalties according to your policy.

An organization can attempt to block ports 22 and 3128 and then block any outbound HTTP connections to a short list of well-known secure proxy sites, such as http://Anonymizer.com.

Behavioral science can assist in mitigating the insider threat. All computer usage should be recorded and history logs retained for two months, including e-mails, IM, temporary files, and print jobs logs. Spyware, such as "keystroke loggers," should be utilized on a periodic basis and in specific audits. These audits should be merited only when a user exhibits suspicious behavior as defined in Section 2.5.4 ("Warning Signs"). To take it a step further, audits should be performed by an auditor outside of the target business unit at least, and, ideally, from an independent, third-party service. Third-party scrutiny of the system might discourage the perpetrator in the best case, or at least lead to discovery of the questionable activity.

Employee training, strong policy management, and enforcement of security policies are critical to help prevent insider attacks. A complete multilayered "Information Security Policy" must be in place against both outsider and insider attacks. This plan should correctly identify assets at risk and security items for all known scenarios and entry points, and have policies and plans in place to effectively prevent, monitor, audit, and enforce the tenets of the security policy. Personnel should be trained on the potential signs of social engineering, safe home computing, proper procedure for remote access, and proper storage and security of authentication mechanisms. Those who truly understand the psychology of their peers can only mitigate the insider threat; management of this threat is a truly dynamic process.

2.6 Conclusion

The highlights of this chapter included the following, based on the Insider Threat Study from the U.S. Secret Service and Carnegie Mellon Software Engineering Institute:

■ Most incidents were not technically sophisticated or complex.
■ The majority of the incidents were thought out and planned in advance.
■ Most insiders were motivated by financial gain.
■ A wide variety of individuals perpetrated insider incidents.

The highlights of the Eugene Schultz document entitled "A Framework for Understanding and Predicting Insider Attacks"[2] states the following:

■ An insider attack is a deliberate misuse by those who are authorized to use computers and networks.
■ "Insider jobs" have turned out to be the result of complicity between an insider and an outsider.
■ More attacks come from the inside than from anywhere else.

The Shaw, Ruby, and Post research indicates that computer criminals possess traits of introversion and depression.

A Krauss and Macgahan study on computer fraud manipulation indicated that there are three categories that include input transaction manipulation schemes, unauthorized program modification schemes, and file alteration and substitution schemes. This study has particular significance for this research, as it refers to the input transaction manipulation schemes that are the primary focus of all of the various insider computer fraud categories.

Tom Kellerman's work on *Managing the Insider Threat* discussed in detail the need for authentication, privileges, and physical security to thwart the insider threat. Kellerman detailed the warning signs for detecting the insider threat through the identification of several red flags. He also identified the risks associated with HTTP tunneling that could be used by an insider for covert communications. Also noted was that it becomes very difficult to discern how an insider might attack one's network from within the perimeter without conducting a comprehensive penetration test that mimics the insider attack vectors.

Additional Resources

Compiled in the list below are documents that may be of value in evaluating the insider threat and the adequacy of information security controls needed to reduce internal and external risks and controls. The resource listing order was organized randomly and is not based on significance. The following literature may be of assistance in further understanding the topic of the insider threat and computer fraud:

■ EMERALD: Event Monitoring Enabling Responses to Anomalous Live Disturbances (www.sdl.sri.com).
■ The Insider Threat to Information Systems by Eric D. Shaw, Keven G. Ruby, and Jerrold M. Post.
■ *Computers & Security*, 20(8), 715–723, 2001.
■ The Insider Threat by Terrance A. Roebuck (http://all.net/CID/Threat/papers/Insider.html).

- CERT Coordination Center—Intruder Detection Checklist (http://www. cert.org/tech_tips/intruder_detection_checklist.html).
- Manage Logging and Other Data Collection Mechanisms (http://www.cert. org/security-improvement/practices/p092.html).
- Ghost in the Machine: An Analysis of IT Fraud and Abuse. U.K. Audit Commission, London, February 1998.
- The Growing Security Threat: Your Employees. META Group, January 2004.
- Elsevier Advanced Technology *Computers & Security*, 21(1), 62–73, 2002.
- A Detection-Oriented Classification of Insider IT Misues by A.H. Phyo and S.M. Furnell. Network Research Group, School of Computing, Communications and Electronics, University of Plymouth, Drake Circus, Plymouth, U.K., 2004.
- A Framework for Understanding and Predicting Insider Attacks by E. Eugene Schultz, *Computers & Security*, 21(6), 526–531, 2002.
- Methodology for the Optimization of Resources in the Detection of Computer Fraud by Thurman Stanley Dunn. University Microfilms International (UMI) Doctoral Dissertation, 1982.
- A Guide to Building Secure Web Applications: Event Logging. OWASP (www.cgisecurity.com/owasp/html/plht).
- Computer Fraud: Analyzing Perpetrators and Methods by Harold E. Davis and Robert L. Braun. *The CPA Journal*.
- How to Systematically Classify Computer Security Intrusions by Ulf Lindqvist and Erland Jonsson. Chalmers University of Technology, Sweden, 1996.
- Synthesizing Test Data for Fraud Detection Systems by Emilie Landin Barse, Hakan Kvarnstrom, and Erland Jonsson. Chalmers University of Technology, Sweden.
- Intrusion and Fraud Detection by Hakan Kvarnstrom. Chalmers University of Technology, Sweden, 2004.
- A Generalized Application Security Audit Program for Any Computing Platform with Comments by Laura Sioma. SANS Institute, September 2000.
- A Paper on the Promotion of Application Security Awareness by Man-Sau Yi. SANS Institute, 2001.
- Information Technology: Code of Practice for Information Security Management, ISO/IEC 17799, December 2000.
- The Computer Forensics and CyberSecurity Governance Model by Kenneth C. Brancik. August 2002.
- New Basel Accord: Operational Risk Management—Emerging Frontiers for the Profession, Vol. 1, 2002 (www.isaca.org/@member/journal.jrnlv102f2.htm).
- Guidance Concerning the Reporting of Computer Related Crimes by Financial Institutions, Board of Governors of the Federal Reserve System, Washington, D.C., Supervisory Letter SR 97-28 (www.federalreserve.gov/ boarddocs/srletters/1997/sr9728.htm).

- Computer Assisted Techniques for Fraud Detection by David Coderre. *The CPA Journal,* 1999 (www.nysscpa.org/epajournal/1999/0899/departments/D57899. html).
- Fraud Detection: I've Got Your Number by Mark J. Nigrini. AICPA, 1999.
- Logging for Intrusion and Fraud Detection by Emilie Laudin Barse. Chalmers University of Technology, School of Computer Science and Engineering, 2004.
- An Analysis of the Effectiveness of Specific Auditing Techniques for Detecting Fraud as Perceived by Three Different Auditor Groups by Glen D. Moyes. Doctoral Dissertation, 1991.
- Relationships of Internal Accounting Controls and Occurrences of Computer Fraud by Donald R. Baker. Friedt School of Business and Entrepreneurship, Nova University, 1990.
- Global Technology Audit Guide (GTAG), The Institute of Internal Auditors (IIA) (www.theiia.org).
- Towards a Theory of Insider Threat Assessment by Ramkumar Chinchani, Anusha Iyer, Hung Q. Ngo, and Shambhu Upadhyaya. *Proceedings from the 2005 International Conference on Dependable Systems and Networks,* University of Buffalo.
- Honeypots: Catching the Insider Threat by Lance Spitzner. *Proceedings of the 19th Annual Computer Security Applications Conference (ACSAC)* 2003, Honeypot Technologies, Inc.
- Web Application Security Consortium: Threat Classification, 2004 (www. webappsec.org).
- A Framework for Role-Based Monitoring of Insider Misuse by Aung Htike Phyo, Steven M. Furnell, and Francisco Portilla. Network Research Group, School of Computing, Communications and Electronics, University of Plymouth, Drake Circus, Plymouth, U.K.
- A Study of Vulnerability Factors in Espionage by the Trusted Insider by Terry Thompson. Presented to the Dean of the Union Institute and University Graduate School, Cincinnati, OH, June 2005.
- Security Countermeasures and Their Impact on Information Systems Misuse: A Deterrence Perspective by John P. D'Arcy. Dissertation submitted to the Temple University Graduate Board, 2005.
- The Inside Job is the Real Threat by Poonam Khanna. *Computing Canada,* 2005.
- VA Breach Shows Growing Insider Threats by Sean Steele. *Network World,* 2006.
- Misuse of Insurer's Data Points to Insider Threats by Jaikumar Vijayan. *Computerworld,* April 2006.
- Position Paper, Insider Threat by Irene Schwarting. Pacific Northwest National Laboratory, ACM, 2006.
- Preventing Insider Sabotage: Lessons Learned from Actual Attacks by Dawn Cappelli. CERT, 2005.

- Insider Threat Study: Computer System Sabotage in Critical Infrastructure Sectors. Carnegie Mellon Software Engineering Institute (SEI), 2005.
- Insider Threat: Real Data on a Real Problem by Dawn Cappelli, Carnegie Mellon University and Michelle Keeney, U.S. Secret Service.
- Security Experts: Insider Threat Looms Largest by Ellen Messmer. *NetworkWorldFusion*, 2003.
- Business Continuity: Inside the Mind of the Insider by Eric D. Shaw, Jerrold M. Post, and Keven G. Ruby. *Security Management* (www.securitymanagement.com).
- CyberCrimes and Misdemeanors: A Reevaluation of the Computer Fraud and Abuse Act by Reid Skibell.
- Insider Threat Analysis and Strategies for Autonomic Policy Formulation by Birendra Mishra and T.S. Raghu.
- Risk from the Trusted Insider, Information Privacy, Compliance, and Acceptable Use. Vericept (www.vericept.com).
- Securing against Insider Attacks by David M. Lynch. EDPACS, 2006.
- Masquerade Detection Using Enriched Command Lines. International Conference on Dependable Systems and Networks, San Francisco, CA, June 22–25, 2003.
- ICT Fraud and Abuse 2004. Audit Commission, London, 2005.
- Information Security Breaches Survey 2006—Technical Report. PricewaterhouseCoopers.
- Are Employees the Biggest Threat in Network Security? by Joseph Ansanelli and Jonathan Bingham. *Network World*, 2005.
- Attacking the Hacking from the Inside Out by Richard C. Bulman Jr. and Jonathan Lehman. *Journal of Internet Law*, 2004.
- 2005 E-Crime Watch Survey—Survey Results. Conducted by *CSO Magazine* in Cooperation with the U.S. Secret Service and CERT Coordination Center.
- Insider Threats Mount by Jaikumar Vijayan. *Computerworld*, 2005.
- Techniques for Detecting Malicious or Improper Data Modifications, Dissertation, Rajni S. Goel, Master of Science, George Mason University, VA, 1991.
- Dissecting Computer Fraud: From Definitional Issues to a Taxonomy by Lucian Vasiu and Ioana Vasiu. *Proceedings of the 37th Hawaii International Conference on Systems Sciences*, 2004.
- The Insider Threat by Bruce V. Hartley. CISSP, PowerPoint Presentation, Privisec, Inc., 2003.
- The Insider Threat to Information Systems: The Psychology of the Dangerous Insider, Security Awareness Bulletin by Eric Shaw, Kevin G. Ruby, and Jerrold M. Post.
- The Insider Threat to U.S. Government Information Systems (unclassified), NSTISSAM INFOSEC/1-99, 1999.
- The FFIEC Information Security IT Handbook, 2006.
- INFOSEC Research Council (IRC), Hard Problems List, 2005.

References

1. Randazzo, Marisa Reddy. Insider Threat Study: Illicit Cyber Activity in the Banking and Finance Sector, The U.S. Secret Service and CERT Coordination Center, Software Engineering Institute (SEI), Carnegie Mellon, Pittsburgh, PA, 2004.
2. Schultz, Eugene. A Framework for Understanding and Predicting Insider Attacks, *Computers & Security,* 21(6), 526–531, 2002.
3. Dunn, Thurman Stanley. Methodology for the Optimization of Resources in the Detecting of Computer Fraud, Dissertation, 1982.
4. Kellerman, Tom. Managing the Insider Threat. This White Paper was written when Kellerman was working for The World Bank, however, the White Paper was never published.

Chapter 3

Chapter 3

The Insider Threat Strategic Planning Process

3.1   Introduction

The primary purpose of this chapter is to introduce the concept of information security governance, with an emphasis and goal in providing a more accurate and cost-effective methodology for conducting an integrated (business/technology) risk assessment, threat assessment (internal and external threats), and privacy impact assessment evaluation. There are two common risk assessment methodology mistakes made by the management of many organizations, which are centered around performing only a technical versus a business risk evaluation to conclude on the integrated risk profile of that organization. The second mistake also being made by organizations is the absence of management's comprehensive threat analysis, which includes the identification of not only external threats but internal threats as well. The component within the information technology (IT) infrastructure that has received the least amount of consideration when evaluating risk within an organization is analyzing the impact of the insider threat. Applications and systems are, in my opinion, the most vulnerable to internal threats because of their existence and access behind the firewall or an enterprise and the higher potential for that application or system to be accessed directly or social engineered by a trusted insider.

This chapter will then leverage off the reader's understanding of the principles involved in completing a thorough integrated risk assessment by deploying the concepts associated with the tailored risk integration process (TRIP). A primary benefit of the TRIP methodology is the ability of any organization to easily deploy a cost-effective and logical approach for the identification, measuring, monitoring, and controlling of both insider and external threats. The TRIP process focuses on understanding the risk profile of a business and the technology used to support a business. Emphasized here is that the risk evaluation within any organization does not end with understanding the risks and controls within one application or system. Through the TRIP methodology, an InfoSec professional will be able to more accurately understand the risk profile of not only a single application, but every IT infrastructure component that supports the transmission and storage of that data.

By the end of this chapter, the reader will be able to understand the concept of performing an integrated risk assessment along with linking management's technical analysis of the integrated risk profile of an application to the business objectives and activities of an organization. The concept of threat assessment will be discussed in significant detail to emphasize its importance in understanding both the inherent (gross) and residual risk levels. The term "net residual risk" (NRR) will be introduced, which emphasizes the importance of considering the risks of critical applications. Through the mapping of the data flows of nonpublic private information (NPPI or NPI) data and core data transaction flow, the critical path of the journey of the NPPI and core transaction data can be tracked beyond the application into other components of the IT infrastructure within an organization and to third parties.

Bayes' Theorem will be introduced and discussion will proceed on how it can be used in a practical and meaningful way through its integration with the Defense in Depth Security Efficiency Calculation. The calculation will provide a quantitative measure for management's assessment of its integrated risk profile, based on the efficiency of each level in the Defense in Depth Model.

3.2 Security Objectives

The insider threat does not have a clear division between external and internal threats. When you evaluate the origin of the insider threat, it does not exclusively originate within the confines of the brick-and-mortar building in which employees work. In Chapter 8, you will notice that many of the insider threats originate from former employees who are conducting their malicious activity from outside of the organization.

The goal of information security and the risk assessment process is to enable organizations to meet all business objectives by implementing business systems with due care consideration of IT-related risks to the organization, its business and trading partners, vendors, and customers. Organizations can achieve the information security goals by considering the following objectives:

■ *Availability*: The ongoing availability of systems addresses the processes, policies, and controls used to ensure authorized users have prompt access to information. This objective protects against intentional or accidental attempts to deny legitimate users access to information and systems.

■ *Integrity of Data or Systems*: System and data integrity relates to the processes, policies, and controls used to ensure information has not been altered in an unauthorized manner and that systems are free from unauthorized manipulation that will compromise accuracy, completeness, and reliability.

■ *Confidentiality of Data or Systems*: Confidentiality covers the processes, policies, and controls employed to protect customers' and organizations' information from any anticipated threats or hazards, including unauthorized access to or use of the information that would result in substantial harm or inconvenience to any customer or institution.

■ *Accountability*: Clear accountability involves the processes, policies, and controls necessary to trace actions to their source. Accountability directly supports nonrepudiation, deterrence, intrusion detection and prevention, after-action recovery, and legal admissibility of records.

■ *Assurance*: Assurance addresses the processes, policies, and controls used to develop confidence that technical and operational security measures work as intended. Assurance levels are part of the system design and include the four elements listed above (availability, integrity, confidentiality, and accountability). Assurance highlights the notion that secure systems provide the intended functionality while preventing undesired actions.

A comprehensive enterprise-wide risk assessment is a vital process that needs to be created and continually reassessed to ensure the enterprise business needs are being accomplished and the appropriate security controls exist. An enterprisewide risk assessment process will likely not have a risk assessment process dedicated exclusively to addressing the insider threat, but will hopefully be closer to an integrated business and technology risk assessment that will address both the internal and external threats for the network, operating system, applications and systems, and the rest of the IT infrastructure components.

Maintaining confidentiality, integrity, and availability of data are key pillars for determining whether or not an enterprise has the appropriate safeguards in place to achieve these goals. An example of how an enterprise can achieve both integrity and accountability for any transactions originating by an insider or outsider would be the control of nonrepudiation. Nonrepudiation occurs when an enterprise demonstrates that the originator of a message is who they say they are, the recipient who received the message is the intended recipient, and no changes occurred in transit. Nonrepudiation is a fundamental requirement for electronic commerce. It can reduce fraud and promote the legal enforceability of electronic agreements and transactions. Although nonrepudiation is a goal and is conceptually clear, the manner in which nonrepudiation can be achieved for electronic systems in a practical, legal sense may have to wait for further judicial clarification.

3.3   Understanding the Information Security Governance Process

An IT professional needs to understand the components of a financial institution's IT infrastructure. The list below may not address all aspects of an enterprise's technology infrastructure but it does include a minimum list of technology risks, which should be considered by bank management for inclusion within their information security risk assessment.

The analyst should consult with management about how they determine the integrated business and technology risk profile of their organization by assessing whether:

- IT is aligned with the enterprise business objectives and to deliver value and security within the final product.
- Information technology risks are clearly identified and mitigated and managed on a continuous basis, as needs dictate.
- Comprehensive information security policies and procedures exist, which at the minimum address the need for an information security risk assessment process that will evaluate the integrated business and technology risk profile of the financial institution. For example, at the minimum, management should consider the following components within their technology infrastructure, when determining the bank's risk profile:
  - Logical Access Controls
  - Intrusion Detection Systems, Vulnerability and Other Network Testing
  - Firewall Security
  - Journaling and Computer Forensics
  - Computer Incident Response

Each of these components should be evaluated by management either internally within an enterprise or externally by an independent and competent third party.

3.4   Cyber-Security Risk Governance Processes for Web-Based Application Protection (Understanding the External Risks and Internal Information Security Risks)

An important component of the risk assessment process involves cyber-security (Figure 3.1). Electronic security or "cyber-security" refers to the protection of information assets from internal and external threats. Protection of these assets includes managing risks not only to information, but also to critical information systems

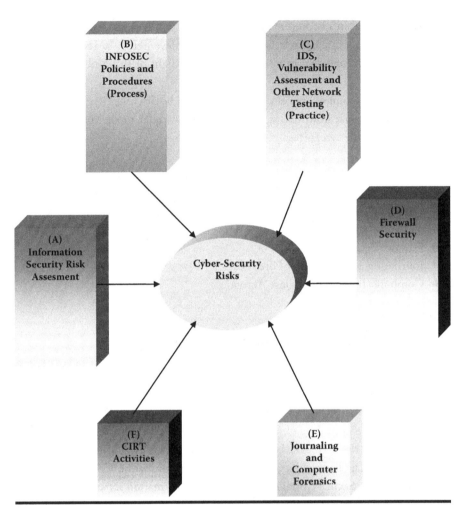

Figure 3.1 Cyber-security risks.

infrastructure, processes, and platforms such as networks, applications, databases, and operation systems, wherever information is collected, processed, stored, transmitted, and destroyed.

Cyber-security threats and incidents have risen dramatically in recent years. This is due primarily to growth of the Internet, which exposes firms, including financial institutions, to a growing number and wider variety of threats and vulnerabilities.

Risk to the financial services sector is particularly high given its role in the critical infrastructure and the potential for monetary gains and systemic disruptions. In February 2003, the White House released its final National Strategy to Secure Cyberspace that outlines a high-level strategy for protecting our nation's critical infrastructure. The banking and finance sector is a major component of the national critical infrastructure plan (CIP) and is taking steps, along with other critical sectors (for example, telecommunications, power, etc.), to secure its electronic security infrastructure from cyber-attacks in light of this and other recent developments.

Each of the six components of cyber-security will be discussed in greater length throughout this book; however, as an initial preview, refer to the diagram above and the listing of the categories:

- An Information Security Risk Assessment
- Information Security Policies and Procedures
- Intrusion Detection Systems (IDS), Vulnerability Assessment, and Other Network Testing
- Firewall Security
- Journaling and Computer Forensics
- Computer Incident Response Activities

3.5 The Risk Management Process (Risk 101—Concepts)

The concept of risk management and governance can be best described as the process of identifying, measuring, monitoring, and controlling vulnerabilities and threats as they impact the objectives of a business or organization. The basic formula for determining total risk is Total Risk = Threats × Vulnerability × Asset Value.

According to the Federal Financial Institution Examination Council (FFIEC) 2006 Information Security Booklet,[3] an ongoing information security risk assessment program is one that effectively

- Gathers data regarding the information and technology assets of the organization, threats to those assets, vulnerabilities, existing security controls and processes, and the current security standards and requirements.
- Analyzes the probability and impact associated with the known threats and vulnerabilities to its assets.
- Prioritizes the risk present due to threats and vulnerabilities to determine the appropriate level of training, controls, and testing necessary for effective mitigation.
- Classifies and ranks sensitive data, systems, and applications.
- Assesses threats and vulnerabilities.
- Assigns risk ratings.

3.5.1 What Should Be Included in the Risk Management Process?

The risk management process should evaluate the universe of critical risks which support the business goals of an enterprise. The technology risks that support the needs of the business must be identified, measured, monitored, and controlled, which is an enormous undertaking because the process does not begin after only one initial risk assessment, but rather needs to be an iterative and continuous process.

The significant overhead associated with management, audit, and compliance working together to provide a continuous assessment of risk processes, practices, and controls is noteworthy. Most organizations have finite budgets to support the risk management and governance processes, and the financial and human cost factor is significant for maintaining an effective and continuous risk governance process through the integration of management and technical controls.

The primary goal of this chapter is not to provide a solution to solving the risk management and governance process challenges, but rather to offer one structure that logically approaches the risk governance challenge and could potentially result in cost savings to an organization based on management's willingness to accept, transfer, or eliminate risks that will not have a high negative operational, strategic, or reputational risk.

The entire premise and benefit of introducing the concept of deploying the TRIP that will be discussed and illustrated within this chapter is to provide a framework for management and audit to consider when seeking ways to develop a new or refine an existing risk management and governance process, without being prescriptive.

Prior to reviewing and potentially incorporating the TRIP methodology, it is advisable to review the Global Technology Audit Guide (GTAG) (2005) on information technology controls, particularly as it relates to the discussion on risk considerations in determining the adequacy of IT controls, Carnegie Mellon University's Operationally Critical Threat, Asset, and Vulnerability Evaluation (OCTAVE), NIST Publication SP 800-30, and other credible resources which reflect industry sound and best practices governing the risk governance process.

Additionally, prior to reviewing the TRIP risk assessment methodology, it is important to understand the basic security control categories as listed in Table 3.1.

3.5.2 The Tailored Risk Integrated Process (TRIP)

The following discussion evaluates risk from a unique perspective whereby an approach is used that is materially different than that seen at many and perhaps most organizations.

Table 3.1 Security Controls

Security Control Class	Security Control Family
Management Security	• Risk Assessment • Security Planning • System and Services Acquisition • Security Control Review • Processing Authorization
Operational Security	• Personnel Security • Physical and Environmental Protection • Contingency Planning and Operations • Configuration Management • Hardware and Software Maintenance • System and Data Integrity • Media Protection • Incident Response • Security Awareness and Training
Technical Security	• Identification and Authentication • Logical Access Control • Accountability (Including Audit Trails) • System and Communication Protection

3.5.2.1 Broad-Brush Approach (Macro Approach)

Typically, in many organizations, technology infrastructure components (i.e., firewalls, routers, local area networks [LANs], wide area networks [WANs], etc.) are evaluated within the risk assessment process, regardless of their criticality level or direct relevance to business unit operations or linkage to critical applications or systems supporting a business unit.

When using the broad-brush approach, the risk assessment process attempts to cover the entire universe of IT technology risks (macro approach) versus a more localized risk assessment of critical applications (micro approach) that supports a specific business process. The universe of IT technology risks (macro approach) typically includes only general (IT infrastructure) versus production application risks and controls.

The following steps are typically included within the broad-brush risk assessment approach for organizations:

- ▪ Enterprise-Wide InfoSec Risk Assessment of All IT Infrastructure Components
- ▪ Application Risks (sometimes)

- Inherent Risk (gross risk)
- Control Identification
- Threat and Vulnerability Modeling
- Residual Risk Identification (net of mitigating application controls)
- Risk Acceptance, Transfer, and Elimination

The integrated business/technology risk and its business impact is commonly overlooked, thereby creating significant gaps in the InfoSec risk assessment process. The technology centric (macro) risk assessments usually have little or no linkage back to the critical applications supporting a business operation.

3.5.2.2 The Recommended Integrated Business/Technology Approach (Application to Infrastructure)

The TRIP methodology would bridge the current risk assessment InfoSec gaps not only to ensure accurate identification of technology, but also to ensure business risks are identified (integrated risk approach). Ideally, any risk assessment needs to begin with an assessment of business-critical applications, privacy considerations, and core data elements within an application or system.

The recommended industry approach is as follows:

- **The TRIP Approach**
  - Identification of critical business processes.
  - Identification of critical applications and systems and data that support a business unit's operations.
  - Identification of critical IT infrastructure components that support the critical applications and systems.
  - Inherent risk identification.
  - Control identification.
  - Threat and vulnerability modeling.
  - Residual risk identification.
  - Net residual identification (factors IT infrastructure components).
  - Risk acceptance, transfer, and elimination.
- **TRIP Advantages**
  - Provides more focused and efficient risk identification process by analyzing InfoSec risks locally at each business unit first through a TRIP versus evaluating all integrated risks—evaluating all integrated risks may include an evaluation of InfoSec risks and controls governing IT infrastructure components and applications which may not represent the high risks within the enterprise.
  - Provides a more accurate integrated enterprise-wide risk assessment by evaluating a business operation and supporting applications and systems

first and then selecting only those IT infrastructure components that directly or indirectly impact the critical business operations and supporting applications and systems.

- Provides cost savings of not having the increased financial overhead of performing an enterprise-wide risk assessment that covers the entire IT universe compared to the more efficient, logical, and risk-based approach using the TRIP methodology.

The process applies the concepts of ISO 27001 as it relates to understanding application risks.

The following approach is a paradigm shift for many people who may not fully understand the concept of integrated risk, and it starts with the concept of technology being used to support the business versus the converse.

The primary premise of this proof of concept methodology is to have a risk analyst or person with equivalent credentials perform an integrated risk assessment (IRA) to fully understand the enterprise technology and business risk, starting from critical business applications to the risk analysis of select IT infrastructure components that support that application or system.

3.5.2.3 The TRIP Strategy

Periodic security testing based on integrated business and technology risks engages either an internal evaluation (i.e., audit/compliance) or third-party technology production application risk assessments.

The scope of controls testing includes at the minimum an assessment of control objectives and points identified for each critical production application and system, as described below:

- Control Points
- Application Access Controls
- Data Origination and Input Controls
- Processing Controls
- Output and Management Information Systems (MISs)

3.6 Security Controls in Application Systems Controls (ISO 27001)

The control objective is to prevent loss, modification, or misuse of user data in application systems controls.[1] Following are methods to achieve that objective:

■ *Input Data Validation Data*: Input to application systems will be validated to ensure that it is correct and appropriate.
■ *Control of Internal Process*: Validation checks will be incorporated into systems to detect any corruption of the data processed.
■ *Message Authentication*: Message authentication will be used for applications where there is a security requirement to protect the integrity of the message content.
■ *Output Data Validation*: Data output from an application system will be validated to ensure that the processing of stored information is correct and appropriate to the circumstances.

3.6.1 Security in Application Systems Controls Needs to Be Clearly Articulated within an InfoSec Policy

Security in application system controls needs to be clearly articulated in an InfoSec policy. A typical InfoSec policy should, at minimum, detail data and systems confidentiality criteria (based on confidentiality, integrity, and availability factors), as detailed in the scorecard in Table 3.2.

■ *Application Criticality Matrix:* A typical Application Criticality Matrix should detail all the criticality factors that are included within the risk evaluation process. Table 3.3 illustrates a few criticality factors but is not an exclusive list. Management, audit, compliance, and legal should determine what is most critical to an organization.
■ *Critical Application and Interfaces Report:* This report is not typical of what you will see within an organization, but its existence is important when evaluating residual risk.

Table 3.2   Dashboard Rating Criteria

Fully Implemented	Partially Implemented	Not Implemented
Confidentiality		
INFOSEC Policies, Procedures, and Practices provide strong documented controls to protect data confidentiality. Strong indication of favorable practices governing data confidentiality.	INFOSEC Policies, Procedures, and Practices need strengthening to ensure the existence of strong documented controls to protect data confidentiality. Preliminary indication of unfavorable practices governing data confidentiality.	INFOSEC Policies, Procedures, and Practices are Critically Deficient to ensure the existence of strong documented controls to protect data confidentiality. Clearly defined weaknesses governing data confidentiality.
Integrity		
INFOSEC Policies, Procedures, and Practices strongly protect data integrity through a high level of controls governing authenticity, non-repudiation, and accountability. Strong indication of favorable practices governing data integrity.	INFOSEC Policies, Procedures, and Practices need strengthening to ensure a strong level of data integrity exists through a high level of controls governing authenticity, nonrepudiation, and accountability. Preliminary indication of unfavorable practices governing data integrity.	INFOSEC Policies, Procedures, and Practices are Critically Deficient to ensure a strong level of data integrity exists through a high level of controls governing authenticity, nonrepudiation, and accountability. Clearly defined weaknesses governing data integrity.
Availability		
INFOSEC Policies, Procedures, and Practices provide a strong internal control standard to protect the timely availability of information technology resources (system & data). Strong indication of favorable practices governing data availability.	INFOSEC Policies, Procedures, and Practices need strengthening to protect the timely availability of information technology resources (system & data). Preliminary indication of unfavorable practices governing data availability.	INFOSEC Policies, Procedures, and Practices require fundamental improvement to protect the timely availability of information technology resources (system & data). Clearly defined weaknesses governing data availability.

Table 3.3 Application Criticality Matrix

1. The Taxonomy (category) of Application	11. Bank Regulatory Implications (Two-Factor Authentication Implications)	21. Significance to Internal Threats
2. O/S[a] Platform	12. Health Care Industry (HIPAA[d]) Implications	22. Impact on the Information Security Scorecard Rating
3. Data Classification	13. Bank Regulatory Implications (BASEL II)	23. Access Controls Safeguards
4. Age of Application	14. Bank Regulatory Implications (FFIEC[e])	24. Data Origination/Input Safeguards
5. Significance to Disaster Recovery	15. Federal Government Implications (i.e., Office of Management and Budget, National Institute of Standards and Technology, Presidential Decision Directives, Federal Information Security Management Act [FISMA])	25. Processing Safeguards
6. Financial and Regulatory Reporting	16. Education/Experience of Technology Personnel	26. Output Safeguards
7. Impact to Operational Risk	17. Attrition Rate of Technology Personnel	27. Data Confidentiality
8. Impact to Reputation Risk	18. History of Audit Findings (Internal/External)	28. Data Integrity
9. SEC SOX 404[b] Implications	19. Application External/ Internal Interfaces	29. Data Availability
10. GLB[c] Act Implications	20. Significance to External Threats	30. Threat Modeling Results (i.e., Probability and Impact of Attacks, Based on Application and Network Vulnerabilities to Attacks)

Source: © Dr. Kenneth C. Brancik, CISA, CISSP.
Note: Factors are not prioritized.

[a] O/S, operating system.
[b] SEC SOX 404, U.S. Securities and Exchange Commission, Sarbanes–Oxley Act, Section 404.
[c] GLB, Gramm–Leach–Bliley Act.
[d] HIPAA, Health Insurance Portability and Accountability Act.
[e] FFIEC, Federal Financial Institution Examination Council.

Table 3.4 Critical Applications for Information Security Purposes

Critical Applications[a]	Platform	Data Flow Source	Data Flow Destination	Data Flow Frequency	Encrypted	Taxonomy (Category)
Crit-App1(A)	Windows	Crit-App5(B)	Crit-App8(C)	Daily	No	**Web-based application (internal)**
Crit-App2						**Web-based application (internal)**
Crit-App3						**Web-based application (external–Internet facing)**
Crit-App4						**Commercial off-the-shelf (COTS)**
Crit-App5						**Home-grown (internal)**
Crit-App6						**Home-grown (external)**
Crit-App7						**Web services (external)**
Crit-App8						**Web services (internal)**
Crit-App9						**Open source (Linux)**

Source: © Dr. Kenneth C. Brancik, CISA, CISSP.

[a] Application criticality. (Refer to the *Application Criticality Factors Matrix* for details.)

3.7 Security and SOX 404 Designated Applications and Systems

This is a report (Table 3.5) that identifies critical production applications for SOX 404 testing purposes. This sample report may be more comprehensive in its contents than is typically seen, particularly within the identification of primary and related applications; however, many organizations do not adequately identify the interrelationships between critical applications (data transfers), which is particularly important when evaluating net residual risk (NRR) (to be discussed later in this chapter). There should be a correlation between critical applications identified for the TRIP process, SOX 404 testing, the audit universe, and for business continuity planning and disaster recovery (BCP/DR) testing; however, it is management's final determination as to whether uniformity is needed for all four reports.

3.8 Application Risk Weightings for Criticality Factors Report

This report is important because it takes each application's criticality factor component from the Application Criticality Matrix document and assigns qualitative and quantitative ratings (see Table 3.6).

3.9 The Inherent Risk Valuation Report

The qualitative and quantitative ratings will then be used in determining the inherent risk valuation. The specific quantitative values are used only as an illustration and should be assigned initially by the management of each organization.

The most important value in this calculation is the total listed of 21.25 (see Table 3.7—"Inherent Risk Valuation") report, which ranks the highest in Inherent Risk Value (also refer to Table 3.11—"Risk Ranking of Critical Production Applications").

One important aspect of Table 3.7—"Inherent Risk Valuation" is to understand each application's criticality factors. For example, one application criticality factor is financial and regulatory reporting (D-6) within Table 3.5—"SOX Production Application (D) Crit-Appl." You can see the key business processes related to Crit-App1, along with other related IT infrastructure components such as the operating system which that application uses for data processing, related applications, and so forth. Additionally, the qualitative assessments contained within Table 3.7—"Inherent Risk Valuation," has hooks to various companion and support tables (see Table 3.8—"Inherent Risk Valuation Legend [for Table 3.7]" and Table 3.9—"Threat Probability/Likelihood").

Table 3.5 SOX Production Application (D) Crit-App1

Number	Category	Key Business Processes	Primary Application	Platform	Data Center	Related Applications	Platform by Application	Data Center
I.	Financial & Regulatory Reporting (D-6)	1. Financial Consolidation (E)	Crit-Appl1 (A)	Unix AIX/ Win2000/ Mainframe	Teleport, Staten Island	Crit-App5 (B) Crit-App8 (C)	Mainframe	Somers, NY
		2. Subsidiary Accounting						
		3. International Accounting						
		4. Expense Analysis/Accruals						
		5. Regulatory Reporting						
II.	Securities Group/ Broker Dealers							
III.	Retail Banking							

Table 3.6 Application Risk Weightings for Criticality Factors: Crit-App1

Application Criticality Factor	Qualitative Rating (H,M,L)	Quantitative Rating (1,2,3,4)
Financial and Regulatory Reporting (D-6)	M (Moderate) = 0.75	3*
Data Confidentiality (D-27)	TBD	TBD
Data Integrity (D-28)	TBD	TBD

Notes: TBD, to be determined.
    Qualitative Rating:
      Inherent Risk: Low = 0.25; Moderate = 0.75; High = 1.0.
    Quantitative Rating:
      Inherent Risk: None = 1; Small <10 million = 2; *Moderate 11 to 30 million = 3;
      Large >30 million = 4.

Financial exposure pertains to the amount of gross revenue generated for the year by the business that has ownership of the application or system. By extension, the greater the amount of revenue generation capability of an application or system, the greater the potential for an application or system to create both current and future financial losses.

3.10 An Example of Various Web Application Threats

Table 3.10 supports the threat analysis evaluation in determining the IR value, which is directly linked to the information found in Table 3.7.

The classes of Web application threats represent a small subset of a significant universe of Web application threats. Management's development and maintenance of a similar type of report is important because it will serve as a baseline to evaluate the probability and likelihood of threats impacting an application and business operation.

Table 3.7 Inherent Risk Valuation—Application Risk Weightings for Criticality Factors Crit-App1

Application Criticality Factor	*Qualitative Assessment*			*Quantitative Assessment*	
	Qualitative Rating Inherent Risk: Low = .25 Mod = .75 High = 1.0			**Quantitative Rating** Inherent Risk: None = 1 Small <10 million = 2 *Moderate 11–30 million = 3 Large >30 million = 4	
	**Gross Qualitative Rating (H,M,L) (1)	**Threats & Probability/ Likelihood Analysis (H,M,L) (2)	**Vulnerabilities & Impact Analysis (H,M,L) (3)	Quantitative Rating (1,2,3,4) (4)	Inherent Risk (IR) Value Multiply Columns Avg (1–3) × 4
Financial & Regulatory Reporting (D-6)	M (Moderate) = .75	M (Moderate) = .75	M (Moderate) = .75	3	= 2.25 (.75 × 3)
Data Confidentiality (D-27)	TBD			TBD	= 5.00
Data Integrity (D-28)	TBD			TBD	= 8.00
Other	TBD			TBD	= 6.00
Total					**21.25** (Cross-Ref. *Risk Ranking of Critical Productions Applications Diagrams*)

Table 3.8   Inherent Risk Valuation (Legend for Table 3.7)

Legend *Qualitative assessment (high, moderate, low):* A qualitative rating (H, M, L) should be predicated on the estimated financial gross revenue generated for the year by the business. By extension, the greater the amount of revenue generation capability of an application or system, the greater the potential for an application or system to create financial losses.

**Threats and vulnerabilities:* Columns 1 through 3 should have weighted values assigned depending on their risk rating.

Example: Low = 0.25, moderate = 0.75, high = 1.0

Probability/likelihood definition:

Note: For a complete listing of vulnerabilities, reference should be made to the Mitre Corporation's Common Vulnerabilities and Exposure (CVE) listing or the SecurityFocus database or other credible listing of vulnerabilities contained in various databases.

Table 3.9   Threat Probability/Likelihood Table

Level	Definition
High	The threat source is highly motivated and sufficiently capable, and controls to prevent the vulnerability from being exercised are ineffective.
Medium	The threat source is motivated and capable, but controls are in place that may impede successful exercise of the vulnerability.
Low	The threat source lacks motivation or capability, or controls are in place to prevent, or at least significantly impede, the vulnerability from being exercised.

Source: National Institute of Standards and Technology NIST SP 800-30 (Risk Management Guide for Information Technology Systems).

Table 3.10   An Example of Various Classes of Web Application Threats

Technique	Description
1. Cross-Site Scripting	Cross-site scripting takes advantage of a vulnerable Web site to attack clients who visit that Web site. The most frequent goal is to steal the credentials of users who visit the site.
2. Structure Query Language (SQL) Injection	SQL injection allows commands to be executed directly against the database, allowing disclosure and modification of data in the database.
3. Command Injection	Operating system and platform commands can often be used to give attackers access to data and escalate privileges on back-end servers.

Table 3.11   Risk Ranking of Critical Production Applications

Name	Ranking	Numeric Rating	Audit Universe	HIPAA[a]	Other	Comment
Crit-App1	1	21.25	Yes	N/A	No	
Crit-App8	2	20.00	Yes	N/A	No	
Crit-App5	3	17.00	Yes	N/A	No	

Note: N/A, not applicable.

[a] HIPAA, Health Insurance Portability and Accountability Act.

3.11   An Example of a Risk Ranking of Critical Production Applications

The starting point for determining application criticality can be found within Table 3.4—"Critical Applications for Information Security Purposes," which provides an example of various critical applications. Table 3.6—"Application Risk Weightings for Criticality Factors: Crit-App1"—supports the threat analysis evaluation in determining the applications' criticality and IR. In Table 3.11, Crit-App1 has the highest numerical score, and based on this assessment would be considered the most critical of the three applications listed. It is important to note that any application considered critical needs to be included within the audit universes based on its significance and importance to an organization. Although this chart does not reflect a separate column for compliance, in reality, this application would also need to be evaluated to ensure compliance with various laws, rules, and regulations.

3.12   The Risk Assessment HeatMap

The Risk Assessment HeatMap Report (Figure 3.2) supports the prerequisite processes that should be involved in executing the TRIP methodology. The listing of general and application controls is not intended to be an all-inclusive list, but rather is a listing of representative controls for illustrative purposes. In reality, a full inventory of controls should be considered in evaluating the residual risk (application or system only) and the NRR (application and IT general controls, which relate to those IT infrastructure components that are used by that application or system). This report shows the relationship between the risk assessment HeatMap and the InfoSec scorecard.

The results of the HeatMap rating should directly correlate with the production application system security rating component of the InfoSec dashboard/scorecard (see Table 3.12).

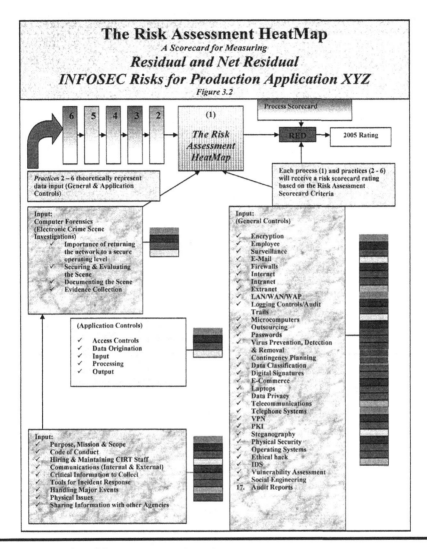

Figure 3.2   The Risk Assessment HeatMap.

An example of the linkage between the HeatMap and the InfoSec scorecard can be seen in 2005, when the Production Application System Security HeatMap ratings was rated RED, which in turn mapped directly to the InfoSec scorecard rating of red. An important distinction to make between the production application HeatMap and the InfoSec scorecard is the dual role played by the HeatMap. Specifically, the HeatMap served double duty in not only providing the support and justification for rating a production application through the scorecard, but also in being used to evaluate residual risk (application alone) and the NRR (application risk coupled with an analysis of the impact of the IT infrastructure components

Table 3.12 Information Security Scorecard Production Applications XYZ

Number	Category	2006	2005	Security Trend
1	Security Policies and Standards	G	G	⟩
2	System Development and Security Architecture	R	Y	
*3	Production Application System Security	Y	R	
4	Network Security	G	Y	
5	User Authentication and Access Controls	G	G	⟩
6	Security Monitoring	R	Y	
7	Vendor Management for Security	R	Y	
8	Incident Response (including computer forensics)	R	R	⟩
	OVERALL	R	Y	

used by that critical application or system). Details on where the results of the HeatMap and residual risk levels fit into the overall risk assessment process will be presented in Section 3.13.

3.13 The Risk Assessment (Acceptance) Process

The risk acceptance process includes the following:

Step 1: Perform a critical application risk assessment (inherent risk).

Step 2: Assess the existence and adequacy of mitigating application controls.

Step 3: Determine the level of residual application risk. (Refer to the forms covering access controls, data origination and input, processing, and output/MIS risk testing for details.)

Step 4: Determine the level of NRR, which incorporates the risks and controls of the supporting IT infrastructure used by a critical application or system.

Step 5: Ensure that the results of the Heatmap are consistent with the InfoSec dashboard/scorecard rating.

Step 6: Evaluate the integrated NRR (business/technology) in context of the entire enterprise risk profile and formalize the risk acceptance process (i.e., acceptance of low to moderate risk or less-significant high-risk areas or risk elimination or transference).

The following reports show important relationships:

Access Controls Residual Risk Form: This report shows the relationship between the level of inherent versus residual application risks, after factoring the risk-mitigating actions (see Table 3.13).

Data Origination and Input Residual Risk Form: This report shows the relationship between the levels of inherent versus residual application risks, after factoring the risk-mitigating actions (see Table 3.14).

Data Processing Residual Risk Form: This report shows the relationship between the level of inherent versus residual application risks, after factoring the risk-mitigating actions (see Table 3.15).

Data Output and MIS Residual Risk Form: This report shows the relationship between the levels of inherent versus residual application risks, after factoring the risk-mitigating actions (see Table 3.16).

Table 3.13 Application Residual Risk: Access Controls Testing Residual Risk Form

Risk Reference Number	Key Risks	Level of Inherent Application Risks (H, M, L)	Key Controls	Risk-Mitigating Actions	Level of Residual Risk (H, M, L)
1	Inappropriate logical security controls could present an opportunity for unauthorized modification, destruction, or disclosure of information assets.	H	Written policies and standards governing logical access controls should exist within the firm, be approved by senior management, and be disseminated to the business lines for implementation.	Determine that the organization has appropriate policies and procedures in place to ensure that effective security standards are consistent across the business.	M

Table 3.14 Application Residual Risk: Data Origination and Input Risk Form

Risk Reference Number	Key Risks	Level of Inherent Application Risks (H, M, L)	Key Controls	Risk-Mitigating Actions	Level of Residual Risk (H, M, L)
1	Inappropriate segregation of duties.	H	All stages of information processing are segregated.	Ensure that duties are separated so that no one individual performs more than one of the following operations: data origination, data input, data processing, and output distribution.	M
2	Source documents are not controlled and do not require authorizing.	H	Access to blank source documents is restricted to authorized personnel.	Review written procedures and observe source document preparation.	M

Table 3.15 Application Residual Risk: Data Processing Risk Form

Risk Reference Number	Key Risks	Level of Inherent Application Risks (H, M, L)	Key Controls	Risk-Mitigating Actions	Level of Residual Risk (H, M, L)
1	Record count and control totals are accurate.	H	User-prepared record count and control totals established over source documents are used to help determine the completeness of data entry and processing.	Review application documentation and observe activity for developing record counts and control totals.	M

Table 3.16 Application Residual Risk for Output/MIS

Risk Reference Number	Key Risks	Level of Inherent Application Risks (H, M, L)	Key Controls	Risk-Mitigating Actions	Level of Residual Risk (H, M, L)
1	MIS report disposition is not properly controlled.	H	Ensure adequate policies, practices, and procedures govern MIS distribution and use.	Select and review samples of ongoing transaction processing systems/operational reports for the targeted MIS area(s).Determine if the source of the information collected originates from the expected business area.	M

Note: MIS, management information system.

3.14 Net Residual Risk (NRR)

The NRR goal is to evaluate application risk in context with the IT infrastructure components that interface with a critical application or system.

Determine the level of NRR that incorporates the risks and controls of the supporting IT infrastructure used by a critical application or system:

Step 1:   Determine the ***Inherent Risk Rating***
Step 2:   Internal Controls Rating
Step 3:   ***Residual Risk Rating***
Step 4:   Risk Assessment Rating
Step 5:   Probability of Occurrence (Refer to Section 3.14.1)
Step 6:   Business Impact Assessment (Refer to Section 3.14.2)
Step 7:   Business Continuity Planning (BCP) Assessment (Refer to Section 3.14.3)
Step 8:   IT Infrastructure Components
Step 9:   Technology Impact Assessment
Step 10: Interfacing Applications
Step 11: Platforms (Operating Systems [O/S])
Step 12: Architecture
Step 13: ***Net Residual Risk (NRR)***
Step 14: Risk Acceptance, Transference, or Elimination

The term NRR needs to be evaluated in the context of high, medium, and low after considering various factors such as probability of occurrence, business impact assessment, and BCP.

3.14.1 Probability of Occurrence

You want to evaluate the impact of a threat and vulnerability assessment (TVA) and the probability of a security exploit actually occurring when assessing the NRR of an organization. For example, a low probability of an exploit actually occurring will not likely contribute significantly to increasing the overall risk profile or NRR of that enterprise. Conversely, a high probability of a significant exploit occurring may increase the integrated risk profile of that organization and increase the NRR. Obviously, the probability of occurrence of an exploit represents only one risk factor in a multitude of a number of risk factors and should be considered in the context of all integrated risk factors in terms of increasing or decreasing the NRR.

3.14.2 Business Impact Assessment (BIA)

The BIA is typically associated with business resumption planning; however, the BIA concept is important because of its interrelationship with InfoSec. The BIA also considers the impact of legal and regulatory requirements, such as the privacy and availability of customer data and required notifications to the institution's primary regulators and customers. The BIA is also important from the context of documenting mission-critical functions, which is obviously important in the early stages of the InfoSec risk assessment where you want to evaluate the most critical business processes and the technology and the critical business applications and systems that support those mission-critical functions.

3.14.3 Business Continuity Planning

During the risk assessment step, business processes and the business impact analysis assumptions are stress tested with various threat scenarios. Not only should organizations analyze a threat and its impact from the business resumption planning perspective, but they should conduct an assessment if the BCP-related threat has an InfoSec consideration as well.

A few reasons for management's inability to secure the necessary financial funding to adequately secure the security of their enterprise include the following:

■ Attempt to oversecure their enterprise.
■ Inability to effectively balance risk and control.

The root causes for unsuccessful management efforts may include the following three factors:

■ The absence of a formalized and documented risk assessment process.
■ An incomplete risk assessment process that covers technology but not the integrated business and technology risk.
■ A point in time versus a continuous risk assessment process that more accurately captures security issues.

Based on the completion of a comprehensive risk assessment and threat modeling that will be described in more detail later in this chapter, there is a need for management to strategize on what are the most effective management and technology controls to reduce the risk profile of an enterprise.

3.15 Application-Based Controls: The 2005 Global Technology Audit Guide (GTAG), The Institute of Internal Auditors (IIA)

One source for determining the adequacy of application controls is through GTAG.[2] In brief, all applications that support business activity need to be controlled. The objective of internal controls over application systems is to ensure the following:

- All input data is accurate, complete, authorized, and correct.
- All data is processed as intended.
- All data stored is accurate and complete.
- All output is accurate and complete.
- A record is maintained to track the process of data from input to storage, and to the eventual output.

However, because application controls now represent a huge percentage of business controls, they should be the priority of every internal auditor.

3.15.1 Application Controls

There are several types of generic controls that should be expected in an application (Table 3.17).

3.15.1.1 BS ISO/IEC 27001:2005

This BS ISO standard[1] addresses information technology, security techniques, information security management systems, and requirements.

The following excerpts within ISO 27001 are included in Table 3.18 and Table 3.19a,b to illustrate various industry guidance relative to application controls.

Implementing ISO 27001 standards requires some level of technical controls. Application security was intentionally selected from the complete ISO specification to simply illustrate that application security is probably one of the most vulnerable components of the IT infrastructure, particularly as it relates to the insider threat. However, with that premise being said, general controls are extremely important because there is obviously a symbiotic relationship for all general and application IT risks and controls.

The trusted insider may have the institutional knowledge of operational activities and have the opportunity to social engineer within the organization to take advantage of perceived weaknesses within the organization. For example, an insider may know that a particular function within an organization has a lack of segregation of duties in a particular area, thereby creating a lack of checks and balances in a particular area. The absence of segregation of duties is a general controls shortcoming and could easily

Table 3.17   Types of Application Controls

Access Controls	• Computer security access control includes authentication, authorization, and audit. It also includes additional measures such as physical devices (including biometric scans and metal locks, hidden paths, digital signatures, encryption, social barriers, and monitoring by humans and automated systems). • Access control is the ability to permit or deny the use of an object (a passive entity, such as a system or file) by a subject (an active entity, such as an individual or process). • Access control systems provide the essential services of identification and authentication (I&A), authorization, and accountability, where identification and authentication determine who can log onto a system, authorization determines what an authenticated user can do, and accountability identifies what a user did.
Data Origination/ Input Controls	• These controls are used mainly to check the integrity of data entered into a business application, whether the source is input directly by staff, remotely by a business partner, or through a Web-enabled application. Input is checked to ensure that it remains within specified parameters. • Data input controls ensure the accuracy, completeness, and timeliness of data during its conversion from its original source into computer data, or entry into a computer application. Data can be entered into a computer application from either manual online input or by batch processing (automated). • Someone reviewing input controls should determine the adequacy of both manual and automated controls over data input to ensure that data is input accurately with optimum use of computerized validation and editing and that error-handling procedures facilitate the timely and accurate resubmission of all corrected data.
Data Processing	• Data processing controls are used to ensure the accuracy, completeness, and timeliness of data during either batch or real-time processing by the computer application. • Someone reviewing these controls should determine the adequacy of controls over application programs and related computer operations to ensure that data is accurately processed through the application and that no data is added, lost, or altered during processing.
Output	• Data output controls are used to ensure the integrity of output and the correct and timely distribution of any output produced. • Output can be in hard-copy form, in the form of files used as input to other systems, or information available for online viewing.

Table 3.18   BS ISO/IEC 27001:2005 (Application and Information Access Controls)

A.11.6 Application and Information Access Control Objective: To Prevent Unauthorized Access to Information Held in Application Systems

A.11.6.1	Information Access Restriction	Control: Access to information and application system functions by users and support personnel shall be restricted in accordance with the defined access control policy.
A.11.6.2	Sensitive System Isolation	Control: Sensitive systems shall have a dedicated (isolated) computing environment.

Source: BS ISO/IEC 27001:2005. (With permission.)

Table 3.19a   BS ISO/IEC 27001:2005 (Correct Processing in Applications)

A.12. Correct Processing in Applications Objective: To Prevent Errors, Loss, Unauthorized Modification or Misuse of Information in Applications

A.12.2.1	Input Data Validation	Control: Data input to applications shall be validated to ensure that this data is correct and appropriate.
A.12.2.2	Control of Internal Processing	Control: Validation checks shall be incorporated into applications to detect any corruption of information through processing errors or deliberate acts.
A.12.2.3	Message Integrity	Control: Requirements for ensuring authenticity and protecting message integrity in applications shall be identified, and appropriate controls will be identified and implemented.
A.12.2.4	Output Data Validation	Control: Data output from an application shall be validated to ensure that the processing of stored information is correct and appropriate to the circumstances.

Source: BS ISO/IEC 27001:2005. (With permission.)

be exploited to benefit an insider. For example, a trusted insider could engage in the manipulation of sensitive data values that he or she is responsible for entering into an application or system if that system does not receive a second check by another employee—that is, an independent validation—to assess the integrity of the data entered.

Table 3.19b   BS ISO/IEC 27001:2005 (Security in Development and Support Processes)

A.12.5 Security in Development and Support Processes Objective: To Maintain the Security of Application System Software and Information

A.12.5.1	Change Control Procedures	Control: The implementation of changes shall be controlled by the use of formal change control procedures.
A.12.5.2	Technical Review of Applications after Operating System Changes	Control: When operating systems are changed, business critical applications shall be reviewed and tested to ensure there is no adverse impact on organizational operations or security.
A.12.5.3	Restrictions on Changes to Software Packages	Control: Modifications to software packages shall be discouraged, limited to necessary changes, and all changes shall be strictly controlled.
A.12.5.4	Information Leakage	Control: Outsourced software development shall be supervised and monitored by the organization.
A.12.5.5	Outsourced Soft- ware Development	Control: Outsourced software development shall be supervised and monitored by the organization.

Source: BS ISO/IEC 27001:2005. (With permission.)

3.16 Laws, Rules, and Regulations

Complying with technical controls in any environment for any sector of the critical infrastructure of the United States will likely require some blend of management and technical controls. Consider, for example, a financial services company (i.e., banking, brokerage, and insurance) that is likely to share, at minimum, three common regulations that impact its industry. The three common regulations may include the following: the Gramm–Leach–Bliley (GLB) Act, the Health Insurance Portability and Accountability Act (HIPAA), and the Sarbanes–Oxley Act, section 404 (SOX 404). Additionally, assume that the company resides in a state that has legislation for breach notification in the event NPPI data was compromised or after passage of the proposed national Data Accountability and Trust Act (DATA) that would require customer notification in the event of a security breach into an organization's database holding NPPI data.

3.16.1 H.R. 4127 (Data Accountability and Trust Act [DATA]) October 25, 2005

The goal of this legislation is to protect consumers by requiring reasonable security policies and procedures to protect computerized data containing personal information and to provide for nationwide notice in the event of a security breach.

Personal information is taken to include an individual's first and last names in combination with any one or more of the following data elements:

- Social security number.
- Driver's license or other state identification number.
- Financial account number or credit or debit card number and any required security access code or password used to access a financial account.

The regulations set forth require the following policies and procedures:

- A security policy with respect to the collection, use, sale, other dissemination, and maintenance of such personal information.
- The identification of an officer or other individual as the point of contact with responsibility for the management of information security.
- A process for identifying and assessing any reasonably foreseeable vulnerabilities in the system maintained by such person that contains such electronic data.
- A process for taking preventive and corrective action to mitigate against any vulnerabilities identified in the process required by subparagraph C, which include encryption of such data, implementing any changes to security practices and the architecture, installation, or implementation of network or operating software.

3.16.2 Notification of Information Security Breach

Nationwide notification is necessary if any person engaged in interstate commerce who owns or possesses data in electronic form containing personal information discovers a breach of security of the system that is maintained by such person and that contains such data.

Once management determines the requirements of each of these regulations, an assessment will need to be performed on how internal processes and practices within an enterprise may reduce the level of risk for a particular area and be in compliance with the letter and spirit of the regulation. Management should perform a gap analysis that measures what mitigating controls they currently possess versus what they need to reduce the level of risk to an acceptable level.

For illustrative purposes, consider the three regulations involving privacy, which include GLB, HIPAA, and the Breach Notification Act currently mandated for 29 states within the United States. Each of the respective regulations and laws share a common purpose—to safeguard NPPI in transit and in storage, whether the data is used for financial transactions or a patient's medical records.

Based on the aforementioned example, management's risk assessment will need to perform three primary tasks as part of a privacy impact assessment (PIA):

- Identify which data elements within GLB and HIPAA contain NPPI data that could be viewed, altered, stolen, and eventually sold in the marketplace to an interested third party for identity theft purposes.
- Identify the NPPI data's critical path or journey from the original point of data entry into an application or system to its transmission to an application service provider for processing and then to its transmission back to another internal application.
- Identify the NPPI data's critical path or journey to its final place of rest within some repository.

The Government Accountability Office (GAO) testimony to the Committee on Government Reform, House of Representatives, stipulated within the E-Government Act of 2002, the PIA guidance, highlights of which are as follows:

- Protect personal information in government systems.
- Require that agencies conduct PIAs.
- Ensure that handling conforms to applicable legal, regulatory, and policy requirements regarding privacy.
- Determine the risks and effects of collecting, maintaining, and disseminating information in an identifiable forum in an electronic information system.
- Examine and evaluate protections and alternative procedures for handling information to mitigate privacy risks.

Measures for preventing inadvertent data breaches include the following:

- Limit data retention.
- Limit access to personnel information and train personnel accordingly.
- Consider using technology controls such as encryption when data needs to be stored on mobile devices.

3.17 Critical Path of NPPI and Core Business Transactions

3.17.1 NPPI Data

The concept of the critical path of data is very important, because it basically maps out the journey of sensitive customer and patient data throughout the IT applications, systems, and IT infrastructure components to its final place at rest within some database of a server. Understanding the critical path will provide the initial roadmap for management to develop a clear security strategy for deciding which layers of security are desired within the Defense in Depth Model to safeguard NPPI in transit and in storage.

It is important to identify NPPI data and map its entire journey for regulatory, audit, and compliance purposes, and it is equally as important to perform a similar process for core business transactions.

Performing data transaction flows of each transaction that contains NPPI and core business transaction data will allow management to make the appropriate decisions relative to which means of safeguarding controls would be the most effective for any given transaction that involves NPPI and core business transaction data.

The benefits of performing a data flow diagram on NPPI and core transaction data are as follows:

- Mapping transaction flows is the precursor step for determining the identification of "control points" throughout the journey of data within an IT infrastructure.
- A control point is defined as any place along the path of the journey of data throughout the IT infrastructure of an organization or service provider, which encompasses any one of the following criteria:
  - Data origination
  - Access control
  - Input
  - Processing
  - Output
  - A place where data confidentiality is required
  - A place where data integrity is required
  - A place where data availability is required
  - A place where auditability or some type of journaling is required

3.18 Information Security Theory and Control Point Identification

No information security theory exists today which discusses the concept of data criticality and how data values are not static but are dynamic and constantly change throughout the data transactions life cycle. Specifically, data is enriched in many ways through additional processing performed within an application or system. That same data previously processed within one application is now being transmitted to a second or third application for continued processing. As such, data is constantly modified or enriched, receiving pre- and postprocessing. Additionally, NPPI and core business data transactions could be deleted at some point in their transaction journey. The significance of understanding the dynamic changing behavior of data throughout its journey is noteworthy, because it will determine what control points should be added, modified, or deleted, based upon the changes in the data flows.

3.19 Control Points and the Key Risk Indicator (KRI)

A control point, as previously defined, represents a point in the data's transmission or storage where data needs to be assessed to effectively understand the behavior of data for audit, investigation, verification, and validation and computer forensic purposes.

The concept of KRI for the Insider Computer Fraud Framework is noteworthy because it represents the general term used for identifying all the components used to evaluate data privacy through the transmission and storage of sensitive data. The term or concept of KRI for business data value monitoring is significant because of management's need to monitor core business data throughout the IT infrastructure, applications, and systems.

Keep the following in mind:

KRIs are changes in values for core business data, key fraud indicator (KFI), key fraud metrics (KFM), and key fraud signature (KFS).

A control point represents processes or functions relating to data prior to entry into a system, during and after processing, where risks need to be identified, measured, monitored, and controlled. KRIs may include the following operational processes or functions: data origination, access control, input, processing, output, confidentiality, integrity, availability, and auditability.

3.20 The Relationship between KRIs, Control Points, and IT Infrastructure

The initial selection, modification, or deletion of KRIs should have a direct correlation to the layers of defense and the Defense in Depth Model. Similarly, any significant changes to the control points may directly impact the layers within the Defense in Depth Model that may be used to safeguard critical and sensitive data, applications, and systems. There are no absolutes in terms of when a change in a KRI or control point would necessitate a reevaluation or assessment for either adding or deleting another layer of defense within the Defense in Depth Model. However, significant changes in KRIs and control points should serve as trigger points or early warning signs that an IT infrastructure reassessment may be warranted.

3.21 The Relationship between the Risk Evaluation Process and the Defense in Depth (DiD) Efficiency Calculation

The Defense in Depth (DiD) Efficiency Calculation is a good method for pulling together a number of different qualitative workflows. There were previous discussions on a number of distinct areas, such as KRIs, control points, the IT infrastructure, residual risk, NRR, and many other qualitative factors. Until now, the analysis has been primarily qualitative, and now we need to show the convergence between the qualitative and the quantitative aspects of risk. Performing a quantitative assessment is important for understanding the effectiveness of each layer within the Defense in Depth Model (that is, applications, network, database, etc.) and for showing how collectively all the layers in the Defense in Depth Model assist in reducing enterprise risks in total.

3.22 Background on the Origin of Bayes' Theorem and Practical InfoSec Application of the Theorem Using the DiD Efficiency Calculation

Bayes' Theorem (also known as Bayes' rule or Bayes' law) is a result in probability theory, which relates the conditional and marginal probability distributions of random variables. In some interpretations of probability, Bayes' Theorem tells how to update or revise beliefs in light of new evidence: the probability of an event A conditional on another event B is generally different from the probability of B conditional on A. However, there is a definite relationship between the two, and Bayes' Theorem is the statement of that relationship.

As a formal theorem, Bayes' Theorem is valid in all interpretations of probability. However, frequentist and Bayesian interpretations disagree about the kinds of things to which probabilities should be assigned in applications: Frequentists assign probabilities to random events according to their frequencies of occurrence or to subsets of populations as proportions of the whole; Bayesians assign probabilities to propositions that are uncertain. A consequence is that Bayesians have more frequent occasion to use Bayes' Theorem.

According to Jim Nelms, chief information security officer (CISO) of the World Bank, who developed the DiD efficiency calculation that is a practical adaptation of Bayes' rule, the DiD calculation applies unrelated probabilities to the five layers (application, middleware, database manager, operating system, and network) of custody transfer within any given system. Nelms states that the five-layer model is distinct because of the technological interface between layers and the requirement of custody transfer between layers, as these are not arbitrary layers of definition but physically and programmatically separated layers for evaluation based on the technology used.

3.23 Determining an Applications Residual Risk (Inherent Risk-Mitigating Controls)

Our initial judgmental qualitative risk assessment for an application or system was important for determining the inherent risk assessment rating (that is, low, moderate, and high). For details refer to the Inherent Risk Valuation Matrix (Table 3.7) to see how the qualitative ratings are used in assigning a numeric value. Additionally, the qualitative risk assessment for an application is used to assign a numeric value to the threats and probability/likelihood analysis and the vulnerabilities and impact analysis values also included within the Inherent Risk Valuation Matrix.

Determining the type of mitigating controls to reduce the level of inherent risk is an important second step in assigning a qualitative value (low, moderate, and high) for the residual risk level. We are determining the type of mitigating controls through completion of the Application Control Point Rating Matrix.

Using the example (Table 3.20) below for the Application Control Point Rating Matrix, the application identified as CML-APP1 has a calculated rating of 47 percent out of a possible 100 percent, which would be considered low and indicative of an application with poor controls. Therefore, for illustrative purposes, if we have an application with a high inherent risk value and poor mitigating controls, we will assign a qualitative rating of low, leaving a residual risk value of high.

- Inherent Risk = High
- Mitigating Controls = Low
- Residual Risk = High

The process described below will provide an illustration and working example of the close interrelationship between the risk evaluation process, Bayes' Theorem, and the DiD calculation.

3.24 Determining an Application's Net Residual Risk (Inherent Risk-Mitigating Controls ± IT Infrastructure and Software Controls (Optimizers)

The residual risk level is unacceptable at "high," and evaluating the mitigating controls within the application does not by itself reduce the risk exposure for that application or system. However, when factoring the impact of the optimizers, the NRR level has greatly improved from high to moderate or low:

- Inherent Risk = High
- Mitigating Controls = Low (poor application controls)
- Residual Risk = High
- ±Optimizers = High (strong controls from the IT infrastructure and software)
- Net Residual Risk = Moderate or Low (a favorable improvement in reducing the risk level of the application or system through the use of additional layers of defense found within the IT infrastructure)

3.25 A Quantitative Analysis (Defense in Depth Efficiency Calculation)

For illustrative purposes, let us review the steps needed for computing the Defense in Depth Efficiency Calculation.

3.25.1 Step 1: Complete the Application Control Point Ratings Matrix

Basically, this step establishes the initial ratings percentage for a given application. Note that this calculation is for determining the efficiency or effectiveness of security controls within an application or system. The effectiveness of the control points is directly correlated to the controls used to assess the level of the application's residual risk. The percentage range from 0 to 100 that management will assign to each critical application will be initially judgmental and probably predicated, for the most part, on internal audits and SOX 404 testing on the critical application. It is important to note that the control points used within the Application Control Point Ratings Matrix represent only a starting point for assessing an application's risk/control profile. Management should consider other factors in their assessment; however, it is important to ensure that there is at least consistent criteria in how applications are assessed. Consequently, if changes in control points are made for one application or system, those same control point changes should also be made when evaluating other applications or systems for consistency purposes.

To illustrate the concepts and terms mentioned in this chapter, we will refer to the Application Control Point Rating Matrix presented in Table 3.20, which is the first step toward calculating the Defense in Depth Efficiency Calculation. The efficiency percentage values assigned to each control point category will be subjective; however, once the control point concept is inculcated in the terminology and culture of both management and audit, the assigning of numeric values will likely evolve from art to science, but this will likely take time within an organization.

The calculation value of 47 percent was determined after taking each subtotal (420) and dividing the subtotal by the total number of control points (9). The value of 47 percent represents the efficiency of Layer 1 in this Defense in Depth Model, which is obviously below average using the scale of 0 (lowest) to 100 (highest). (Refer to Table 3.21 for the operating system for Layer 2.)

The calculation of the efficiency of security in Layer 1 (application) cannot be viewed alone in a vacuum because it represents only the controls when evaluating the level of an applications residual risk assessment (application inherent risk–application controls) and excludes any reference to any interrelated IT infrastructure components. Consequently, we now need to evaluate the impact of application security in context with the rest of the IT infrastructure components (that is, firewalls, middleware, databases, etc.), which may either increase or decrease the level of risk by integrating various optimizers into the equation, as detailed in Step 2.

One of the goals in assessing the impact of the Defense in Depth calculation optimizers (IT infrastructure components) is to more accurately evaluate the integrated risk by tracing NPPI and core business transaction data from the initial point of entry within an application or system to the operating system being used for processing the application and data, to the network segments that are transporting the data, to the transmission of that data to other applications, to its final point of storage within some repository.

3.25.2 Step 2: Complete the IT Infrastructure and Software Control Point Rating Matrix Operating System (Application Security Optimizer)

In Step 1, we focused exclusively on the first layer of defense, which included a measure of the effectiveness of a particular application, which we determined to be at 47 percent, which is indicative of an application that appears to have a high degree of risk. By extension, we will leverage off the 47 percent efficiency rating assigned to an application and then determine what IT infrastructure components the application uses to process, transmit, and store data within the enterprise and to external third parties—individuals or organizations—via the network (that is, LAN, WAN), firewalls, routers, middleware, databases, or other applications within the organization

Table 3.20 Application Control Point Rating Matrix: A Quantitative Analysis (Defense in Depth Efficiency Calculation)—The Commercial Loan Application (Critical Application)

Application Control Point[a]	Layer 1	Efficiency Percentage										
Application Risks	CML_APP1[b]	0	10	20	30	40	50	60	70	80	90	100
Data Origination				X								
Access Controls							X					
Input					X							
Processing			X									
Output									X			
Confidentiality					X							
Integrity										X		
Availability										X		
Auditability							X					
Subtotal	420		10	20	60		100		70	160		
AVG (%)	47											

[a] The AVG percentage represents the efficiency level of various controls as determined by the nine identified control points; however, there is no definitive number that is acceptable, and they should be determined primarily by management, audit, and the compliance departments of a given institution, based on the results of a previously performed comprehensive integrated (business/technology) risk assessment

[b] Layer 1: CML_APP1 represents a management-determined critical application used for processing commercial loans within a bank. The application was determined to be critical based on a criticality matrix of several factors. The CML_APP1 application will not only receive an assessment of the "Application Control Points," as determined from this matrix, but will receive a similar control point assessment as detailed in the companion Infrastructure Control Point Rating Matrix.

Table 3.21 Infrastructure Control Point Rating Matrix: A Quantitative Analysis (Defense in Depth Efficiency Calculation)—The Commercial Loan Application (Critical Application)

Infrastructure Control Point	Layer 2										
Operating System	CML_APP1										
					Efficiency Percentage						
	0	10	20	30	40	50	60	70	80	90	100
Data origination										X	
Access controls									X		
Input								X			
Processing									X		
Output								X			
Confidentiality				X							
Integrity									X		
Availability									X		
Auditability									X		
Subtotal				30				140	400	90	
	660										
AVG (%)	73										

or external to it. The IT infrastructure components will be called *application control optimizers*, or simply *optimizers*. The term *optimizers* is being used because an attempt is being made to increase the accuracy of our application risk assessment by factoring the risks associated with other IT infrastructure components.

Using the first optimizer, the operating system used to process the NPPI and core business data, the second layer of protection in the Defense in Depth calculation has strengthened and reflects 73 percent, which will improve the aggregate Defense in Depth calculation that factors each layer. Having strong control over the operating system is noteworthy, because certain legacy applications may rely heavily on the strength of the access control and security provisioning process based on sound operating system parameter settings and other related controls.

3.25.2.1 Network Perimeter (Application Security Optimizer)

Continuing the IT infrastructure control point assessment process we previously completed for the operating system in Step 2, we need to assess other layers of the Defense in Depth Model which may provide additional layers of protection, such as the network perimeter (Table 3.22).

In this example, we are now factoring the third layer of defense in the Defense in Depth Model calculation, where we are now evaluating the security efficiency and effectiveness of the network perimeter optimizer.

We started with the application (Layer 1) that represented the starting point of the journey of NPPI and core business transaction data. Through the development of data flow diagrams, we then traced the aforementioned key data elements within the critical path of their journey to other components of the IT infrastructure (optimizers) and the data's journey to potential third parties for additional processing. In our example, we show the second layer of defense as the operating system (application security optimizer). The third layer is the inclusion of the network perimeter optimizer.

This is an iterative process in evaluating the security strength and efficiency of each layer in the Defense in Depth Model, using the same control points for each layer of defense, starting with the application and then continuing to each IT infrastructure component. The next layer in the Defense in Depth Model might be Layer 4, which includes firewalls, and then Layer 5 for routers, and so forth. It is important to note that a direct correlation exists between the critical path of NPPI and core business application data as it starts and completes its journey from point of entry to its final place of rest within a repository. Therefore, depending on the journey of NPPI and core business data, you could conceivably have numerous other layers in this Defense in Depth Efficiency Calculation.

Using a simple Web-based electronic banking application as an example, determine how many potential layers of the Defense in Depth Model could exist. We always start with the first layer of the Defense in Depth Model (Table 3.23) being the critical business application. Ideally, for consistency in application classification

Table 3.22 Infrastructure Control Point Rating Matrix (Network Perimeter): A Quantitative Analysis (Defense in Depth Efficiency Calculation)—The Commercial Loan Application (Critical Application)

Infrastructure Control Point	Layer 3	Efficiency Percentage										
Network Perimeter	CML_APP1	0	10	20	30	40	50	60	70	80	90	100
Data Origination							Not applicable					
Access Controls		X										
Input		X										
Processing							Not applicable					
Output							Not applicable					
Confidentiality												
Integrity		X										
Availability		X										
Auditability		X										
Subtotal		X										
AVG (%)		0										

Table 3.23 Defense in Depth IT Infrastructure and Software (Applications and Modifiers): A Quantitative Analysis—E-Banking Application Matrix

Layer	Application	Rating[a]
1	Application	47
Optimizers (IT Infrastructure)		
2	Operating System	73
3	Network Perimeter	0
4	Web Server	TBD
5	Web Authentication	TBD
6	Firewalls	TBD
7	IDs	TBD
8	Internal Network Servers (i.e., LAN)	TBD
9	Internet Banking Servers	TBD
10	Domain Name Server	TBD
11	E-mail Server	TBD
12	External Routers	TBD
13	Informational Web Server	TBD
14	Transactional Web Server	TBD
Optimizers (Software)		
15	Active X Controls	TBD
16	Database Management System	TBD
17	Application Programming Interfaces (APIs)	TBD
18	Web Browser	TBD
19	Middleware	TBD
20	Embedded Script within Web Page	TBD
21	Java Applets	TBD

Note: TBD, to be determined.

[a] Cross-reference the computed ratings for each layer from respective infrastructure control matrix.

and treatment, it would be good to have a commonly used and consistent criteria for classifying a critical application or system to ensure standards are applied equally for production applications that are subject to various regulatory and audit constraints, such as those imposed by SOX 404, GLB, HIPAA, and BCP/DR purposes.

The Defense in Depth IT Infrastructure and Software Modifier E-Banking Application Matrix is not intended to reflect all of the potential optimizers for this example; however, if this process was used in a real-life application within an organization, then it would be important to ensure that each application or system and all of their optimizers have been identified.

In this matrix, the term *software optimizer* is introduced in the attempt to expand the defense in depth security risk and controls analysis from just the application and the IT infrastructure components to include software risks and controls. Data is constantly being enriched or modified in some way, through a formula or algorithm in some application or system. Therefore, the combined risk evaluation of an application or system in totality may be significantly different when the effect and impact of the IT infrastructure and software optimizers are factored in.

It is clear that by looking at the application security controls on a stand-alone basis, the 47 percent rating reviewed in a vacuum would leave the impression that the application's security profile is poor and in need of additional controls to reduce the level of residual risk.

This is where the concept of NRR becomes very important, because our security analysis should require us to understand not only the holistic risk profile of the application or system, but also what IT infrastructure and software control points need to be considered in our analysis so as not to inaccurately classify the risk level of a production application by myopically analyzing only the application risks.

Without calculating the Total Defense in Depth Model Security Efficiency Ratio, it is clear that the application controls appear weak based on the Layer 1 rating of 47 percent. However, the positive contributions made by the IT infrastructure *optimizers* appear noteworthy and based on the ratings determined for Layer 2 at 74 percent (operating system) and Layer 3 (network perimeter) at 95 percent. We can now see a marked improvement in the total defense in depth effectiveness and efficiency.

3.25.3 Step 3: Calculate the DiD Security Effectiveness Percentage Using All Five Layers of Protection and with Two Out of the Five Layers of Protection

The calculations below are based primarily on Bayes' Theorem, which describes a "new" probability (control effectiveness) given a "prior" set of probabilities, when operating together. Achieving layered protection requires a layered evaluation that can be calculated based on the Defense in Depth Formula.

The effectiveness of an individual layer in the Defense in Depth Model was previously calculated, but the synergistic effect of all the layers of controls and defense was not calculated.

Bayes' Theorem is used to calculate the total synergistic effect of security protection after determining the appropriate percentage for each layer of defense that was previously determined. The first example will illustrate the Defense in Depth Security Control Efficiency Calculation using two layers of defense; the second example will add an additional variable or security layer for a total of three layers within the model and calculation. Based on the additional layer of security, the differences in security protection having two versus three layers of protection will be compared.

The illustrated examples will provide two points for discussion. The first is that application security should not be assessed in a vacuum and requires an understanding of the critical path of NPPI and core business transaction data and the identification of control points within the application or system, in addition to analyzing the impact of optimizers that represent components of the IT infrastructure and software security controls.

The second point is that finding the elusive integrated (business and technology) risk is achievable. A precursor step to determining the control points within applications, IT infrastructure components, and software will not only aide in solving the Defense in Depth calculation, but should serve as the basis for identifying the appropriate management and technology controls. Additionally, the control points identified should serve as the basis for determining the universe for internal and external audits.

For the examples listed below, and the goal of keeping the illustrations simple, the impact of software controls as an optimizer was not factored into this analysis; however, in real-life analysis, the effectiveness and efficiency of software control should be considered in the calculation.

Bayes' Theorem:

$$E_{total} = \frac{C * (1 - ((1 - E1) * (1 - E2)...))}{L}$$

where E is the effectiveness of a single layer, C is the number of layers with controls implemented, and L is the total number of layers.

The scenarios in the following sections are based on the previously determined layers of the defense percentages as illustrated in Table 3.24.

Table 3.24 A Quantitative Analysis E-Banking Application Matrix: Defense In Depth IT Infrastructure and Software—Modifiers

Layer	IT Infrastructure Component	Rating[a]
1	Application	47
Optimizers (IT Infrastructure)		
2	Operating system	73
3	Network	85
4	Middleware	66
5	Database Manager	75

[a] Cross-reference the computed ratings for each layer from respective infrastructure control matrix.

3.25.3.1 Scenario 1: Calculating the Defense in Depth Security Efficiency Ratio with Five Layers

A bank has five layers of defense in their Defense in Depth Security Model, with the first being a critical application that has a rating of 47, the second layer being the operating system with a rating of 73 percent, the third layer being the network with a rating of 85, the fourth layer being the middleware with a rating of 66, and the fifth layer being the database manager with a rating of 75. The aforementioned situation is realistic, as most organizations would likely have some level of defense at each layer. The actual percentages of strength for each individual layer is the question mark in the equation, with 0 assigned to the lack of any substantive security controls and with 100 percent assigned to a layer that has very strong controls.

$$
\begin{aligned}
E_{total} &= \frac{5*(1-((1-.47)*(1-.73)*(1-.85)*(1-.66)*(1-.75)))}{5} \\[2mm]
&= \frac{5*(1-(.53)*(.27)*(.15)*(.34)*(.25))}{5} \\[2mm]
&= \frac{5*(1-.0018)}{5} \\[2mm]
&= \frac{5*.9982}{5} \\[2mm]
&= \frac{4.991}{5}
\end{aligned}
$$

$= 100\%$ (Total Defense in Depth Security Efficiency Percentage)

This calculation reflects the benefits enjoyed through having all five layers of defense working at varying capacities, and operating synergistically. The 100 percent Defense in Depth Efficiency Calculation using all five layers of defenses based on this formula and calculation provides a strong level of defense for this organization.

3.25.3.2 Scenario 2: Calculating the Defense in Depth Security Efficiency Ratio with Only Two Layers of Defense

The same bank decided on maintaining only two layers of information security defense in a three-layer system (three layers used for simplicity of calculation, as typically five layers must be addressed in any given system) to protect its organization, which as previously noted will have a deleterious impact on the overall Defense in Depth Efficiency Calculation. (Note that using only two layers of defense has the impact of defeating the effectiveness of the other layers, with an assigned "0" given to the third layer or variable in the calculation.)

Therefore, using the same formula in calculating the total Defense in Depth security efficiency percentage, the network perimeter is strong and has a 95 percent efficiency rating. Note that you must adjust the "C" variable to a value of two in order to accurately reflect the number of layers with controls implemented of the three layers present in this model.

$$E_{total} = \frac{2*(1-((1-.47)*(1-.73)*(1-0)))}{3}$$

$$= \frac{2*(1-((.53)*(.27)*(1)))}{3}$$

$$= \frac{2*(1-(.1431))}{3}$$

$$= \frac{2*(.8569)}{3}$$

$$= \frac{1.7138}{3}$$

$$= .57 \text{ or } 57\% \text{ (Total Defense in Depth Security Efficiency Percentage)}$$

This calculation, although using only two layers of defense, reflects the negative impact of not having all layers present (normally five) of defense when computing the Defense in Depth Security Efficiency Calculation. The impact of assigning a

"0" for the nonexistent third layer of defense reduced the DiD Efficiency Ratio from 100 percent to 57 percent.

To further illustrate the dramatic impact of ignoring one or more layers within a system, consider the following calculation using the standard five-layer model where three layers are measured at 98 percent efficiency and two layers are ignored:

$$E_{total} = \frac{3*(1-((1-.98)*(1-.98)*(1-.98)*(1-0)*(1-0)))}{5}$$

$$= \frac{3*(1-(.02*.02*.02*1*1))}{5}$$

$$= \frac{3*(1-.000008)}{5}$$

$$= \frac{3*.999992}{5}$$

$$= \frac{2.9999}{5}$$

$$= 0.59998 \text{ or } 59\% \text{ efficiency}$$

Lesson learned—You may choose to ignore one or more areas of your system; however, you may not choose to exclude the consequences of doing so.

Although not illustrated in the two aforementioned examples, it is important to comment on the impact to the efficiency relative to identical flaws in multiple layers. The existence of identical flaws in multiple layers does not change Bayes' algorithm, but it does affect the evaluation criteria for establishing layer efficiency. Table 3.25 can be used to target a desired security efficiency.

Table 3.25   Desired Security Table Efficiency Table

Number of Layers	60%	70%	80%	90%
1	60.0%	70.0%	80.0%	90.0%
2	84.0%	91.0%	96.0%	99.0%
3	93.6%	97.3%	99.2%	99.9%
4	94.7%	99.2%	99.8%	100.0%
5	99.0%	99.8%	100.0%	100.0%

Source: Jim Helms. (The CSO of The World Bank.)

3.25.4 Step 4: Assign a Qualitative Rating to the Total Defense in Depth Security Efficiency Percentage

Under the first scenario, the total defense in depth security efficiency percentage of 100 percent, which is obviously very strong and based not on the strength of the application, but rather the strength is the IT infrastructure controls and the software controls (optimizers), as appropriate. Therefore, based on the calculation of 100 percent, we will conclude with some level of assurance that the controls used for determining the NRR (risk level after factoring the IT infrastructure components and software controls) is favorably low (low risk and strong controls). Similarly, under the second scenario, with a total defense in depth efficiency percentage of 85 percent being good and all factors being equal to those in the first scenario, we would still conclude that the NRR level remains favorably low (albeit not as strong as the first scenario with a 100 percent DiD rating).

3.25.5 Step 5: Perform an Update on the Threat Modeling Rating Based on the Results of the Defense in Depth Calculation and the Net Residual Risk Rating Assessment

Initially we performed an assessment of the threat modeling process when we evaluated the inherent risk valuation for critical applications and systems. (Refer to the Inherent Risk Valuation Matrix for details.) The purpose of evaluating the threat modeling process at the earliest stages in the risk assessment process was to calculate the application risk weightings for criticality factors.

Determining the appropriate application and system criticality factors is important for ensuring that a consistent process exists in the identification and updating of critical systems for SOX 404 testing, GLB, HIPAA compliance, and disaster recovery testing, to name a few. By extension, any data determined to be critical or sensitive based on business, regulatory, compliance, and management drivers must have the appropriate safeguards in place to ensure the confidentiality, integrity, and availability of this information is in place.

Based on our increased knowledge of the InfoSec risk landscape of both the application or system and key data flows between other critical applications within the enterprise and to external third parties, we are now in a position where we can assess the threat landscape as it impacts the inherent risk level, but more importantly the impact of threats on the NRR level. Understanding the impact of threats on the NRR has particular significance because it is evaluating the likelihood and probability of threats after we identified our inherent (gross) risk and mitigating controls provided through the IT infrastructure and software.

Ostensibly at this point we are saying that we have protected our enterprise both externally and internally against known and potentially unknown threats based on our NRR rating and our total Defense in Depth security efficiency percentage.

3.26 The Threat Assessment Process (The Integration Process)

A common omission in the threat modeling process is to focus exclusively on identifying known versus the unknown external threats and to exclude an evaluation of the insider threat (known and unknown).

The primary goal of this chapter and book is to provide a workable and practical framework for identifying, measuring, monitoring, and controlling the insider threat. Therefore, our discussion on the topic of threat modeling will be more in line with providing a high-level framework to incorporate within an actual threat model which should then encapsulate the appropriate minimum standards for evaluating the insider threat.

However, at this point in our risk assessment analysis, we are well beyond the stage of determining the criticality and sensitivity of data and the applications or systems that process that data. The incorporation of threat modeling was important at that early stage of assessing the inherent risk valuation. Our risk assessment evaluation process at this stage of the analysis has matured, and at this point in our risk assessment, the residual risk and NRR levels were determined and the defense in depth security efficiency ratio was calculated.

Therefore, at this stage in our analysis, we basically performed a significant number of the preliminary critical steps needed for completing a thorough risk modeling process, which includes the following steps (the steps are not in sequence order as this will be contingent upon each organization based upon its existing operational processes and practices):

- *Identify Key Business Assets*: This is the first important step required for performing an integrated risk assessment.
- *Identify Critical Data and Systems*: This step was performed during the integrated risk assessment process.
- *Identify Core Business Transaction Data Elements*: The identification of core business transaction data elements was completed during the integrated risk assessment process.
- *Identify Sensitive Data Elements that are NPPI*: Sensitive data elements were identified so as to ensure compliance with GLB, HIPAA, and the breach notification requirements.

- *Data Flows*: The data flows of critical core business transaction data elements and sensitive data elements were determined during the integrated risk assessment process.

- *Metadata*: Any available metadata should be collected on core business transaction data and NPPI data for compliance and regulatory purposes.

- *Key Fraud Indicators (KFIs)*: KFIs are data elements that have been determined to contain NPPI information that would be the most vulnerable to an external or internal defalcation or breach. There should be a direct correlation between the values identified as KFIs and the total of NPPI data. The KFIs can be thought of as a subset of the total NPPI data. However, the total set of NPPI data should include sensitive data elements used for monitoring compliance with HIPAA (such as medical records), as applicable, and the requirements of either a state or proposed national legislation (Data Availability and Transport Act [DATA]) or similar legislation that is required by companies for notification in the event of a breach.

- *Key Fraud Metrics (KFMs)*: The KFM is a by-product of the identification of KFIs and is used to establish a means for establishing a numerical baseline for what is a normal value for a particular area.

- *Key Risk Indicators (KRIs)*: Key risk indicator is the parent term used to describe the key core business and sensitive NPPI and KFI data flows within an enterprise application or with external third parties.

- *Control Point Determination*: Control points are identified at each stage of a transactions journey through the application and components of the IT infrastructure (i.e., network through to a third party, to its final resting or storage repository).

- *Optimizers*: Optimizers (IT infrastructure and software controls) are identified.

- *Residual Risk Rating*: A completed qualitative assessment through a residual risk rating (inherent risk-mitigating controls); a completed qualitative residual risk rating gives values of high, moderate, and low.

- *Net Residual Risk Rating*: A completed qualitative NRR rating designates values of high, moderate, and low.

- *Completed Layer 1 (application) Defense in Depth Security Efficiency Calculation*: A completed quantitative rating for a critical application (Layer 1 controls) is based upon the Defense in Depth Security Efficiency Calculation.

- *Completed Optimizer (all IT infrastructure and software) Layer 2 and above*: A completed quantitative rating for a critical application and its optimizers (IT infrastructure components and software controls) is based on Layer 2 and beyond, using the Defense in Depth Security Efficiency Calculation.

- *Completed Total Defense in Depth Security Efficiency Percentage*: A completed total Defense in Depth security efficiency percentage reflects the synergistic effect on the entire security within a critical application and its critical path throughout the IT infrastructure and software security within each identified control for each layer of security.

Prior to developing a strategy or action plan to reduce the level of threats, our universe of risks is narrowly focused on the key integrated risk (business and technology) areas presented below.

3.27 Critical Applications or Systems

The data flow and critical path of only key core transactions within the critical applications or systems, NPPI data (financial and medical), and the collection of the metadata associated with all the core and NPPI data is important data to collect and analyze in understanding the behavior of data and its journey throughout the IT infrastructure within the organizations and to external third parties.

By narrowing our threat modeling universe to include only the key critical applications, core transactions, and NPPI data and metadata for regulatory and compliance purposes, the bold statement has been made at this point that we engaged in either risk acceptance, elimination, or the transference of risks found within the other critical applications or systems, IT infrastructure, and software.

An important point to mention prior to discussing the nuances of threat modeling is that up to this point, we have spoken specifically to the roles and responsibilities of management relative to the risk assessment process and have not given equal time to discussing what roles corporate internal audit and compliance and the Chief Privacy Officer play in this process. Specifically, audit, compliance, privacy, and legal departments of a corporation should be actively engaged throughout the risk assessment and threat modeling process. Each of the aforementioned departments within an organization should treat the risk assessment and threat modeling process as a perpetual project. Perhaps one day when the risk assessment and threat modeling process matures to a science, then management and the audit, compliance, privacy, and legal departments can become less engaged in the process. However, the processes identified for many organizations are not effectively implemented and are certainly not fully operational in an automated manner.

3.28 The Strategic Planning Process for Reducing the Insider Threat

The strategic planning process basically involves completion of the risk assessment process using the TRIP methodology or equivalent, completion of the Threat Assessment Matrix (see Section 3.29), completion of the insider computer fraud threat assessment (ICFTA), utilization of the Strategic, Legal/Regulatory, and

Operational Risk Matrix, performance of an application and code review penetration test, completion of an InfoSec scorecard, and finally, use of management's analysis and strategic plan for InfoSec, which factors the impact of both external and internal threats against the level of NRR.

The strategic planning process should be an iterative and dynamic process that has several moving parts as detailed in Figure 3.3. Any changes within any component will have a ripple effect on each of the interconnected processes; consequently, each dependent process needs to be reevaluated against those changes.

Figure 3.3 provides a general framework for the steps involved in establishing a method for identifying, measuring, monitoring, and controlling the insider threat. Each of the steps identified in Figure 3.3 are mutually inclusive and as

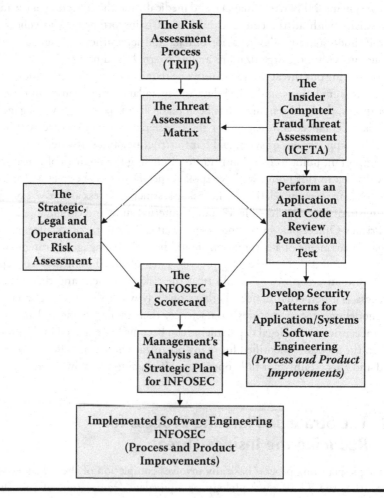

Figure 3.3   The strategic planning process for reducing the insider threat.

such have important interdependencies that need to be understood. It would be relatively easy to perform any of these steps in a vacuum; however, one of the more challenging aspects is to find the interrelationships and integration between each of these steps.

3.29 The Threat Assessment Matrix

Throughout our discussion of risk assessment, the importance of control points and their role in tracing the flow of critical data between various applications and systems has been highlighted. In order to be consistent in applying the concepts discussed in previous sections of this chapter, we will continue the use of the term "control points" in this section, given its significance and interrelationship to the risk assessment process, security pattern analysis (to be discussed later in this chapter) and based on the results of the pattern analysis, be able to conduct some level of predictive analysis of day zero insider and external threats.

One of the primary goals of the Threat Assessment Matrix is to crystallize what criteria should be used to evaluate the severity of a particular threat so that uniformity and consistency can be applied in the ratings assessment across an enterprise, regardless of its source.

Table 3.26   The Threat Assessment Matrix—A Guide for Completing the ICFTA

Control Point	High (3)	Moderate (2)	Low (1)	Direction
Access Controls (For illustration purposes, the rating criteria associated with access controls are broken out within a separate document—see Table 3.27)			Refer to Table 3.27 for details	
Data Origination/Input Controls				
Processing Controls				
Output Controls				

Note: Ratings criteria are as follows: high (3)—high risk level (refer to Table 3.27 for the ratings assessment criteria; weak controls); moderate (2)—moderate risk level (moderate controls); low (1)—low risk level (strong controls). To obtain rating criteria, cross-reference the threat assessment rating reference table.

The Threat Assessment Matrix is structured so that each control point rating will be consistent in format. Specifically, the following ratings criteria will be itemized for each control point:

1. Summary
2. Probability
3. Impact
4. Confidentiality
5. Integrity
6. Availability
7. Auditability

As indicated in the Threat Assessment Matrix (Table 3.26), one of the primary goals in completing this table is to achieve uniformity in criteria without jeopardizing the ability of management to decide how to assess the qualitative ratings and their associated numeric values based on perceived or actual risks.

3.30 The Threat Assessment Rating Reference Table

The threat assessment rating reference table is presented in Table 3.27. The results of completing the Threat Assessment Matrix will have particular significance in three separate but related areas, which include the following:

■ *Insider Computer Fraud Threat Assessment (ICFTA)*: The ICFTA should be used to assess what applications or systems are vulnerable to ICF activities. Analyzing the ratings concluded from the completion of ICFTA (high, moderate, low) and considering the level of NRR should establish the basis for determining how effective each is against an insider threat to an application or system.

■ *Application and Code Review*: One of the primary goals in penetration testing is to identify security vulnerabilities in a network and to assess how an outsider or insider to an enterprise may either deny service or gain access to information to which the attacker is not authorized. For discussion purposes, given the high level of vulnerability of applications and systems to the insider threat, our focus will be on performing an application and code review penetration test (Table 3.28). In Chapter 5, the methodology used to determine what type of penetration test to perform based on the threat management process is described.

■ *Strategic, Legal/Regulatory, and Operational Risk Ratings*: Evaluating the impact of ICFTA will be manifested within each family of IT risks, which are the strategic, legal/regulatory, and operational risk ratings (Table 3.29). The aforementioned risk families were intentionally excluded from the ICFTA detailed threat assessment so that the application controls could be viewed in totality instead of having to assess each application control ICF risk individually.

Table 3.27   The Threat Assessment Rating Reference Table: A Guide for Completing the ICFTA (Cross-Reference the Strategic, Legal, and Operational Risk Assessment)

Control Point: Access Controls	Low Risk, Strong Controls (1)
Summary	Rating: (1) Low risk, based on strong controls and the threat source not possessing either the motivation or technical skills to commit the defalcation. Strong security defenses governing the ability to permit or deny access to a system or file. Thorough controls for the effective identification, authentication, authorization, and accountability.
Probability	The threat source is not highly motivated or does not possess the capability of violating access controls to exploit an application or system vulnerability.
Impact	Exploitation of a vulnerability (1) will not result in a high cost for major tangible assets or resources, (2) will not violate, harm, or impede an organization's mission, reputation, or interest, or (3) is not likely to ever result in human death or serious injury.
Confidentiality	InfoSec policies, procedures, and practices provide strong documented controls to protect data confidentiality; strong indication of favorable practices governing data confidentiality.
Integrity	InfoSec policies, procedures, and practices are strong to protect data integrity based on a high level of controls governing authenticity, nonrepudiation, and accountability. Overall, a strong level of favorable practices govern data integrity and exist throughout the enterprise.
Availability	InfoSec policies, procedures, and practices provide strong internal control guidance to protect the timely availability of information technology resources (systems and data). Strong indication of favorable practices governing data availability.
Auditability	Audit trails are available on screen and printed and are also searchable. The data contained in the audit trails can be investigated using various data storage and access methods (i.e., data missing). Based on the ease and completeness of obtaining key data for computer forensic purposes during internal or law enforcement investigations, there should be no problem in collecting and analyzing critical application systems journaling for evidentiary purposes.

Table 3.28 Performing an Application and Code Review Penetration Test for Web-Based and Web Services Applications

Process	Criteria
Web-Based Applications	
Discovery:	Analysis of the technology, architecture, and functionality that comprise the application.
a. Technology	Identify the operating system, Web server version, and additional enabled technology associated with the application.
b. Server Scans	Server scans to identify known application functionality or exposures using the appropriate tools.
c. URL Harvesting	Identifying all known universal resource locators (URLs) within the application.
d. Path Disclosure	Identify the path to document Web roots within the operating system.
e. Directory Listing/ Traversal	Attempt to obtain and traverse directory trees.
f. Virtual Directories	Determine use of virtual directories and their limitations.
g. Functionality Mapping	A functionality map outlines the functions that an area performs and the subcomponents that make up that function.
h. Site Mapping	Create a map that logically portrays the application and identifies pages by type (such as static, dynamic, forms, or common gateway interface [CGI]).
i. Application Interfaces	Several methods can be used to establish a link between the Web server and an application, through CGI, server application programming interface (API), integrated application server, and server-side scripting.
j. Functionality ID used for Security Testing	Based on the previous step performed on functionality mapping, identify and document all application level functionality for later security testing.
k. Hidden Tags	Search for the misuse of hidden tags and take advantage of them to subvert the design of the application (i.e., purchasing a product for a lower cost than was advertised).

Process	Criteria
l. SSL Configuration/ Type	Determine Secure Sockets Layer (SSL) configuration/type to determine possible entry points of attack.
m. Session Traffic	Determine the sensitivity of session traffic to evaluate whether or not it can be sniffed.
Source Code Review:	Examining the source code of pages.
a. Hidden Fields	Hidden fields may reveal data structure (i.e., <meta content = "JavaScript". Developers may want to « hide data sent from the client to the server from the user. The data is only hidden from view and viewing the source code will show the hidden fields.
b. Comments	Search for unnecessary comments/information in the source, providing an attacker inside knowledge of the application.
c. Unnecessary External Links	Search for unnecessary external links that may direct an attacker to an alternate path of attack.
d. Scripting Language Evaluation	Evaluate scripting language usage such as JavaScript, Visual Basic Script, which may provide an alternate form of attack.
Input Validation	Ensuring the input supplied by the user and input into the browser for use within a Web application are the expected or normal values.
Server-Side Passing of Special Characters	Determine whether server-side passing of special metacharacters can compromise processing programs.
Buffer Overflow Conditions	Determine whether possible buffer overflow conditions exist in the server-side applications.
Error Message Generation	Attempt to generate error messages that may provide valuable information about a site's design, such as directory names.
HEX Value Replacements	Determine whether hex values can be replaced for ASCII or Unicode characters to circumvent the security of server-side applications.
Hidden Tags	Change hidden tags to determine if the server-side application correctly validates the data.

(continued)

Table 3.28 Performing an Application and Code Review Penetration Test for Web-Based and Web Services Applications (*Continued*)

Process	Criteria
Cross-Site Scripting Attacks	To prevent cross-site scripting attacks, determine if the Web site application filters the user input (i.e., the user-supplied data should be filtered for script code such as HTML <SCRIPT> tags).
Structure Query Language (SQL) Injection	Attempt to run SQL queries through input fields on the Web page. The error page returned from the SQL injection may provide insight into how the database is constructed, indicate the POST data that triggered the error, or provide someone's sensitive data (i.e., account information), assuming the SQL query is accepted.
Arbitrary Commands	Attempt to execute arbitrary commands via any noted vulnerable server-side applications.
Hypertext Markup Language (HTML) Embedding	The process of adding extra HTML-based content that will be rendered in the recipient's browser and pretends to come from the vulnerable application. Typically used to conduct virtual defacements of Web sites.
Session Management	Managing Hypertext Transfer Protocol (HTTP)-based client sessions are stateless; however, there are various methods that can be used to control the session management process.
Determine and Verify the Method Used to Maintain State	There are basically three methods available to both allocate and receive session ID information, which include: session ID information is embedded in the URL which is received by the application through HTTP GET requests when the client clicks on links embedded within a page; session ID information is stored within the fields of a form and submitted to the application. Typically the session ID information would be embedded within the form as a hidden field and submitted with HTTP POST command through the use of cookies.
Encryption of Session	Determine if the session IDs are encrypted.
Session Characteristics	Determine if the session IDs are incremental, predictable, or able to be played again.
Session Timeouts	Analyze session time-outs for adequacy.

Process	Criteria
Session Caching	Check for and analyze session caching.
Concurrent Sessions	Determine the session management information — number of concurrent sessions, Internet Protocol (IP)-based authentication, role-based authentication, identity-based authentication, cookie usage, session ID in URL encoding string, session ID in hidden HTML, field variable, etc.
Linkage between Session ID and IP Address	Determine the session management limitations — bandwidth usages, file download/upload limitations, transaction limitations, etc.
Session Management Limitations	Determine the session management limitations — bandwidth usages, file download/upload limitations, transaction limitations, etc.
Man-in-the-Middle Attacks	Gather sensitive information with man-in-the-middle attacks and then replay this gathered information to fool the application.
Input Manipulation	Make changes to data input to evaluate the effectiveness of the Web-based applications controls.
Limitations of Defined Variables	Find the limitations of the defined variables and protocol payload — data length, data type, construct format, etc.
Long Characters	Use exceptionally long character strings to find buffer overflows vulnerability in the applications.
Concatenate Commands	Concatenate commands in the input strings of the applications.
Bypass Input Validation Mechanisms	Use specific URL-encoded strings or Unicoded strings to bypass input validation mechanisms of the applications.
Functionality Perversion	Evaluation of application functionality for potential security concerns.
Basic Application Functionality	Analysis of basic application functionality for potential security issues with the interface, behavior, and architecture.
Programmatic Attacks	Identification of opportunities to programmatically attack any weaknesses noted during application test (i.e., buffer overflow conditions, brute force credential guessing, or token spoofing, etc.).

(continued)

Table 3.28 Performing an Application and Code Review Penetration Test for Web-Based and Web Services Applications (*Continued*)

Process	Criteria
Write to Application	Identify any ability to write to applications to the host file system and any ability to execute uploaded files.
Client-Side Data	Examination of client-side cached files, temporary files, or other information that potentially yields sensitive information or that could be altered maliciously and resubmitted to the application at a later time (i.e., reverse engineering of encrypted cookies).
Metacharacters	Determine whether command execution is possible through applications, for example, by using metacharacters to bypass application controls.
Uploaded or Appended Files	Identify the ability to upload or append files to server.
Download or View Files	Identify the ability to download or view arbitrary files on the server.
Random Number Analysis/ Prediction Techniques	Use a random number analysis/prediction technique to determine the predictability of any random but recurring variable or session management facility.
Authentication	Establish controls to reduce the risks associated with the Internet delivery channel, by authenticating users by more than one method.
Web ID Authentication	Authenticating the identity of a customer in a retail and commercial business environment to prevent incidents of fraud, including identity theft. Additionally to prevent an attacker from bypassing authentication and viewing protected files and executing programs on the Web server.
Cookie	Ensures the persistent cookie that stores the user's ID and time of last log-in requires the users to reauthenticate themselves if they left the computer without logging off or were inactive for a period of time.
Cookies	Provide a means of time-based authentication. Function by sending parcels of text sent by a server to a Web browser and then sends back the text unchanged by the browser each time it accesses that server.

Process	Criteria
Passing Cookies	Determine whether the server-side application is passing cookie information to the client's browser.
Manipulate Cookies	Attempt to manipulate cookie information to "spoof" any associated server-side authentication mechanism.
Disable Cookie	Disable client cookie support in the client browser and note any session data that is passed via the URL.
Persistent Cookies	Determine whether persistent cookies are used and if excess information is left on the user's system.
Buffer Overflow Attacks	Determine whether cookies are susceptible to buffer overflow attacks.
User Variables	Variables are temporary holders of information which include numeric, true/false, and objects.
Encrypted Variables	Determine whether user variables are encrypted.
Variable Characteristics	Determine whether user variables are incremental, predictable, or able to be played again.
Buffer Overflow Attacks	Determine whether variables are susceptible to buffer overflow attacks.
Input Manipulation	Attempts to bypass the normal data input controls that ensure the accuracy, completeness, and timeliness of data during its conversion from its original source into computer data, or entry into a computer application.
Limitations of the Defined Variables and Protocol Payload	Find the limitations of the defined variables and protocol payload (data length, data type, construct format, etc.).
Character Strings	Use exceptionally long character strings to find buffer overflow vulnerability in the applications.
Concatenate Commands	Concatenate commands in the input strings of the applications.
SQL Injection	Inject SQL language in the input strings of data-base-tiered Web applications.
Cross-Site Scripting	Examine cross-site scripting in the Web applications of the system.

(continued)

Table 3.28 Performing an Application and Code Review Penetration Test for Web-Based and Web Services Applications (*Continued*)

Process	Criteria
Unauthorized Directory/ File Access	Examine unauthorized directory/file access with path/directory traversal in the input strings of the applications.
URL-Encoded and Unicoded Strings	Use specific URL-encoded strings or Unicode-encoded strings to bypass input validation mechanisms of the applications.
Manipulate the Session/ Persistent Cookies	Manipulate the session/persistent cookies to fool or modify the logic in the server-side Web applications.
Manipulate the (Hidden) Field Variable	Manipulate the (hidden) field variable in the HTML forms to fool or modify the logic in the server-side Web applications.
Manipulate Hypertext Transfer Protocol (HTTP) Variables	Manipulate HTTP variables to fool or modify the logic in the server-side Web applications.
Illogical/Illegal Input	Use illogical/illegal input to test the application error-handling routines and to find useful debug/ error messages from the applications.
Output Manipulation	Attempts to bypass the normal data output controls for ensuring the integrity of the output and the correct and timely distribution of any output produced.
Cookies	Retrieve valuable information stored in cookies.
Cache	Retrieve valuable information from the client application cache.
Serialized Objects	Retrieve valuable information stored in the serialized objects.
Temporary Files and Objects	Retrieve valuable information stored in the temporary files and objects.
Information Leakage	Evaluating the appropriateness of the information that is viewable within the Web application.
HTML Forms	Find useful information in the hidden field variables of the HTML forms and comments in the HTML documents.
Viewable Application Information	Examine the information contained in the application banners, usage instructions, welcome messages, farewell messages, application help messages, debug/error messages, etc.

Process	Criteria
Web Services Applications[a]	
Reconnaissance Attacks	Gain access to Web service interfaces and to Web service messages in transit.
Directory Traversal Attack	Access the Web services host server and access the host server's password files and executables on the server to execute arbitrary commands.
Web Services Definition Language (WSDL) Scanning	Locate Web services that have been removed from the pregenerated WSDL and access them.
Format String Attacks	Send unexpected inputs to the Web application program in the form of strings specifically crafted to enable privilege escalation and take control of the program and the host on which it runs.
Attacks on Integrity	Attempt to make unauthorized changes to information accessed/handled by the application, based on the absence of such controls as cryptography, WS-Security, and other safeguards.

[a] Web services applications: The following section includes only a small subset of the total security risks involved in deploying Web services; however, for the purpose of showing Web-based application security concerns, a few of the many Web services, Web-based application threats were identified, but not an exhaustive list. This document is a companion document to further support the discussion within Chapter 6.

Notes: Management is encouraged to perform a thorough integrated (business and technology) application risk assessment, privacy impact assessment, and a comprehensive threat assessment prior to deploying Web services (internal and external). The learning curve for understanding Web services is steep, and the few application threats contained within this matrix only scratch the surface of application and other related threats.

Specifically, excluded from this document is a discussion of Web services-related threats including input validation; session management; general security policy and guidance for the presentation tier, business logic tier, and data tier; filtering requirements for all Simple Object Access Protocol/eXtensible Markup Language (SOAP/XML) messages for threats/information leaks; attack prevention for XML DoS; admission controls through antivirus and other malicious content; authentication and access controls; interoperability; Web Services Interoperability Organization (WS-I) and WS-Security and trust management; integrity and privacy; authorization; policy/governance enforcement; XML/SOAP testing requirements; and so forth.

A more comprehensive discussion on Web services may be found by accessing the following Web sites: www.nist.gov (A Guide to Secure Web Services), www.oasis-open.org, www.projectliberty.org, and www.ws-i.org. (All penetration tests should receive approval by the appropriate management/board/legal personnel within the organization prior to conducting an actual testing process.)

Table 3.29 The Strategic, Legal, and Operational Risk Assessment Matrix—Low Risk, Strong Controls (1)

General Risk Category[a]	Area of Concern	Related Controls[b]
Strategic: The risk to earnings or capital arising from adverse business decisions or improper implementation of those decisions. This risk is a function of the compatibility of an organization's strategic goals, the business strategies developed to achieve those goals, the resources deployed against these goals, and the quality of implementation	Business case	Strategic technology planning; establish goals and monitor performance; conduct research and consult with experts
	Internal/external resources	Provide adequate training; provide adequate support staff; administration of software updates; insurance coverage (e.g., Fidelity Bond)
	Outsourcing arrangements	Perform due diligence on vendors; audit performance; back-up arrangements
	Technological developments	Monitor new developments; budget for technology upgrades
Legal/regulatory/compliance:The risk to earnings or capital arising from violations of, or nonconformance with, laws, rules, regulations, prescribed practices, or ethical standards	Legal framework	Detailed contracts; digital signature; comprehensive disclosure
	Jurisdiction (e.g., laws, taxes)	Consult with legal counsel; well-defined trade area
	Regulatory compliance	Policies and procedures; consult with regulatory agencies; internal and external audit

General Risk Category[a]	Area of Concern	Related Controls[b]
Operational risk	Security	Authorization; access control (e.g., passwords, log-on IS); authentication; secure data storage; encryption; firewalls/filtering routers
	Operations	Policies and procedures; client accounting; contingency plans; back-up training; audit procedures

[a] OCC 98-3 Technology Risk Management (Guidance for Bankers and Examiners).
[b] The Federal Financial Institution Examination Council (FFIEC) Interagency Statement on Retail On-Line Banking.

3.30.1 Performing an Application and Code Review Penetration Test for Web-Based and Web Services Applications

Provided in Table 3.28 is an example of what the scope of an application and code review penetration test may include and it is intended to illustrate the interrelationships and dependencies that exist between the Threat Assessment Matrix, the ICFTA, and the application and code review penetration test methodology.

The application and code review penetration test methodology contains several key Web application testing criteria. It should not be considered to be the unabridged list of every risk, but rather a listing of several key test criteria that should be considered along with any industry sound and best practices and the institutional knowledge of each organization that may have fallen victim to the insider threat.

3.30.2 The Information Security Scorecard

The information security scorecard (Table 3.30) is a diagnostic tool for management to evaluate the effectiveness of management's policies and standards and practices to identify measure, monitor, and control information risks and controls. The scorecard rating criteria and its companion "INFOSEC Scorecard for Corporation XYZ" are intended to establish an enterprise-wide information security component and composite ratings based on a combined total of eight general and application control components.

There are two application components: one for the software development process (preimplementation projects) and the other for production applications and

Table 3.30 The Information Security Scorecard for Corporation XYZ

Number	Category	2006	2005	Security Trend
1	Security policies and standards	G	G	❯
2	System development and security architecture	R	Y	
*3	Production application system security	Y	R	
4	Network security	G	Y	
5	User authentication and access controls	G	G	❯
6	Security monitoring	R	Y	
7	Vendor management for security	R	Y	
8	Incident response (including computer forensics)	R	R	❯
	Overall	R	Y	

systems. The remaining components should be placed in the generic category of general controls.

The purpose of the information security scorecard differs from the ICF threat assessment (ICFTA) scorecard that is exclusively limited to evaluating the insider threat on production applications. Obviously, a symbiotic relationship exists between the ICFTA (production application focused) and the InfoSec scorecard (all general and application controls).

So far in this chapter we covered a significant amount of ground and incorporated many concepts. The interrelationships between each of the processes, practices, and documents were discussed. *The Strategic Planning Process for Reducing the Insider Threat* document traces our processes to this point to collect the prerequisite data to accurately complete the InfoSec scorecard.

However, one step remains in the insider threat identification and analysis process, which involves developing security patterns for establishing strategies and plans to strengthen the software development process and improve products. The output of the security pattern analysis will feed into the final step of management's development of a comprehensive and integrated strategic plan for InfoSec. Additionally, as indicated in *The Strategic Planning Process for Reducing the Insider Threat*, the final results of the completed InfoSec scorecard will also be an important source document for management's information security analysis and development of a strategic plan for reducing InfoSec risks.

3.31 Develop Security Patterns for Applications/ Systems Software Engineering (Process and Product Improvements)

The concept of "pattern" is a solution to a problem in a context. The concept of developing patterns is relatively new but is growing in popularity, particularly among those who work in the computer science community. The work in computer science, particularly in the object-oriented community, is based on the work of Christopher Alexander of University of California–Berkeley, an architect and professor of architecture who uses patterns to solve various architectural problems.

From a computer science perspective, software engineering has benefited from the use of design patterns, by using developed patterns to capture, reuse, and teach software design expertise. Patterns from a software development perspective might use Unified Modeling Language (UML) diagrams as a tool for implementing software design issues and sample code implementing the pattern and proposed solution.

Through Alexander, the concept of pattern languages is discussed and relates to expressing collections of interrelated patterns to define families of solutions. In the design pattern, community patterns and pattern languages provide a means for communicating detailed problem-solving knowledge by someone who is considered an expert in one domain to individuals or groups in another area, who may not possess the domain expertise. Ostensibly, a pattern attempts to develop a "best practice" in regards to a particular category or class of problems or related problems.

Based on the concept of software development design patterns has evolved the idea of security patterns, which provides a well-understood solution to a recurring information security problem. The general precepts outlined by Alexander also apply to the development and design of information security patterns; however, the pattern may not necessarily take the form utilizing a UML diagram or describe a solution in terms of source code.

A pattern definition, whether involving a design pattern for software engineering or security purposes, generally includes the following basic elements:

Context: Environmental assumptions, policy statements
Problem: Security objectives, threats, attacks
Forces: Functional security requirements
Solution: To be determined

From an application development perspective, security patterns fall into two general categories, with the first being structural and the second being procedural. In brief, the structural patterns take the more traditional use of software design patterns through the use of UML and source code to illustrate solutions. The primary goal of procedural patterns is to strengthen the process used to develop software with the appropriate level of security.

However, to introduce the concept of security patterns and to be aligned with the topic of this chapter, the example below will be focused on illustrating more of a procedural or process level pattern that has relevance to defined security practices and procedures.

In an article written by Sasha Romanosky, dated June 4, 2002, entitled "Enterprise Security Patterns,"[4] a pattern was identified that has relevance to the topic of this chapter governing the risk assessment process, with the pattern entitled "Risk Assessment and Management."

3.31.1 Security Pattern (Risk Assessment and Management)

- ■ Alias
- ■ Risk analysis

3.31.2 Motivation

Not all information requires the same degree of protection. Patient records, Web log files, military tactics, and hourly weather reports all have varying degrees of sensitivity. The proper security of all of this information requires risk analysis. Naturally, if the risk is high, the effort to protect the data should be great. If the risk is low, the protection should be low.

Similarly, hardware and software throughout the enterprise will require varying degrees of hardening. The security requirements of a front-end application server are different than those of an internal development machine. A front-line firewall is secured differently than a quality assurance (QA) router.

It is worth noting that this could be considered a catch-all pattern. Because security is all about risk management, every resource file, servlet, object, datastore, application, server, and so forth, warrants a risk assessment.

3.31.3 Problem

Whenever information needs to be transferred, stored, or manipulated, the privacy and integrity of that data need to be reasonably assured. Hardware and software require protection from misconfiguration, neglect, and attack. Underprotection of any of these could drive a company to bankruptcy (or legal battle), and overprotection becomes a waste of resources.

3.31.4 Forces

- If the relative risks of attacks are not known, time and money may be improperly allocated to protecting certain resources.
- Management may not understand or appreciate the potential for loss or theft of enterprise information or resources.

3.31.5 Solution

Identifying and assessing risk is the first step to better security. Although many formulas exist to determine risk, they invariably include threat, vulnerability, and cost (value). For example,

$$Risk = Threat * Cost * Vulnerability$$

where *Threat* is the frequency of attempts or successes; *Cost* is the total cost of a successful breach by this mechanism, and *Cost* also accounts for the value of the resource or information being protected; and *Vulnerability* is the likelihood of success.

Begin by recognizing what is valuable and to whom. Different attackers will have different motives and will therefore target different resources. Youth hackers are typically motivated by publicity or mischief and seek to deface Web pages or spread malware. Professional criminals, motivated by financial reward, may seek to steal credit card numbers or specialized information (secret recipes, blueprints, etc.). Terrorists care little for Web page defacement but more for infrastructure denial of service and destruction.

With effective application and networking monitoring (operated either in-house or outsourced), threat can be reasonably determined and (if necessary) projected. There will be more attack attempts (and therefore successful attacks) made by youth hackers than other attackers, simply because of their numbers. Terrorist attacks, thankfully, are much less frequent, but their effects are far more severe.

Cost, to an extent, can also be calculated, or at least estimated. The cost (due to time lost) of restoring a single server, rebuilding a data center, or replacing stolen or corrupt data is quantifiable. Additional costs are those due to (the hopefully temporary) loss of business, publicity, and media fees.

Vulnerability, however, can be more difficult to determine. The likelihood of success would be determined by the type of attacker (previously determined by the value of the resources) and the grade of defenses of an enterprise infrastructure. An attacker with a low level of sophistication and funding who is targeting an enterprise with very strong defenses will have little success. However, vulnerability will be much higher when a sophisticated terrorist with potentially unlimited funding targets an enterprise with the same defenses.

Once threat, cost, and vulnerability have been determined (or approximated) for different attacks, priority can be given to the greater exposures.

3.31.6 Consequences

- Only the appropriate amount of effort is spent to protect data.
- A better understanding is gained of the profiles of attackers and the value of data they seek.
- Recognition of ownership and accountability of data within the organization are achieved.

3.31.7 Known Uses

- Production Web and application servers are severely hardened, kept up to date with patches and actively monitored, whereas QA and development machines have a reduced (from default) set of services running but may be behind on patch updates.
- Human resources and confidential financial information reside on highly protected machines behind departmental firewalls with very limited access.

3.31.8 Related Patterns

White Hat, Hack Thyself: A risk assessment will help determine relative threat areas. A penetration test (audit) can uncover vulnerable areas of an enterprise's environment. Together this information will assist in identifying and prioritizing the major exposures of an enterprise.

Roles (RBAC): Once the relative value of data is understood, appropriate access needs to be provided. The roles pattern is a method by which this can be accomplished—that is, by associating individuals with common sets of privileges, data is protected.

For additional information on patterns, refer to the following resources:

- Technical Guide—Security Design Patterns, Bob Blakley, Craig Heath, and members of The Open Group Security Forum, the Open Group, UK, April 2004.
- Enterprise Security Patterns, Sasha Romanosky, June 4, 2002.
- Security Patterns for Web Application Development, Darrell M. Kienzle and Mathew C. Elder.

■ www.securitypatterns.org
■ www.csis.pace.edu/~bergin

3.32 The Strategic, Legal, and Operational Risk Assessment

According to the FFIEC 2006 Information Security Booklet[3]:

> An information security strategy is a plan to mitigate risks while complying with legal, statutory, contractual, and internally developed requirements. Typical steps to building a strategy include the definition of control objectives, the identification and assessment of approaches to meet the objectives, the selection of controls, the establishment of benchmarks and metrics, and the preparation of implementation and testing plans. Security strategies include prevention, detection, and response, and all three are needed for a comprehensive and robust security framework.

The final point in the risk assessment and threat assessment and modeling process is developing a strategic plan for InfoSec. Management needs to develop a comprehensive road map to reduce their level of NRR for an application or system to reduce the potential for insider abuse (that is, fraud).

All of the predecessor steps are now complete in the risk assessment and threat modeling process and should all eventually feed into the management analysis and strategic plan for InfoSec governance.

Management should analyze the following minimum considerations when evaluating insider computer fraud and evaluate its impact on the Strategic, Legal, and Operational Risk Matrix criteria below:

■ The results of the risk assessment process.
■ The results of the PIA.
■ The results of the threat assessment.
■ The qualitative assessment of residual risk and NRR ratings.
■ The adequacy of existing management controls.
■ The adequacy of existing technical controls.
■ The results of the Defense in Depth Model calculation.
■ The assessment of the strength of controls in the existing IT architecture.
■ The analysis of internal and external audit reports relating to general and application controls.
■ The analysis of compliance-related reports that conclude on data privacy risks and control the regulatory and legal landscape.

Based on the results of the aforementioned minimum considerations, a qualitative assessment needs to be made for evaluating the level of strategic, legal, and operational risk. Every organization has unique processes and practices, and the consideration of those unique risk factors in the assessment factors should be determined by management, as appropriate.

3.33 Implemented Software Engineering InfoSec Process and Product Improvements

The last phase of the integrated business and technology risk, threat, and privacy impact assessments should consider the following minimum factors prior to deciding to implement the following controls to reduce risks associated with the insider threat:

- *Reevaluation of Software Development Policies, Procedures, and Practices*: Ensure security controls are "baked" into the software development life cycle.
- *Architectural Considerations*: Evaluate additional layers of defense in the Defense in Depth Model.
- *Stricter Access Controls*: Implement more restrictive access controls.
- *Quarantine and Isolation*: Determine the need for compartmentalizing systems and data to reduce the potential for insider misuse.
- *Misuse Detection*: Determine the need for selective application and system journaling of KFIs and deployment of various computer forensic techniques for tracking and trace-back purposes.
- *Anomaly Detection*: Determine the need for developing and deploying advanced technologies to capture information on day zero attack vectors from insiders (i.e., neural networks and behavioral modeling).
- *Recovery of Information*: Possess the technology needed for decrypting sensitive data that may be hidden and protected by the insider in a distributed and fragmented manner of storage.

Listed above are just a few potential strategies that could be deployed by management to combat risks associated with the insider threat.

3.34 Conclusion

This chapter included many highlights: The concept of information security governance was introduced. A central focus was placed on emphasizing the importance of evaluating the integrated (business/technology) risk assessment process. The concept of determining integrated risk was illustrated using the TRIP methodology.

An Application Criticality Matrix was developed which reflected key factors for prioritizing the significance of key applications. The importance of performing a PIA to ensure NPPI was identified, measured, monitored, and controlled to ensure regulatory compliance requirements were successfully achieved. Throughout the chapter, various tools were displayed that will aid in conducting a comprehensive risk assessment such as a HeatMap and the information security scorecard. The concepts of residual risk and NRR were discussed to demonstrate the importance of evaluating not only application risks, but also the IT infrastructure and software components (optimizers) that the application uses in the data processing and transmission process. The importance of developing data flow diagrams was emphasized to determine NPPI and core transaction data used in the processing and transmission of that data within the organization and to third parties. Use of NPPI and core transaction data was discussed in the context of understanding KFIs, KFMs, KFSs, and KRIs. The concept of determining the critical path was also emphasized, which traces the journey of the critical data from point of entry into an application or system to its final resting place within a repository. A thorough discussion also occurred in computing the Defense in Depth Security Efficiency Calculation.

A brief discussion of industry sound and best practices for information security and application controls was conducted using ISO 27001 and GTAG. The threat assessment process was discussed in determining the inherent risk rating as well as for determining the NRR rating. The strategic planning process for reducing the insider threat was discussed which covered many areas, involving the completion of the ICFTA, performing an application and code penetration test, in addition to evaluating the strategic and the operational risk assessments. The concept of developing security patterns was also introduced for strengthening the software engineering process. Finally, a discussion was conducted for implementing software engineering InfoSec process and product improvements.

References

1. Permission to reproduce extracts from BS ISO/IEC/2700: 2005 is granted by BSI. British Standards can be obtained in PDF format from the BSI Online Shop: http://www.BS 1-Global.com/en/shop or by contacting Customer Service for hard copies call +44 (0) 20 8996 9001, via e-mail: cservices@bsielobal.com.
2. GTAG (Global Technology Audit Guide), Application Based Controls. The Institute of Internal Auditors, 2005.
3. The FFIEC Information Security Booklet, 2006.
4. Komanosky, Sasha. Enterprise Security Patterns, June 2004. The original source for the security pattern was the 3/03I SSA Password/Journal *Enterprise Security Patterns*.

Chapter 4

Information Technology Architecture and Insider Computer Fraud Prevention

4.1   Introduction

Introduced in this chapter will be the fundamentals of system architecture and the importance of designing an application or system that embodies several key considerations, primarily at the network level, that will aid in facilitating perimeter protection which is vulnerable to both internal and external exploits. The concept of the Zachman Framework, will also be introduced, and the importance of network security within the architectural design of the network to reduce all types of internal and external threats will be stressed.

4.2   Components of an Information Technology Infrastructure

The components of an information technology infrastructure and its security risks and controls are unique to every enterprise and particularly noteworthy in terms of how an architectural framework is designed and deployed to identify and mitigate the risks associated with insider computer fraud (ICF). Many organizations have Internet facing Web-based applications that can be accessed remotely by the insider either within the confines of the organization or remotely. Conversely, there are many applications within organizations that are not network based or Web based and function as stand-alone applications, which can also be used to perpetrate computer fraud. Consequently, the risk exposure for insider abuse is significantly higher for organizations that have Web-based versus traditional applications that can be accessed only within the organization.

The following list of information technology (IT) infrastructure components is by no means exhaustive, and the primary intent is not necessarily to inform of the unique security risks associated with each component, but rather to have it function as a refresher and to provide equal footing and foundation for other aspects of the ICF framework throughout this chapter and the entire book.

- *Firewall*: A system designed to prevent unauthorized access to or from a private network. Firewalls can be implemented in both hardware and software, or a combination of both. Firewalls are frequently used to prevent unauthorized Internet users from accessing private networks connected to the Internet, especially intranets. All messages entering or leaving the intranet pass through the firewall, which examines each message and blocks those that do not meet the specified security criteria. There are several types of firewall techniques:
  - *Packet Filter*: Looks at each packet entering or leaving the network and accepts or rejects it based on user-defined rules. Packet filtering is fairly effective and transparent to users, but it is difficult to configure. In addition, it is susceptible to Internet Protocol (IP) spoofing.
  - *Application Gateway*: Applies security mechanisms to specific applications, such as File Transfer Protocol (FTP) and Telnet servers. This is very effective but can impose performance degradation.
  - *Circuit-Level Gateway*: Applies security mechanisms when a Transmission Control Protocol (TCP) or User Datagram Protocol (UDP) connection is established. Once the connection has been made, packets can flow between the hosts without further checking.
  - *Proxy Server*: Intercepts all messages entering and leaving the network. The proxy server effectively hides the true network addresses.
- *Router*: A router is a special purpose computer or software device that enables two or more dissimilar networks to communicate. Routers route traffic, which consists of Transmission Control Protocol/Internet Protocol (TCP/IP) packets.
- *Host*: A computer that is connected to a TCP/IP network, including the Internet.

■ *Servers*: A server is a dedicated computer that allows other computers to connect to it. Various types of servers exist which include the following:
  • Domain Name System
  • Web servers
  • Internet banking servers
  • E-mail servers
  • Proxy servers
■ *PC Workstations*: In networking, workstation refers to any computer connected to a local area network. It could be a workstation or a personal computer.
■ *Intrusion Detection Systems*: Intrusion detection is fundamentally the process of monitoring computer networks and systems for violations of computer policy.

4.3 A Primer for Enterprise Architecture Using Zachman's Framework—Architectural Strategies to Prevent and Detect ICF

As seen from the defense in depth interrelationships diagram, the first layer of defense is the macro taxonomy. Conducting this taxonomy is an important first step in establishing the appropriate risk-based InfoSec architectural blueprint. Additionally, an important preliminary step in this ICF framework is to conduct an initial risk assessment. Collectively, between the macro and micro taxonomies developed on specific ICF cases, the architectural analyst can determine what strategies would be best suited to detect and hopefully prevent ICF activities, by leveraging and modifying where appropriate, the necessary enhancements to an existing architectural design.

In general, the industry lacks any best practices for application and IT infrastructure architectural design, and this presents some unique challenges in terms of knowledge sharing on this elusive topic. Even less is written about how there should be a symbiotic relationship between the risk assessment process and architectural design and the selection of key IT components to mitigate those risks. Before engaging in the selection and deployment of any IT infrastructure components (that is, firewalls, management console, demilitarized zone [DMZ] server hosts, etc.), an overview of a few basic concepts and definitions for developing an Enterprise Architecture, particularly for applications, will be introduced.

When developing a system architectural design for an enterprise, there are several key considerations:

■ *Scalability*: This is the ease by which additional system processing capacity, throughput, or transactions can be increased (or decreased) over time.

- *Replication*: Add processing resources that replicate and share part of the workload.
- *Clustering*: Physically centralize but logically distribute the processing load.
- *Locality of Decision-Making Authority*: Distribute the ability to affect modification, while centralizing the decision for which modifications to incorporate.
- *Adaptability*: This is the ease by which the existing architectural design or configuration of a system can be updated to respond to changing conditions, performance congestion, security attacks, and so forth.
- *Mitigating Architectural Mismatches*: This may occur when system components cannot interconnect to exchange data.
- *Architectural Security Gaps*: There may be architectural security gaps that allow for unauthorized access and update capabilities to system resources.
- *Component Based*: Configuring architecture using separable components.
- *Multitier*: Configuring architecture into tiers that separate user interface from network access gateways (i.e., Web servers, security firewalls), from data storage/retrieval repositories.

4.4 The Zachman Framework

There are many different approaches to describing the elements of an enterprise architecture, including the original framework developed by John Zachman. The goal of this section presents the original Zachman Architectural Framework along with the interpretation and modification of that framework by David Hay, author of *Introduction—The System Development Life Cycle*.

The Zachman Enterprise Architecture Framework has become popular because it provides a model of how all of the component parts of an organization fit together and is not simply a description of a collection of documents and plans.

A framework for modeling information systems architecture was devised by John Zachman in 1987. The Zachman Framework provides a structured way for any organization to acquire the necessary knowledge about itself with respect to the Enterprise Architecture. John Zachman proposes a logical structure for classifying and organizing the descriptive representations of an enterprise, in different dimensions, and each dimension can be perceived in different perspectives. As noted in Table 4.1, the process is not depicted as a series of steps but instead is approached from the point of view taken by various individuals within an enterprise, including the Chief Executive Officer (CEO), the businesspeople who run the organization, the systems analyst, the designer, and the system itself.

- *Scope (Ballpark View)*: This is a definition of the enterprise's direction and business purpose.

Table 4.1 The Zachman Framework

	Data	Function	Network	People	Time	Motivation
1. Scope (planner)	List of things important to the business	List of processes the business performs	List of locations in which the business operates	List of organizations and agents important to the business	List of events significant to the business	List of business goals
2. Enterprise Model (owner)	For example, entity relationship (ER) diagram	For example, process flow diagram	For example, logistics network	For example, organization chart	For example, master schedule	For example, business plan
3. System Model (designer)	For example, Data Model	For example, data flow diagram	For example, distributed system architecture	For example, Human Interface Architecture	For example, processing structure	For example, Knowledge Architecture
4. Technology Model (builder)	For example, data design	For example, structure chart	For example, systems architecture	For example, human/technology interface	For example, control structure	For example, knowledge design
5. Detailed description (out-of-context view)	For example, database description	For example, Network Architecture	For example, Security Architecture	For example, Security Architecture	For example, timing definition	For example, knowledge definition
6. Functioning system	For example, data	For example, function	For example, network	For example, organization	For example, schedule	For example, strategy

- *Model of the Business (Owner's View)*: This defines in business terms the nature of the business, including its structure, functions, and organization.
- *Model of the Information System (Architect's View)*: This defines the business described in Step 2, but in more rigorous information terms.
- *Technology Model (Designer's View)*: This describes how technology may be used to address the information processing needs identified in the rows.
- *Detailed Representations (Builder's View)*: Choice is made of a particular language and the program listings, database specifications, and networks.
- *Functioning System*: A system is implemented and made part of an organization.

The columns in the Zachman Framework represent different areas of interest for each perspective:

- *Data*: Each of the rows in this column address understanding of and dealing with an enterprise's data.
- *Function*: The rows in the function column describe the process of translating the mission of the enterprise into successively more detailed definitions of its operations.
- *Network*: This column is concerned with the geographical distribution of the enterprise's activities.
- *People*: The fourth column describes who is involved in the business and in the introduction of new technology.
- *Time*: The fifth column describes the effects of time on the enterprise.
- *Motivation*: This is concerned with the translation of business goals and strategies into specific ends and means.

4.5 Types of System Architectural Designs for Information Processing

The primary types of system architectures for information processing include Service Oriented Architecture (SOA), distributive (client–server), and centralized information systems processing more commonly associated with mainframe and midrange computers. Management's decision to choose one or both of the architectural designs is a business decision and should be primarily based on the mission statement and the business goals and objectives of the enterprise. Whichever information processing is selected, management's architectural decisions to accommodate the processing need to consider the features, advantages, and disadvantages of each information processing mode.

Listed below are the three primary architectures and processes that can assist management in achieving their stated business goals and objectives.

4.5.1 Service Oriented Architecture (SOA)

The primary focus of this research is a SOA, which is essentially a collection of services. These services communicate with each other. The communication can involve either simple data exchange or it could involve two or more services coordinating some activity. By definition, a service is a function that is well defined, self-contained, and does not depend on the context or state of other services. Web services is the most likely connection of SOAs and uses eXtensible Markup Language (XML) to create a robust connection. A Web service is a software system designed to support interoperable machine-to-machine interaction over a network. It has an interface described in a machine-processable format (specifically Web Services Description Language [WSDL]). Other systems interact with the Web service in a manner prescribed by its description using Simple Object Access Protocol (SOAP) messages, typically conveyed using Hypertext Transfer Protocol (HTTP) with an XML serialization in conjunction with other Web-related standards.

The conventional wisdom in the marketplace today is that Web services apply only to business-to-business (B2B) external Internet facing applications; however, that is only partly correct. Specifically, Web services can be used for internal communication between newer applications with legacy applications and production applications that need to interface with each other given their coding and other differences. Ostensibly, Web services would provide the glue that would facilitate the communication between various disparate applications and systems, both internally and externally.

An organization using Web services internally could easily have those services disrupted through the insider threat. Refer to the SOA diagram detailed in Figure 4.1 for a graphical illustration of the proposed SOA developed specifically for this research along with detailed discussions of risks, vulnerabilities, and the potential for an insider to exploit those weaknesses. The SOA below reflects several control points where higher than normal risks may occur, involving access controls, input, processing, and output, which could result in some type of data input manipulation and resulting data integrity issues.

4.5.2 Centralized Processing

This refers to the processing of all data at one single central location by a large mainframe computer. During the 1990s, the mainframe computer was in demand after a varied history. Mainframes became popular in the 1960s and 1970s because of their unprecedented computer power. During the 1980s and early 1990s, concepts such as client–server and distributed computing caused many to realize that although computing power could be purchased at a significantly lower capital cost, there were hidden costs involved. Mainframes are now making a comeback, because

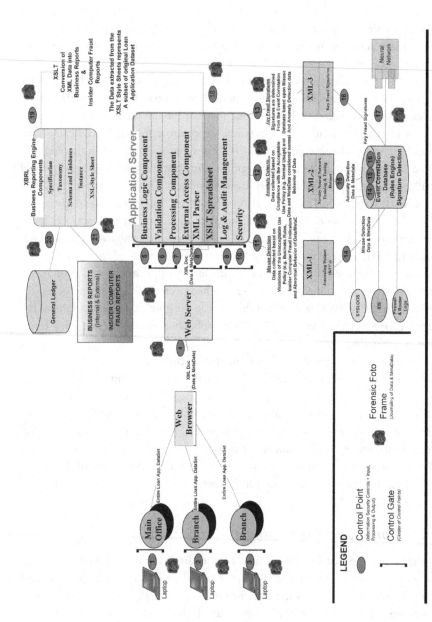

Figure 4.1 Insider computer fraud Service Oriented Architecture (SOA).

business applications need the power to perform thousands of transactions a minute in computing environments that are becoming increasingly more complex.

4.5.3 Distributive Systems Architecture

A Distributive Systems Architecture refers to any of a variety of computer systems that use more than one computer, or processor, to run an application. This includes parallel processing, in which a single computer uses more than one central processing unit (CPU) to execute programs. More often, however, distributed processing refers to local area networks (LANs) designed so that a single program can run simultaneously at various sites. Most distributed processing systems contain sophisticated software that detects idle CPUs on the network and parcels out programs to utilize them. Another form of distributed processing involves distributed databases—databases in which the data is stored across two or more computer systems. The database system keeps track of where the data is so that the distributed nature of the database is not apparent to users.

4.5.4 Client–Server Architecture

This is a network architecture in which each computer or process on the network is either a client or a server. Servers are powerful computers or processes dedicated to managing disk drives (file servers), printers (print servers), or network traffic (network servers). Clients are PCs or workstations on which users run applications. Clients rely on servers for resources, such as files, devices, and even processing power.

Another type of network architecture is known as a peer-to-peer architecture because each node has equivalent responsibilities. Both client–server and peer-to-peer architectures are widely used, and each has unique advantages and disadvantages. Client–server architectures are sometimes called two-tier architectures. "Two-tier" refers to client–server architectures in which the user interface runs on the client and the database is stored on the server. The actual application logic can run on either the client or the server. A newer client–server architecture, called a three-tier architecture, introduces a middle tier for the application logic. A special type of client–server architecture consists of three well-defined and separate processes, each running on a different platform:

- The user interface, which runs on the user's computer (the client).
- The functional modules that actually process data (this middle tier runs on a server and is often called the application server).
- A database management system (DBMS) that stores the data required by the middle tier (this tier runs on a second server called the database server).

The three-tier design has many advantages over traditional two-tier or single-tier designs, the chief ones being as follows:

■ The added modularity makes it easier to modify or replace one tier without affecting the other tiers.
■ Separating the application functions from the database functions makes it easier to implement load balancing.

4.6 Conclusion

This chapter included the following key areas:

■ The information technology infrastructure and its security risks and controls are unique to every enterprise and particularly noteworthy in terms of how an architectural framework is designed and deployed to identify and mitigate the risks associated with ICF.
■ Maintaining comprehensive and effective controls over each component of the IT infrastructure (i.e., firewalls, filters, gateways, proxy servers, routers, servers, PC workstations, and intrusion detection systems) will reduce both insider and external risks to an enterprise.
■ Conceptually understanding Zachman's Framework can be an important component toward developing and implementing a framework for modeling information systems architecture for reducing both insider and external threats. Particular focus is paid to describing the importance of the Web-services SOA, which is the primary architectural foundation to describe this ICF framework.

Understanding an organization's technology architecture directly relates to the Defense in Depth Model for defending against both internal and external threats.

References

1. Hay, David. *Introduction—The System Development Life Cycle*, Essential Strategies, Inc., Houston, TX, 2000.
2. The Zachman Institute for Framework Advancement (www.pinnaclebusgrp.com).

Chapter 5

Protection of Web Sites from Insider Abuse and the Information Technology Infrastructure

5.1 Introduction

In this chapter, insider computer fraud (ICF) is discussed in the context of the risks and controls needed for each component of the ICF infrastructure. The importance of existing cyber-related controls will be discussed, which can be mutually beneficial for reducing the risks associated with both insider and external threats. The methods of detection of weak controls within an enterprise are introduced to allow the reader to gain a fundamental knowledge of what controls can be used within an enterprise to reduce ICF exposure.

5.2 Insider Attacks

Based on the results of the ICF taxonomy, there were several incidents involving former insiders who hacked into their former employers' systems. Although external hacking attacks by former employees occur less frequently than other forms of insider misuse, there were seven cases detected from research involving hacking activities, which points out the insider threat and the need to ensure that the appropriate level of safeguards and controls exist on network security. Although the focus here is primarily on ICF conducted primarily within an organization and behind the corporate firewalls, the occurrence of these seven cases illustrates the importance of application as well as cyber-security preparedness.

5.3   Intrusion Detection Systems, Vulnerability Assessments, and Other Network Testing

Intrusion detection systems (IDS) perform a number of different functions, including the following:

- Monitoring and analysis of user and system activity.
- Auditing of system configurations and vulnerabilities.
- Assessment of the integrity of critical system and data files.
- Recognition of activity patterns reflecting known attacks.
- Statistical analysis for abnormal activity patterns.
- Operating system audit trail management, with recognition of user activity reflecting policy violations.

Network intrusion detection systems (NIDS) use raw network packets as the primary data source. Additionally, the IDS uses a network adapter in promiscuous mode that listens and analyzes all traffic in real-time as it travels across the network. Through the use of an IDS filter, a determination is made regarding what traffic is discarded or passed on to an attack recognition module. The network IDS usually has two logical components: the sensor and the management station. The sensor sits on a network segment, monitoring it for suspicious traffic.

The management station receives alarms from the sensors and displays them to an operator. The sensors are usually dedicated systems that exist only to monitor the network.

5.4   Network Intrustion Detection Systems (NIDS)—Strengths and Weaknesses

5.4.1   Strengths

- *Network Attack Detection*: The NIDS can detect some of the external and internal attacks that use the network, particularly new attack forms. A NIDS will alert for an external attack or an insider accessing the network remotely and wishing to conduct potential ICF activities.

- *Anomaly Detectors—Detection Ability*: Anomaly detectors have the ability to detect unusual behavior and therefore the ability to detect symptoms of attacks without specific knowledge of details.
- *Anomaly Detectors—Attack Signatures*: Anomaly detectors have the ability to produce information that serves as the basis for the development of new attack signatures.
- *No Modifications of Production Servers or Hosts*: A network-based IDS does not require modification of production servers or hosts.
- *No Production Impact*: NIDS will generally not negatively impact any production services or processes, because the device does not function as a router.
- *Self-Contained*: NIDS runs on a dedicated system that is simple to install, generally plug-and-play after some configuration changes, and then is set to monitor network traffic.

5.4.2 Weaknesses

- *Limited to a Network Segment*: NIDS examines only network traffic on the segment to which it is directly connected. It cannot detect an attack that travels through a different network segment.
- *Expensive*: The problem may require that an organization purchase many sensors in order to meet its network coverage goals.
- *Limited Detection*: Detection is limited to programmed attacks from external sources; however, it is not considered effective for detecting the more complex information threats.
- *Limited Coordination*: There is little coordination among sensors, which creates a significant amount of analysis traffic.
- *Difficulty with Encryption*: A network-based IDS may have a difficult time handling attacks within encrypted sessions.
- *False Positives*: Anomaly detection generates a significant number of false positives.

5.5 Host-Based Intrusion Detection Systems (HIDS)—Strengths and Weaknesses

Host-based IDSs operate on information collected from within a computer system, which gives this HIDS a distinct advantage over NIDS, due to the fact that it is easy for a target to see the intended outcome of the attempted attack compared to network attack.

5.5.1 Host IDS (HIDS)

The host-based IDS looks for signs of intrusion on the local host system. These frequently use the host operating system audit trails and system logs as sources of information for analysis. They look for unusual activity that is confined to the local host, such as log-ins, improper file access, unapproved privilege escalation, or alterations on system privileges. Every platform is different in terms of what system audit trails and system log reports are produced; however, in Windows NT, there are system, event, and security logs, and in UNIX there are Syslog and other operating-specific log files. When changes occur to any file, it will be compared to what is configured in the current security policy. Alerts to the changes can be done in real-time or performed periodically. Additionally, there are some host-based IDSs that can listen to port activity and alert when specific ports are accessed, which also provides a form of network-type attack detection.

This IDS architecture generally uses rule-based engines for analyzing activity; an example of such a rule might be, "superuser privilege can only be attained through the su command." Therefore, successive log-in attempts to the root account might be considered an initial attempt to perpetrate computer fraud or misuse.

5.5.1.1 Strengths—HIDS

- A host-based IDS usually provides much more detailed and relevant information than a network-based IDS.
- Host-based systems tend to have lower false-positive rates than do network-based systems.
- Host-based systems can be used in environments where broad intrusion detection is not needed, or where the bandwidth is not available for sensor-to-analysis communications.
- Finally, a host-based system may be less risky to configure with an active response, such as terminating a service or logging off an offending user.

5.5.1.2 Weaknesses

- Host-based systems require installation on the particular device that you wish to protect.
- If the server is not configured to do adequate logging and monitoring, you have to change the configuration of, possibly, a production machine, which is a tremendous change management problem.
- Host-based systems are relatively expensive.
- They are almost totally ignorant of the network environment. Thus, the analysis time required to evaluate damage from a potential intrusion increases linearly with the number of protected hosts.

5.5.2 Vulnerability Assessment Phases

There are three basic phases involved in vulnerability assessment processes, which include planning, discovery, and reporting, which make up the reconnaissance phase of a comprehensive penetration test, prior to conducting the actual penetration tests.

5.5.2.1 Planning

The first stage of the vulnerability assessment (VA) process involves the planning process. Basically, during the planning phase, you want to determine which VA tools will be used, outlining the goals and objectives of VA (for example, establishing test goals based on the results of the VA), and to manage other logistical matters to set the groundwork for successful penetration testing.

5.5.2.2 Discovery

There are basically two primary steps involved in the vulnerability testing. (Note that these two steps are also typically performed during a penetration test, although the results of an independent VA, if performed close in time to the actual penetration test, could be used as input into the penetration testing planning process.) Specifically, the two primary steps include mapping and identifying active devices on the network and then scanning the active devices for vulnerabilities.

5.5.2.3 Mapping and Identifying Active Devices on the Network

The goal of this phase is to discover all devices associated with the network, including hosts, firewall routers, and network infrastructure (such as Domain Name System [DNS] and management systems). Important components of this step are as follows:

Sniffing: An important component within the VA process is packet sniffing. In brief, packet sniffing tools are used typically by the system administrators (SA) of an enterprise or other network manager to capture packets off the network and analyze them. In the past, diagnostic tools used for sniffing were either very expensive, proprietary, or both. Open-source tools are available that can be used for this purpose. (See Section 5.6 for further details.)

Scanning: The purpose of scanning tools is to perform an analysis of vulnerabilities that could be exploited remotely through the network. Port scanning utilities will be executed to determine which Transmission Control Protocol (TCP) ports and services are available. Additionally, User Datagram Protocol (UDP) port scanners will be used to evaluate which UDP ports are open on the target systems. There are numerous open-source scanning tools, and a few of these tools will be described in Section 5.6.

It is important to note that both of the two aforementioned steps (mapping, sniffing, and scanning), although designated as processes performed in a separate vulnerability scan, are also typically performed as important preliminary components prior to the actual penetration test.

5.6 The Penetration Testing Process

Penetration testing is an emerging practice used in organizations to attempt to identify and test their vulnerabilities before a malicious agent has the opportunity to exploit it. The various techniques presented here attempt to penetrate a target network from a particular frame of reference, both internal and external to the organization.

Fundamentally, during a penetration (Pen) test, an attempt is made to gain unauthorized access to a system or product based on information obtained during VA in order to demonstrate whether the network infrastructure protection is adequate. The Pen testing process and objective at its most fundamental level is trying to emulate a hacker by assessing the security strengths and weaknesses of a target network. A comprehensive Pen test will surface and test for real-world vulnerabilities (for example, open services) detected during the network security scan.

5.6.1 Goals

One of the primary goals in Pen testing is to identify security vulnerabilities in a network and to assess how an outsider or insider to an enterprise may either deny service or gain access to information to which the attacker is not authorized.

5.6.2 Methodology

Determining what type of Pen test to perform will be largely attributed to the threat management is trying to replicate and how the test should be conducted (internal versus external) and who should be conducting the test. Different types of Pen tests are as follows:

Internal (Consultant Scenario): Typically, during an internal Pen test, an attempt will be made to emulate a consultant with zero knowledge of the entity; however, the person making the attempt will possess a sufficient skill level to perform the ethical hack but will have no access rights to the network other than physical access.

Internal (Internal Employee Scenario): Another threat profile that should be tested within an internal threat scenario would be that of an internal employee. An internal Pen test searches for potential security vulnerabilities within the internal (trusted) network.

The trusted network is typically protected from unauthorized intrusion from the Internet by firewalls; however, the insider threat (e.g., disgruntled employee) represents the greatest risk to an enterprise. As such, access controls need to be evaluated to ensure the existence and adequacy of controls governing host systems (e.g., client–server, Web, e-mail), mainframe and legacy systems, network servers (e.g., file, print, and directory services), workstations, routers, switches, and private branch exchange (PBX). Using the scenario of an internal employee who has moderate familiarity and knowledge of the Federal Reserve System is assumed. The emulated entity's skill level will be low to moderate. The tools and techniques used by the emulated entity will be on par with the typical skill set of a "script kiddy."

Additionally, internal Pen tests should include vulnerabilities and physical access or exposures to social engineering. Through the use of social engineering, passwords can be compromised and insiders can gain unauthorized access to systems and applications. For example, systems running Internet Relay Chat (IRC) or Instant Messaging (IM) are vulnerable. Based on a computer emergency response team (CERT) vulnerability detected during 2002, through social engineering attacks on users of IRC and IM services, intruders tricked unsuspecting users into downloading and executing malicious software, which allowed the intruders to use the systems as attack platforms for launching distributed denial-of-service (DDoS) attacks. CERT indicates that tens of thousands of systems have been compromised in this manner.

External: External Pen tests are intended to identify vulnerabilities that were established through the organization connection to the Internet via a firewall or gateway. Fundamentally, external Pen tests are designed to test the adequacy of the perimeter defense mechanisms, such as remote access controls, firewalls, encryption, intrusion detection, and incident response. There will be an attempt to emulate an external entity attempting to gain unauthorized access to an entity's public Web site and to gain unauthorized access to the entity's network remotely. The individual performing the ethical hack will possess a sufficient skill level of low to moderate, thereby recreating the skills similar to those of a "script kiddy." One method of external testing that would simulate a hacker attack intrusion attempt is war dialing. This test checks for modems or PBXs and then attempts to gain unauthorized access to the network resources. Additionally, firewall scanning checks various ports on the firewall to determine whether potential entry points exist to gain access to trust networks.

Pen Teams: The Pen Test teams are performed by the Final Four accounting firms and other consulting firms. The term "Tiger team" is typically used to describe Pen testing teams. The term "Spider team" is commonly used to refer to those individuals involved in Pen testing against Web servers that are located outside of the enterprise's network. A few considerations for when to use a Pen testing company should include evaluating the reputation of the firm or consultants hired. Organizations need to carefully screen through potential firms, consultants, and subcontractors who have been given permission to sensitive data. Consideration should also be made relative to obtaining liability insurance in the event of something going wrong during the test.

5.7 Firewall Security

5.7.1 What Is a Firewall?

- A firewall is a group of measures that enforces access control between two networks or systems.
- A firewall controls access between the Internet and a bank's Internet site, a bank's Internet site and the internal networks, and intranet network segments.
- A firewall enforces security rules between two or more networks.
- A firewall evaluates each network packet against a network security policy.

5.7.2 Address Screening Routers

Routers examine every packet coming into and going out of an intranet and decide where to send those packets so that they can be delivered to the proper address.

They can control the type and direction of traffic permitted and, essentially, can also decide whether packets should even be delivered.

In other words, they can block certain packets from coming into or going out of an intranet.

When routers are used in this way to protect an intranet by blocking certain packets, they are called filtering routers or screening routers.

5.7.3 Circuit-Level Gateway

A circuit-level gateway operates at Level 5 (session layer) of the open system interconnection (OSI) Reference Model. The gateway establishes connections between trusted hosts and clients.

- Similar to the proxy, there is no direct connection between the systems.
  - It applies security mechanisms when a TCP or UDP connection is established.

- Once the connection has been made, packets can flow between the hosts without further checking.
■ One example of a compatible relay mechanism is SOCKS-compliant applications. SOCKS is a protocol for handling TCP traffic through a proxy server.

5.7.4 Application-Level Gateway

An application-level gateway applies security mechanisms to specific applications, such as FTP and Telnet servers. This is an effective process, but it can impose performance degradation.

5.7.5 Stateful Inspection Gateway

The stateful inspection firewall is capable of working at all seven layers of the OSI Reference Model, making this a very versatile firewall. Most stateful inspection firewalls operate at Layers 3 and 4. Stateful firewalls will also close all ports to unsolicited incoming data and keep a table of requests from inside the network, like the two gateway methods. The state table is consulted and used to make decisions to allow or reject a given packet. If a response packet is received at the firewall, there must be an entry in the state table or the packet is rejected.

5.8   Conclusion

The highlights of this chapter include the following:

■ The ICF taxonomy discussed in Chapter 8 is developed and includes several cited cases of where former employees externally hacked into their former bosses' computers to conduct nefarious activities.
■ Risks associated with ICF activities can be reduced with the use of various detection tools and processes that can assist in reducing ICF-related activities, which includes the deployment of IDS, VAs, and other network testing.
■ The concepts presented in this chapter provide background information on various components of cyber-security, which plays an important role in assessing net residual risk (inherent risk within an application less the risk level of related network information technology infrastructure components). The net residual risk of an application will determine how susceptible an application is to ICF activities.

Chapter 6

Web Services Security and Control Considerations for Reducing Transaction Risks

6.1 Introduction

The architecture of Web services is introduced in this chapter, given its growing importance within the marketplace, although it has been slower to gain traction in the financial services sector than perhaps in other sectors of the critical infrastructure of this nation. Also, the concept of the Forensic Foto Frame, which captures data at key control points in the path of a particular transaction, is introduced. The goal of this chapter is not to prematurely inundate the reader with an extended discussion of the Forensic Foto Frame concept, but to briefly introduce the topic conceptually in context to the much broader topic of Web services and the Service Oriented Architecture (SOA).

Each topic in this chapter is approached with the presumption that neophytes and subject matter experts (SME) alike will be reading. As such, this document provides a thorough overview of the many facets of Web services as a prerequisite educational foundation, with particular emphasis on security implications.

6.2 Web Services Security for a Service Oriented Architecture

Web services were selected as the primary architecture based upon its growing use within the marketplace. However, the concept of the Forensic Foto Frame, which captures data at various control points and control gates along the path of a particular transaction, would apply in a distributed client–server environment equally as well.

The standards can be incorporated in an interface with an existing application, allowing any other application with a similar interface to connect with it and exchange data. The Web services middleware is less expensive to implement than customized code. Through the use of Web services, businesses are closer to a real-time data sharing among trading partners without having the burden of integration that has been the historical problem. There is an emphasis within organizations to leverage the benefits of low-cost integration and SOA.

The primary players in the Web services space include Microsoft, IBM, Oracle, BEA, and others. There is concern in the marketplace that reliance on vendor alliances is questionable, which may lead to vendor politics, thereby preventing a single, consistent set of standards. The front-runners in Web services design and development tools vendors are Microsoft VS.net, BEA WebLogic Workshop, and IBM/Rational Websphere.

6.3 Web Services and the Financial Services Sector

Based on the Gartner Group's Giga Web research, there appears to be great interest in Web services within the financial services area; however, intercompany usage has barely started to happen. According to the Gartner Group research, the major impediment to wider usage within the financial services group is the lack of implemented security standards (WS-Security). It is anticipated that it will take from one to two years for such standards to be widely implemented by vendors and a few years beyond that for its use to hit any type of critical mass within the marketplace.

Currently, the primary players within the Web services space for financial institutions include Streetline, a Credit Suisse Group technology services company, through their Web services order-management application to connect institutional clients to the global-brokerage firm for real-time, straight-through processing (STP). Fidelity is also using Web services for software infrastructure to enable integration with external computing systems, where they have found that it has decreased its application development time. Other vendors such as Corillian, an online banking vendor, and Diebold, an automated teller machine (ATM) vendor, have started to incorporate Web services into their product offerings. Cape Clear Software, a provider of Web services technology, announced in September 2002 that it partnered with the Society for Worldwide Interbank Financial Telecommunications (SWIFT) to provide SWIFT members the ability to use SWIFT as a true Web services tool, linking its applications with those of other members through Web services standards like eXtensible Markup Language (XML), Simple Object Access Protocol (SOAP), and Universal Description, Discovery, and Integration (UDDI).

6.4 Major Groups Involved in Establishing Standards for Web Services Security

Listed below are the major groups working toward the establishment of standards for Web services security:

- *OASIS (Organization for the Advancement of Structured Information Standards)*: A global consortium that drives the development and adaption of e-business standards. OASIS produces worldwide standards for security, Web services, XML conformance, business transactions, electronic publishing, topic maps, and interoperability within and between marketplaces. Key standards include extensible rights markup language, WS-Security, Security Assertion Markup Language (SAML) provisioning, biometrics, and eXtensible Access Control Markup Language (www.oasis-open.org).
- *W3C (World Wide Web Consortium)*: Develops interoperable technologies (specifications, guidelines, software, and tools). Key standards include XML encryption, XML signature, and XKMS (XML Key Management Specifications) (www.w3c.org).
- *Liberty Alliance*: The Liberty Alliance project was formed in 2001 to establish an open standard for federated network identity. Key standards include SAML to pass standards-based security tokens between identity and authentication systems (www.projectliberty.org).
- *WS-I (Web Services Interoperability Organization)*: An open-industry organization chartered to promote Web services interoperability across platforms, operating systems, and programming languages. The organization works across all industries and standards organizations to respond to customer needs by providing guidance, best practices, and resources for developing solutions for Web services (www.ws-i.org).

6.5   Current Uses of Web Services

Although Web services currently do not have the capability of handling complex business transactions involving multiple parties, they have allowed for the point-to-point integration between business partners over the Internet, which involves organizations that already have trusted relationships (i.e., an airline employee making a reservation for a rental car for a customer). In those circumstances, security over such activity may be limited to Secure Socket Layer (SSL) protocol over Hypertext Transfer Protocol (HTTP). More recently, some companies enabled Web services, which allow customers to directly access back-end applications, without the customer having to access the Hypertext Markup Language (HTML) interface (i.e., Amazon allows certain business partners to access their catalogs and ordering service and Google provides a Web services interface to its search functionality).

6.6   Web Services Security—Industry Concerns

The Financial Services Technology Consortium (FSTC) and the Liberty Alliance Project in a Final Report, dated July 8, 2003, entitled: "Identity Management in Financial Services—An Assessment of the Liberty Alliance and SAML Specifications" (www.fstc.org), established a goal to assess the effectiveness of two Web services security specifications measured against common business use scenarios and known industry requirements. Specifically, particular emphasis was placed on assessing the effectiveness of how well the Liberty Alliance and SAML specifications meet the needs of the financial services industry and others (that is, technology vendors and standards bodies).

The next phase of the project is to move the phase 1 deliverables into a multibank, customer pilot operation with treasury workstation and portal vendors to include security features. Currently, Netegrity and Entrust are Web single sign-on (SSO) vendors that are active players in developing visions for support of secure Web services. It is believed that the best Web SSO will leverage the strengths of Web SSO vendors being built in the next several years and will include an integration of identity management strategies, rules-based authorization engines, and other authentication types.

Liberty was formed to promote the concept of federation to network identity. Many industry proponents were concerned that emerging centralized ownership models of identity credentials could be damaging to public privacy and the success of Web services. This defines a set of specifications for protocols on which services such as account linkage and SSO are built. It incorporates SAML technology as a key foundation element, leveraging both the Web browser and Web service profiles.

6.7   Web Services Security—General Concerns

Web services are concerned on several fronts:

- *Standards Lack Maturity*: Areas that need further development are security and quality of service, which may restrict the scope of its implementation so that it fits within the limitations of its protocols.
- *Security*: Web services are based on standards that are considered simple and portable and provide no built-in security mechanisms. As such, data that is transferred via Web services is vulnerable to many threats.
- *Information Technology (IT) Staff Training*: Inexperience of IT staff involved in the implementation of Web services is considered a major challenge for the rapid adoption of this technology.
- *Malicious Intent*: Current standards do not address the problem of malicious content. WS-Security and other initiatives focus on protecting the privacy and security of nonmalicious Web services connections.

6.8   Web Services Security—Technical Security Concerns

The technical security governing Web Services continues to evolve and mature (i.e., SAML). There are some organizations that are moving slowly into Web services, by deploying such activity internally as a pilot prior to engaging directly into external e-commerce and data transmissions.

- *Transmission of Executables*: Web services allow the hidden transmission of executables and other malicious content. Web services allow for the transmission of any kind of data within the flow of message transactions.
- *Cyber Attacks*: Web services security vendors and other perimeter security vendors have not yet achieved a significant level of sophistication with regard to the aforementioned types of attacks.

6.8.1   Security Assertion Markup Language (SAML)

SAML is an XML vocabulary used to convey trustworthy, digitally signed authentication and user credential information between applications or domains and independent from actual authentication mechanisms, user directories, or security policies. SAML adds bindings to various messages and transport mechanisms and profiles for using SAML in different real-world applications, including the following:

■ *Browser-Based SSO*: The browser-based SSO usage of SAML allows an identity provider to transparently pass identity attributes to service providers as part of a SSO environment. The underlying mechanics of SAML allow the service provider to validate that the information has integrity.

■ *SOAP-Based Web Services*: A SAML assertion can be directly attached to the header of a SOAP envelope to indicate who the end user is behind any particular transaction.

■ *Other Web Services Security Proposals*: There are other efforts underway to evaluate the security aspects of Web services, which include evaluating a Web services proof of concept, which involves interoperability testing between Java and .NET platforms across financial firewalls. There are extensions of SOAP being designed to provide data confidentiality, integrity, authentication, and message reliability. The goal of this operational proof of concept system is to determine whether Web services technologies are suitable for core banking applications.

6.8.2 Specific Types of Web Services Security Solutions

Specific security criteria may include the following:

■ *Security Infrastructure*: A number of existing standards can be used to enhance the security of Web services. Although some like SSL and HTTPS can be used on their own to provide point-to-point security, all of the following can be incorporated in the more elaborate schemes currently being developed.

■ *SSL (Secure Sockets Layer)*: SSL is a network encryption and authentication mechanism developed by Netscape, which is used in HTTPS. Currently a de facto standard, SSL has been submitted to the Internet Engineering Task Force (IETF) for standardization, which will take the form of Transport Layer Security (TLS) Protocol.

■ *TLS (Transport Layer Security)*: A Transport Layer Security Protocol was adopted by IETF as RFC 2246. TLS is based on SSL, which it may eventually supersede.

■ *HTTPS*: HTTPS is a secure form of HTTP, implemented by the use of SSL instead of plain text. Data is encrypted in both directions, and the server is authenticated by an SSL certificate. SOAP can be rendered more secure by running over HTTPS instead of HTTP, but this technique protects only the data on the wire; it becomes vulnerable once it reaches the computers at each end. WS-Security, in contrast, protects messages from end to end.

- *XML Digital Signature*: This is a set of XML syntax and processing rules for creating and representing digital signatures (a necessary building block for the WS-Security Framework). As well as its obvious purpose of guaranteeing message integrity, XML Digital Signature can be used to implement nonrepudiation. It is a W3C recommendation and an IETF draft standard (RFC 3275).
- *XKMS (XML Key Management Specification)*: A specification submitted to W3C by Microsoft, VeriSign, and webMethods in March 2001, XKMS aims to provide a Web service public key infrastructure (PKI) interface in such a way as to hide as much complexity as possible from the client. The W3C XML Key Management Working Group is basing its work on XKMS.
- *Passport*: Microsoft's SSO service, launched in 1999, now has 200 million accounts and performs more than 3.5 billion authentications every month. Originally based on "vanilla" Web standards such as SSL, Passport was updated in 2002 to interoperate with Kerberos. Some people feel Passport concentrates too much power in the hands of Microsoft, and they prefer Liberty's more transparent approach of publishing specifications that can be implemented by any vendor who wishes to do so and deployed by them or others.
- *Bidirectional SSL/TLS*: This is transport-level authentication (bidirectional SSL/TLS).
- *Message-Level Authentication*: This includes HTTP basic and HTTP digest.
- *Security Assertion Markup Language (SAML)*
- *X509*
- *Data-Element Level Encryption and Digital Signatures*
- *Ability to Secure*: There is the ability to secure SOAP messages and plain XML messages.
- *XML Application Firewall*: An XML application firewall fits well as a noninvasive drop-in solution in front of any XML or Web services interface. Most of the security solutions currently in the marketplace remain at the basic level and do not provide the low level of message scanning and hardware acceleration that the gateways provide.

6.9 Extensible Markup Language (XML)

XML is derived from Standard Generalized Markup Language (SGML), which has been an International Organization for Standardization (ISO) standard since 1986 and for the World Wide Web Consortium (W3C) which was adopted since February 1998. AXML is a metalanguage that provides rules for creating a set of tags that indicate the description of each data element.

XML provides a context by which applications can send and receive messages and documents that describe the nature of their content in machine-readable form. Web services provide a standardized mechanism through which applications can discover other applications, initiate remote procedures, and exchange XML-defined data. Basically, Web services enable interoperability between software written in different programming languages, developed by different vendors, or running on different operating systems or platforms. A few of the benefits of using Web services may include business-to-business integration, enhanced business process automation, a flexible approach to outsourcing, and access to business functions.

The concept of Web services was first proposed by Microsoft and IBM in 2000 as a method for connecting applications across the Internet. During 2002 and early 2003, Web services became accepted as a strategic initiative within many organizations, primarily used to integrate enterprise applications and to create simple, point-to-point connections between trusted business partners. The Web services development platform was either a Java-based application server or Microsoft's Windows 2000 Server.

Web services will define how data will be requested and passed, with the standards incorporated in an interface within an existing application, which will allow any other application with a similar interface to connect with it and to exchange data. Web services are sometimes referred to as "XML in motion" because Web services protocols define the transport mechanisms for XML-based communications.

There are two formats for defining XML document declarations: XML document-type definition (DTD) and XML Schema. The XML DTD was the original representation that provided a road map to the syntax used within a given class of XML document. Because XML tags are not predefined as in HTML, a DTD describes tag names and distinguishes the required and optional elements that may appear in a document.

6.10 XML and Security

At the current time, encrypting a complete XML document, testing its integrity, and confirming the authenticity of its sender is fairly straightforward; however, at times it may be necessary to use encryption and authenticate in arbitrary sequences and involve different users and originators. At the present time, the most important sets of developing specifications in the area of XML-related security are XML encryption, XML signatures, XACL (eXtensible Access Control Language), SAML, and XKMS.

With general encryption, there is no problem in digitally signing an XML document as a whole. The difficulty arises when parts of a document need to be signed, perhaps by different people, and when selective encryption needs to be performed. For example, a signer may want to view the document in plain text, which means decrypting part of a document that has already been encrypted. XML encryption will allow encryption of digital content, such as GIF, SVG, or XML fragments, while leaving other parts of the XML document not encrypted.

6.11   Simple Object Access Protocol (SOAP)

SOAP is an XML-based protocol for document-based messaging and remote procedure calls across distributing computing environments. SOAP-based messages are transport independent: designed for use over HTTP, SOAP also can be used with other transport mechanisms, such as the Simple Mail Transfer Protocol (SMTP) that may be required when traversing corporate firewalls.

SOAP is used by applications to invoke remote object methods and functions using an XML request that is routed to a remote SOAP server, typically over HTTP. When remote execution completes, an XML-formatted response is returned to the calling application. A SOAP message has three sections: a general message container, called an envelope, that is used to specify the encoding style of the message data; the body containing the actual message data; and an envelope header designed to carry additional transaction-specific information, such as authentication, routing, and scope detail.

6.12   SOAP and Security

When securing SOAP messages, various types of threats should be considered:

■ The message could be modified or read by antagonists or an antagonist could send messages to a service that, while well-formed, lacks appropriate security claims to warrant processing.
■ Based on the OASIS Web Services Security Model, which applies the use of message security tokens combined with digital signatures to protect and authenticate SOAP messages. Security tokens assert claims and can be used to assert the binding between authentication secrets or keys and security identities. Protecting the message content (confidentiality) from being disclosed or modified without detection (integrity) is a primary security concern.

6.13   Problems with Web Services Security

There are no industry best or even sound processes or practices for risk mitigation for Web services threats and vulnerabilities within the financial services sector or other industries. Despite data being shared among partners and sent over public networks, companies still have security concerns. Web services are based on standards that are simple and portable but provide no built-in security mechanisms. Therefore, data transferred via Web services can be exposed to threats. Security standards for Web services are being developed that attempt to define a standard set of message headers to achieve integrity and security, but they are not yet available.

Risk mitigation is the ultimate goal in reducing the threats and vulnerabilities within Web services; however, the means by which that goal can be partially accomplished is through the development of a process that continually identifies, measures, monitors, and controls Web services weaknesses.

The primary process many organizations use to identify, measure, monitor, and control information security and business process weaknesses is a risk assessment process. The three primary risk categories that apply to Web services security include authentication, authorization, administration, and cyber-security concerns. A few of the primary solutions to the security-related problems noted below (authentication, authorization, administration, and cyber-security) were previously identified and discussed in the previous section.

The risk assessment process should include, at the minimum, the following general categories involved in Web services:

- *Authentication*: Authentication is a core requirement of a secure Web services architecture—only free and public Web services do not require some form of authentication. The major choices for authentication include how credentials are bound to the Web services request, the type of credentials, whether a session token is used, and where and how authentications are processed.
- *Authorization*: Web services architects must decide on the richness of authorization policy and where and how authorization is performed.
- *Richness of Authorization*: The business situation drives authorization policy requirements. This can range from simple implied entitlement to complex policy-based and instance-based authorization. The terms "implied entitlement" and "implied authorization" refer to a service protected by authentication only, with no explicit authorization checks, such that all authenticated principals are granted access by default.

6.14 Administration

Determining the appropriate Web services administration is a security challenge. A comprehensive secure Web services architecture involves securing more than an independent, stand-alone Web services tier, which in turn involves multiple software infrastructure elements, each with its own security. For example, a business partner security infrastructure integration (federation) provides emerging solutions and standards for federated security. A security infrastructure is needed to enable business partners (or divisions within a single enterprise) to recognize and trust each other's users.

6.15 Conclusion

This chapter introduces the reader to the topic of Web services with the primary goals of establishing an introductory foundation on the topic and of introducing and discussing key security concerns that may introduce insider computer fraud risks. Web services are the nucleus of this book, based primarily on the concept of the Forensic Foto Frame, which will capture data at various points in a transaction within a Service Oriented Architecture.

6.16 Conclusion

Chapter 7

Application Security and Methods for Reducing Insider Computer Fraud

7.1 Introduction

This chapter presents the following key preventive and detective controls needed to safeguard an enterprise against insider computer fraud (ICF):

- The policies, procedures, and practices used to safeguard the confidentiality, integrity, and availability of data.
- The strengthening of the software development life-cycle methodology to address InfoSec.
- The findings of the U.S. Secret Service/computer emergency response team (CERT) Insider Threat Study.
- The application risk assessment process and net residual risk.
- The Insider Fraud Model.
- The risk assessment process and ICF prevention and detection.
- The development of application-specific acceptable and unacceptable use policies.
- The ICF threat assessment—Preliminary Risk Scorecard.

7.2 An Overview of Application Security

Application security is the policies, procedures, and practices used to safeguard the confidentiality, integrity, and availability of data. Unfortunately, many InfoSec policies are somewhat silent in addressing application security controls in both the preimplementation and postimplementation processes.

One of the greatest threats to organizations is insiders exploiting applications behind the firewall, within their organizations. The ICF threat is particularly noteworthy within applications, given the absence of software methodologies that ensure security is baked into the security engineering process from a preimplementation process. A second source of control that is absent in many organizations is the use of any source code analyzers prior to an application migrating into production. Organizations should conduct not only desktop checks of the application source code prior to cutover to production, but additionally, the use of software that will scan the source code, with a particular focus on detecting vulnerabilities (that is, cross-site scripting [XSS], Structure Query Language [SQL] injection, cookie poisoning, etc.).

7.3 The Current State of Application Security and the Prevention and Detection of the Insider Threat

Historically, applications in general (preproduction and production) have not received the attention they should from a risk perspective. Many organizations have not spent a great deal of time evaluating the risk profile of applications architecture as it pertains to the design of access, input, processing, and output controls throughout the software development life cycle. Despite the need in the industry for information security standards that address security requirements or guidelines for the software development life cycle, very few guidelines even remotely approach methods or a framework for addressing the what, when, and how of "baking" InfoSec controls within the preimplementation process. More recently, the issuance of NIST Special Publication 800-64, Security Considerations in the Information Systems Development Life Cycle, issued in October 2003 (www.nist.gov),[1] offers a framework for evaluating InfoSec risks and controls throughout the software development life cycle (SDLC).

The outlook for ensuring InfoSec is included within the SDLC is looking considerably more promising today and in the near future than ever before, and it is being driven by a number of factors, but unfortunately most are on a voluntary basis by organizations, not mandated through legislation. A sample of legislation pertaining to InfoSec includes Section 404 of Sarbanes–Oxley (SOX), Health Insurance Portability and Accountability Act (HIPAA) for the health-care industry, the Federal Financial Institution Examination Council (FFIEC), the Director of Central Intelligence Directives (DCID) 6/3 Standards, and the Federal Information Security Management Act (FISMA).

Unfortunately, although the aforementioned security guidance provides general InfoSec guidance, there is generally only minimal reference and guidance to application security, where the insider threat is most prevalent. Certainly, the passage of the Sarbanes–Oxley Act (SOX) (required the Public Company Accounting Oversight Board [PCAOB]) has contributed to the assurance process of ensuring the existence and adequacy of internal controls over financial reporting. Specifically, PCAOB ¶108—*Fraud Considerations in an Audit of Internal Controls over Financial Reporting*[2] represents an important first step legislatively that presents one of the first substantive down payments for mandating that companies maintain the appropriate level of internal controls over financial reporting.

The auditing standard requires the auditor to do the following:

■ Examine controls specifically designed to restrain the inappropriate use of company assets.
■ Review the company's risk assessment process.
■ Understand the company's code of ethics.
■ Evaluate the adequacy of the company's internal audit activities, internal audit's reporting relationship to the audit committee, and the audit committee's involvement and interaction with internal audit.
■ Consider the adequacy of the company's procedures for handling complaints and confidential submissions of concerns about questionable accounting and auditing practices.

A positive component of SOX is the inclusion of evaluation access controls of critical production applications within an enterprise. Up to the onset of SOX, in the private sector, there was no previous substantive voluntary effort by many organizations to even consider the evaluation of InfoSec controls within production applications, unless perhaps there was a noticed breach within a particular application or system or a significant volume of software patches or a notable number of programmatic changes made to the application.

7.4 Application Security and the Federal Insider Threat Study

During August 2004, the U.S. Secret Service National Threat Assessment Center (NTAC) and the CERT Coordination Center of Carnegie Mellon University's Software Engineering Institute (CERT/CC) joined efforts to conduct a unique study of insider incidents. The Insider Threat Study (ITS) then examined each case from both a behavioral perspective and a technical perspective. The cases examined within this study were incidents perpetrated by insiders (current or former employees or contractors) who intentionally exceeded or misused an authorized level of network, system, or data access in a manner that affected the security of the organizations' data, systems, or daily business operations.[3]

The following conclusions listed below were reached based upon this study:

In 70 percent of cases studied, the insiders exploited or attempted to exploit systemic vulnerabilities in applications or processes or procedures (e.g., business rule checks, authorized overrides) to carry out the incidents. In 61 percent of the cases, the insiders exploited vulnerabilities inherent in the design of the hardware, software, or network.

In 78 percent of the incidents, the insiders were authorized users with active computer accounts at the time of the incident. In 43 percent of the cases, the insider used his or her own username and password to carry out the incident.

There were some cases in which the insider used other means beyond his or her user account to perpetrate the harm. Twenty six percent of the cases involved the use of someone else's computer account, physical use of an unattended terminal with an open user account, or social engineering (i.e., gaining access through manipulation of a person or persons who can permit or facilitate access to a system or data).

Only 23 percent of the insiders were employed in technical positions, with 17 percent of the insiders possessing system administrator or root access within the organization.

Thirty-nine percent of the insiders were unaware of the organizations' technical security measures.

Particularly noteworthy is the fact that insider misuse was conducted by those employees with only a minimal level of technical knowledge or training. This statement is quite alarming, because it reflects the ease by which insiders can misuse the applications and systems of their employers with only a modicum of skills required. This statement should put organizations on notice that a comprehensive defense in depth strategy does not stop at the network's perimeter, which has been the primary point of focus for many InfoSec risk assessments, but through extension, should also include a review of logical security controls inherent in production applications and throughout the SDLC process.

7.5 The Application Risk Assessment Process and Net Residual Risk

Included within this chapter are two documents to aid the security architect to assess application security risks. The processes for evaluating application security risks are as follows:

- *Micro ICF Taxonomy Completion*: Complete a micro ICF taxonomy of a particular application. (Refer to Chapter 8 for details.)
- *Macro Taxonomy*: Evaluate the risks associated with the macro taxonomy (presented in Chapter 8) and determine their applicability to potential ICF activities.
- *ICFTA Completion (Inherent Risk)*: Complete the ICF threat assessment (ICFTA) for evaluating inherent (gross) application controls risk, which involves completion of a self-assessment of an application's risks and controls that are subject to potential or actual ICF activities. (Refer to Table 7.1 for details.)
- *CTRRF Completion (Residual Risk)*: The completion of the controls testing residual risk form (CTRRF) identifies the existence and adequacy of internal controls for determining the residual application controls risk rating. The primary purpose of this diagnostic tool is to allow the information technology (IT) professional to become aware of the similarities and differences between risks and controls over traditional, Web-based, and Web services software applications. Regardless of which application is involved in the risk assessment process, the completion of the CTRRF will determine the existence and adequacy of internal controls that should reduce the level of inherent risk in an application.
- *Risk Assessment Evaluation*: The cyber-security risk assessment ("Health-Check") evaluates all the interrelated environmental processes and other components that either directly or indirectly impact application security and ICF risks. Too often, risk assessment at many organizations considers just the inherent risk or, on occasion, the residual risk evaluation. One of the benefits of computing the net residual risk (NRR) within an application is to leverage off the residual risk value that was already determined by many organizations and to then integrate into the risk evaluation process the impact of the several major categories contained within the cyber-security HealthCheck. (Refer to Appendix F for details.)
- *Net Residual Risk (NRR)*: The NRR is a qualitative assessment and not a quantitative value. There are too many intangibles to accurately assign precise value and statistical probabilities to any of the criteria listed below (at least initially); consequently, conducting a more simplified qualitative assessment initially is more prudent and realistic. When assessing the NRR of an application, the following areas must be considered, including determination of the inherent risk rating, controls, the risk assessment process, the probability of occurrence, a business impact assessment (BIA), and the NRR.

Listed below is an example of the interrelationships that exist between the several components mentioned above for evaluating the NRR:

Step 1: Inherent risk rating (i.e., Rating = High).
Step 2: Internal controls rating (i.e., Rating = Strong).
Step 3: Residual risk rating (i.e., Rating = Moderate).

Step 4: Risk assessment rating (cyber-security HealthCheck) (i.e., Rating = Low).

Step 5: Probability of occurrence (i.e., Rating = Low).

Step 6: Business impact assessment (BIA) (i.e., Rating = Low).

Step 7: Net residual risk (NRR) (i.e., Rating = Low).

Step 8: Risk acceptance or risk rejection (i.e., Risk Acceptance).

Step 9: Software engineering considerations: Based on the results of the NRR conclusion, a final evaluation should be made relative to whether management is willing to accept or reject the risks introduced by a particular ICF threat. Based on the example above, the decision is clear that expending additional time and financial resources to enhance the security features within an application that has a low NRR should probably not receive the benefit of any additional InfoSec enhancements to prevent or detect ICF activities. Now, conversely, if the NRR was high and management decided not to accept the risk (risk rejection), then the application InfoSec deficiencies would have to be considered to be included within the software engineering process to reduce the level of NRR.

7.6 Software Engineering Considerations for Ensuring Application Security

Application security requirements need to be clearly identified and defined early within the software development life cycle. By definition, application security can be both manual and programmed activities intended to ensure the completeness and accuracy of the books and records of an enterprise. All phases of the software development life cycle need to incorporate the appropriate level of security within each application or system to mitigate against software vulnerabilities and the risks associated with insiders who attempt to exploit these vulnerabilities through computer fraud. Presented in this chapter are a number of considerations for ensuring that security is built into the software development life cycle to reduce the risks associated with application security.

As previously noted, based on the results of the NRR and management's decision to proceed with the software engineering process to address the ICF threat, each phase of the software development life cycle will need to reflect the appropriate security considerations that should be included within the application's development. Although we have primarily been discussing application preimplementation, the risk assessment processes (NRR) that should follow would apply to production applications as well. One of the unfortunate realities for many organizations is that their software development methodologies exclude evaluating InfoSec considerations within their SDLC.

Typically, application security risk assessments play a minor role in the risk evaluation processes, and changes to software development policy and practices

Table 7.1 Insider Computer Fraud Threat Assessment (ICFTA): Preliminary Risk Scorecard—A Self-Assessed Diagnostic Tool for Evaluating Inherent Application Risks Subject to Insider Computer Fraud

| | Application Controls (Preliminary Self-Assessed Controls for Determining Inherent Application Risk) | | | | |
	Access Controls	Data Origination and Input Controls	Processing	Output/MIS	Journaling
ICF Risks					
Macro Taxonomy Risks (Generic Risks Application to All Applications and Threats)					
Unauthorized system access	X				X
Inappropriate use of confidential corporate data stored in one computer system	X				X
Computer data manipulation within an application or system		X			X
Ease of access to a computer system/application entry due to security weaknesses of an older version of an application		X			X
Software code modification: "Trojan Horse" was built into a system to terminate users' sessions and cause a loss of data	X				X
Terminate user sessions in a seemingly random way, causing loss of data	X				X

(continued)

Table 7.1 Insider Computer Fraud Threat Assessment (ICFTA): Preliminary Risk Scorecard—A Self-Assessed Diagnostic Tool for Evaluating Inherent Application Risks Subject to Insider Computer Fraud (Continued)

ICF Risks	Application Controls (Preliminary Self-Assessed Controls for Determining Inherent Application Risk)				
	Access Controls	Data Origination and Input Controls	Processing	Output/MIS	Journaling
Misuse of system's capabilities (impersonation of another insider to send threatening e-mails to another insider)	X				X
Inadequate network journaling for forensic purposes	X				X
Illegal data transaction	X	X			X
Computer data manipulation within an application or system (i.e., change system data relating to the status of rebate claims from "paid" to "unpaid")	X	X	X	X	X
Acquisition of data (i.e., obtained credit card account numbers and other information)	X				X
Inappropriate use of confidential data in a computer system (i.e., acquired data was illegally distributed and transmitted to third parties)	X			X	X
Computer data destruction within an application or system (i.e., deletion of company's customers database and other records)		X	X	X	X

Self-dealing transaction to capitalize on the destruction created by the software code modification	X		X
Software code modification: "Logic Bomb" was built into a system to terminate users' sessions and cause a loss of data	X		X
Inappropriate acquisition of data (i.e., accessing and reading e-mails of company executives to gain a commercial advantage)	X	X	X
Employee impersonation and transmission of unauthorized e-mails to corporate clients	X		X
Computer access level modifications	X		
Damage to system availability (i.e., DDos attack)	X		
Exploitation of operating system vulnerabilities	X		
Circumvention of security controls (i.e., bypass the audit mechanism of the funding records database)	X		
Misuse of system capabilities (i.e., ability to make contra entries to the system which are used to suppress evidence of takings of account numbers of regular payers, who would not normally receive a payment reminder)	X		X
Unauthorized system access (i.e., access to supervisor's password)	X		X

(continued)

Table 7.1 Insider Computer Fraud Threat Assessment (ICFTA): Preliminary Risk Scorecard—A Self-Assessed Diagnostic Tool for Evaluating Inherent Application Risks Subject to Insider Computer Fraud (Continued)

ICF Risks	Application Controls (Preliminary Self-Assessed Controls for Determining Inherent Application Risk)				
	Access Controls	Data Origination and Input Controls	Processing	Output/MIS	Journaling
Inappropriate viewing of data outside the normal usage (i.e., computer monitoring, which revealed user file accesses outside the norm)	X				X
Inappropriate account provisioning (i.e., programmers had access to live programs and data files)	X				X
Masquerading as an employee	X				X
Hardware destruction (i.e., shutdown of computer server)	X				X
Hardware malfunction (i.e., resulted from deletion of programs)	X				X
Unauthorized system access (i.e., hacking)	X				X
Inappropriate viewing of data outside the normal usage (i.e., insider obtained confidential customer account and credit card information)	X			X	X

Description					
Collusion between an insider and an outsider (i.e., insider provided the outsider the confidential customer account information)	X				X
Illegal distribution and transmission of acquired financial information to one or more individuals outside of the company, who in turn used the credit card accounts and other financial information to fraudulently obtain goods	X		X		X
Malcode software injection (i.e., a computer programmer designed a virus to erase portions of the company's mainframe)	X				X
Micro ICF Taxonomy (This section was specifically focused on the insider loan fraud example; however, the contents of this section will be unique to the specific taxonomy performed for each application based on the results of the overall risk assessment results for each specific application.)					
A large discrepancy between the number and dollar amount of past due and nonaccrual loans from the loan data download and information reported to the board of directors	X	X	X	X	X
Loans with chronic past due loan histories are reported as current and do not appear on the institution's problem loan list	X	X	X	X	X
Loans with excessive number of payment extensions	X	X	X	X	X
Loans with excessive number of renewals and increasing loan balances	X	X	X	X	X

(continued)

Table 7.1 Insider Computer Fraud Threat Assessment (ICFTA): Preliminary Risk Scorecard—A Self-Assessed Diagnostic Tool for Evaluating Inherent Application Risks Subject to Insider Computer Fraud *(Continued)*

| ICF Risks | Application Controls (Preliminary Self-Assessed Controls for Determining Inherent Application Risk) | | | | |
	Access Controls	Data Origination and Input Controls	Processing	Output/MIS	Journaling
Loans with partial charge-offs that do not appear on the institution's problem loan list	X	X	X	X	X
Accrued interest is too high in relation to delinquency status	X	X	X	X	X
Paid ahead status is inconsistent with loan type and terms	X	X	X	X	X
Multiple borrowers with the same mailing address and different customer identification numbers	X	X	X	X	X
Different borrowers with identical social security or taxpayer identification numbers	X	X	X	X	X
Relationships exist that are not identified by social security numbers or addresses	X	X	X	X	X
The financial institution is unable to contact or notify customer by mail	X	X	X	X	X

These accounts may not be grouped by loan officer and monitored for activity	X	X	X	X
Senior management and subordinates may not question the loan officer due to high production or profitability of the portfolio	X	X	X	X
A significant increase in loan originations occurring on or about the date the institution received capital funding	X	X	X	X
Preferential interest rates	X	X	X	X
Frequent changes in loan review personnel may prevent them from becoming familiar enough with the institution's lending practices to identify insider schemes. Also, they may be close to uncovering an insider loan fraud and have been dismissed for this reason	X	X	X	
Collusion between the insider and the appraiser to falsify appraisals	X	X	X	X
To maximize compensation, insider may camouflage poor quality loans with forged, altered, or fraudulent documents, or originate loans to fictitious borrowers	X	X	X	X
A particular insider may be prone to engage in dishonest or unethical behavior	X	X	X	X
An attempt to conceal identity of delinquent borrowers to avoid board scrutiny	X	X	X	X

(continued)

Table 7.1 Insider Computer Fraud Threat Assessment (ICFTA): Preliminary Risk Scorecard—A Self-Assessed Diagnostic Tool for Evaluating Inherent Application Risks Subject to Insider Computer Fraud (*Continued*)

ICF Risks	Application Controls (Preliminary Self-Assessed Controls for Determining Inherent Application Risk)				
	Access Controls	Data Origination and Input Controls	Processing	Output/MIS	Journaling
An insider's financial condition may be strained and provide a motive to engage in loan fraud	X	X	X	X	X
Loans may be omitted to conceal insiders' strained financial positions and avoid board scrutiny	X	X	X	X	X
Insider attempting to conceal charged-off fraudulent loans	X	X	X	X	X
All new loans are not being reported to the board	X	X	X	X	X
Inadequate monitoring of policy exceptions	X	X	X	X	X
An insider may be involved in a kickback scheme where loans are granted in exchange for personal benefits or cash	X	X	X	X	X
Employees may have knowledge of irregular loan transactions	X	X	X	X	X
An insider with this level of control can force alteration of institution records to his or her benefit	X	X	X	X	X

Might signify working conditions or ethical compromises that employees are unwilling to accept	X	X	X	X	X
Insider may be booking fictitious loans or involved in a kickback scheme	X	X	X	X	X
Insider may be trying to discourage or impede in-depth review of institution records	X	X	X	X	X
An insider attempting to control access to records, which gives him or her the ability to shift and manipulate data to cover loan fraud	X	X	X	X	X
Indicates possible existence of fictitious loans and insider manipulation of loan status to hide irregularities	X	X	X	X	X
Loan purpose or insider's involvement is concealed to circumvent institution's legal lending limits	X	X	X	X	X
An insider may have violated a fiduciary duty by placing his or her own interest above that of the financial institution. An insider may be applying borrowed funds to conceal fraudulent loans	X	X	X		
An insider may extend preferential treatment to a customer in exchange for kickbacks or a reciprocal arrangement	X	X	X	X	X
An insider could be concealing information relevant to uncovering lending irregularities	X	X	X	X	X
Nominee, straw borrower, or fictitious borrower	X	X	X	X	X

(continued)

Table 7.1 Insider Computer Fraud Threat Assessment (ICFTA): Preliminary Risk Scorecard—A Self-Assessed Diagnostic Tool for Evaluating Inherent Application Risks Subject to Insider Computer Fraud (Continued)

ICF Risks	Application Controls (Preliminary Self-Assessed Controls for Determining Inherent Application Risk)				
	Access Controls	Data Origination and Input Controls	Processing	Output/MIS	Journaling
An insider can conceal exceptions and fraudulent loans	X	X	X	X	X
Insider can divert loan payments and proceeds or post or alter institution records	X	X	X	X	X
An insider may have motive to commit loan fraud	X	X	X	X	X
An insider may have financial difficulties and be motivated to engage in fraudulent lending activities	X	X	X	X	X
An insider knowingly accepting unreliable financial information in order to grant loan approval. There may be financial incentive or reciprocal favors	X	X	X	X	X
An insider knowingly accepting unreliable financial information in order to grant loan approval. Financial incentives or reciprocal favors may be involved	X	X	X	X	X
An insider knowingly accepting unreliable financial information in order to grant loan approval. Financial incentives or reciprocal favors may be involved	X	X	X	X	X

Insider may be unable to service debt to the institution if required to repay related interest's debt	X	X	X	X
Circumvention of an institution's legal lending limits. Masking of true financial condition	X	X	X	X
Borrowers do not exist; loans are to fictitious borrowers or nominees	X	X	X	X
An insider is involved in kickback or a fraudulent loan scheme. Blackmail may be involved	X	X	X	X
An insider attempting to conceal a questionable or fraudulent loan, policy exceptions, or legal lending limit violation	X	X	X	X
Fraudulent transaction	X	X	X	X
Collateral is inadequate or does not exist	X	X	X	X
Loan is to a nominee or straw borrower	X	X	X	X
An insider attempting to conceal documentation, underwriting, or collateral problems. Loan transaction may be fraudulent	X	X	X	X
Documents may be used for fictitious loans	X	X	X	X
Insider circumvents controls to receive preferential treatment of prohibited transaction	X	X	X	X
Insider collusion involving possible kickbacks, bribes, or other fraudulent schemes	X	X	X	X

(continued)

Table 7.1 Insider Computer Fraud Threat Assessment (ICFTA): Preliminary Risk Scorecard—A Self-Assessed Diagnostic Tool for Evaluating Inherent Application Risks Subject to Insider Computer Fraud (*Continued*)

ICF Risks	Application Controls (Preliminary Self-Assessed Controls for Determining Inherent Application Risk)				
	Access Controls	Data Origination and Input Controls	Processing	Output/MIS	Journaling
An insider influencing an appraiser to conceal inadequate collateral position. This may involve a kickback scheme	X	X	X	X	X
Purpose does not comply with lending policies or violates the law. True purpose may be to pay accrued interest on other loans to borrower	X	X	X	X	X
Self-dealing. Concealment of loans that do not meet policy guidelines. Violation of code of conduct	X	X	X	X	X
Self-dealing. Fraudulent loan transaction	X	X	X	X	X
Fraudulent loan transaction	X	X	X	X	X
An insider knowingly accepting or preparing forged or falsified documents	X	X	X	X	X
Fraudulent transaction. Borrower's true credit history may be concealed by using fictitious social security number to generate credit report. Forged letters and forged earnings statements.	X	X	X	X	X

True beneficiary of funds may be hidden	X	X	X		X
False information used as basis for loan decision	X	X	X		X
Insider using loan proceeds for personal benefit, hiding problem loans, or lending limit violation	X	X	X		X
Insider having financial difficulties and motive to commit fraud	X	X	X		X
Insider attempting to conceal fraudulent loans	X	X	X		X
Insider attempts to conceal lending limit violations, delinquency or fraudulent loans	X	X	X		X
Loan proceeds not used to stated purpose. Fraudulent transaction	X	X	X		X
Charge-off of fraudulent loans. A loan officer directed by senior officer or director to grant loans that normally would be declined. There could be financial incentives or reciprocal benefits involved	X	X	X		X
Insider using dormant or inactive accounts for fraudulent lending activities. Possible use of customer information to generate fictitious loans could be involved	X	X	X		X
Conceal delinquent or fraudulent loans	X	X	X		X
Fraudulent transactions. Insider receiving kickbacks from loan customer or embezzling loan proceeds or funds from deposit accounts	X	X			X

(continued)

Table 7.1 Insider Computer Fraud Threat Assessment (ICFTA): Preliminary Risk Scorecard—A Self-Assessed Diagnostic Tool for Evaluating Inherent Application Risks Subject to Insider Computer Fraud (Continued)

ICF Risks	Application Controls (Preliminary Self-Assessed Controls for Determining Inherent Application Risk)				
	Access Controls	Data Origination and Input Controls	Processing	Output/MIS	Journaling
May be partially attributable to fraudulent lending transactions	X	X	X	X	X
Fraudulent loan activity may be processed within these accounts	X	X	X	X	X
Other Computer Fraud Risks and Controls (Generic Risks Applicable to All Applications and Threats)					
Applications do not undergo a formal security design review prior to coding	Pre-Imp controls				
Extraneous transactions		X			X
Failure to enter transactions		X			X
Misuse of adjustment transaction		X			X
Misuse of error-correction procedures	X	X			X
Breakage (siphoning off small sums from numerous sources)	X	X			X
Undocumented transaction codes	X	X			X

Control		General application Pre-Imp controls	
Deliberate misreporting	X		X
Fudging control totals	X		X
Access to a live master file	X		X
Input validation	X		X
Session management	X		X
Authentication and authorization	X		X
Password standards	X		X
Design and code review			
Application and server error handling			
Application auditing and logging	X		X
Application backup and restore		X	X
Private data encryption	X	X	X
Web-Based Applications			
Data validation (input and output from a Web application). Ensure the Web-based application (server not client side) only accepts known valid and sanitized data and checks for the following minimum criteria:	X		X
Data type			
Min and Max lengths			
Required fields			
Any enumerated list of possible values are on that list			
Data values conform to the specific format			
Rejection of known bad data (i.e., malicious payloads)			

(continued)

Table 7.1 Insider Computer Fraud Threat Assessment (ICFTA): Preliminary Risk Scorecard—A Self-Assessed Diagnostic Tool for Evaluating Inherent Application Risks Subject to Insider Computer Fraud (*Continued*)

ICF Risks	Application Controls (Preliminary Self-Assessed Controls for Determining Inherent Application Risk)				
	Access Controls	Data Origination and Input Controls	Processing	Output/MIS	Journaling
Enterprise load testing for Web applications: Particularly important for preventing ICF in the form of a DDos attack. Risks may include: No goals have been established for: Testing strategy for application performance (i.e., projection of the number of concurrent users, estimate of growth pattern rates and consideration of application integration issues—internally and third-party applications) Validation of the application design: Usability, functionality, and ensuring there are no code sequences that may degrade performance Development: In addition to testing for functional correctness, they should test the same component with a small number of users for an early check on the scalability of the application Performance tuning and acceptance: Different transaction scenarios of real-life usage are emulated during this phase	X	X	X	X	X

Performance regression testing: The Web application is continuously retested in preproduction and measured against the established benchmarks to ensure that any preproduction application changes or infrastructure modifications do not result in any degradation of performance			
Production and postdeployment: Modifications to ensure the application can handle daily fluctuations in transactions and its impact on central processing unit (CPU) utilization, memory and disk space, and on application and database servers.			
Command execution attacks (i.e., Structure Query Language [SQL] injection, which is a direct database call to the database, which can allow an attacker to change SQL values, concatenate SQL statements, add function call and stored-procedures to a statement, etc.). The best way to protect a system against SQL injection attacks is to construct all queries with prepared statements or parameterized stored procedures, which encapsulates variables that in a manner suited to the target database	X		X
Control of format and type of data	X	X	
Attacks on session-dependent information	X	X	X
Cookie tampering			
Prevention of form field tampering used for accepting user input for processing, storage, and display			

(continued)

Table 7.1 Insider Computer Fraud Threat Assessment (ICFTA): Preliminary Risk Scorecard—A Self-Assessed Diagnostic Tool for Evaluating Inherent Application Risks Subject to Insider Computer Fraud (*Continued*)

ICF Risks	Application Controls (Preliminary Self-Assessed Controls for Determining Inherent Application Risk)				
	Access Controls	Data Origination and Input Controls	Processing	Output/MIS	Journaling
Graphical user interface (GUI) restricts the type of data the user is able to access	X				X
Either the application or server conducts data integrity checks, to include but not be limited to: Data type (i.e., string, integer, etc.) Whether a null value is entered Numeric values		X			X
Session management: Hypertext Transfer Protocol (HTTP) does not provide, but applications should through session tokens, which need protection from attackers taking over a session	X				X
HTML injection—cross-site scripting: attacker's use of a Web site to send malicious code (i.e., JavaScript) to another user. Users are tricked into clicking on a link that causes the injected code to travel to the vulnerable Web server and the Web server then reflects the attack back to the unsuspecting user's browser	X				X

Buffer overflows: an attacker can cause a Web application to execute malicious code that is designed to take over a system. Failure to apply the latest patches may create the potential for buffer overflows	X	X
Command injection flaws: attacker embeds malicious commands in the message parameters and the external system can be made to execute these commands on behalf of the Web application	X	X
No error handling problems (i.e., error messages should be generated and logged for future analysis, such as user inputs into the application)	X	X
No use of encryption for storage in the application's file system (as applicable)	X	X
Denial of service: lack of use of any load testing tools to generate Web traffic so that you can test certain aspects of how your site performs under heavy load	X	X
Session hijacking: no method for users to log out of an application. Logging out does not clear all session states and remove or invalidate any residual cookies	X	X
Session authentication attacks: no checks made to ensure that the currently logged-on user has the authorization to access, update, or delete data or certain functions	X	X

(continued)

Table 7.1 Insider Computer Fraud Threat Assessment (ICFTA): Preliminary Risk Scorecard—A Self-Assessed Diagnostic Tool for Evaluating Inherent Application Risks Subject to Insider Computer Fraud (*Continued*)

	Application Controls (Preliminary Self-Assessed Controls for Determining Inherent Application Risk)				
	Access Controls	Data Origination and Input Controls	Processing	Output/MIS	Journaling
ICF Risks					
Session validation attacks: no checks to determine that the session variable is validated to ensure the correct form is being used, with no unexpected characters. No checks made to ensure that the current logged-on user has the authorization to access, update, or delete data or certain functions	X				X
Man in the middle attacks: occurring when an attacker tries to insert him- or herself between the server and the client. Acting as the client for the server and acting as a server for the client. No Secure Sockets Layer (SSL) used for sites needing high privacy or possessing high-value transactions	X				X
Brute force: use of weak session ID controls with no cryptographically sound token-generation algorithm	X				X
Session token replay: no session token time-outs and token regeneration to reduce the window of opportunity to replay tokens. No use of nonpersistent cookies to store the session token. Sessions do not expire after a given point in time, usually ranging from five to twenty minutes of inactivity	X				X

Description			
Input validation: high susceptibility of a Web-based application for manipulating the data sent between the browser and the Web application from various input sources such as: URL query strings Form fields Cookies HTTP headers	X	X	X
URL query strings: HTML forms submit their results using one of two methods: GET or POST. If the method is GET, all form element names and values will appear in the query string of the next URL the user sees. Tampering with query strings is as easy as modifying the URL in the browser's address bar. Increased risks are involved when an application would not recheck the account number, thereby increasing the potential for the balance of the other user's account to be exposed to an attacker. A request will have a query string with parameters just like a form and a user can simply look in the "address" window of the browser and change the parameter values. When parameters need to be sent from a client to a server, they should be accompanied by a valid session token	X	X	X
Form fields: there is no use of a secret key within a form field and appended to a string (outgoing form message) along with an MD5 digest or other one-way hash that is generated for the outgoing form message and stored as a hidden field	X		X

(continued)

Table 7.1 Insider Computer Fraud Threat Assessment (ICFTA): Preliminary Risk Scorecard—A Self-Assessed Diagnostic Tool for Evaluating Inherent Application Risks Subject to Insider Computer Fraud (Continued)

ICF Risks	Application Controls (Preliminary Self-Assessed Controls for Determining Inherent Application Risk)				
	Access Controls	Data Origination and Input Controls	Processing	Output/MIS	Journaling
No security scanning tools are used of code by the program development team to identify known exploits (i.e., code injection attacks, cross-site scripting, denial of service, buffer overruns)	X				X
Cookie content can be manipulated by a malicious user through the absence of any encryption of the cookie or by other means (i.e., linkage to an intrusion detection system [IDS] to evaluate the cookie for any impossible combination of values that would indicate tampering. Cookies are used to maintain state in a stateless HTTP protocol; however, both persistent and nonpersistent cookies can be used to store user preferences and data such as session tokens	X	X			X

Web Services Risks and Controls (Generic Risks Applicable to All Web-Based Applications and Threats; Web Services* operate on Layer 7 of the Open Systems Interconnection [OSI] Model That Includes Description [WSDL], Messaging [SOAP], Transmission [XML], and Protocol [HTTP, FTP])

	Col 1	Col 2	Col 3
Ensuring message reliability: To determine the validity of a message, the following three considerations should be made: Was the message received the same as the one sent? (i.e., byte counts, check sums, and digital signatures) Does the message conform to the formats specified by the agreed-upon protocol for the message? Does the message conform to the business rules expected by the receiver?	X		X
Coercive parsing: an insider may parse a Simple Object Access Protocol (SOAP) message to extract parameters and determine what method to invoke, insert content into a database, or perform some other function. The insider can now conduct a hack via a DoS attack or simply just degrade the applications performance	X	X	X
Oversize payloads: an insider can transmit a large eXtensible Markup Language (XML) file to deplete the CPU resources as a result of parsing and validating each entry	X		X
Replay attack: an insider may engage in a "ping of death," where repetitive SOAP messages are made to overload the Web service	X		X
Malicious content: an insider can spread viruses or Trojan horse programs within valid XML messages, which may create problems for the Web services application. Attachments that contain executables, images, and other binary code can be used for malicious purposes within a Web services application	X		X

(continued)

Table 7.1 Insider Computer Fraud Threat Assessment (ICFTA): Preliminary Risk Scorecard—A Self-Assessed Diagnostic Tool for Evaluating Inherent Application Risks Subject to Insider Computer Fraud (Continued)

	Application Controls (Preliminary Self-Assessed Controls for Determining Inherent Application Risk)				
ICF Risks	Access Controls	Data Origination and Input Controls	Processing	Output/MIS	Journaling
Transmission of SOAP messages via HTTP may increase risk of interception in addition to not being reliable. Other methods of transmission that could reduce security risks include Simple Mail Transfer Protocol (SMTP) or message queues	X	X			X
SOAP/XML does not provide any granular message-level access control, because SSL certificates and HTTP user-names and passwords used for each session do not interrogate the payload	X	X			X
No use of Security Assertion Markup Language (SAML) for authentication: SAML allows for a single sign-on method of authentication by embedding authentication status and authorization permissions	X				X
Firewalls will not inspect the contents of a SOAP message, but only whether the transport (HTTP) is valid according to the syntax of the HTTP (RFC) protocol. This situation could be problematic for a Web services application based on the potential for a SOAP message being malicious, corrupted, or potentially damaging					

	Col 1	Col 2	Col 3
Scanning for patterns and anomalies in the data being exchanged versus just packet flow monitoring is one method for identifying anomalies in the data being exchanged. Monitoring traffic exclusively at the packet level will not help detect Web services-related security incursions	X		
The lack of proper content filtering controls to spot syntax errors in SOAP and XML result in significant damage to a system or multiple systems. Examples of improper syntax may include a data string that is too long, contains illegal characters, etc.	X	X	
Insiders may exploit Web services where identities are being hijacked and data is being stolen	X	X	X
The absence of a Web services-capable firewall to reduce the risk of receiving undesirable network traffic (i.e., SOAP messages, XML data, and Web Services Description Language [WSDL] files). Web services allow any kind of data to be transported using the Transmission Control Protocol/Internet Protocol (TCP/IP) ports for standard Web traffic (80 and 443), which effectively makes traditional firewalls blind to many attack methods. Both XML data and WSDL descriptions are rich with information, and firewalls do not have the ability to conduct any significant level of XML data filtering or WSDL validation	X		
The enterprise does not use SSL for Web services for point-to-point external connections	X	X	

(continued)

Table 7.1 Insider Computer Fraud Threat Assessment (ICFTA): Preliminary Risk Scorecard—A Self-Assessed Diagnostic Tool for Evaluating Inherent Application Risks Subject to Insider Computer Fraud (*Continued*)

ICF Risks	Application Controls (Preliminary Self-Assessed Controls for Determining Inherent Application Risk)				
	Access Controls	Data Origination and Input Controls	Processing	Output/MIS	Journaling
The enterprise does not use a virtual private network (VPN) internally within the organization for its Web services	X				X
The enterprise does not use XML encryption to protect message secrecy. A public key infrastructure (PKI) can be used to provide authentication, digital signatures, and key distribution. The PKI is based on XML key management specification (XKMS), which is intended for the integration of PKI and digital certificates	X				X
The enterprise does not maintain a Web services policy that discusses the following areas: Availability Authentication Authorization Privacy Nonrepudiation	X	X	X	X	X

The enterprise does not maintain the most basic level of WS-Security, which includes the use of XML-encryption and XML-digital signatures within the SOAP message headers and a mechanism for transferring security tokens between participants X

* Web services: Based on a definition provided by Chris Kwabi, "XML Web Services Security and Web Based Application Security, SANS Practical Assignment," dated 2003, "The term 'Web Service' can apply to a wide variety of network base application topology. In this context, the term 'Web Service' describes application components whose functionality and interfaces are exposed to potential users through the use of existing and emerging Web Technology standards including XML, SOAP, WSDL, and HTTP. In contrast to Web sites, browser-based interactions, or platform-dependent solutions, Web services are computer-to-computer-based services that are generated via defined formats and protocols in a platform independent and language neutral manner."
A second and closely aligned definition of Web services came from Hugo Haas (www.w3.org) who states: "A Web service is a software system designed to support interoperable machine-to-machine interaction over a network. It has an interface described in a machine-processable format (specifically WSDL). Other systems interact with the Web service in a manner prescribed by its description using SOAP messages, typically conveyed using HTTP with an XML serialization in conjunction with other Web-related standards."

Application Journaling: Generic Risks Application to All Applications and Threats (The Absence of Proper Journaling and Audit Trails Could Represent an Operational Risk from an Incident Response and Computer Forensic Perspective)

Key fraud indicator (KFI) (attribute) CREATION X

Date X

Time X

Last save time X

Revision number X

Total edit time (minutes) X

(continued)

Table 7.1 Insider Computer Fraud Threat Assessment (ICFTA): Preliminary Risk Scorecard—A Self-Assessed Diagnostic Tool for Evaluating Inherent Application Risks Subject to Insider Computer Fraud (Continued)

ICF Risks	Application Controls (Preliminary Self-Assessed Controls for Determining Inherent Application Risk)				
	Access Controls	Data Origination and Input Controls	Processing	Output/MIS	Journaling
Total metadata object CREATION					X
KFI (attribute) ACCESS					X
Date					X
Time					X
Last save time					X
Revision number					X
Total edit time (minutes)					X
Total metadata object, ACCESS					X
KFI (attribute) DELETIONS					X
Date					X
Time					X
Last save time					X

Revision number	X
Total edit time (minutes)	X
Total metadata object DELETIONS	X
KFI (attribute) ADDITIONS	X
Date	X
Time	X
Last save time	X
Revision number	X
Total edit time (minutes)	X
Total metadata object ADDITIONS	X
KFI (attribute) MODIFICATIONS	X
Date	X
Time	X
Last save time	X
Revision number	X
Total edit time (minutes)	X
Total data object MODIFICATIONS	X
Document embedded graphics or objects	X

(continued)

Table 7.1 Insider Computer Fraud Threat Assessment (ICFTA): Preliminary Risk Scorecard—A Self-Assessed Diagnostic Tool for Evaluating Inherent Application Risks Subject to Insider Computer Fraud (*Continued*)

ICF Risks	Application Controls (Preliminary Self-Assessed Controls for Determining Inherent Application Risk)				
	Access Controls	Data Origination and Input Controls	Processing	Output/MIS	Journaling
Total number of document embedded graphics or objects					X
Embedded graphics/OBJECTS CREATION					X
Date					X
Time					X
Last save time					X
Revision number					X
Total edit time (minutes)					X
Total number of embedded graphics CREATED					X
Embedded graphics/OBJECTS ACCESSES					X
Date					X
Time					X
Last save time					X

Revision number	X
Total edit time (minutes)	X
Total number of embedded graphics ACCESSED	X
Embedded graphics/OBJECTS DELETIONS	X
Date	X
Time	X
Last save time	X
Revision number	X
Total edit time (minutes)	X
Total number of embedded graphics DELETIONS	X
Embedded graphics/OBJECTS ADDITIONS	X
Date	X
Time	X
Last save time	X
Revision number	X
Total edit time (minutes)	X
Total number of embedded graphics ADDITIONS	X
Embedded graphics/OBJECTS MODIFICATIONS	X

(continued)

Table 7.1 Insider Computer Fraud Threat Assessment (ICFTA): Preliminary Risk Scorecard—A Self-Assessed Diagnostic Tool for Evaluating Inherent Application Risks Subject to Insider Computer Fraud (Continued)

| ICF Risks | Application Controls (Preliminary Self-Assessed Controls for Determining Inherent Application Risk) | | | | |
	Access Controls	Data Origination and Input Controls	Processing	Output/MIS	Journaling
Date					X
Time					X
Last save time					X
Revision number					X
Total edit time (minutes)					X
Total number of embedded graphics MODIFICATIONS					X
DOCUMENT ALGORITHMIC TRANSFORMATIONS (i.e., Calcs)					X
Algorithmic transformations CREATION					X
Date					X
Time					X
Last save time					X

Revision number	X
Total edit time (minutes)	X
Total number of algorithmic transformations CREATION	X
Algorithmic transformations ACCESSES	X
Date	X
Time	X
Last save time	X
Revision number	X
Total edit time (minutes)	X
Total number of algorithmic transformations ACCESSES	X
Algorithmic transformations DELETIONS	X
Date	X
Time	X
Last save time	X
Revision number	X
Total edit time (minutes)	X
Total number of algorithmic transformations DELETIONS	X
Algorithmic transformations ADDITIONS	X

(continued)

Table 7.1   Insider Computer Fraud Threat Assessment (ICFTA): Preliminary Risk Scorecard—A Self-Assessed Diagnostic Tool for Evaluating Inherent Application Risks Subject to Insider Computer Fraud (*Continued*)

ICF Risks	Application Controls (Preliminary Self-Assessed Controls for Determining Inherent Application Risk)				
	Access Controls	Data Origination and Input Controls	Processing	Output/MIS	Journaling
Date					X
Time					X
Last save time					X
Revision number					X
Total edit time (minutes)					X
Total number of algorithmic transformations ADDITIONS					X
Algorithmic transformations MODIFICATIONS					X
Date					X
Time					X

Last save time	X
Revision number	X
Total edit time (minutes)	X
Total number of algorithmic transformations ADDITIONS	X
DATA ACCESS RULES VIOLATIONS	X
(Access Level 1—CREATE)	X
(Access Level 2—ACCESS)	X
(Access Level 3—DELETE)	X
(Access Level 4—ADD)	X
(Access Level 5—MODIFY)	X

Note: Fully implemented, low risk; partially implemented, moderate risk; not implemented, high risk.

usually do not occur until application vulnerabilities or exploits are detected. However, the decision to proceed with actually implementing a security solution for an application is a personal choice, but one that should be predicated by a careful risk evaluation of that application or system (i.e., a NRR of high and management's risk rejection decision). Based on what I perceive as being a systemic problem for many organizations, it is appropriate then to review the criteria outlined within NIST SP 800-64, which discusses a framework for evaluating InfoSec through each phase of the software development life cycle.

7.6.1 National Institute of Standards and Technology (NIST) Special Publication (SP) 800-64

7.6.1.1 Security Considerations in the Initiation Phase

- *Needs Determination*: A needs determination is an analytical activity that evaluates the capacity of an organization's assets to satisfy existing and emerging demands. The security part of needs determination will result in a high-level description of the security controls in the proposed system and the assurance requirements.
- *Security Categorization*: This defines three levels of potential impact on organizations or individuals should there be a breach of security (a loss of confidentiality, integrity, or availability). Security categorization standards assist organizations in making the appropriate selection of security controls for their information systems.
- *Preliminary Risk Assessment*: These are results in an initial description of the basic security needs of the system. A preliminary risk assessment should define the threat environment in which the system will operate. This assessment is followed by an initial identification of required security controls that must be met to protect the product or system in the intended operational environment.
- *Security Considerations in the Acquisition/Development Phase*
  - *Risk Assessment*: Risk assessment is analysis that identifies the protection requirements for the system through a formal risk assessment process. This analysis builds on the initial risk assessment performed during the initiation phase but will be a more in-depth and specific report.
  - *Security Functional Requirements Analysis*: This is an analysis of requirements that may include the following components: (1) system security environment (i.e., enterprise information security policy and enterprise security architecture) and (2) security functional requirements.
  - *Security Assurance Requirements Analysis*: This is an analysis of requirements that address the developmental activities required and assurance evidence needed to produce the desired level of confidence that the information security will work correctly and effectively. The analysis, based on

legal and functional security requirements, will be used as the basis for determining how much and what kinds of assurance are required.

- *Cost Considerations and Reporting*: In this step, how much of the development cost can be attributed to information security over the life cycle of the system is determined. These costs include hardware, software, personnel, and training.

■ *Security Planning*: Security planning ensures that agreed-upon security controls, planned or in place, are fully documented. The security plan provides a complete characterization or description of the information system as well as attachments or references to key documents supporting the agency's information security program (e.g., configuration, management plan, contingency plan, incident response plan, security awareness and training plan, rules of behavior, risk assessment, security test and evaluation results, system interconnection agreements, security authorization, accreditations, and plan of action and milestones).

■ *Security Control Development*: Security control development ensures that security controls described in the respective security plans are designed, developed, and implemented. For information systems currently in operation, the security plans for those systems may call for the development of additional security controls to supplement the controls already in place or the modification of selected controls that are deemed to be less than effective.

■ *Developmental Security Test and Evaluation*: This test and evaluation ensure that security controls developed for a new information system are working properly and are effective. Some types of security controls (primarily those controls of a nontechnical nature) cannot be tested and evaluated until the information system is deployed. These controls are typically management and operational controls.

■ *Other Planning Components*: Other planning components ensure that all necessary components of the development process are considered when incorporating security into the life cycle. These components include selection of the appropriate contract type, participation by all necessary functional groups within an organization, participation by the certifier and accreditor, and the development and execution of necessary contracting and processes.

7.6.1.2 Security Considerations of the Operations/Maintenance Phase

■ *Configuration Management and Control*: Ensure adequate consideration of the potential security impacts due to specific changes to an information system or its surrounding environment. Configuration management and configuration control procedures are critical to establishing an initial baseline of hardware, software, and firmware components for the information system and subsequently controlling and maintaining an accurate inventory of any changes to the system.

■ *Continuous Monitoring*: Ensures that controls continue to be effective in their application through periodic testing and evaluation. Security control monitoring (i.e., verifying the continued effectiveness of those controls over time) and reporting the security status of the information system to appropriate agency officials are essential activities of a comprehensive information security program.

7.6.1.3 Security Considerations of the Disposition Phase

■ *Information Preservation*: Ensures that information is retained, as necessary, to conform to current legal requirements and to accommodate future technology changes that may render the retrieval method obsolete.
■ *Media Sanitization*: Ensures that data is deleted, erased, and written over as necessary.
■ *Hardware and Software Disposal*: Ensures that hardware and software are disposed of as directed by the information security officer.

7.6.2 ICF Framework

There are numerous forms of ICF (see Chapter 8), and the software engineering process needs to clearly identify what aspects of the ICF Framework are needed. Obviously a good place to start is with the completion of a comprehensive risk assessment process. However, during this research, this ICF Framework is primarily geared toward identifying and detecting data input manipulation within an application. Prior to discussing how this framework can assist in the software engineering consideration, we need to clearly identify the types of applications in today's marketplace.

Production application reviews are unfortunately the orphans of all of IT and not reviewed to any great extent by many organizations. Many organizations need to strengthen their ability to evaluate risks associated with commercial off-the-shelf (COTS) and may only be slightly better with home-grown applications from a production perspective. Anyway, rarely do you see an institution perform Post-Implementation reviews; however, this practice has been changing recently, perhaps as a result of SOX 404 and perhaps as a result of applications and systems receiving additional code through patches and programmatic version changes.

The audit function of an enterprise should be involved in Pre-Imps depending on the risk of the system or application. Ideally, the audit department should be involved in production applications during their integrated business and technology audits. An IT infrastructure audit is typically performed as a stand-alone audit.

Again, Sarbanes–Oxley reviews are in the production application review space now and the internal audit department of an enterprise should be leveraging off of their reviews. Internal audit departments should be considering the following six classes of production applications in scoping their reviews, as applicable:

- Home grown (traditional "Non-Web"-based application or system)
- COTS (traditional "Non-Web"-based application or system with or without customization for the institution's particular needs)
- Home grown (Web-based application)
- COTS (Web-based application or system with or without customization for the institution's particular needs)
- Home grown (Web services application)
- COTS (Web services application or system with or without customization for the institution's particular needs)

Then there is the application service provider (ASP) who actually maintains the application and conducts data processing for the client, and addresses the question of how to evaluate the adequacy of their risks and controls given the outsourcing relationship between the enterprise and the ASP. The client in an ASP relationship may have a service-level agreement or a service contract, which includes a right to audit clause that would provide the client access to the software vendor. This would be one potential avenue for an organization to assess the risk profile of that ASP in that outsourcing relationship. A client's ability to obtain supporting documentation regarding the ASP's software development methodology could be difficult given the potential for that ASP to cite intellectual property rights (IPF).

Another concern presented in this chapter is the general approach to the evaluation of software applications to detect ICF activities. A general discussion of application risks and controls is presented in this chapter; however, the specific application risks will require the security architect to completely understand the business purpose of the application within the organization, access level, input, processing and output controls for the application, and then for interfacing the application. In order to gain a sound understanding of the aforementioned, risks and controls will likely require process mapping and the development of data flow diagrams.

7.7   The Risk Assessment Process and ICF Prevention and Detection

Provided in Figure 7.1 is a high-level overview of various key components of the ICF Model, including the following general areas:

- Enterprise risk assessment process
- Unacceptable use policy for an application
- Acceptable use policy for an application
- Development of taxonomies (macro and micro)
- Development of data flow diagrams to determine control points and gates for capturing data behavior from Forensic Foto Frames

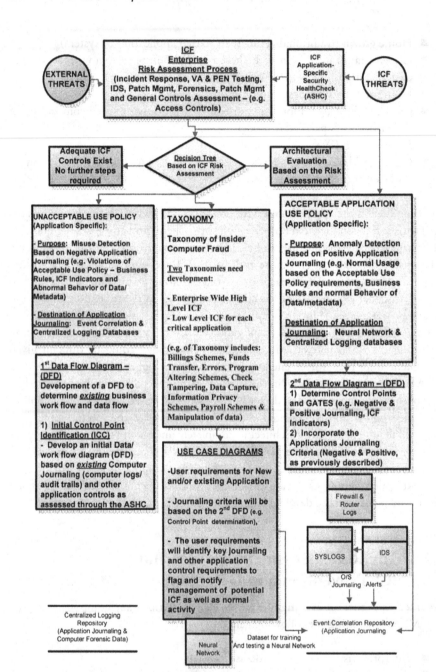

Figure 7.1   ICF Model—a macro view.

7.7.1 *Inherent Risk Rating: ICF Threat Assessment (ICFTA)*

The ICFTA (Table 7.1) is the first step used for determining the NRR qualitative rating for a particular application (Section 7.5). It represents a preliminary risk scorecard used by the IT professional to perform an initial evaluation of application risks and controls. Currently, there is only a minimal amount of information in the public domain relative to evaluating application risks and controls, and the ICFTA has incorporated all types of applications risks and controls. The ICFTA is a diagnostic tool for the IT professional to use in conducting their initial application risk evaluation to determine the level of inherent risks, using the color scorecard rating, which includes fully implemented—low risk, partially implemented—moderate risk, and not implemented—high risk).

7.7.2 *Risk Assessment Rating (Cyber-Security HealthCheck)*

The cyber-security HealthCheck (Appendix F) was developed to evaluate the adequacy of the network infrastructure and related IT components (i.e., patch management, computer incident response team [CIRT] processes, risk assessment process, and vulnerability and penetration testing). The qualitative results from the cyber-security HealthCheck will either lower or increase the overall NRR assessment rating.

The reviews for Web-based and Web services production and Pre-Imp applications or systems are significantly more complex than the traditional. In addition to the use of the ICFTA and the CTRRF, if the enterprise is a service provider, having a Level II SAS70 audit can be of value to address the adequacy of internal controls governing a particular application. Additionally, the AICPA's WebTrust/SysTrust certification can also add value in evaluating the risks and controls governing an organization's business-to-business (B2B) and business-to-consumer (B2C) Web-based applications.

7.8 Developing Application-Specific Acceptable and Unacceptable Use Policies

A key finding in the U.S. Secret Service and CERT Insider Threat Study[4] is that insider attacks on organizations in the banking and finance sector required minimal technical skill to execute. Many of the cases involved the simple exploitation of inadequate practices, policies, or procedures. The insider threat activity examined in the banking and finance sector appears to involve an interaction among organizational culture, business practices, policies, and technology, as well as the insiders' motivations and external influences.

As reflected by the ICF Model diagram (Figure 7.1), there should be the development of acceptable and unacceptable use policies related to the use of a particular application or system. Listed below is a brief distinction between the two policies:

Acceptable Use Policy (AUP): This is the opportunity for identification of what should ostensibly be the business rules of the enterprise governing normal usage by an employee and the trusted insider of the enterprise. This is an opportunity for an organization to clearly define how an application works, identify control points (i.e., access, input, processing, and output controls), and designate acceptable practices of how an insider should be using this application or system. Specifically, the policy at the highest level may include a discussion of the roles and responsibilities of employee end users, supervisors, managers, or directors, and the procedural steps they need to follow to ensure company policy and standards are being met.

Unacceptable Use Policy (UUP): A discussion of the various business rules would be appropriate, similar to the AUP. The policy should address what constitutes a violation of the policy and the designation of ICF indicators and abnormal behavior of data and metadata.

7.9 Conclusion

The highlights of this chapter include the following areas:

■ Application security controls for ICF risk identification and reduction involve ensuring that the software development methodologies include InfoSec controls that are baked into the process to reduce ICF threat.

■ Based on the 2004 U.S. Secret Service Nation Threat Assessment Center (NTAC) and CERT Coordination Center Insider Threat Study, in 70 percent of the cases studied, the insiders exploited or attempted to exploit systemic vulnerabilities in applications or processes or procedures.

■ The determination of net residual value will provide a more comprehensive understanding of application and system security risk by reviewing application security risks in context to all cyber-security risks.

■ The Preliminary ICF Threat Assessment (ICFTA) will greatly aid in management's ability to understand application risks that are subject to ICF.

■ Application security lies at the heart of ICF abuse. Consequently, to effectively address reducing the potential of misuse of applications by insiders, there is a need to address the underlying problem within applications which involves management and audit evaluating the risks and controls within critical applications and determining methods to reduce those risks. In this chapter, the ICFTA is identified as a diagnostic tool for evaluating risks within an application, which will aid in the determination of net residual value of an application. Based on the net residual value rating (high, moderate, or low) assigned to an application, a determination of the appropriate level of controls can then be made as a risk reduction strategy for an application. The lower the application risk level, the chances are reduced that an insider will successfully achieve ICF.

References

1. Security Considerations in the Information Systems Development Life Cycle, NIST SP 800-64, 2004.
2. Avellanet, Wayne A. *Guide to the PCAOB Internal Control Standard,* Warren, Gorham & Lamont, New York, 2004.
3. Randazzo, Marisa Reddy. Insider Threat Study: Illicit Cyber Activity in the Banking and Finance Sector, The U.S. Secret Service and CERT Coordination Center, Software Engineering Institute (SEI), Carnegie Mellon, Pittsburgh, PA, 2004.

Chapter 8

Insider Computer Fraud Taxonomy and the Art of the Key Fraud Indicator (KFI) Selection Process

8.1   Introduction

In this chapter, application security is discussed at length, and how, historically, applications and systems in general (preproduction and production) have not received the attention they should from a risk perspective and have been overshadowed by network security. Additionally, there is discussion on the tight cohesion between seemingly disparate topics such as software vulnerabilities, application security, taxonomy, and insider computer fraud (ICF), versus collective and interrelated topics that are all inextricably connected.

8.2 Insider Computer Fraud (ICF) Taxonomy

8.2.1 The Nexus between Software Vulnerabilities, Application Security, Taxonomy, and ICF

8.2.1.1 Software Vulnerabilities and ICF

Insiders of an organization have access to software vulnerabilities exposure listings (i.e., www.cve.mitre.org/cve) and can easily perform a review of the database of various commercial off-the-shelf (COTS) products that have vulnerabilities and potential exploits within an application. Although insider software code manipulation does not rank as high as data manipulation in terms of the results of the ICF taxonomy, contained within this chapter, it does represent a potential threat, and those risks need to be surfaced and effectively controlled.

In terms of gaining access to information about a software application or system from within an organization, an insider may also gain access to a projects software development documentation (i.e., user requirements, vulnerabilities, etc.), assuming the project documentation is located on the organization's intranet Web site and is not password controlled. Even if the project documentation is located on the intranet Web site and the user identification (UID) and password are tightly controlled, a trusted insider would potentially have an easier time in accessing this information than an outsider to the organization. Based on an insider's review, that supporting application documentation could identify vulnerabilities within an application that may not have been resolved to the preimplementation testing, and an attempt to exploit those vulnerabilities could be made by that insider.

Although details of how the software engineering processes are beginning to show signs of improvement are presented in Chapter 7, it is this author's opinion that the software industry in general still has a long way to go to prove to the public that COTS has evolved in reducing the volume of preventable security vulnerabilities. There are many indications in the industry that companies and individuals are becoming more acutely aware of the inherent weaknesses within not only the software products being produced, but also the underlying root cause of these problems. The jury is still out on the effectiveness of the push toward strengthening the software engineering processes behind software development; however, there are currently noteworthy efforts to address these fundamental process-related problems.

8.2.1.2 Application Security and ICF

There is a direct correlation between inadequate software design processes, application security flaws that are introduced, and the increased risk of ICF activities. For many organizations, there tends to be a greater emphasis on ensuring the adequacy of controls over the operating system platform to control access into applications and systems, with less emphasis on providing secure application authentication and access control safeguards.

Based on a document written by Andrew Jaquith (Program Director with @stake, Inc.,[1] but recently acquired by Symantec; now a Programmer Manager at Yankee Group), the following commentary was made.

First, most firms do not adequately provide secure authentication and access control features within applications. Nearly two-thirds (62 percent) of applications we assessed suffered from poor design and implementation choices that allowed access controls to be bypassed. Over one-quarter of the applications permitted user passwords to travel over the network unencrypted, where they could easily be stolen. Twenty-seven percent of applications lacked password policies or controls that would have helped lock out would-be intruders trying to brute-force the log-in process. And despite the widespread popularity of cryptography for use with Secure Sockets Layer (SSL), one-third of companies stored sensitive information such as user passwords, confidential data, and encryption key insecurely.

Second, e-business applications typically trust user input implicitly or rely on client-side validation, rather than having the server check for inappropriate data. For example, a common trick with attackers is to submit Web forms that contain embedded Hypertext Markup Language (HTML), JavaScript, or overly long strings that do not conform to what the developer intended. Under the right conditions, this can cause the Web server to fail, inadvertently disclose confidential information, or redirect unsuspecting users to a server of the attacker's choosing (referred to as a "cross-site scripting" vulnerability). Input validation errors plagued over two-thirds (71 percent) of the applications in our sample.

Third, a user's session security remains the Achilles heel of most e-business applications. Most Web application servers assign a unique, random number (called a session identifier) for users when they log in, which is used over the duration of the session to identify them. The application typically associates the session identifiers with the user's state—that is, which pages have been visited, the contents of a shopping cart, and where the user is in the purchase process. The session identifier is normally stored in a cookie in the user's browser or in an encoded universal resource locator (URL). However, when the session is being conducted in the clear—unencrypted, without using SSL—a malicious attacker need only steal the session identifier to be able to masquerade as the user; obtaining the password is unnecessary. Session hijacking, therefore, is a serious risk. Thirty-one percent of the applications we examined contained security defects that left them vulnerable to this form of attack.

8.2.2 Software Vulnerabilities, Application Security, Taxonomy, and ICF Prevention and Detection

The inextricably close interrelationships that exist between software vulnerabilities, application security, and the taxonomical processes that need to be identified, analyzed, and implemented between application defects, absent or weak security processes during the software engineering process, and the need for ICF prevention and detection strategies all play a crucial role in reducing ICF risk.

As an extension to the previous paragraphs that discussed software vulnerabilities, application security, and ICF, the next few paragraphs will pertain to various taxonomies relating to application defects, a generic taxonomy of computer fraud, and the ICF taxonomy developed based on the research conducted.

8.2.3 Ontology

Prior to reviewing the several taxonomies below, it is important to define and discuss a few foundational concepts involving ontology in information security and characteristics of satisfactory taxonomies. (Refer to Figure 8.1—"Ontology.")

Based on a definition identified by Victor Raskin, Center for Education and Research in Information Assurance and Security (CERIAS), Purdue University, and Sergei Nirenburg, Computing Research Laboratory, New Mexico State University, in their article: "Ontology in information security: a useful theoretical foundation and methodological tool,"[2] the following explanation is provided.

Not to be confused with the philosophical discipline of metaphysics, the laughingstock of empiricist philosophy and recently experiencing a spectacular comeback, ontology is a constructed model of reality, a theory of the world—more practically, a theory of a domain. In still more practical terms, it is a highly structured system of concepts covering the processes, objects, and attributes of a domain in all of their pertinent complex relations, to the grain size determined by such considerations as the need of an application or computational complexity. Thus, an ontology may divide the root concept ALL into EVENTs, OBJECTs, and PROPERTYs (Figure 8.1); EVENTs into MENTAL-EVENTs, PHYSICAL-EVENTs, and SOCIAL-EVENTs; OBJECTs into INTANGIBLE-OBJECTs, MENTAL-OBJECTs, PHYSICAL-OBJECTs, and SOCIAL-OBJECTS; and so on, to finer and finer details.

8.2.4 Taxonomy

The use of taxonomies within this research was pervasive and probably one of the most critical foundational components within this book. There was a need for developing several taxonomies to effectively navigate through many different aspects of ICF activities that assisted in clarifying and decomposing the topic to its functional primitive components. With the exception of the application defect taxonomy, every other taxonomy and its actual applied use throughout this book were developed as original thought for this research.

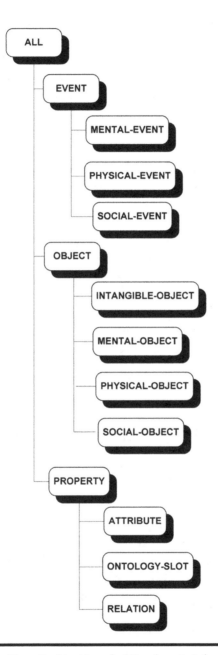

Figure 8.1 Ontology. (From Raskin, V. et al., "Ontology in Information Security: A Useful Theoretical Foundation…" (Figure 5 and text excerpt) *Proceedings of the 2001 Workshop on New Security Paradigms* (NSPW'01) pp. 53–59. © 2001, ACM, Inc.

In its simplest terms, a taxonomy is a classification scheme that partitions a body of knowledge and defines the relationship of the pieces. The classification component is the process of using a taxonomy for separating and ordering.

One of the clearest explanations I came across of the characteristics of a taxonomy includes the following criteria, as described in Edward G. Amoroso's 1994 publication, *Fundamentals of Computer Security Technology* and used within the Sandia Report, A Common Language for Computer Security Incidents,[3] which states the following:

Our experience has indicated that satisfactory taxonomies have classification categories with the following characteristics:

- *Mutually Exclusive*: Classifying in one category excludes all others because categories do not overlap.
- *Exhaustive*: Taken together, the categories include all possibilities.
- *Unambiguous*: Clear and precise so that classification is not uncertain, regardless of who is classifying.
- *Repeatable*: Repeated applications result in the same classification, regardless of who is classifying.
- *Accepted*: Logical and intuitive so that categories could be generally approved.
- *Useful*: Could be used to gain insight into the field of inquiry.

8.2.5 Customized Taxonomies for Detecting ICF

The following taxonomies were created within this research to assist in gaining a clearer understanding of the many facets of this complex and elusive topic:

1. The Universal ICF Taxonomy (Original Diagram)
2. Macro ICF Taxonomy (Original Diagram)
3. Taxonomy of Computer Fraud—Perpetration Platform (Lucian Vasiu, Deakin University, Australia, and Ioana Vasiu, Babeş-Bolyai University, Romania)
4. Taxonomy of Computer Fraud—Perpetration Method (Lucian Vasiu, Deakin University, Australia, and Ioana Vasiu, Babeş-Bolyai University, Romania)
5. Micro Insider Computer Loan Fraud Taxonomy
6. Insider Loan Taxonomy (Key Fraud Indicators [KFIs] and Key Fraud Metrics [KFMs])
7. Forensic Foto Frame Taxonomy (Original Diagram)
8. Metadata Taxonomy (Original Diagram)
9. Application Defect Taxonomy (Lucian Vasiu, Deakin University, Australia, and Ioana Vasiu, Babeş-Bolyai University, Romania)

8.2.6 Practical Uses of the Customized Applications Taxonomies for Detecting ICF

Listed below are the primary areas in which the use of the taxonomies developed for this research were applied:

ICF Journaling Workflow Diagram
Development and Use of KFIs
Development and Use of KFMs
Development and Use of Key Fraud Signatures (KFSs)

8.2.7 Customized Taxonomies for Detecting ICF—The Universal ICF Taxonomy

This taxonomy provides a comprehensive listing of potential ICF activities. However, the primary focus of this research is on the manipulation of data input, which is one the most prevalent forms of ICF.

8.2.7.1 Macro Computer Fraud Taxonomy

This taxonomy (Figure 8.2) provides a comprehensive listing of potential ICF threats. The contents of these criteria represent a roll-up of the categories of ICF activities based upon the results of the *ICF Summary Report* and the *ICF Taxonomy* documents listed below. All of the criteria contained within the ICF Summary Report and the ICF Taxonomy were based on a collection of actual cited cases of ICF activities and listed in the public domain.

Listed below are the names and sequences of reports prepared in support of developing the macro ICF taxonomy (Table 8.1):

- Macro ICF Taxonomy (Final Step)
- ICF Summary Report (Summary Report)
- ICF Taxonomy Heatmap (Interim Report)
- ICF Decomposition—ICF Case Analysis Report (Detailed Case Listing)

According to Lucian Vasiu and Ioana Vasiu,[4] a perpetration platform occurs in a taxonomy of computer fraud when accessing a protected computer without authorization, which is not approved by the system owner or administrator, or exceeding authorization for a legitimate user (Table 8.2).

The perpetration methods in a taxonomy of computer fraud are generally described by the authors as input, program, and output. The authors state that the greatest concerns are the frauds that involve manipulation of data records or computer programs to disguise the true nature of transactions, cracking into an organization's computer system to manipulate business information, and unauthorized transfers of funds electronically (Table 8.3).

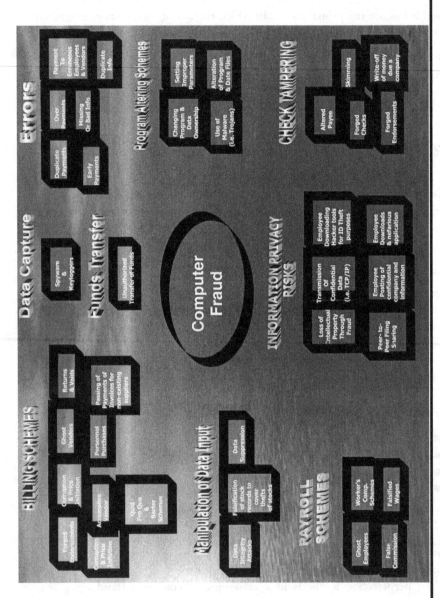

Figure 8.2 The universal ICF taxonomy.

Table 8.1 Macro ICF Taxonomy

Ontological Category (Parent)	Ontological Category (Child)
Data	Data input manipulation
	Data destruction
System	Misuse of system capabilities (authorized users)
	Hardware destruction or damage
	Access control misuse
	Hacking (unauthorized user)
	Unauthorized system access through the fraudulent use of ex-employees
Software	Code manipulation
	Logic bomb
	Malcode injection
	Trojan horse

GENESIS — HYBRID ICF

Table 8.2 Taxonomy of Computer Fraud (Perpetration Platform)

WOA (Without Authorization)	Masquerade	Impersonation	Password attacks	Guess
				Crack
				Harvest
			Password trafficking	
		Spoofing attacks		
	Vulnerability exploitation	Software		
		Personnel		
		Communications		
		Physical		
	Exceeding authorization			

Source: Vasiu, Lucian and Vasiu, Ioana. Dissecting computer fraud from definitional issues to a taxonomy, *Proceedings of the 37th Annual Hawaii International Conference on Systems Sciences.* © 2004 IEEE. (Reprinted by permission.)

Table 8.3   Taxonomy of Computer Fraud (Perpetration Method)

Data	Insert	Improper data	
		Data improperly	
	Improper obtaining or use		
	Integrity attacks		
	Availability attacks		
Program	Run attacks	Without authorization	
		In excess of authorization	
		Improper parameters	
		Transit attacks	Interruption
			Interception
			Modification
			Fabrication
	Integrity attacks		
	Availability attacks		

Source: Vasiu, Lucian and Vasiu, Ioana. Dissecting computer fraud from definitional issues to a taxonomy, *Proceedings of the 37th Annual Hawaii International Conference on Systems Sciences.* © 2004 IEEE. (Reprinted by permission.)

Table 8.4   Micro Taxonomy of Insider Computer Fraud—Bank Insider Loan Fraud

Data Manipulation	Insert	Falsified data
		Nominee loan name
	Improper use of loan proceeds	
	Integrity issues	
	Preferential rate and term for loan	

8.2.7.2   Micro Insider Computer Loan Fraud Taxonomy

The bank insider loan fraud taxonomy was developed based upon a review and analysis of a white paper produced by the Federal Financial Institution Examination Council (FFIEC), entitled "Insider detection, investigation and prevention of insider loan fraud," for the FFIEC fraud investigation symposium, held October 20–November 1, 2002. (See Table 8.4.)

8.2.7.3   Insider Loan Taxonomy (KFI and KFM)

This taxonomy (Figure 8.3) was developed based upon my analysis of the aforementioned FFIEC document that was used as the basis for determining KFIs and

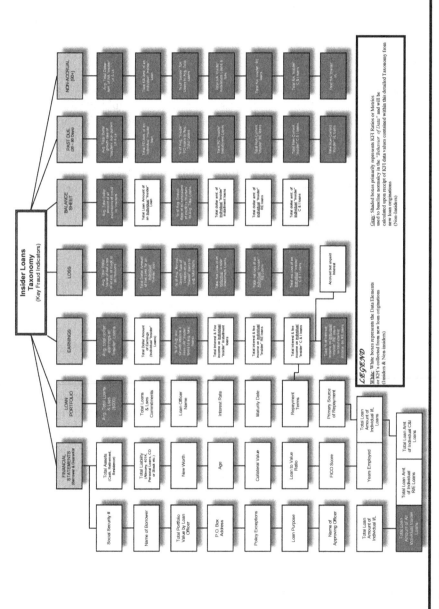

Figure 8.3   Insider loan taxonomy.

KFMs, which assisted in the illustration of how the framework could be implemented, using insider loan fraud within banks.

8.2.8 Forensic Foto Frame Taxonomy (Source: Kenneth C. Brancik)

The Forensic Foto Frame was developed in conjunction with the generic process that should be followed prior to deciding what KFI and KFM should be considered for data capture at various control points throughout the journey of a data transaction. The Forensic Foto Frame concept and application are graphically illustrated within the Service Oriented Architecture (SOA) diagram, for use in illustrating insider bank loan originations. Each Forensic Foto will capture data during the control point/gating process to determine normalcy in data behavior at various integral points in the data's journey. Through the use of the data captured from each Forensic Foto and being ingested through the use of the novelty neural network, a data normalcy evaluation can then be made to either prevent or detect suspicious insider activity. (See Table 8.5.)

8.2.9 Metadata Taxonomy

The metadata taxonomy (Figure 8.4) provided an integral component in establishing the criteria for the attribute selection for each KFI, KFM, KFS, and training and testing dataset for the novelty neural network. A good analogy between identifying the role of metadata and data is closely aligned with relational database design, where the primary key in the database schema would equate to the data element, and the attributes of the table would equate to the metadata. Together the primary key and its supporting attributes make up the relational database schema, while collectively the data and metadata attributes make up the KFIs and KFMs, which can then be used for a multitude of purposes (that is, KFS, neural network training and testing dataset, data capture with the Forensic Foto Frame, etc.).

Table 8.5   A Taxonomy of a Forensic Foto Frame

Data	ICF Risk Analysis	Key Fraud Indicator and Key Fraud Metric Attribute Selection	Metadata	Administrative
				Attribute activity
				Frame statistics
				Data access rules
				Graphics/objects
				Algorithmic transformations

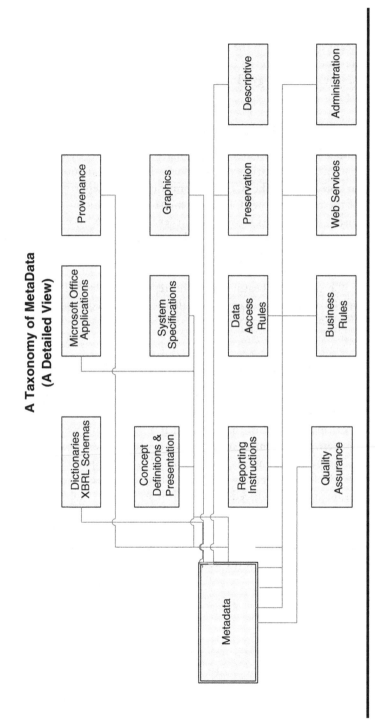

Figure 8.4 A taxonomy of metadata (a detailed view).

This taxonomy, although not developed as part of this book, provides added value to the software engineering process. Presented in Chapter 7, Section 7.6, is a significant discussion on the need and importance of having a software development life cycle that addresses information security controls baked into the software development methodology (Table 8.6).

8.2.10 ICF Taxonomy (Summary Report)

The results of the ICF Taxonomy Summary Report directly feed into the roll-up process used in preparation of the Macro Insider Computer Fraud Taxonomy diagram noted above. The ICF Taxonomy Summary Report provides a high-level recap of the results of the ICF taxonomy (Decomposition—ICF Case Analysis) report listed below, at its most granular level (i.e., case-by-case reporting of ICF activity). A third report used within the taxonomy development process was the IFC taxonomy (HeatMap), used in preparation of this ICF taxonomy (summary report). (See Table 8.7.)

The ICF taxonomy heatmap (interim report) and the ICF taxonomy (decomposition–ICF case analysis) are reports that were prepared in support of developing the ICF taxonomy (summary report).

8.2.11 ICF Taxonomy (Decomposition—ICF Case Analysis)

The ICF taxonomy report provides a case-by-case recap of several months of research in finding legitimate sources of information that reflected ICF cases. As part of this research in finding cited ICF cases, calls were placed to various federal government agencies to request a release of cases involving ICF, with the names of perpetrators and suspect individuals and companies having anonymity. However, the federal agencies that were contacted refused to provide any detailed information under the Freedom of Information Act (FOIA), which exempted any release of such information. As such, data to help in determining the specific modus operandi used by the perpetrators in such ICF cases was not available for collection and analysis. As such, the cases cited below primarily originated from the sources detailed within the document.

Table 8.6   Application Defect Taxonomy

Administrative Interfaces
– Administrative channels
– Log storage and retrieval
– Public interfaces

Authentication and Access Control
– Brute force
– E-mail interception
– Implicit component trust
– No authentication
– Password controls
– Password sniffing
– Authentication (other)

Configuration Management
– Class path misconfiguration
– Configuration file integrity
– Default accounts
– Default services

File Permissions
– License checking
– Privileged applications
– Sample code
– Untrusted service reliance
– Vendor patches
– Configuration management—other
– Cryptographic Algorithms
– Hard-coded credentials
– Random number generation
– Weak encryption
– Cryptographic—other

Information Gathering
– Account enumeration
– Browser cache
– Browser history
– Client-side comments

– Debug commands
– Error codes
– Files/application enumeration
– System and user information—other

Input Validation
– Buffer overflows
– Case sensitivity
– Client-side validation
– Cross-site scripting
– Direct operating system commands
– Direct Structure Query Language
  (SQL) commands
– Metacharacters
– Null characters
– Path traversal
– Unicode encoding
– Universal resource locator (URL)
  encoding
– Input validation—other

Parameter Manipulation
– Cookie manipulation
– Form field manipulation
– URL manipulation
– Parameter manipulation—other

Sensitive Data Handling
– Credential storage
– Data segregation
– Database misconfiguration
– Sensitive data handling—other

Session Management
– Cleartext data
– Session replay/hijacking
– Session management—other

Source: From Vasiu, Lucian and Vasiu, Ioana, in *Proceedings of the 37th Annual Hawaii International Conference on Systems Sciences,* 2004. (With permission.)

Table 8.7 Insider Computer Fraud Taxonomy (Summary Report)

Genesis

Ontological Category (Parent)	Ontological Category (Child)	Hybrid ICF (Data, System, and Software)		Count	Case ID
		Ontological Category (Child) SWD Software and Data (A)	Ontological Category (Child) SD System and Data (B)		(A) & (B)
Data	Data input manipulation	(1) Software code modified to create an intentional loss of data Terminate user sessions in a seemingly random way, causing a loss of data	(1) Unauthorized use or misuse of system access privileges or capability to change access controls to perpetrate fraud	(A1) 1 (B1) 39	(A1) SWD-1 (B1) SD-1-45 (except 2, 26, 30, 38, 41, and 42)
	Data destruction	(2) Software code modified to create a self-dealing financial opportunity	(2) Inappropriate use of confidential data	(B2) 6	(A2) N/A (B2) SD-1, 4, 10, 37, 38, 39
System	Misuse of system capabilities (Authorized users)	(3) Intentional system modification to suppression disclosure of key financial data	(3) Misuse of system capabilities	(B3) 8	(A3) N/A (B3) SD-5, 18–21, 28, 35, 36
	Hardware destruction or damage	(4) Software code modification to delete data	(4) Illegal financial transaction	(A4) 3 (B4) 4	(A4) SWD-1, SWD-2, SWD-8 (B4) SD-6, 7, 9, 10

	Threat	Description (A)	(A) No.	(A) Code	Description (B)	(B) No.	(B) Code
	Access control mouse	(5) Software code modification using a "logic bomb"	(A5) 3	(A5) SWD-3, SWD-5, SWD-6	(5) Inappropriate acquisition of data	(B5) 4	(B5) SD-3, 12, 15, 17
	Hacking (Unauthorized user)	(6) Software code modification using a "time bomb"	(A6) 1	(A6) SWD-4	(6) Access level modifications	(B6) 2	(B6) SD-14 and 26
	Unauthorized system access through the fraudulent use of ex-employees' passwords	(7) Malcode software injection	(A7) 1	(A7) SWD-7	(7) Employee impersonation	(B7) 2	(B7) SD-14 and 29
Software	Code manipulation				(8) Transmission of unauthorized e-mails	N/A	(B8) N/A
	Logic bomb				(9) Damage to system availability	(B9) 3	(B9) SD-32, 36, 41
	Malcode injection				(10) Illegal distribution and transmission of source code to another company	(B10) 1	(B10) SD-43
	Trojan horse				(11) Exploitation of software vulnerabilities	(B11) 2	(B11) SD-2 and 17
					(12) Circumvention of security controls	(B12) 1	(B12) SD-17

(continued)

Table 8.7   Insider Computer Fraud Taxonomy (Summary Report) (*Continued*)

Ontological Category (Parent)	Ontological Category (Child)	Ontological Category (Child)	Ontological Category (Child)	Count	Case ID
Genesis		Hybrid ICF (Data, System, and Software)			
			(13) Illegal use of system to make payments to legitimate or bogus accounts	N/A	(B13) N/A
			(14) Illegal use of system to redirect funds	(B14) 2	(B14) SD-25 and 27
			(15) Deletion of audit trails/ forensic journaling	(B15) 1	(B15) N/A
			(16) Inappropriate data viewing	(B16) 1	(B16) SD-23
			(17) Dormant account reactivation	(B17) 2	(B17) SD-25 and 27
			(18) Programmer access to live programs and production data	N/A	(B18) N/A
			(19) Transmission of large files to intentionally slow the system down	(B19) 1	(B19) SD-44

(20) Diversion of credit proceeds from a suspended account to another insider	N/A	(B20) N/A
(21) Access level privilege escalation	(B21) 1	(B21) SD-29
(22) E-mail account modification by an insider of another insider's account	(B22) 1	(B22) SD-29
(23) Financial "Window-Dressing" to mask problems	(B23) 1	(B23) SD-30
(24) Application or system destruction	(B24) 7	(B24) SD-11, 13, 14, 16, 22, 31, 45
(25) Damage to system availability	(B25) 5	(B25) SD-31, 32, 33, 36, 40
(26) Password trafficking by insiders on a Yahoo Internet bulletin board	N/A	(B26) N/A
(27) Collusion between an insider and an outsider	(B27) 2	(B27) SD-33 and 38

(continued)

Table 8.7   Insider Computer Fraud Taxonomy (Summary Report) (Continued)

Ontological Category (Parent)	Ontological Category (Child)	Ontological Category (Child)	Ontological Category (Child)	Count	Case ID
Genesis		Hybrid ICF (Data, System, and Software)	(28) Illegal distribution and transmission of acquired financial information	(B28) 1	(B28) SD-39
			(29) Computer data manipulation	(B29) 11	(B29) SD-2, 8, 9, 14, 17, 22, 24, 26, 27, 30, 41
			(30) Programmer copied passwords, which allowed users to create, change, or delete any file on the network and post the file on the Internet	(N/A)	(B30) N/A

8.2.12 Insider Computer Fraud Taxonomy—ICF Cases

Presented in Table 8.8 are ICF case analyses.

Table 8.8 Insider Computer Fraud Taxonomy (Decomposition—ICF Case Analysis)

Issue	Source	Category	Comments
A former Telecom employee was indicted by a federal grand jury on charges he stole more than $20MM from the company's prepaid cellular telephone service As a corporate social responsibility (CSR) employee working at a large Telecom company, the individual had access to a password-protected Telecom computer account in which the company kept a record of prepaid cell phone minutes. This individual copied more than $20MM worth of the 15-digit personal identification numbers and then sold them on his own	Associated Press (AP)	Hybrid insider computer fraud (system and data) Unauthorized system access, inappropriate use of confidential corporate data stored in a computer system, copy and sale of personal identification numbers (PINs)	SD-1
A trader working for a bank hid $691 million in losses. Using an older version of a well-known trading system, which allowed the insider into the system to manipulate the data feeds, the insider was able to manipulate his value-at-risk (VAR) calculations	U.S. Secret Service Insider Threat Report and Wall Street & Technology	Hybrid insider computer fraud (system and data) (18 USC 1030) Ease of access into a computer system or application entry due to the apparent security weaknesses of an older version of the	SD-2

(continued)

Table 8.8   Insider Computer Fraud Taxonomy (Decomposition—ICF Case Analysis) (*Continued*)

Issue	Source	Category	Comments
that estimated the maximum range of losses to be suffered in a certain portfolio and keep his trading going, as his losses mounted. The insider entered into fake options entries that appeared to hedge his real options and reduced the limit numbers		application; computer data manipulation within an application or system; financial "window-dressing" to mask FX trading losses	
The law enforcement agency suggests that such crimes could have been prevented through the use of group rather than individual trading, by making it easier to detect illegal or suspicious trading practices because there are multiple team members trading from the same account			
A contract employee of a local authority was allowed back to the office to complete a CV after her contract had expired. Two weeks later, staff noticed that computer files and disks were missing and, unfortunately, not all work had been saved. The police investigated and found evidence of the missing files at the employee's address. Although an information technology (IT) expert	U.K. Audit Commission, "Ghost in the Machine— An Analysis of IT Fraud and Abuse," 1999	Hybrid insider computer fraud (system and data) Unauthorized system access; inappropriate acquisition of data	SD-3

Issue	Source	Category	Comments
was able to establish that some of these files had been accessed on the day the employee left, there was insufficient evidence to prosecute under the Computer Misuse Act of 1990			
A "Trojan horse" (one program masquerading as another) was illicitly built into a system and the effect of running the program was to terminate users' sessions in a seemingly random way, causing a loss of data. The problems were initially misdiagnosed and technical staff started an investigation into the way that the software had been set up. This investigation proved fruitless and it was only the suspicion of one member of staff that led to the discovery of an unusual piece of program code in an obscure part of the system. Investigation of this code suggested malicious activity. Additional security was introduced to find out exactly what the errant code was doing and which user was running it. This pointed suspicion at a member of the IT section.	U.K. Audit Commission, "Ghost in the Machine— An Analysis of IT Fraud and Abuse," 1999	Hybrid insider computer fraud (software and data) Software code modification: "Trojan horse" was built into a system to terminate users' sessions and cause a loss of data; terminate user sessions in a seemingly random way, causing a loss of data	SWD-1

(continued)

Table 8.8 Insider Computer Fraud Taxonomy (Decomposition—ICF Case Analysis) (*Continued*)

Issue	Source	Category	Comments
A nurse on night duty at a hospital was using her authorized access to the patient administration system to search for names of friends and family. She then discussed the health problems of individuals with other members of her family. This was regarded as a breach of confidentiality and the nurse was given a written warning	U.K. Audit Commission, "Ghost in the Machine— An Analysis of IT Fraud and Abuse," 1999	Hybrid insider computer fraud (system and data) Unauthorized system access (i.e., patient information); inappropriate use of confidential data in a computer system (i.e., disclosure of patient information to third parties)	SD-4
An employee of a company used the e-mail system to send a threatening message to another member of staff. The origin of the message had been disguised by misusing the proxy rights of another e-mail user which had not been adequately secured. The incident came to light when the recipient complained to a supervisor. The individual suspected of sending the message was not at work when it was written and was quickly eliminated from the inquiry. However, because the audit trail on the network used to facilitate access to the e-mail network was inadequate, it was not possible to prove who had sent the message	U.K. Audit Commission, "Ghost in the Machine— An Analysis of IT Fraud and Abuse," 1999	Insider computer fraud (system and data) Inadequate system access controls (i.e., employee's misuse of proxy rights of another employee/e-mail user); misuse of system's capabilities (impersonation of another insider to send threatening e-mails to another insider); inadequate network, adequate trails for forensic purposes	SD-5

Issue	Source	Category	Comments
In a collusion case involving four employ-ees of a certain currency exchange and one outsider, a computer was used to create phony currency exchange transactions and then cover them with real ones. They stole the differences that resulted from the rate changes. The act involved tamper-ing with programs and the erasure of tapes	Vasiu, Lucian and Vasiu, Ioana, Dissecting computer fraud: from definitional issues to a taxonomy, Proceedings of the 37th Annual Hawaii International Conference on Systems Sciences, 2004	Hybrid insider computer fraud (software and data) Computer data manipulation within an application or system (creating phony currency exchange transac-tions and then converting them to real transactions); software code modification (create the erasure of tapes)	SWD-2
In one case of exceeding authorization, an individual pled guilty to exceeding their autho-rized access to the computer systems of a particular company in order to illegally issue almost $8MM in that company's stock	Vasiu, Lucian and Vasiu, Ioana, Dissecting computer fraud: from definitional issues to a taxonomy, Proceedings of the 37th Annual Hawaii International Conference on Systems Sciences, 2004	Hybrid insider computer fraud (system and data) Unauthorized system access (exceeding authorized access levels); illegal data transaction (stock issuance)	SD-6
A financial consultant defrauded the Common-wealth by transferring $8,735,692 electronically to private companies in which he held an interest. He did this by logging on to the department's network using another person's name and password. To	Vasiu, Lucian and Vasiu, Ioana, Dissecting computer fraud: from definitional issues to a taxonomy, Proceedings of the 37th	Hybrid insider computer fraud (system and data) Unauthorized system access (impersonation of another employee and use of his or her UID and password); illegal data transaction	SD-7

(continued)

Table 8.8 Insider Computer Fraud Taxonomy (Decomposition—ICF Case Analysis) (*Continued*)

Issue	Source	Category	Comments
obscure the audit trail, he used other employees' log-on codes and passwords	Annual Hawaii International Conference on Systems Sciences, 2004	(electronic money transfer)	
In January 2003, a former employee of a company used the username and password he held while employed at the company to remotely log into the company's network, then changed customers' credit card details, and proceeded to make refunds to his credit card through the altered accounts. The perpetrator modified various pricing and availability of the products, reducing the price of some to $0	Vasiu, Lucian and Vasiu, Ioana, Dissecting computer fraud: from definitional issues to a taxonomy, Proceedings of the 37th Annual Hawaii International Conference on Systems Sciences, 2004	Hybrid insider computer fraud (system and data) Unauthorized system access; computer data manipulation within an application or system (credit card refunds through altered accounts and modification of pricing and availability of the products)	SD-8
A contractor working for a Commonwealth agency was convicted of defrauding the Commonwealth of $1.4 million. The contractor, while performing his regular duties, was able to access and alter system data to change the status of rebate claims from "paid" to "unpaid" on the system, and transfer bogus rebate payments into his own account. The contractor was then able	Vasiu, Lucian and Vasiu, Ioana, Dissecting computer fraud: from definitional issues to a taxonomy, Proceedings of the 37th Annual Hawaii International Conference on Systems Sciences, 2004	Hybrid insider computer fraud (system and data) Computer data manipulation within an application or system (i.e., change system data relating to the status of rebate claims from "paid" to "unpaid"); illegal data transaction (transfer of rebate payments)	SD-9

Issue	Source	Category	Comments
to delete the record of the illegal transaction and return the "paid" status and dates to their original state			
In *U.S. v. John Doe*, the defendants, while employed by a financial services organization, had the intent to further a scheme to defraud through access to one or more financial systems, computer systems without authorization or in excess of their authorized access on said computer systems, thereby obtaining credit card account numbers and other information, which they were not authorized to access in connection with their duties at the financial institution. That information was distributed and transmitted to one or more individuals who, in turn, used that information to fraudulently obtain goods and services	Vasiu, Lucian and Vasiu, Ioana, Dissecting computer fraud: from definitional issues to a taxonomy, Proceedings of the 37th Annual Hawaii International Conference on Systems Sciences, 2004	Hybrid insider computer fraud (system and data) Unauthorized system access; inappropriate acquisition of data (i.e., obtained credit card account numbers and other information); inappropriate use of confidential data in a computer system (i.e., acquired data was illegally distributed and transmitted to third parties)	SD-10
An ex-employee of an airport transportation company is guilty of hacking into the company's computer. A man previously employed at the administrative and operations center of the carrier's Coach transportation company pleaded	www.cyber-crime.gov (4/18/03)	Hybrid insider computer fraud (system and data) Unauthorized system access (i.e., hacking); computer data destruction within an application or system (i.e.,	SD-11

(continued)

Table 8.8 Insider Computer Fraud Taxonomy (Decomposition—ICF Case Analysis) (*Continued*)

Issue	Source	Category	Comments
guilty to a federal charge of hacking into the company's computer system and wiping out critical data. The hack wiped out the company's customer database and other records and effectively shut down the company's computer server, Internet-based credit card processing system, and Web site. The network administrator at the companies' facility had administrator-level passwords and privileges for all of the company's computer operations. The employee was terminated by the company		deletion of company's customers database and other records)	
Disgruntled financial services company unleashed a "logic bomb" on a company's computers. A disgruntled computer systems administrator for a large financial services company was charged today with using a "logic bomb" to cause more than $3M in damage to the company's computer network, and with securities fraud for his failed plan to drive down the company's stock with activation of the logic bomb	www.cyber-crime.gov	Hybrid insider computer fraud (software and data) Software code modification: "logic bomb" was built into a system to terminate users' sessions and cause	SWD-3

Issue	Source	Category	Comments
Specifically, the employee purchased more than $21M of "put option" contracts for particular bank stock, according to the charging document. A put option is a type of security that increases in value when the stock price drops.		a loss of data; self-dealing transaction to capitalize on the destruction created by the software code modification	
A California-based man pleaded guilty to illegally accessing former employer's computers. This former employee was found guilty of accessing the computer system of his former employer and reading the e-mail messages of company executives for the purpose of gaining a commercial advantage at his new job at a competitor	www.cyber-crime.gov	Hybrid insider computer fraud (system and data) Unauthorized system access (i.e., former employee); inappropriate acquisition of data (i.e., accessing and reading e-mails of company executives to gain a commercial advantage)	SD-12
U.S. charges engineer with computer intrusion, destruction of database at an apparel company located in Manhattan. The U.S. Attorney for the Southern District of New York announced that John Doe was arrested and charged in Manhattan's federal court with the unauthorized intrusion of the computer network of his former employer. John Doe was hired as the controller on September 1, 2001. In	www.cyber-crime.gov	Hybrid insider computer fraud (system and data) Unauthorized system and database access; computer data destruction within an application or system (i.e., deletion of customers' orders within a database)	SD-13

(continued)

Table 8.8 Insider Computer Fraud Taxonomy (Decomposition—ICF Case Analysis) (*Continued*)

Issue	Source	Category	Comments
connection with his work at the firm, this individual was given the password to permit him to remotely access the computer system from his home. On its computer network, the insider manages different databases relating to its business, including its customers' orders. On April 11, 2002, the employee accessed the company database containing customer orders and found that the records of all of the orders had disappeared. The computer records allegedly indicated that an individual accessed the MP computer system using a password from at or about 9:21 P.M. until at or about 9:46 P.M. on April 10, 2002, and that orders in the database were deleted during this computer session			
A man convicted and sentenced for hacking into a former employer's computer server was convicted and sentenced for "unauthorized computer intrusion," or "hacking," into the computer database of his employer	www.cyber-crime.gov	Hybrid insider computer fraud (system and data) Unauthorized system access (i.e., hacking); computer data destruction within an application or system (i.e., deletion of company's customer database);	SD-14

Issue	Source	Category	Comments
		computer access level modifications; data manipulation (i.e., altered billing records); employee impersonation and transmission of unauthorized e-mails to corporate clients	
There was an announcement that a former employee pleaded guilty today to exceeding his authorized access to company's computer systems and obtaining valuable information	www.cyber-crime.gov	Hybrid insider computer fraud (system and data) Unauthorized system access; inappropriate acquisition of data (i.e., accessing proprietary information beyond the user's authorization level)	SD-15
A database engineer who worked with a technology organization had personal differences with his employer and decided to take revenge by using the computers of his previous employer to launch a DoS attack causing several hours of downtime (and lost revenue) over a three-day period	Magklaras, G.B. and Furnell, S.M., Insider threat prediction tool: evaluating the probability of IT misuse, *Computers and Security, 21*(1), 62–73, 2001	Hybrid computer fraud (system and data) Unauthorized system access (i.e., hacking); damage to system availability (i.e., DDos attack)	SD-16
Two investment traders working together for two major financial organizations. They made risky investments and lost large amounts of	Magklaras, G.B. and Furnell, S.M., Insider threat prediction tool:	Hybrid insider computer fraud (system and data) Computer data manipulation within an application	SD-17

(continued)

Table 8.8   Insider Computer Fraud Taxonomy (Decomposition—ICF Case Analysis) (*Continued*)

Issue	Source	Category	Comments
investment capital. However, instead of admitting their losses, they illegitimately modified computer records in order to obtain more money to cover their losses	evaluation the probability of IT misuse, *Computers and Security,* *21*(1), 62–73, 2001	or system (i.e., modified computer records in order to obtain more money to cover their losses) Inappropriate acquisition of data exploitation of operating system vulnerabilities; circumvention of security controls (i.e., bypass the audit mechanism of the funding records database)	
Temporary staff used an online system to suppress action in respect of arrears on their own accounts and those of relatives and friends.	"Opportunity Makes a Thief: An Analysis of Computer Abuse," 1994, printed in the United Kingdom for the Audit Commission at Press On Printers	Insider computer fraud (system and data) Misuse of system's capabilities (i.e., use of online system to suppress action in respect of arrears on their own accounts and those of relatives and friends)	SD-18
A cashier at a remote office had access to the supervisor's password to enable her to close down the system and, among other things, to initiate contra entries to correct mistakes, and so forth. She used this facility to suppress	"Opportunity Makes a Thief: An Analysis of Computer Abuse," 1994, printed in the United Kingdom for the Audit	Hybrid insider computer fraud (system and data) Unauthorized system access (i.e., access to supervisor's password); misuse of system's capabilities (i.e., ability to make	SD-19

Issue	Source	Category	Comments
evidence of takings in respect of account numbers of regular payers who would not normally receive a payment reminder	Commission at Press On Printers	contra entries to the system which are used to suppress evidence of takings of account numbers of regular payers, who would not normally receive a payment reminder)	
A clerk defrauded an organization from its purchases system for over a period of five years	"Opportunity Makes a Thief: An Analysis of Computer Abuse," 1994, printed in the United Kingdom for the Audit Commission at Press On Printers	Insider computer fraud (data) Computer data manipulation within an application or system (i.e., adding a bogus invoice with a forged approval slip to batches prepared by the payments division, subsequently switching the bogus invoice for an approved invoice of an identical amount)	D-1
A clerk in a student awards payments section managed to obtain, by deception, the system password to gain access to prohibited data files. She used this access to arrange for payments to be made into her own bank account	"Opportunity Makes a Thief: An Analysis of Computer Abuse," 1994, printed in the United Kingdom for the Audit Commission at Press On Printers	Hybrid insider computer fraud (system and data) Unauthorized system access (i.e., access to system password to gain access to prohibited data files involving student awards payments); misuse of system's capabilities (i.e.,	SD-20

(continued)

Table 8.8 Insider Computer Fraud Taxonomy (Decomposition—ICF Case Analysis) (Continued)

Issue	Source	Category	Comments
		ability to initiate payments of student awards to the benefit of the employee)	
A manager ignored the organization's security guidelines and left his password to the purchases system on a note by his workstation. Another employee used the password to arrange payments to fictitious accounts	"Opportunity Makes a Thief: An Analysis of Computer Abuse," 1994, printed in the United Kingdom for the Audit Commission at Press On Printers	Hybrid insider computer fraud (system and data) Unauthorized system access (i.e., access to system password via password writing on note); misuse of system's capabilities (i.e., ability to initiate payments to employee via fictitious account)	SD-21
The perpetrator was a system administrator in the computer department with full access to all the system's facilities. He input false student awards claims into the creditor payment system and when the checks were produced he went back into the system and removed all evidence of the transactions. Reconciliation procedures were weak and the payments were not identified. An interesting characteristic of this case was that the perpetrator had previously reported the weaknesses in the	"Opportunity Makes a Thief: An Analysis of Computer Abuse," 1994, printed in the United Kingdom for the Audit Commission at Press On Printers	Hybrid insider computer fraud (system and data) Misuse of user access privileges and system's capabilities (i.e., system administration; in computer department with full access to system's facilities); computer data manipulation within an application or system (i.e., input false student awards claims into the creditor payment system); computer data	SD-22

Issue	Source	Category	Comments
system to management but as nothing was done, he took advantage of the opportunity		destruction within an application or system (i.e., deletion of audit trails/forensic journaling from system)	
The perpetrator, a clerk in a section dealing with insurance policies, had managed to access his girlfriend's insurance policy details and overwritten certain information	"Opportunity Makes a Thief: An Analysis of Computer Abuse," 1994, printed in the United Kingdom for the Audit Commission at Press On Printers	Hybrid insider computer fraud (system and data) Misuse of user access privileges and system's capabilities (i.e., wrongful access of girlfriend's insurance policy details and overwriting of certain information); inappropriate viewing of data outside the normal usage (i.e., computer monitoring, which revealed user file accesses outside the norm)	SD-23
To help with the implementation of a new system, a high-level password was granted to a system support member of the computer department. This password was never cancelled when the implementation was completed, and the member used the password to access the stock system and defraud the organization	"Opportunity Makes a Thief: An Analysis of Computer Abuse," 1994, printed in the United Kingdom for the Audit Commission at Press On Printers	Hybrid insider computer fraud (system and data) Misuse of user access privileges and system's capabilities (i.e., initial high-level password issued to insider but never revoked); computer data manipulation within an application or system (i.e.,	SD-24

(continued)

Table 8.8 Insider Computer Fraud Taxonomy (Decomposition—ICF Case Analysis) (*Continued*)

Issue	Source	Category	Comments
		unrevoked password used by employee to perpetrate fraud within stock system)	
A store manager moved stock with the collusion of other employees and altered the computer records to suggest the stock had been sold	"Opportunity Makes a Thief: An Analysis of Computer Abuse," 1994, printed in the United Kingdom for the Audit Commission at Press On Printers	Insider computer fraud (data) Computer data manipulation within an application or system (i.e., falsification of computer records to reflect store inventory/stock was in fact sold but was recorded as a loss, which resulted in a financial recovery to the benefit of the store manager)	D-2
A supervisor at one of the company's manufacturing branches was paying nonexistent canteen staff through the company's payroll system	"Opportunity Makes a Thief: An Analysis of Computer Abuse," 1994, printed in the United Kingdom for the Audit Commission at Press On Printers	Insider computer fraud (data) Computer data manipulation within an application or system (i.e., falsification of computer records to reflect nonexistent payroll expenses of fictitious employees)	D-3

Issue	Source	Category	Comments
A payroll clerk reactivated retired employees' records and changed their bank account details to one of three accounts she controlled (including her own account).	"Opportunity Makes a Thief: An Analysis of Computer Abuse," 1994, printed in the United Kingdom for the Audit Commission at Press On Printers	Insider computer fraud (system and data) Computer data manipulation within an application or system; dormant account reactivation; payment account modification and funds redirection	SD-25
A trainee programmer left within the two-year stipulated period and was therefore responsible for repaying an agency introduction fee and interview expenses that were incurred. The debtor's section discovered when they conducted a periodic balancing of the Sundry Debtor's Control Account that the debt had been deleted from the system. Programmers had access to the live programs and data files and the organization's management were convinced that the trainee programmer had deleted the record from the system before he left	"Opportunity Makes a Thief: An Analysis of Computer Abuse," 1994, printed in the United Kingdom for the Audit Commission at Press On Printers	Hybrid insider computer fraud (systems and data) Inappropriate account provisioning (i.e., programmers had access to live programs and data files); computer data manipulation within an application or system employee account/debt	SD-26

(continued)

Table 8.8   Insider Computer Fraud Taxonomy (Decomposition—ICF Case Analysis) (continued)

Issue	Source	Category	Comments
A clerk in the Rents Section realized that a high level of credits existed in a suspense account. He gained access to the system by using another's password and transferred a balance from a "dead" file to a friend's account	"Opportunity Makes a Thief: An Analysis of Computer Abuse," 1994, printed in the United Kingdom for the Audit Commission at Press On Printers	Hybrid insider computer fraud (systems and data) Unauthorized system access (i.e., use of another friend's password); computer data manipulation within an application or system (i.e., dormant account reactivation and refund of credit proceeds from a suspended account to a friend's account and then split the proceeds with the employee)	SD-27
A member of the IT department and her boyfriend accessed dormant accounts in a financial organization and transferred investors' funds to a bogus account	"Opportunity Makes a Thief: An Analysis of Computer Abuse," 1994, printed in the United Kingdom for the Audit Commission at Press On Printers	Hybrid insider computer fraud (system and data) Unauthorized system access (i.e., access to dormant accounts); misuse of system's capabilities (i.e., transfer of funds to a bogus account)	SD-28
A student at another university hacked into the college's computer system via access to an academic network. He then found the account	"Opportunity Makes a Thief: An Analysis of Computer Abuse," 1994,	Hybrid insider computer fraud (system and data) Unauthorized system access (i.e., hacking);	SD-29

Issue	Source	Category	Comments
and password of a member of the academic staff who had not used the system for some months. He used the enhanced access rights held by the member of staff to modify his mail address and then "leap-frogged" to another JANET site masquerading as the member of staff	printed in the United Kingdom for the Audit Commission at Press On Printers	masquerading as an employee; access level privilege escalation; account modification of mail address of a member of the university's academic staff	
Over a three-year period, an institution's quarter-end past-due loan ratio was consistently around one percent. Closer review by examiners revealed that the chief executive officer was refinancing loans and extending loan payments to maintain a low past-due loan ratio	The Federal Financial Institutions Examination Councils (FFIEC), Examiner Education: "The Detection, Investigation and Prevention of Insider Loan Fraud: A White Paper"	Hybrid insider computer fraud (system and data) Computer data manipulation within an application or system; financial "window-dressing" to mask their past-due loans (i.e., loan refinancing and extending loan payments to maintain a low past-due loan ratio)	SD-30
Former employee of a company sentenced to one year for hacking into company's computer, destroying data. An employee from the company was sentenced for hacking into the company's computer system and wiping out critical data, an act that shut down a computer	www.cyber-crime.gov	Hybrid insider computer fraud (system and data) Unauthorized system access (i.e., hacking); computer data destruction within an application or system (i.e., deletion of critical data); hardware destruction (i.e.,	SD-31

(continued)

Table 8.8 Insider Computer Fraud Taxonomy (Decomposition—ICF Case Analysis) (*Continued*)

Issue	Source	Category	Comments
server that was central to the company's foreign operations		shut down of computer server)	
A former AS/400 computer programmer who worked at the IT department of a company was arrested by the federal law enforcement, after having broken into the company's computer system from a remote location. During the unauthorized intrusion, the programmer deleted several programs which resulted in the malfunction of several crucial applications	www.cyber-crime.gov	Hybrid insider computer fraud (system and data) Unauthorized system access (i.e., hacking); computer data destruction within an application or system (i.e., deletion of several programs); hardware malfunction (i.e., resulted from deletion of programs)	SD-32
A former employee of a clothing company was sentenced to prison for password trafficking and computer damage	www.cyber-crime.gov	Hybrid insider computer fraud (system and data) Unauthorized system access (i.e., hacking); damage to system availability (i.e., DDos attack); and was also involved in password trafficking by insiders on an Internet bulletin board	SD-33
Local law enforcement employee was indicted for public corruption. According to an indictment, the law enforcement employee accessed key files and computer	www.cyber-crime.gov	Hybrid insider computer fraud (system and data) Unauthorized system access (i.e., data searching for confidential	SD-34

Issue	Source	Category	Comments
programs on active or pending, pending inactive, closed, and nonexistent law enforcement investigations and files and disclosed information from the files to friends and family members.		information— pending investigations by the law enforcement); falsification of information to law enforcement agents pertaining to an investigation	
Three indicted in conspiracy to commit bank fraud and identity theft. Former financial institution employee Thomas is charged with one count of conspiring (1) to obtain unauthorized computer access to financial institution information, (2) to commit computer fraud, (3) to unlawfully use a means of identification of another person, and (4) to commit bank fraud	www.cyber-crime.gov	Hybrid insider computer fraud (system and data) (18 USC 1030) Unauthorized system access (i.e., unauthorized computer access to financial information); misuse of user access privileges and system's capabilities (i.e., misuse of confidential member profile information of account holders through financial institution computers and providing it to others)	SD-35
Ex-employee of airport transportation company guilty of hacking into company's computer	www.cyber-crime.gov	Hybrid insider computer fraud (system and data) Unauthorized system access (i.e., hacking); misuse of user access privileges and system's capabilities (i.e., former	SD-36

(continued)

Table 8.8 Insider Computer Fraud Taxonomy (Decomposition—ICF Case Analysis) (Continued)

Issue	Source	Category	Comments
		systems administrator [SA] had administrator-level passwords and privileges for all of the company's computer operations, which allowed this individual to change passwords on the system and delete specialized software applications)	
A man pleaded guilty to illegally accessing former employer's computers The man pleaded guilty to illegally accessing a computer system of his former employer and reading the e-mail messages of company executives for the purposes of gaining a commercial advantage at his new job at a competitor	www.cybercrime.gov	Hybrid insider computer fraud (system and data) Unauthorized system access (i.e., hacking); inappropriate viewing of data outside the normal usage (i.e., reading e-mail messages of company executives for competitive advantage)	SD-37
Twenty-seven-month sentence in Internet fraud scheme to defraud an e-commerce company	www.cybercrime.gov	Hybrid insider computer fraud (system and data) Inappropriate viewing of data outside the normal usage (i.e., insider obtained confidential customer	SD-38

Issue	Source	Category	Comments
		account and credit card information); collusion between an insider and an outsider (insider provided the outsider the confidential customer account information); outsider made fraudulent Internet credit card charges for hotel and airline reservations	
Former financial corporation employees sentenced for scheme to defraud a bank	www.cyber-crime.gov	Hybrid insider computer fraud (system and data) (18 USC 1030)	SD-39
Engaged in a scheme to defraud a bank by accessing one or more of their computer systems, thereby obtaining credit card account numbers and other customer account information pertaining to many accounts		Unauthorized system access (i.e., former bank employee is restricted from using former employer's systems); inappropriate viewing of data outside the normal usage (i.e., insider viewed data they were not authorized to view based upon their duties. Obtained credit card account numbers and other customer account information); obtained goods	

(continued)

Table 8.8 Insider Computer Fraud Taxonomy (Decomposition—ICF Case Analysis) (*Continued*)

Issue	Source	Category	Comments
The largest (known) computer crime in the world occurred several years ago which resulted in the destruction of an equity funding and insurance company, with losses of $2 billion. The company's management tried to make Equity Funding the fastest-growing and largest company in the industry. Unfortunately, they attempted to gain that position by engaging in virtually every type of known business fraud.	www.cyber-crime.gov	Insider computer fraud (data) Computer data manipulation within an application or system (management created 64K fake people in their computer system and insured them with policies that they sold off to reinsurers)	D-4
A watch engineer launched an insider attack motivated by revenge. The engineer was a man with approximately 11 years of service. He became disillusioned and decided to respond by planning a time bomb within a vital computer system. When it was triggered, the bomb destroyed the manufacturing programs and left the company unable to produce further products.	www.cyber-crime.gov	Insider computer fraud (software and data) Software code modification: an insider (engineer) placed a "time bomb" within a vital computer system, which had the affect of destroying the manufacturing programs and left the company unable to produce further products	SWD-4
A U.S. software company was compromised using passwords belonging to ex-employees. The intruders were traced to an online company.	*Computer Fraud and Security* magazine	Insider computer fraud (system and data) Unauthorized system access (i.e., two former	SD-40

Issue	Source	Category	Comments
The attack caused the e-mail systems to go down and important files disappeared. The attack highlights the importance of deactiving ex-employee passwords		corporate employees, SAs, used passwords belonging to ex-employees); the attack caused the e-mail systems to go down and important files disappeared	
A programmer for a missile program reportedly felt unappreciated for his programming work on a parts-tracking system. He planted a "logic bomb" in the system designed to erase critical data after he resigned. He then anticipated returning to rescue the company as a high-paid and valued consultant	Shaw, Eric D., Ruby, Keven G., and Post, Jerrold M., The Insider Threat to Information Systems, Security Awareness Bulletin 2-98	Computer fraud (software and data) Software code modification: "logic bomb" was built into a system for the purpose of erasing critical data after he resigned from the company	SWD-5
A regional PC manager for the supermarket chain was charged in an intricate computer fraud that cost the supermarket over $2 million over two years. Among the strategies used was manipulating the computer accounting system to funnel certain purchases into a dummy account. At the end of the day, the perpetrators would take the amount funneled into the dummy account right out of the cash registers and then delete the account, also erasing any trace of their fraud	Shaw, Eric D., Ruby, Keven G., and Post, Jerrold M., The Insider Threat to Information Systems, Security Awareness Bulletin 2-98	Hybrid insider computer fraud (system and data) Computer data manipulation within an application or system (i.e., manipulate the computer accounting system to funnel certain purchases into a dummy account); computer data destruction within an application or system (i.e., deletion of the dummy account and then erasing any trace of their fraud)	SD-41

(continued)

Table 8.8 Insider Computer Fraud Taxonomy (Decomposition—ICF Case Analysis) (*Continued*)

Issue	Source	Category	Comments
A major international energy company recently discovered a logic bomb in software created by a contracted employee. It was installed as "job insurance" by the contracted employee with five prior convictions related to hacking. The contractor's firm failed to screen this employee who installed the code in anticipation of using it as leverage against his employer in case his criminal record was discovered	Shaw, Eric D., Ruby, Keven G., and Post, Jerrold M., The Insider Threat to Information Systems, Security Awareness Bulletin 2-98	Computer fraud (software and data) Software code modification: "logic bomb" was built into a system	SWD-6
A computer programmer working as a subcontractor for a company illegally accessed sensitive military information on combat readiness. He also copied passwords, which allow users to create, change, or delete any file on the network, and posted them on the Internet	Shaw, Eric D., Ruby, Keven G., and Post, Jerrold M., The Insider Threat to Information Systems, Security Awareness Bulletin 2-98	Hybrid insider computer fraud (system and data) Unauthorized system access (i.e., a computer programmer working as a subcontractor for a corporation illegally accessed sensitive Air Force information on combat readiness); misuse of user access privileges and system's capabilities (i.e., programmer copied passwords, which allowed the	SD-42

Issue	Source	Category	Comments
		users to create, change, or delete any file on the network, and post them on the Internet)	
A computer programmer for a company designed a virus after being repri-manded for storing personal letters on his company computer. The virus was designed to erase portions of the company's mainframe and then repeat the process if a predetermined value was not reset in a specific location. After being fired, the former employee used a duplicate set of keys to return to the facility at 3 A.M. and created an unauthorized back-door password to reenter the system and execute a virus	Shaw, Eric D., Ruby, Keven G., and Post, Jerrold M., The Insider Threat to Information Systems, Security Awareness Bulletin 2-98	Computer fraud (software and data) Malcode software injection (i.e., a computer pro-grammer designed a virus to erase portions of the company's main-frame)	SWD-7
A programmer working on advanced distributed computing software transferred via the Internet the firm's entire proprietary source code to another individual	Shaw, Eric D., Ruby, Keven G., and Post, Jerrold M., The Insider Threat to Information Systems, Security Awareness Bulletin 2-98	Computer fraud (system and data) Unauthorized system access (i.e., a computer programmer gained access to a company's source code); illegal distribution and transmission of the source code to another company	SD-43

(continued)

Table 8.8 Insider Computer Fraud Taxonomy (Decomposition—ICF Case Analysis) (*Continued*)

Issue	Source	Category	Comments
A contract employee within a computer company knowingly and willfully violated the federal regulations within a federal government agency by downloading a compressed or "zipped" computer file called "ZIP-42" from the Internet, and transmitted said zipped file to an e-mail account on the government agency's e-mail server on at least seven different occasions, knowing that the zipped file in question would cause the computer system to drastically slow down or completely stop processing e-mail messages at a government research center	www.cyber-crime.gov	Insider computer fraud (system and data) Unauthorized system access (i.e., a contract employee knowingly and willfully violated the federal government regulations by downloading a compressed or zipped computer file); misuse of user access privileges and system's capabilities (i.e., the contract employee intentionally transmitted the zip file with the goal of slowing the computer system down and to stop processing e-mail messages)	SD-44
A computer programmer at a retail chain in a foreign country found himself facing a 50 percent cut in his salary. As a result of his "silent sabotage," the national retail chain was literally brought to its knees when the employee successfully activated a Trojan-horse-type program, thereby "causing all points-of-	*Computer Fraud & Security, 10, October, 2003.*	Hybrid insider computer fraud (software and data) Software code modification: "Trojan horse" was built into a system that caused all points-of-sale terminals to stop working on the busiest shopping day of the week	SWD-8

Issue	Source	Category	Comments
sale (terminals) to stop working on the busiest shopping day of the week, resulting in a monetary loss			
A government employee was suspected of creating false invoices on behalf of veterans. An examination of his laptop computer revealed several deleted files and fragments of files that could be reconstructed to recreate the invoices. A report was issued along with the recreated invoices. The suspect was arrested and later pled guilty	Department of Veterans Affairs, United States of America Office of Inspector General Semiannual Report to Congress October 1, 2003–March 31, 2004	Insider computer fraud (data) Computer data destruction within an application or system (i.e., deletion of files/invoices)	D-5
An ex-official of a local computer consulting firm pleaded guilty to a computer attack charge. A former network administrator of a Manhattan-based computer network consulting firm was charged with a felony involving a computer intrusion of a company's computer system in April 2003		Insider computer fraud (system) Unauthorized system access (i.e., hacking), which destroyed portions of the computer hardware	SD-45

8.3   Misuse of Typical Application Features

This report, although not prepared directly by the author, was useful in gaining a specific understanding of what factors and criteria should be considered as part of the software engineering process to ensure security is baked into the software development methodologies. (See Table 8.9.[5])

Table 8.9 Misuse of Typical Application Features

Legitimate Action	Misuse	
	Client/Server Applications	
Message exchange	Unusual exchange of messages that degrades performance	V
Connectivity to server	Exceeding possible number of connections to cause a denial of service	L
Execution of tasks	Executing privileged procedures	V
	Word Processors	
Writing a document	Insertion of illegal content	L
	Insertion of malicious code	L
	Link to restricted information in other document	V
Reading a document	Bypassing permissions to obtain privileges in the document	V
	Mail Clients	
Sending and receiving e-mails	Inserting illegal content	L
	Setting up remote attack	L
	Private use/gain	L
	Overload of e-mails to degrade network performance	V
	Browsers	
Browsing the Internet	Access to illegal content	L
Access to cached files and history	Displaying other user's viewed files and previous accesses	V
	Multimedia Players	
Playing video/audio file	Viewing illegal content	L
	Programming Tools	
Developing programs	Creation of malware	L
Displaying memory segments	Access to memory segments with sensitive info	V
	General-Purpose Applications	
Reading a file	Opening temporary files with sensitive information	V
Writing a file	Modifying temporary files to change program flow	A
Input strings	Buffer overflow for elevation of privileges	A
	Buffer overflow for code execution	A
	Buffer overflow for denial of service	A
	Database Applications	
Data access	Use of legitimate access rights to access data improperly	L

L: Use of legitimate rights; V: Exploitation of vulnerability through common interaction; A: Exploitation of vulnerability through advanced mechanisms.

Source: Modified from Portilla, Francisco, Furnell, Steven M., and Phyo, Aung H. Analysis of insider misuse in commercial application. In *Advances in Network & Communication Engineering*, University of Plymouth, UK, 2004, pp. 46–54. (With permission.)

8.4 Conclusion

This comprehensive chapter provided a unique insight into the various taxonomies of ICF. Listed below are a few of the highlights of this chapter:

■ Insiders of an organization have access to software vulnerabilities exposure listings (i.e., www.cve.mitre.org/cve) and can easily perform a review of the database of various COTS products that have vulnerabilities and potential exploits.
■ There is a direct correlation between inadequate software design processes, application security flaws that are introduced, and the increased risk of ICF activities.
■ There is an inextricably close relationship that exists between software vulnerabilities, application security, and the taxonomical processes and ICF prevention and detection.
■ Several taxonomies were provided to illustrate the varying research on the topic and the categorization of ICF.
■ Based on this research, the high volume of ICF activities involved hybrid ICF (system and data) activities, specifically involving unauthorized or misuse of system access privileges or capability to change access controls to perpetrate fraud.

References

1. A. Jaquith, *The Security of Applications: Not All Are Created Equal*, @stake, Inc., 2002.
2. Raskin, V. et al., "Ontology in Information Security: A Useful Theoretical Foundation..." (Figure 5 and text excerpt) *Proceedings of the 2001 Workshop on New Security Paradigms* (NSPW'01) pp. 53–59. © 2001, ACM, Inc. Reprinted by permission. DOI: http://doi.acm.org/10.1145/508171.508180
3. Amoroso, Edward. *Fundamentals of Computer Security Technology*, Prentice Hall, New York, 1994. The original cite was sourced from *Fundamentals of Computer Security Technology and used within the Sandia Report, A Common Language for Computer Security Incidents*.
4. Vasiu, Lucian and Vasiu, Ioana. Dissecting computer fraud from definitional issues to a taxonomy, *Proceedings of the 37th Annual Hawaii International Conference on Systems Sciences*. © 2004 IEEE. Reprinted by permission.
5. Modified from Portilla, Francisco, Furnell, Steven M., and Phyo, Aung H. "Analysis of insider misuse in commercial applications," 2004. In *Advances in Network & Communication Engineering*, University of Plymouth, UK (ISBN 1-84102-118-0), pp. 46–54. With permission.

Chapter 9

Key Fraud Signature (KFS) Selection Process for Detecting Insider Computer Fraud

9.1   Introduction

The KFS selection and implementation processes are significant components to Layer 2 of this Defense in Depth insider computer fraud (ICF) Framework. The topic of application journaling goes beyond just selecting a KFS, and a more in-depth discussion will occur on this topic in Chapter 10. However, for the purpose of this discussion, only the KFS selection process will be discussed.

Just as a recap, the levels of my Defense in Depth Model include the following three components; however, it is important to note that each of these three layers do not have to be performed sequentially, but rather should be performed in concert given their close interrelationships:

Layer 1: Application and information technology (IT) control risk assessment
Layer 2: Application journaling
Layer 3: Training and testing the novelty neural network

9.2   KFS Selection Process

9.2.1   KFS Background

The KFS selection process is initially more of an art than a science and will need the benefit of time and experience for users to more fully gain from the benefits of its use. Over time, when the ICF architectural framework has seen refinements based on a clearer understanding of the risks of a particular application or system, the identification, deletion, and refinement of an existing KFS will become more mature and repeatable and this process will eventually evolve into more of a science. However, given the number of variables involved in the KFS selection process, the selection of KFS will always have some component of judgment present. It is important to note at this point that an initial selection of KFS candidates is an important first step in defining what is most relevant to journal from a risk perspective and the initially selected KFS will change over time.

It would be beneficial at this point to introduce the KFS triangle (Figure 9.1) that graphically depicts the interrelationships between a KFS, key fraud metrics (KFMs), and key fraud indicators (KFIs). One approach for introducing any new method or process is to illustrate through example. Consequently, I will attempt to briefly recap the preliminary steps I took in selecting my preliminary KFS. The

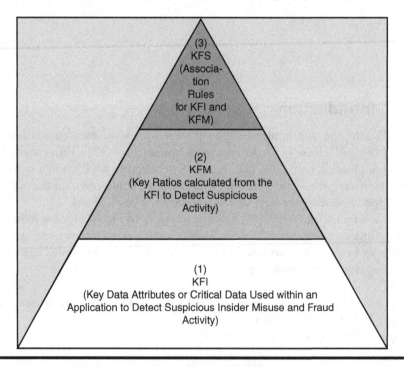

Figure 9.1   The key fraud signature (KFS) pyramid.

topic I selected involved insider loan fraud, but this topic may not be the area of highest risk within every organization; therefore, the completion of the initial application/system risk assessment process is crucial.

9.2.1.1 Phase I: Asset Risk Prioritization

Listed below are the phases of my KFS selection that may assist others who are embarking on establishing an ICF Framework.

This first phase of the KFS selection process begins with a management team that is representative of all key aspects of the enterprise's operation. It is not sufficient to have only a technology professional unilaterally make the important decision of selecting an assets risk prioritization. In my example, I selected the banking industry, given its financial significance to the economy and its importance to the critical infrastructure. Then within the banking sector, I intentionally chose loans, given the fact that loans for most banks represent the greatest earning asset on the balance sheet.

Further to that end, I needed to more narrowly focus my attention on a more specific aspect of loans that I felt would possess the greatest risk to a financial institution. I finally decided on selecting the topic of loans to insiders of a bank, given the regulatory implication of ensuring insiders comply with the requirements of Regulation "O" which establishes regulatory compliance criteria for directors, senior executive officers, and principal shareholders. This topic was also beneficial in that a comprehensive study was performed on this topic and detailed within the "Federal Financial Institutions Examination Council (FFIEC) Insider Detection, Investigation and Prevention of Insider Loan Fraud: A White Paper Produced by the October 20–November 1, 2002 FFIEC Fraud Investigation Symposium" document. A similar approach should be considered for use in completing the asset risk prioritization.

9.2.1.2 Phase II: Data Criticality

Once the asset risk prioritization has been completed and a specific organizational risk area has been selected (i.e., loans), then research needs to ensue regarding cited cases where computer fraud has been perpetrated. Given the large deficiency of data involving ICF being available within the public domain, in all likelihood, the architect of this framework will need to brainstorm and knowledge share with others within their respective organizations regarding their experiences of ICF relating to that topic. In the absence of any research that has targeted fraud, such as the FFIEC document I used for evaluating my candidate KFS, or the absence of any significant research of computer fraud relating to the topic, then one backup plan will include evaluating the following minimum sources:

- Integrated Business/Technology Risk Assessment Process
- Application Security HealthCheck
- Discussions with the data owners regarding data criticality
- Discussions with the database administrator regarding data criticality
- Information Security Policies and Procedures
- Process Maps
- Data Flow Diagrams
- Network Topology
- Review of the Financial Statements
- Software Development Documentation
- Acceptable and unacceptable use policies for each application/system

9.2.1.3 Phase III: Taxonomy (Macro) of ICF

The foundation of selecting a KFS is partly predicated on first selecting relevant KFIs. Therefore, by the time you reach phase III of the KFS process, you should be familiar with existing documentation (phase II) relevant to your understanding of the risk profile of a specific application or system and how the application or system integrates into the entire IT infrastructure of the enterprise. Having a clear understanding of the broad categories of all fraud types (internal and external) will serve as the basis for more narrowly focusing in on ICF. This will be a challenging process given the likely absence of any documented cases that can be leveraged in developing both the macro and micro taxonomy. Based on my research, I was able to identify several broad categories of ICF, which I feel cover the basic types of computer fraud, including the following:

- Billing schemes
- Data capture
- Funds transfer
- Errors
- Manipulation of Data Input
- Payroll Schemes
- Information Privacy Risks
- Check Tampering
- Program Altering Schemes

Within each of these broad categories, there are several subcategories that are discussed further in Chapter 8, along with a companion diagram.

Given the likely absence of any substantial volume of documented internal or external ICF cases, the systems security architect who plans to develop the macro taxonomy will probably have to speculate on the major ICF categories. In the absence of documented support for specific ICF cases, developing the initial macro taxonomy on a "best effort" basis is acceptable; however, at the micro taxonomy level, the architect needs to make assumptions on what the KFI and KFMs based on their domain expertise. (Refer to the phase IV taxonomy—micro for details.)

9.2.1.4   Phase IV: Taxonomy (Micro) of ICF

Determining accurate and meaningful KFIs is the lynchpin to establishing effective journaling, event correlation, and metrics, and for training and testing a neural network. Furthermore, there is a symbiotic relationship between the KFIs and the use of the neural network. Although the neural network will greatly benefit from being trained and tested through the use of KFIs, the neural networks output also benefits the identification, modification, and potential deletion of the KFIs. Although the symbiotic relationship between the KFIs and the neural network will be discussed in much greater detail in Chapter 11, suffice it to state at this point that when KFIs are created, modified, or deleted, these changes will commonly occur based upon the anomaly detection capabilities of the neural network's output.

The use of the micro taxonomy, as previously mentioned, will aid in the development of effective KFIs. For example, based on the micro taxonomy performed on ICF at banks, a few of the documented cases involved the reactivation of dormant accounts. Therefore, from a KFI selection process, you would want to incorporate a KFI involving dormant accounts.

To extend the discussion of KFIs slightly further, it is important to note that a KFS is basically a collection of related and significant KFIs and KFMs that are judgmentally selected. However, typically one signature will be too narrowly focused and would commonly have one or two primary key attributes, and the other related attributes (data and Metadata) would all be related in some way to the primary key attributes. Therefore, if one "significant" KFI changes in some respect (i.e., value or behavior between other KFIs), then the supporting attributes will likely change as well. A good analogy to KFS behavior is similar in concept to database modeling, where a primary key attribute is selected based on that data element's significance (i.e., social security number) to that relational database, and the attributes of that table then are all related to or in some way associated with the primary key. Although associated attributes may change within a database and within a KFS (a collection of related KFIs), the "significant" or "primary" KFI or primary key, which defines a database table, will probably not change. However, it is important to note that KFSs will change with time as they should based on the specific risks associated with a particular application and through the reevaluation process suggested within this framework (i.e., neural network).

One important aspect to remember is that selecting a KFI does not necessarily indicate the existence of fraud; however, the development of KFSs will aid in the development of another layer of detective controls to spot potential fraudulent activity. However, it is important to note that a KFS will identify known misuse and represents a much stronger indication of ICF than a single KFI.

However, although having performed a micro taxonomy was helpful in narrowing down a "short list" of potential KFI candidates, one of the largest challenges in selecting KFIs without any knowledge of actual details surrounding a documented ICF case is determining in what context you need to capture the data for forensic journaling purposes. In other words, every KFS needs to tell some type of story regarding the suspected or actual ICF cases. To that end, it is important to note that the KFI selection process and the crafting of any KFS is a fluid process and should be refined over time. It is important, however, that the designer of the KFS have an intimate knowledge of the business to know the architecture of the enterprise and the functionality of the application, have completed the "Control Point" identification process, and have used the selected KFI in a journaling capacity prior to considering its use for training and testing a novelty neural network.

Listed below are a few examples of the KFS identification process relating to insider loan fraud; however, regardless of what type of ICF activity, the process that needs to be followed should be similar. The list of KFIs noted below originated from the "Insider Computer Fraud Operational Acceptance Detailed Test Plan," which basically identifies the KFI and predicts in what direction they would expect to see absolute value changes, but it also captures the primary key–attribute interrelationship when KFI modifications occur. The capturing of the interrelationships between the "significant" or anchor key versus the supporting attributes is important for not only developing the KFS, but also identifying the "data behavior" in training and testing the neural network.

Listed below are the general steps that should be followed in developing and maintaining the KFSs:

1. *Identify Application or System Misuse (i.e., Taxonomies)*: As an initial starting point, the macro taxonomy will focus your initial thoughts on the larger-scale risks and vulnerabilities within an application or system.

2. *Develop Key Fraud Signature Association Rules (KFSARs)*: Develop rules that correspond to event correlation rules.

3. *Develop Signatures Based on Misuse Detection*: Specifically, the designer of the signatures should be intimately knowledgeable about the organization's policies and standards governing the use of a particular application or system. A KFS is focusing on known misuses of an application (misuse, not anomaly detection), and the types of misuses commonly found within a particular application should be clearly articulated within various policies within an organization (i.e., unacceptable use policy and other relevant policies and standards). Again, there are close parallels between journaling criteria and selecting standards for KFS development. More specifics about journaling will be discussed in Chapter 10.

4. *Develop Meaningful Metrics*: After developing meaningful metrics, include them as a component of the signature, where appropriate. The development and use of metrics are becoming more pervasive in understanding all types of operational risk within an enterprise; however, their use tends to be too narrowly focused by considering them as a stand-alone barometer of acceptable norms and practices. Their integration into the KFS development process could add another dimension and layer of ICF detection and perhaps time prevention.

5. *Continually Analyze the Results*: The neural network must be continually analyzed for new anomalies. There is a symbiotic relationship between the KFI identification process and the use of a neural network in detecting ICF activities. A key point to note here is that an interrelationship exists between the KFIs, KFSs, and KFMs initially identified and the results of the neural network. You do not want to log every KFI, so it becomes increasingly important to fine-tune the signature process to ensure the methodology you use in the initial KFS identification process also includes a method for updating those signatures. Similar to network intrusion detection signatures, they are continually updated by the software vendors, and so should updates occur for KFS. The only obvious disadvantage to maintaining KFS is that you will be primarily responsible for conducting the KFS updates yourself, given there are few software vendors in existence that have entered into this commercial space.

6. *Develop and Populate the KFS Worksheet*: Leveraging off the Forensic Foto Frame concept as graphically illustrated within the "ICF Service Oriented Diagram for Insider Bank Loan Originations," develop a "KFS Worksheet" (refer to Appendix E for an example) which decomposes each fraud category to ostensibly one or perhaps two individual KFIs. Each simple KFI can be combined, where appropriate, by the key fraud signature association rules (KFSAR) listed below.

9.2.1.5 Phase V: KFSAR Process

In brief, there are no industry standards relative to the identification of signature attacks either from a network perspective or certainly not at the application level. Overall, standardization of control processes governing network security are more mature than at the application level from a number of different fronts (i.e., intrusion detection systems, IDS; intrusion prevention systems, IPS; access controls; etc.); however, at the application level, access controls, type and format of journaling criteria, and audit trails for many applications are still in their infancy.

Although it would be easier to reintroduce and support an existing or equivalent KFSAR for applications, that unfortunately is not the current reality. Consequently, the following sections within phase V will generically describe the process

I followed; however, all processes that are in their incipient stages of development need to evolve and mature, and this process is no exception to that heuristic.

The KFSAR process begins by identifying KFIs (data and metadata) and KFMs and then evaluating how to link each of these attributes to tell a story of suspected ICF. Furthermore, as graphically depicted within the Defense in Depth Interrelationships diagram, policies and procedures also play an important role in establishing business rules, which represents the underlying driving force behind the development and maintenance of the KFSAR. For example, the acceptable and unacceptable use policies should include the business rules of the enterprise which should factor into the KFSAR process for the selection and maintenance of KFIs and KFMs and ultimately the creation of the KFS, which ties together these two attribute categories.

Event correlation and the KFSAR criteria are presented. (See Figure 9.2 for illustration.) There should be a linkage between the KFS selection and the event correlation software. Unfortunately there are organizations that have event correlation software capabilities, but the software may not accept any type of application journaling (KFS

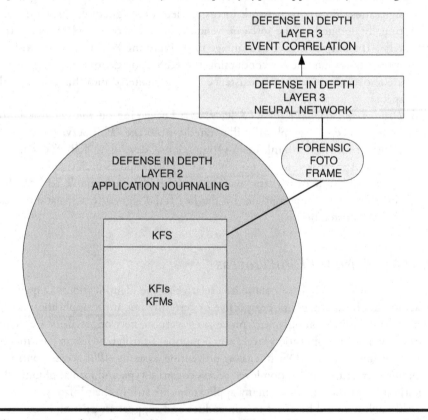

Figure 9.2 Defense in Depth Layer 2 (journaling) and Layer 3 (neural network and event correlation interaction).

or other type of journaling and audit trails), primarily due to the fact that a universal standardized application journaling format has never been established. Consequently, the event correlation software will accept all the network-related journaling (i.e., network intrusion detection systems [NIDS] and host-based intrusion detection systems [HIDS] alerts, firewall and router logs, Syslogs, etc.). However, a big piece of the root cause equation, which involves application journaling, is never considered within the event correlation software. Given the KFI concept is a new concept developed from this research, the evaluation of what data is actually correlated within the algorithms of the event correlation engine will help in determining a root cause analysis. Performing this front-end evaluation of what data is currently being correlated by the network infrastructure will aid in determining what data should be collected from the KFS, parsed, and then included as another important data stream for analysis within the event correlation algorithms. The combination of the network IT infrastructure components, coupled with the application journaling, will provide my data for the event correlation engine to determine a root cause analysis of a suspected intrusion and perhaps ICF activities.

9.2.2 The Neural Network and the Key Fraud Signature Association Rules (KFSAR) Criteria

There is also a close relationship between the KFS selection process and developing the neural network dataset. In brief, the data that has been collected and assigned the title of a KFI will serve double duty. Specifically, there should, under most circumstances, be a close similarity between selected KFIs that will be journaled within an application, and then also applying that same dataset to training and testing a neural network.

Over time, as the system matures, the pool of KFS will continually be refined through additions, deletions, and modifications, to reflect more accurately documented cases that represent misuse detection (application journaling) or anomaly detection (neural networks) of ICF activity. The key to remember at this point is that you want to capture individual KFI and KFM value changes for application journaling. Second, while concurrently journaling KFI value changes within an application or system, you also want to use the same pool of KFIs to train and test the neural network. This relationship between KFI and KFM journaling makes logical sense, given the multipurposes of these values (journaling, neural network dataset, and input into an event correlation database).

9.2.2.1 The KFS Candidate Preparation Document and Its Interrelationship to Other Documents

The KFS candidate preparation document lays out a blueprint of identifying fraud activities relating to a particular application. This KFS candidate preparation document was used within my research to document the insider loan example. Specifically, the KFS candidate preparation document captured all the cited FFIEC insider loan computer fraud cases, which then allowed me to develop KFS candidates. Then through the use of the KFS candidate preparation document, I developed the operational acceptance testing detailed test plan for training and testing a neural network.

9.2.2.2 Timing of KFS Development

The concepts presented within this document are new, and the architects actually deploying such a system should proceed slowly in its actual implementation. Unlike network intrusion signatures that have been identified and refined to reflect attempted or actual network breaches, most organizations will probably not have the same comfort level with ICF within its applications and will need to monitor application journaling and the output of a neural network over a period of time to gain a better understanding of what is legitimate data behavior involving ICF activities and the assignment of KFS.

Both network and application intrusion detection systems inherently possess the same shortcomings relative to the reporting of false negatives and false positives. Whether data preprocessing occurs prior to the entry of this information into the system or the system takes in raw data, the designer of their own enterprise architecture should closely evaluate the results of the neural network. Specifically, establishing KFSARs may be premature without having the benefit of knowing the data behavior through the monitoring of KFI and KFM attributes. Although it is important to develop initial KFSARs, the key is to try and reduce the volume of false negatives and false positives, which are commonplace through the use of NIDS and have an equally high probability of occurring with detecting insider misuse within applications, which tend to have less visibility within organizations.

A strategy for reducing the potential risk of an application or system generating too high a volume of false negatives and false positives within applications (zero is unavoidable) includes the following steps:

- Monitor data behavior of KFIs and KFMs over time prior to selecting a KFS
- The designer of a KFS needs to be fairly confident about the interrelationships between each individual KFI and KFM prior to assigning any KFSAR. Prematurely assigning a KFSAR could be problematic from the standpoint of reporting too many false negatives and false positives. Therefore, to recap, the designer of the application or system should monitor the behavior of data attributes over a period of time prior to developing a KFS.
- Integrate the results of the novelty neural network into the development of KFSAR and the assignment of a KFS.

Given the fact that the KFIs and KFMs have a number of different uses, including journaling, establishing a dataset for training and testing a neural network, and as a data stream for event correlation purposes, it is important to ensure that adjustments to the rule-base and the signatures be periodically made. Specifically, through the use of a novelty neural network, you want to continually evaluate the output of the network, which includes the flagging of novelties or, in other words, new associations between other attributes that were not previously detected. For example, if the total "novelty score" for a particular insider transaction is 1 (indicating only one new anomalistic attribute relationship was detected) and no new subsequent attribute associations were detected involving a selected KFI or KFM, then journaling of the attributes individually may be appropriate; however, this does not pass the litmus test for inclusion within a KFS. By definition, a KFS is a well-defined and documented ICF case, similar to those outlined in the FFIEC document for insider computer loan fraud. As such, it would not make logical sense to include initially identified KFS and KFS attributes within a KFS, given the absence of any tangible negative trend in negative data behavior.

The next step is to finalize the KFSAR and KFS candidate selection. Both the KFSAR and KFS candidates need to be selected and agreed upon by technology and information security professionals, audit, accounting, and management within the enterprise, including legal regarding all aspects of the KFS selection and maintenance process. Management is interested in ensuring KFSs are accurate to protect the data and reputation of the enterprise, and accounting (Section 9.2.3) would be interested in ensuring your KFI and KFS selections are best representative of ICF activity, while legal would be interested in the forensic evidentiary data being produced for potential discovery purposes, based upon the KFSAR and KFS selection and monitoring process to detect ICF activities.

Risk prioritize the KFS as high, moderate, or low or use the equivalent risk rating system. It will be impossible to follow up on determining the legitimacy and impact of every ICF within an enterprise. One viable way of prioritizing what ICF attack signatures are most important is to assign a rating to each ICF attack. It may not be logistically or economically feasible to develop and monitor a KFS for every one insider misuse. Although this is not to say that the insider misuse should be ignored, but rather a rating system should be developed that accurately captures and prioritizes ICF activities. There needs to be a risk/reward analysis on the decision to follow up on any known insider misuse.

9.2.3 Accounting Forensics

The important aspect to note at this point is that under the aforementioned insider loan fraudulent scenario, my analysis reflects speculation regarding which specific accounts would be potentially impacted given the suspected insider misuse of the application and data. However, in reality, to come to some firm conclusion relative to which accounts were involved in insider misuse would likely require a higher level of accounting expertise through a postmortem analysis of the application, the transactions involved, the data flow attributes impacted by the suspected computer fraud, and what data was actually processed within the application. In brief, an impact analysis would have to be performed of the suspected fraudulent transaction, with a financial statement and forensic accounting analysis of that enterprise.

For illustrative purposes, the example below represents a simple format that could be used in identifying a KFS candidate, for use in KFS preparation, journaling, and neural network dataset preparation.

9.2.3.1 Example of KFSAR (Macro and Micro ICF Taxonomy)—Insider Loan Fraud Scenario

Although no KFSAR rules exist, one baseline rule that could be considered would be a basic "If Then Else" statement to determine associations between KFI and KFM attributes. To keep the illustrations simple, the following example will use only KFIs, not KFMs.

To illustrate the "If Then Else" statement, one rule format may take the form of the following:

Example of KFS Format:
> If (Day = Saturday *and* Time = P.M. *and* Item = Beer), *then* cost <$10.00, which just says that on Saturday evenings people normally buy small quantities of beer.

Example KFSAR:
> If (sale values decrease *and* production costs increase *and* marketing costs decrease), *then* the financial risk is low.

Now, for a specific example of how to apply the rule format above, first assume that we are not aware of any cited ICF cases but have the benefit of the macro taxonomy presented in Table 9.1.

The top hybrid ICF cases involving a combined systems- and data-related ICF include the following areas:

Macro Taxonomy:
> Unauthorized use or misuse of system access privileges or capability to change access controls to perpetrate fraud (high risk).
> Software modification to funnel purchases into a "dummy" account and then erase any trace of fraud (moderate risk).
> Misuse of system capabilities (low risk).

Based on the macro taxonomy, one potential KFSAR might include the following:

Table 9.1   Macro Insider Computer Fraud Taxonomy

	Ontological Category (Parent)	Ontological Category (Child)	
Genesis	Data	Data input manipulation Data destruction	*Hybrid ICF*
	System	Misuse of system capabilities (authorized users) Hardware destruction or damage Access control misuse Hacking (unauthorized user) Unauthorized system access through the fraudulent use by ex-employees	
	Software	Code manipulation Logic bomb Malcode injection Trojan horse	

KFSAR 1 (Macro Taxonomy):

If (user access level increases *and* this is a new employee), *then* the financial risk is high.

To illustrate this example in another manner, which more closely aligns with our ICF scenarios involving insider computer loan fraud, perhaps the following format and content would provide another perspective. Look now at an actual KFS that was used within the insider computer fraud operational testing (detailed test plan), suspicious case 4, which reflects the following KFI value changes to give the appearance of a potential insider fraudster, who decided to engage in data input manipulation.

For a specific example of how to apply the KFSAR 1 Micro Taxonomy rule noted below, first review Table 9.2. An insider may have created a fraudulent loan or may be receiving bribes or kickbacks from a borrower who cannot repay the loan. Accrued interest may be capitalized.

Listed below are the KFI candidates that I used in developing the dataset for suspicious case 4:

KFS Candidate (Simple Format)
  a. ➥ Loan balance
  b. Time-stamp the modification to the loan balance data value
  c. ≠ ABUI (accrued but unpaid interest)
  d. Time-stamp the modification to the ABUI data value

Table 9.2 Micro Insider Computer Fraud Taxonomy (Bank Insider Loan Fraud)

Data Manipulation	Insert	Falsified data
		Nominee loan name
	Improper use of loan proceeds	
	Integrity issues	
	Preferential rate and term for loan	

Source: Insider Loan Fraudulent Scenario: *Analysis of Electronic Loan Data—KFS Candidate Preparation,* Federal Financial Institution Examination Council (FFIEC).

Based on the micro taxonomy, one potential KFSAR might include the following:

KFSAR 2 (Micro Taxonomy):

If (FinData _LoanBal declines by 15 percent *and* FinData_LoanBal_IL_ Mod_Time_Meta changes *and* ABUI increases by 5 percent *and* Earn_ ABUI_Mod_Time_Meta changes), *then* Alert KFS 1.

(Additional KFIs and KFMs can be added as appropriate to more accurately reflect new malicious ICF patterns.)

Assuming a transaction meets the criteria of KFSAR 2 and the data behavior is now considered suspicious and meeting the criteria of KFS 1, a KFS 1 alert should be transmitted to notify the appropriate InfoSec personnel to potentially trigger their computer incident response team (CIRT) processes to mitigate the risks associated with this activity.

There are, however, several mitigating factors that may influence the severity of these alerts. They include the following factors:

1. *A KFS Designation Does Not Apply to Each Forensic Foto Frame*: Although the KFS designation might be appropriate and technically meets the criteria outlined within the KFSAR, each KFS does not apply universally to every Forensic Foto Frame. Based on the ICF Service Oriented Architecture diagram listed below, there may be numerous control gates where Forensic Foto Frames will be taken. Each Forensic Foto Frame will be taken at various stages within the journey of the transaction and its data. What might be considered as a KFI or KFS anomaly, indicating a suspicious transaction, for Forensic Foto 1, may paradoxically be considered as normal behavior for Forensic Foto 2, based on different processing activities (i.e., calculations) that will change the behavior of the data. (See Figure 9.1.)
2. *Direct and Indirect Correlation Conditions Have Not Been for a High-Risk KFS Designation*:

a. *Direct Correlation*: A general rule for a direct correlation to exist may require that certain conditions be satisfied. For example, a KFS 1 designation may also require the incorporation of a KFM to be considered a high risk, which may be included within another signature, say KFS 2. These two KFSs (1 and 2) taken individually might be considered as on a low or moderate risk designation. Consequently, now that two conditions have been met and have met the correlation rules, then the combination of these rules can now be considered as a high ICF rules designation. Otherwise, KFS 1 alone is considered as having only a moderate risk level.

b. *Indirect Correlation*: From an indirect correlation perspective, there may be ontological rules that establish pre- and postconditions to occur which taken together would warrant a high risk designation, which has similarities to the concepts of direct correlation. The difference between a direct and an indirect correlation lies predominately in the predictability of what conditions need to be satisfied (i.e., direct correlation) versus actions that may exist, but were not initially anticipated to meet the definition of a direct correlation. For example, say the conditions of KFS 1 have been met, however, a KFM value also changed in an unpredictable way that would not be considered as normal behavior of data. Using the insider loan example, a loan that has been historically past due has been charged off; however, the KFM_Loss-IL ratio increases, which is a contradictory cause and effect. From an accounting and finance perspective, if a loan was charged off, then any ratio that relates to a charge-off, such as the KFM_Loss_IL ratio, should also decline, but the KFM ratio actually increased. These circumstances would warrant the use of indirect correlation between these two events, given the unusual pre- and postcondition that occurred, thereby establishing an association between these two events or activities.

3. *Novelties Detected from the Neural Network Will Change the Significance of KFS*: One of the major advantages of incorporating the use of a novelty neural network within my ICF Framework is to validate the accuracy, relevance, and significance of existing KFSs, KFIs, and KFMs. For example, KFS 1 may have been an appropriate fraud signature at one point in time; however, recently there have been no patterns of novelties detected for a particular Forensic Foto Frame. This situation now raises the question of whether or not the KFS is still relevant given the absence of any pattern of novelties detected by the neural network. Conversely, a consistent pattern of new aggregate novelty (i.e., five new associations occurred between various KFIs and KFMs) recently appeared within the same Forensic Foto Frame as KFS 1. This recurring aggregate novelty was not predicted during the initial KFS designation; however, given this new pattern of novelties now appearing between various attributes, the need for reevaluating the existing universe of KFS should be triggered. Under this new scenario, it may be appropriate to create new KFSs or modify or delete the existing signatures that no longer have relevance to detection of ICF activities. (See Table 9.3.)

Table 9.3 Data Definition Table

	Attributes (Data and Metadata)
ADM	*Administration/Summary Data*
Adm_Tot_Data	The number of data elements within the frame
Adm_Tot_MetaData	The number of metadata elements within the frame
Adm_Author	Author
Adm_Author_Email	Author e-mail
Adm_DataOwner	Data owner/maintainer
Adm_AppOfficer	Name of approving officer
Adm_Desc	Description
Adm_LoanAmt	Total loan amount
KFI	*Data Attributes (KFI)*
	Loan Application Data
FINDATA	Financial statements
FinData_SSN	Social security number
FinData_Borrower	Borrower
FinData_PortfolioValue	Total portfolio value by loan officer
FinData_POBox	P.O. Box address
FinData_PolicyExc	Policy exception
FinData_Purpose	Loan purpose
FinData_AppOfficer	Name of approving officer
FinData_TA	Total assets
FinData_TL	Total liabilities
FinData_BorrowerNW	Borrower net worth
FinData_LTV	Loan-to value (LTV)
FinData_Collateral	Collateral value
FinData_FICO	FICO score
FinData_YRSEmp	Years employed

FinData_Ln Officer	Loan officer's name
FinData_IntRate	Interest rate
FinData_MatDt	Maturity date
FinData_Repay	Repayment terms
FinData_PSOR	Primary source of repayment
FinData_Insiders_All	Loan balance for "insider" loans
FinData_LoanBal_IL	Loan balance for an installment loan
FinData_LoanBal_RE	Loan balance for a real estate loan
FinData_LoanBal_C&I	Loan balance for a commercial and industrial loan
EARN	*Earnings*
Earn_Tot_LN	Total dollar amount of earnings for individual "insider" loans
Earn_Tot_Int&Fes_IL	Total interest and fee income on individual I/L
Earn_Tot_Int&Fees_RE	Total interest and fee income on individual RE loans
Earn_Tot_Int&Fees_CI	Total interest and fee income on individual C&I loans
Earn_ABUI	Accrued but unpaid interest
BS	*Balance Sheet*
BS_TotAllInsiders	Total dollar amount of all extensions of credit to "insiders"
BS_TotIndRE	Total dollar amount of individual, "insider"" real estate loans
BS_TotIndC&I	Total dollar amount of individual, "insider" C&I loans
BS_TotIndIL	Total dollar amount of individual, "insider" I/L

KFI Metadata Attributes (Association with Each Data Attribute)

CREATION (Create)	*KFI (Attribute) Creation*
Create_Date_Meta	Date
Create_Time_Meta	Time

(continued)

Table 9.3   Data Definition Table (*Continued*)

Create_SaveTime_Meta	Last save time
Create_Rev#_Meta	Revision number
Create_TotEditMin_Meta	Total edit time (minutes)
Create_Tot_MetaData_Meta	Total metadata object CREATIONS
ACCESS (Acc)	*KFI (Attribute) Accesses*
Acc_Date_Meta	Date
Acc_Time_Meta	Time
Acc_LastSaveTime_Meta	Last save time
Acc_Rev#Access_Meta	Revision number
Acc_TotEditTime_Meta	Total edit time (minutes)
Acc_FreqTotMetaData_Meta	Total metadata object ACCESS
DELETE (Del)	*KFI (Attribute) Deletions*
Del_Date_Meta	Date
Del_Time_Meta	Time
Del_LastSaveTime_Meta	Last save time
Del_RevNumber_Meta	Revision number
Del_TotEditTime_Meta	Total edit time (minutes)
Del_TotMetaData_Meta	Total metadata object DELETIONS
ADDITION (Add)	*KFI (Attribute) Additions*
Add_Date_Meta	Date
Add_Time_Meta	Time
Add_LastSaveTime_Meta	Last save time
Add_RevNum_Meta	Revision number
Add_TotEditTime_Meta	Total edit time (minutes)
Add_TotMetaData_Meta	Total metadata object ADDITIONS
MODIFICATION (Mod)	*KFI (Attribute) Modifications*
Mod_Date_Meta	Date

Mod_Time_Meta	Time
Mod_LastSaveTime_Meta	Last save time
Mod_RevNum_Meta	Revision number
Mod_TotEditTime_Meta	Total edit time (minutes)
Mod_TotMetaData_Meta	Total data object MODIFICATIONS
GRAPHICS/OBJECTS (Gpf)	*Document Embedded Graphics/Objects*
Gpf_TotMetaData_Meta	Total number of document embedded graphics/objects
CREATION (Create)	*Embedded Graphics/Objects Creation*
Create_Gpf_Date_Meta	Date
Create_Gpf_Time_Meta	Time
Create_Gpf_LastSaveTime_Meta	Last save time
Create_Gpf_RevNum_Meta	Revision number
Create_Gpf_TotEditTime_Meta	Total edit time (minutes)
Create_Gpf_TotGraphics_Meta	Total number of embedded graphics CREATED
ACCESS (Acc)	*Embedded Graphics/Objects Accessed*
Acc_Gpf_Date_Meta	Date
Acc_Gpf_Time_Meta	Time
Acc_Gpf_LastSaveTime_Meta	Last save time
Acc_Gpf_RevNum_Meta	Revision number
Acc_Gpf_TotEditTime_Meta	Total edit time (minutes)
Acc_Gpf_TotGraphics_Meta	Total number of embedded graphics ACCESSED
DELETE (Del)	*Embedded Graphics/Objects Deletions*
Del_Gpf_Date_Meta	Date
Del_Gpf_Time_Meta	Time
Del_Gpf_LastSaveTime_Meta	Last save time
Del_Gpf_RevNum_Meta	Revision number

(continued)

Table 9.3   Data Definition Table (*Continued*)

Del_Gpf_TotEditTime_Meta	Total edit time (minutes)
Del_Gpf_TotGraphics_Meta	Total number of embedded graphics DELETIONS
ADDITION (Add)	*Embedded Graphics/Objects Additions*
Add_Gpf_Date_Meta	Date
Add_Gpf_Time_Meta	Time
Add_Gpf_LastSaveTime_Meta	Last save time
Add_Gpf_RevNum_Meta	Revision number
Add_Gpf_TotEditTime_Meta	Total edit time (minutes)
Add_Gpf_TotGraphics_Meta	Total number of embedded graphics ADDITIONS
MODIFICATION (Mod)	*Embedded Graphics/Objects Modifications*
Mod_Gpf_Dte_Meta	Date
Mod_Gpf_Time_Meta	Time
Mod_Gpf_LastSaveTime_Meta	Last save time
Mod_Gpf_RevNum_Meta	Revision number
Mod_Gpf_TotEditTime_Meta	Total edit time (minutes)
Mod_Gpf_TotGraphics_Meta	Total number of embedded graphics MODIFICATIONS
ALGTRANS (Alg)	*Document Algorithmic Transformations (i.e., Calcs)*
Tot_Alg_Trans_Meta	Total number of document calculations
CREATION (Create)	Algorithmic transformations CREATION
Create_Alg_Date_Meta	Date
Create_Alg_Time_Meta	Time
Create_Alg_LastSaveTime_Meta	Last save time
Create_Alg_RevNum_Meta	Revision number
Create_Alg_TotEditTime_Meta	Total edit time (minutes)
Create_Alg_TotAlg_Meta	Total number of algorithmic transformations CREATION

ACCESS (Acc)	*Algorithmic Transformations Accesses*
Acc_Alg_Date_Meta	Date
Acc_Alg_Time_Meta	Time
Acc_Alg_LastSaveTime_Meta	Last save time
Acc_Alg_RevNum_Meta	Revision number
Acc_Alg_TotEditTime_Meta	Total edit time (minutes)
Acc_Alg_TotAlg_Meta	Total number of algorithmic transformations ACCESSES
DELETE (Del)	*Algorithmic Transformations Deletions*
Del_Alg_Date_Meta	Date
Del_Alg_Time_Meta	Time
Del_Alg_LastSaveTime_Meta	Last save time
Del_Alg_RevNum_Meta	Revision number
Del_Alg_TotEditTime_Meta	Total edit time (minutes)
Del_Alg_TotAlg_Meta	Total number of algorithmic transformations DELETIONS
ADDITION (Add)	*Algorithmic Transformations Additions*
Add_Alg_Date_Meta	Date
Add_Alg_Time_Meta	Time
Add_Alg_LastSaveTime_Meta	Last save time
Alg_RevNum_Meta	Revision number
Alg_TotEditTime_Meta	Total edit time (minutes)
Alg_TotAlg_Meta	Total number of algorithmic transformations ADDITIONS
MODIFICATION (Mod)	*Algorithmic Transformations Modifications*
Mod_Alg_Date_Meta	Date
Mod_Alg_Time_Meta	Time
Mod_Alg_LastSaveTime_Meta	Last save time
Mod_Alg_RevNum_Meta	Revision number

(continued)

Table 9.3   Data Definition Table (*Continued*)

Mod_Alg_TotEditTime_Meta	Total edit time (minutes)
Mod_Alg_TotAlg_Meta	Total number of algorithmic transformations ADDITIONS
DATACCESS	*Data Access Rules Violations (Assigned by Sec. Admin.)*
AL1 (Restricts Access to Data & Metadata)	(Access Level 1 — CREATE)
AL2 (Restricts Access to Data & Metadata)	(Access Level 2 — ACCESS)
AL3 (Restricts Access to Data & Metadata)	(Access Level 3 — DELETE)
AL4 (Restricts Access to Data & MetaData)	(Access Level 4 — ADD)
AL5 (Restricts Access to Data & MetaData)	(Access Level 5 — MODIFY)
DATA	*Data*
AL_SSN	Social security number
AL_Borrower	Name of borrower
ALPortfolio	Total portfolio value by loan officer
AL_P.O. Box	P.O. Box address
AL_Policy Exc.	Policy exceptions
AL_Purpose	Loan purpose
AL_App. Officer	Name of approving officer
AL_TA	Total assets
AL_TL	Total liabilities
AL_BorrowerNW	Borrower net worth
AL_Collateral	Collateral value
AL_LTV	LTV

AL_FICO	FICO score
AL_YRS. Emp	Years employed
AL_Ln Officer	Loan officer name
AL_IR	Interest rate
AL_Mat. Dt	Maturity date
AL_Repay	Repayment terms
AL_PSOR	Primary source of repayment
AL_FinData_Insiders_All	Loan balance for "insider" loans
AL_LoanBal_IL	Loan balance for an installment loan
AL_LoanBal_RE	Loan balance for a real estate loan
AL_LoanBal_C&I	Loan balance for a commercial and industrial loan
AL_TotEarn	Total dollar amount of earnings (individual "insider" loan)
AL_TotIntFI_IL	Total interest and fee income on individual "insider" installment loans
AL_TotIntFI_RE	Total interest and fee income on individual "insider" R/E loans
AL_TotIntFI_CI	Total interest and fee income on commercial and industrial loans
AL_ABUI	Accrued but unpaid interest
METADATA	*Metadata*
Date_Meta	Date of KFI attribute creation
Time_Meta	Time of KFI attribute creation
Last_Save_Meta	Last save time of the KFI attribute
Revision_Number_Meta	Cumulative number of KFI attribute revision
Tot_EditTime_Meta	Total edit time of the KFI attribute
Tot_Embedded Graphics	Total number of embedded graphics/objects

(continued)

Table 9.3   Data Definition Table (*Continued*)

Tot_Alg_Trans.	Total number of algorithmic transformations
KFM	*Key Fraud Metrics (KFM)*
LPM	*Loan Portfolio*
KFM_LPM_Avg. Tot_Ln&Lse	Average total loans and leases ($000s)
KFM_LPM_Tot_Ln&Lse	Total loan and lease commitments
KFM_LPM_Tot_Ln&Lse_Insiders	Total loan and lease outstanding balance to all "insiders"
EARN	*Earnings*
KFM_Earn_AvgEarnLns	Average total dollar earnings on all "insider" loans
KFM_Earn_%AvgLn_IncIntInc	Percent of average annual growth interest and fees (all "insider" loans to average total loans)
KFM_Earn_%IntIncC&I	Total percent of interest income on individual "insider" C&I loans
KFM_Earn_%IntIncIL	Total percent of interest income on individual "insider" I/L
KFM_Earn_%IntIncRELns	Total percent of interest income on individual "insider" RE loans
LOSS	*Loss*
KFM_Loss_AvgLns&Lse	Average total dollar value of net loss of all extensions of credit to all "insiders"
KFM_Loss_TotLns&Lse	Total dollar amount of net loss for an individual "insider" loan
KFM_Loss_%Avg	Percent of average annual growth rate of losses on all "insider" loans to average total loans
KFM_Loss_IL	Total net loss of an individual "insider" installment loan
KFM_Loss_RE	Total net loss of an individual "insider" RE loan
KFM_Loss_C&I	Total net loss of an individual "insider" C&I loan
BS	*Balance Sheet*
KFM_BS_TotAvgLns	Average total dollar amount of all extensions of credit to "insiders"

KFM_BS_AvgGrowthRateLns	Percent of average growth rate of all extensions of credit to "insiders" to average total loans
PD	*Past-due/"Noncurrent" (30 to 60 Days)*
KFM_PD_AvgPDGrowthRate	Average total dollar growth rate of "insider" noncurrent loans and leases
KFM_PD_TotPDAmtLns	Total paid amount of an individual "insider" loan
KFM_PD_%AvgPDLns	Percent of average "insider" paid loans to average total loans
KFM_PD_Tot_IL	Total paid "insider" installment loans
KFM_PD_Tot_RE	Total noncurrent "insider" RE loans
KFM_PD_Tot_CI	Total noncurrent "insider" C&I loans
KFM_PD_Tot_IL	Total noncurrent "insider" I/L
NA	*Nonaccrual (90+ Days)*
KFM_NA_AvgTotNALns	Average total dollar amount of nonaccrual "insider" loans and leases
KFM_NA_TotNA_IL	Total nonaccrual amount of an individual "insider" loan
KFM_NA_%NA_Lns	Percent of "insider" nonaccrual loans to average total loans
KFM_NA_Tot_IL	Total nonaccrual "insider" installment loans and leases
KFM_NA_Tot_RE	Total nonaccrual "insider" RE loans
KFM_NA_Tot_CI	Total nonaccrual "insider" C&I loans

9.2.3.2 Forensic Foto Frame

See Table 9.4 for a presentation of a Forensic Foto Frame.

9.2.3.3 A Key Fraud Signature (KFS)

Presented in Table 9.5 is an analysis of electronic loan data.

Table 9.4 Forensic Foto Frame (Data and Metadata Values for KFIs; Data Values of Both Bank Insiders and the General Public)

Foto Frame	Data Name	Data Value	Metadata Name and Value	Comments
1 (Insider)	Borrower financial statements		Refer to the "metadata extraction" document for details on:	Loan data application (non-KFIs):
			Administration/summary data for each KFI attribute listed within Forensic Foto 1 (e.g., social security number, name of borrower, etc.)	*Applicant data*
	Social security number	1112223333		Date of birth
	Name of borrower	Tom C. Callahan		Citizenship
				Marital status
	Total portfolio value by loan officer	5MM		Home address
				Mailing address
			Frame statistics	Home phone
	P.O. box address	P.O. Box 543		Cell phone
			Data access rule violations	(Rent, live with others, own/buying, landlord/
	Policy exceptions	Exceeds officer lending limit	Graphics	mortgagor)
			Algorithmic transformations	Monthly rent/mortgage payment
	Loan purpose	Purchase money mtg. for residence		Years/months there
				Landlord/mortgagor name
	Name of approving officer	Tom Samuelson		Rent/mortgage account number
	Total assets	$100,000		Balance owed
	Total liabilities	$60,000		Ownership
	Borrower net worth	$40,000		
	Collateral value	$400,000		

LTV	50%	Previous address
FICO score	450	City
Years employed	5	State
		Zip
		Years/months there
Loan officer name	Jean Smith	Name of employer
Interest rate	Prime + 2	Position/occupation
	6.93%	description
		Years/months there
Maturity date	11/05/10	Source of other income
		(describe)
Repayment terms	Monthly P&I	Annual amount
	4M	
		Assets
Primary source of	Cash flow from borrower	Cash
repayment		Retirement/401(k)
Bank earnings		accounts
		Residence
Total dollar amount of	$400,000	Publicly traded stocks
earnings (individual	(P & I)	and bonds
"insider" loan)		Other real estate owned
		Other
Total interest and fee	0	
income on individual		*Collateral*
"insider" installment loan		Automobile (year, make/
		model, body, style, milage,
Total interest and fee	$200,000	trade-in allowance, state
income on individual		registered, VIN, additional
"insider" RE loan		description

(continued)

Table 9.4 Forensic Foto Frame (Data and Metadata Values for KFIs; Data Values of Both Bank Insiders and the General Public) (Continued)

Foto Frame	Data Name	Data Value	Metadata Name and Value	Comments
	Total interest and fee income on individual "insider" C&I loan	0		Manufactured home (year, model, manufacturer, length/width, community/park name)
	Bank balance sheet			Certificate of deposit, stocks/bonds, savings (describe, CUSIP/Cust. No., company, number of shares)
	Total loan amount of all individual "insider" loan(s)	$700,000		Other
	Total loan amount of all individual "insider" I/L	0		*Liabilities*
	Total loan amount of all individual "insider" RE loan(s)	$ 700,000		Child support (name of creditor, current outstanding balance, monthly payment, or other terms, account number and ownership information)
	Total loan amount of all individual "insider" C&I loan(s)	0		Alimony
				401(k) loans
				Personal loans from individuals

CD secured, stock secured, margin accounts
Homeowner association dues/condo fees
Other

List of debts to be paid by this loan
Name of creditor
Description
Account number
Current outstanding balance
Monthly payment (or other term)
Debt will be (paid down or paid off/closed)

Government monitoring information
Applicant data (e.g., ethnicity, race, sex)
Coapplicant (e.g., ethnicity, race, sex)

Occupancy
Owner occupied
Nonowner occupied

(continued)

Table 9.4 Forensic Foto Frame (Data and Metadata Values for KFIs; Data Values of Both Bank Insiders and the General Public) (Continued)

Foto Frame	Data Name	Data Value	Metadata Name and Value	Comments
				Property type
				1–4 family
				Multifamily
				Manufactured housing
				Address of property to be
				purchased, refinanced, or
				improved
				Street address
				City
				County
				State
				Zip
				Coapplicant
				Same data as above
2 (General public)	Same attributes as noted above	Refer to the "novelty neural network" document for details on example values	Same	
3 (insider or general public)	Not completed, as examples of both insider and general public data were previously provided within Forensic Foto Frames 1 and 2			

4   Web server:
Includes all the consolidation of data and metadata originating from Forensic Foto Frames 1–3

5   Application server (Business logic component)
Includes all the consolidation of data and metadata originating from Forensic Foto Frames 1–3
This model excludes any examples of business logic or rules that an organization might establish for collecting or processing data. The business logic component should, however, be completed if this was a production system. Basically the role of business logic may involve three basic layers, including the following:

Process logic: Logic that moves work between a series of stages or steps
Transaction logic: Processes data to move between the input of the transaction to the creation of a file
Data logic: This is the logic that derives, validates, or constrains data values which enforces operational policies

6   Application server (validation component)
Includes all the consolidation of data and metadata originating from Forensic Foto Frames 1–3
Should include steps for performing edit and validation (E&V) procedures on the data. For details on E&V criteria, refer to the "Key Controls for Reducing Insider Computer Fraud" spreadsheet

7   Application server (processing component)
Includes all the consolidation of data and metadata originating from Forensic Foto Frames 1–3
Based on the "Insider Loans Taxonomy—Key Fraud Indicators" document, the following calculations need to be performed based on the data and metadata collected from Forensic Foto Frames 1 (Insider) and 2 (General Public):

Performance ratios (metrics)

Loan portfolio
Average total loans and leases
Total loan and lease commitments

Earnings
Average total dollar earnings for all "insider" loans
Percent of average annual growth in interest and fees (all "insider" loans to average total loans)
Total percent of interest income on individual "insider" RE loans to total interest income on RE loans
Accrued but unpaid interest

(continued)

Table 9.4 Forensic Foto Frame (Data and Metadata Values for KFIs; Data Values of Both Bank Insiders and the General Public) (*Continued*)

Foto Frame	Data Name	Data Value	Metadata Name and Value	Comments
	Loss			
		Average total dollar value of net loss of all extensions of credit to all "insiders"		
		Total dollar amount of net loss for an individual "insider" loan		
		Percent of average annual growth rate of losses on all "insider" loans to average total loans		
		Total net loss of an individual "insider" installment loans		
		Total net loss of an individual "insider" RE loan		
		Total net loss of an individual "insider" commercial and industrial loan		
	Balance sheet			
		Average total dollar amount of all extensions of credit to "insiders"		
		Percent of average growth rate of all extensions of credit to "insiders" to average total loans		
	Past-due (30 to 60 days)			
		Average total dollar growth rate of "insiders" noncurrent loans and leases		
		Total PD amount of an individual "insider" loan		
		Percent of average "insider" PD loans to average total loans		
		Total PD "insider" installment loans		
		Total noncurrent "insider" RE loans		
		Total noncurrent "insider" commercial and industrial loans		
		Total noncurrent "insider" installment loans		
	Nonaccrual (90+ days)			
		Average total dollar amount of NA "insider" loans and leases		
		Total NA amount of an individual "insider" loan		
		Percent of "insider" NA loans to average total loans		
		Total NA "insider" installment loans and leases		

Total NA "insider" RE loans
Total NA "insider" commercial and industrial loans
Total NA "insider" I/L

(*Past-due, nonaccrual, and loss values will obviously not occur during the inception of a loan's origination, but may occur over time as the loan seasons and the insider or guarantor experiences either the financial inability/capacity or unwillingness to repay the outstanding debt.) Once nonperformance is evident in a loan, then the aforementioned calculations will be performed and used as a dataset for training and testing purposes for the novelty neural network. Additionally, the ratio calculations previously noted can serve as baseline performance metrics for use in developing KFSs or used as benchmarks for audit trail/journaling purposes (e.g., a single new loan creates an unusually large spike in one of the aforementioned ratios).

8 | Application server (XML parser)
Includes all the consolidation of data and metadata originating from Forensic Foto Frames 1–3
The XML parser will read and update, create, and manipulate an eXtensible Markup Language (XML) document (i.e., it provides the functionality of recognizing all the attribute start tags and end tags, listing of attributes, where attribute values can be enclosed in single or double quotes, minimal error checking, etc.).

9 | Application server (Log and audit management)
Includes all the consolidation of data and metadata originating from Forensic Foto Frames 1–3
Over time, when the novelty neural network is trained and tested and matures, journaling will function as an early warning device for misuse detection.

10 | Application server (security)
Includes all the consolidation of data and metadata originating from Forensic Foto Frames 1–3
All KFIs will be assigned Access Levels (1–3) that designate the appropriate provisioning level for that data/metadata attribute:

Access Level 1 (read only—loan officer)
Access Level 2 (write only—data entry personnel only)
Access Level 3 (read/write—supervisory loan officer)

(continued)

Table 9.4 Forensic Foto Frame (Data and Metadata Values for KFIs; Data Values of Both Bank Insiders and the General Public) (Continued)

Foto Frame	Data Name	Data Value	Metadata Name and Value	Comments
11	XML parser (misuse detection) XML-1	Parsing creates XML-1 (journaling dataset that "flags" unusual "data behavior" in KFIs) Includes all the consolidation of data and metadata originating from Forensic Foto Frames 1–3 Dataset collected for monitoring misuse detection on a "real-time" basis. Data journaling is based on misuse detection. Specifically, misuse detection will be based on negative application journaling (e.g., violations of the acceptable use policy—business rules, KFIs, and KFSs). "Data behavior" is considered abnormal during misuse detection. Normal behavior will be determined over time by the novelty neural network		
12	XML parser (anomaly detection) XML-2	Parsing creates XML-2 (novelty neural network training and testing dataset) Includes all the consolidation of data and metadata originating from Forensic Foto Frames 1–3 Data collected based on compliance with the acceptable use policy (e.g., normal usage) and reflects normal "behavior of data" as determined over time by the novelty neural network		
13	XML parser (KFSs) XML-3	Parsing creates XML-3 (KFSs) Includes all the consolidation of data and metadata originating from Forensic Foto Frames 1–3 Input into the development of KFSs is determined in three ways: Novelty neural network flags a KFI (e.g., a single or multiple data and metadata attribute) The data and metadata attributes that are flagged are transmitted and stored within the event correlation database Based on the key fraud signature rule set (KFSR, to be developed), the data and metadata attributes that were flagged by the novelty neural network will be analyzed against the criteria identified within the KFSR to determine whether the transaction has met the rules for an existing KFS or perhaps the creation of a new KFS		

14	XML-1 (calculations performed by the event correlation rules engine)
	Includes all the consolidation of data and metadata originating from Forensic Foto Frames 1–3
	If there were any calculations performed at this phase, then a Forensic Foto Frame should be taken, otherwise a Foto is not required (a snapshot of the data would have already been taken at the control point/gate 11)
15	XML-2 (Calculations performed by the Event Correlation Rules Engine)
	Includes all the consolidation of data and metadata originating from Forensic Foto Frames 1–3
	If there were any calculations performed at this phase, then a Forensic Foto Frame should be taken, otherwise a Foto is not required (a snapshot of the data would have already been taken at the control point/gate 12)
16	XML-3 (calculations performed by the event correlation rules engine)
	Includes all the consolidation of data and metadata originating from Forensic Foto Frames 1–3
	If there were any calculations performed at this phase, then a Forensic Foto Frame should be taken, otherwise a Foto is not required (a snapshot of the data would have already been taken at the control point/gate 13)
17	Novelty neural network ("novelty" data and metadata attributes)
	Includes all the consolidation of data and metadata originating from Forensic Foto Frames 1–3
	The "novelty" data and metadata attributes flagged by the neural network will be transmitted and stored within the event correlation database, where the calculations performed by the event correlation rules engine (Forensic Foto Frames 14–16) will be performed
18	XSLT spreadsheet
	Includes all the consolidation of data and metadata originating from Forensic Foto Frames 1–3
	Through the use of XSLT stylesheets, the selected XML data collected will be formatted and then transmitted to the XBRL software application for further processing and reporting
19	XSLT (optional—XBRL preprocessing)
	Includes all the consolidation of data and metadata originating from Forensic Foto Frames 1–3
	This Forensic Foto Frame is optional, if no additional data or metadata processing or calculations have been performed are the XSLT stylesheet processing phase

(continued)

Table 9.4 Forensic Foto Frame (Data and Metadata Values for KFIs; Data Values of Both Bank Insiders and the General Public) (*Continued*)

Foto Frame	Data Name	Data Value	Metadata Name and Value	Comments
20	XBRL (business reporting engine processing: G/L) Includes all the consolidation of data and metadata originating from Forensic Foto Frames 1–3 Based on any data calculations or formatting changes created from the XSLT stylesheets for business reporting purposes, calculations, or generation of any insider computer fraud reports			
21	XBRL (business reporting engine processing: business reports and insider computer fraud reports) Includes all the consolidation of data and metadata originating from Forensic Foto Frames 1–3 Based on any data calculations or formatting changes created from the XSLT stylesheets for business reporting purposes, calculations, or generation of any insider computer fraud reports			

Table 9.5 Analysis of Electronic Loan Data (Key Fraud Signature Candidate Preparation)

Data Analysis	Warning Signs	Potential Problems	Journaling Criteria
Reconcile download data to board reports, call report data, and institution's system-generated reports	A large discrepancy between the number and dollar amount of past-due and nonaccrual loans from the loan data download and information reported to the board of directors	There may be an attempt to conceal problem or fraudulent loans from board of directors	KFI candidate attributes (data and metadata) *Admin/sum data* Loss (all KFIs) PD (30 to 60 days) (all KFIs) Nonaccrual (90+) (all KFIs)
Analyze fields containing past-due loan counters by using search criteria to identify loans with chronic past-due loan histories	Loans with chronic past-due loan histories are reported as current and do not appear on the institution's problem loan list	An insider may be hiding problem or fraudulent loans by manually adjusting due dates or using proceeds from nominee loans to keep loans current and off management monitoring reports	KFI candidate attributes (data and metadata) *Admin/sum data* *Financial statements* FinData_SSN FinData_Borrower FinData_MatDt FinData_LoanBal_IL FinData_LoanBla_RE FinData_LoanBal_C&I FinData_AppOfficer FinData_Ln_Officer FinData_PolicyExc *Balance sheet* BS_TotAllInsiders BS_TotIndREBS_TotIndC&I BS_TotIndIL

(continued)

Table 9.5 Analysis of Electronic Loan Data (Key Fraud Signature Candidate Preparation) (*Continued*)

Data Analysis	Warning Signs	Potential Problems	Journaling Criteria
			Earnings
			Earn_Tot_LN
			Earn_Tot_Int&Fees_IL
			Earn_Tot_Int&Fees_RE
			Earn_Tot_Int&Fees_CI
			Loss (All KFIs)
			PD (30 to 60 days) (all KFIs)
			Nonaccrual (90+) (all KFIs)
			KFI candidate attributes (data and metadata)
			Admin/sum data
			Financial statements
Establish criteria to identify loans with multiple payment extensions	Loans with excessive number of payment extensions	A repayment source does not exist because the loan is to a nominee or is fraudulent	FinData_SSN
			FinData_Borrower
			FinData_PSOR
			FinData_MatDt
			FinData_LoanBal_IL
			FinData_LoanBla_RE
			FinData_LoanBal_C&I
			FinData_AppOfficer
			FinData_Ln_Officer
			FinData_PolicyExc

| Establish criteria to identify loans with multiple renewals and an outstanding loan balance that exceeds the original loan amount | Loans with excessive number of renewals and increasing loan balances | An insider may have created a fraudulent loan or may be receiving bribes or kickbacks from a borrower who cannot repay the loan; accrued interest may be capitalized | *Balance sheet*
BS_TotAllInsiders
BS_TotIndRE
BS_TotIndC&I
BS_TotIndIL

Earnings
Earn_Tot_LN
Earn_Tot_Int&Fees_IL
Earn_Tot_Int&Fees_RE
Earn_Tot_Int&Fees_CI

KFI candidate attributes (data and metadata)

Admin/sum data

Financial statements
FinData_SSN
FinData_Borrower
FinData_MatDt
FinData_LoanBal_IL
FinData_LoanBla_RE
FinData_LoanBal_C&I
FinData_AppOfficer
FinData_Ln_Officer
FinData_PolicyExc

Balance sheet
BS_TotAllInsiders
BS_TotIndRE
BS_TotIndC&I
BS_TotIndIL |

(continued)

Table 9.5 Analysis of Electronic Loan Data (Key Fraud Signature Candidate Preparation) (Continued)

Data Analysis	Warning Signs	Potential Problems	Journaling Criteria
			Earnings
			Earn_ABUI
			Earn_Tot_LN
			Earn_Tot_Int&Fees_IL
			Earn_Tot_Int&Fees_RE
			Earn_Tot_Int&Fees_CI
Identify loans with partial charge-offs	Loans with partial charge-offs that do not appear on the institution's problem loan list	These could be nominees of fraudulent loans where part of the balance was charged off to keep the loan balance below the minimum loan amount subject to routine review	KFI candidate attributes (data and metadata)
			Admin/sum data
			Financial statements
			FinData_SSN
			FinData_Borrower
			FinData_MatDt
			FinData_LoanBal_IL
			FinData_LoanBla_RE
			FinData_LoanBal_C&I
			FinData_AppOfficer
			FinData_Ln_Officer
			FinData_PolicyExc
			Balance sheet
			BS_TotAllInsiders
			BS_TotIndRE
			BS_TotIndC&I
			BS_TotIndIL

Determine reasonableness of accrued interest in relation to loan type, repayment terms, and payment status	Accrued interest is too high in relation to delinquency status	There may be an attempt to conceal problem or fraudulent loans by manually changing payment due dates	*Earnings* Earn_Tot_LN Earn_Tot_Int&Fees_IL Earn_Tot_Int&Fees_RE Earn_Tot_Int&Fees_CI *Loss (all KFIs)* *PD (30 to 60 days) (all KFIs)* *Nonaccrual (90+) (all KFIs)* *KFI candidate attributes (data and metadata)* *Admin/sum data* *Financial statements* FinData_SSN FinData_Borrower FinData_MatDt FinData_LoanBal_IL FinData_LoanBla_RE FinData_LoanBal_C&I FinData_AppOfficer FinData_Ln_Officer FinData_PolicyExc *Balance sheet* BS_TotAllInsiders BS_TotIndRE BS_TotIndC&I BS_TotIndIL

(continued)

Table 9.5 Analysis of Electronic Loan Data (Key Fraud Signature Candidate Preparation) (Continued)

Data Analysis	Warning Signs	Potential Problems	Journaling Criteria
			Earnings
			Earn_ABUI
			Earn_Tot_LN
			Earn_Tot_Int&Fees_IL
			Earn_Tot_Int&Fees_RE
			Earn_Tot_Int&Fees_CI
			Loss (all KFIs)
			PD (30 to 60 days) (all KFIs)
			Nonaccrual (90+) (all KFIs)
Establish criteria to identify loans significantly paid ahead	Paid ahead status is inconsistent with loan type and terms	There could be loans to a straw borrower or fraudulent loan	KFI candidate attributes (data and metadata)
			Admin/sum data
			Financial statements
			FinData_SSN
			FinData_Borrower
			FinData_MatDt
			FinData_LoanBal_IL
			FinData_LoanBla_RE
			FinData_LoanBal_C&I
			FinData_AppOfficer
			FinData_Ln_Officer
			FinData_PolicyExc

Identify loans to different borrowers with the same mailing address but different customer identification numbers

Multiple borrowers with the same mailing address and different customer identification numbers

There could be loans to a straw borrower or fraudulent loan

Balance sheet
BS_TotAllInsiders
BS_TotIndRE
BS_TotIndC&I
BS_TotIndIL

Earnings
Earn_ABUI
Earn_Tot_LN
Earn_Tot_Int&Fees_IL
Earn_Tot_Int&Fees_RE
Earn_Tot_Int&Fees_CI

Loss (all KFIs)
PD (30 to 60 days) (all KFIs)
Nonaccrual (90+) (all KFIs)

KFI candidate attributes (data and metadata)

Admin/sum data

Financial statements
FinData_SSN
FinData_Borrower
FinData_MatDt
FinData_LoanBal_IL
FinData_LoanBla_RE
FinData_LoanBal_C&I
FinData_AppOfficer
FinData_Ln_Officer
FinData_PolicyExc
FinData_POBox

(continued)

Table 9.5 Analysis of Electronic Loan Data (Key Fraud Signature Candidate Preparation) (Continued)

Data Analysis	Warning Signs	Potential Problems	Journaling Criteria
Identify loans to different borrowers with the same social security number or taxpayer identification number and different customer identification numbers	Different borrowers with identical social security or taxpayer identification numbers	This could indicate a fictitious borrower	KFI candidate attributes (data and metadata) *Admin/sum data* *Financial statements* FinData_SSN FinData_MatDt FinData_LoanBal_IL FinData_LoanBla_RE FinData_LoanBal_C&I FinData_AppOfficer FinData_Ln_Officer FinData_PolicyExc
Identify loans with similar names or forms of the same name. Also identify addresses that are similar or the same	Relationships exist that are not identified by social security numbers or addresses	This could indicate fictitious borrowers or undisclosed related borrowers	KFI candidate attributes (data and metadata) *Admin/sum data* *Financial statements* FinData_SSN FinData_Borrower FinData_MatDt FinData_LoanBal_IL FinData_LoanBla_RE FinData_LoanBal_C&I FinData_AppOfficer FinData_Ln_Officer FinData_PolicyExc

			KFI candidate attributes (data and metadata)
Generate a list of loans, by loan officer, with a post office box mailing address or hold mail notation	The financial institution is unable to contact or notify customer by mail	The borrower does not exist or borrower has no knowledge of loan. There could be a nominee or fictitious loan	*Admin/sum data* *Financial statements* 　FinData_SSN 　FinData_MatDt 　FinData_LoanBal_IL 　FinData_LoanBla_RE 　FinData_LoanBal_C&I 　FinData_AppOfficer 　FinData_Ln_Officer 　FinData_PolicyExc 　FinData_POBox
Identify loans by loan officers who may have been terminated or left the institution	These accounts may not be grouped by loan officer and monitored for activity	Possible kiting of payments from one account to another. Borrowers may not exist	*KFI candidate attributes (data and metadata)* *Admin/sum data* *Financial statements* 　FinData_SSN 　FinData_MatDt 　FinData_LoanBal_IL 　FinData_LoanBla_RE 　FinData_LoanBal_C&I 　FinData_AppOfficer 　FinData_Ln_Officer 　FinData_PolicyExc 　FinData_BorrowerNW 　FinData_TAFinData_TL 　FinData_PortfolioValue

(continued)

Table 9.5 Analysis of Electronic Loan Data (Key Fraud Signature Candidate Preparation) (Continued)

Data Analysis	Warning Signs	Potential Problems	Journaling Criteria

Identify loans that are associated with a loan officer who has a substantial portfolio or whose portfolio has experienced rapid growth	Senior management and subordinates may not question the loan officer due to high production or profitability of the portfolio	Loans could be fictitious	KFI candidate attributes (data and metadata)
			
			Admin/sum data
			
			Financial statements
			  FinData_SSN
			  FinData_PortfolioValue
			  FinData_LoanBal_IL
			  FinData_LoanBla_RE
			  FinData_LoanBal_C&I
			  FinData_AppOfficer
			  FinData_Ln_Officer
			  FinData_PolicyExc
			  FinData_BorrowerNW
			  FinData_TAFinData_TL

If the institution recently raised additional capital, determine if insider loans or total loans increased substantially around the same time	A significant increase in loan originations occurring on or about the date the institution received capital funding	These could be insider or shareholder loans granted to fund stock purchases	KFI candidate attributes (data and metadata)
			
			Admin/sum data
			
			Financial statements
			  FinData_SSN
			  FinData_MatDt
			  FinData_LoanBal_IL
			  FinData_LoanBla_RE
			  FinData_LoanBal_C&I
			  FinData_AppOfficer

| Identify loans with compara-bly low interest rates | Preferential interest rates | There could be low interest rates used to minimize cash flow required to service a fraudulent loan | FinData_Ln_Officer
FinData_PolicyExc
FinData_BorrowerNW
FinData_TAFinData_TL

Balance sheet
BS_TotAllInsiders
BS_TotIndRE
BS_TotIndC&I
BS_TotIndIL

Earnings
Earn_Tot_LN
Earn_Tot_Int&Fees_IL
Earn_Tot_Int&Fees_RE
Earn_Tot_Int&Fees_CI

KFI candidate attributes (data and metadata)

Admin/sum data

Financial statements
FinData_SSN
FinData_MatDt
FinData_LoanBal_IL
FinData_LoanBla_RE
FinData_LoanBal_C&I
FinData_AppOfficer
FinData_Ln_Officer
FinData_PolicyExc
FinData_FICO |

(continued)

Table 9.5 Analysis of Electronic Loan Data (Key Fraud Signature Candidate Preparation) (*Continued*)

Data Analysis	Warning Signs	Potential Problems	Journaling Criteria
			FinData_Collateral
			FinData_Repay
			Earnings
			Earn_Tot_LN
			Earn_Tot_Int&Fees_IL
			Earn_Tot_Int&Fees_RE
			Earn_Tot_Int&Fees_CI

Board Minutes and Board Report

Warning Signs	Potential Problems	Ways to Detect	Journaling Criteria
An institution changes loan review personnel or firm without apparent valid reasons	Frequent changes in loan review personnel may prevent them from becoming familiar enough with the institution's lending practices to identify insider schemes. Also, they may be close to uncovering an insider loan fraud and have been dismissed for this reason	Review board, audit committee, or loan committee minutes. Engage in discussions with management and employees	Manual check

			KFI attributes (data and metadata)

An insider inappropriately suggests or resists changes in appraisers	Collusion between the insider and the appraiser to falsify appraisals	Review board minutes. Engage in discussions with management and employees	*Admin/sum data*
			
			Financial statements
			   FinData_SSN
			   FinData_LTV
			
			Earnings
			   Earn_Tot_LN
			   Earn_Tot_Int&Fees_IL
			   Earn_Tot_Int&Fees_RE
			   Earn_Tot_Int&Fees_CI

Insider receives compensation receives compensation based on incentives of bonuses based on new loan volumes without compensating controls	To maximize compensation, insider may camouflage poor quality loans with forged, altered, or fraudulent documents, or originate loans to fictitious borrowers	Review board minutes and compensation plans. Engage in discussions with management	KFI candidate attributes (data and metadata)
			
			Admin/sum data
			
			Financial statements
			   FinData_SSN
			   FinData_MatDt
			   FinData_LoanBal_IL
			   FinData_LoanBla_RE
			   FinData_LoanBal_C&I
			   FinData_AppOfficer
			   FinData_Ln_Officer
			   FinData_PolicyExc
			   FinData_FICO
			   FinData_Collateral
			   FinData_Repay

(continued)

Table 9.5 Analysis of Electronic Loan Data (Key Fraud Signature Candidate Preparation) (Continued)

Warning Signs	Potential Problems	Ways to Detect	Journaling Criteria
			Balance sheet
			BS_TotAllInsiders
			BS_TotIndRE
			BS_TotIndC&I
			BS_TotIndIL
			Earnings
			Earn_Tot_LN
			Earn_Tot_Int&Fees_IL
			Earn_Tot_Int&Fees_RE
			Earn_Tot_Int&Fees_CI
			Loss (all KFIs)
			PD (30 to 60 days) (all KFIs)
			Nonaccrual (90+) (all KFIs)
The insider is a defendant in a lawsuit alleging improper handling of a transaction	A particular insider may be prone to engage in dishonest or unethical behavior	Review board minutes and litigation summaries	Manual check
A past-due loan report does not include an itemized list of past-due loans	An attempt to conceal identity of delinquent borrowers to avoid board scrutiny	Compare board reports to system-generated and departmental reports	KFI candidate attributes (data and metadata)
			Admin/sum data
			Financial statements
			FinData_SSN
			FinData_MatDt
			FinData_LoanBal_IL

Insider's loans appear on past-due loan reports

FinData_LoanBla_RE
FinData_LoanBal_C&I
FinData_AppOfficer
FinData_Ln_Officer
FinData_PolicyExc
FinData_FICO
FinData_Collateral
FinData_Repay

Loss (all KFIs)
PD (30 to 60 days) (all KFIs)
Nonaccrual (90+) (all KFIs)

An insider's financial condition may be strained and provide a motive to engage in loan fraud

Review board and system-generated reports

KFI candidate attributes (data and metadata)

Admin/sum data

Financial statements
FinData_SSN
FinData_MatDt
FinData_LoanBal_IL
FinData_LoanBla_RE
FinData_LoanBal_C&I
FinData_AppOfficer
FinData_Ln_Officer
FinData_PolicyExc
FinData_FICO
FinData_Collateral
FinData_Repay

(continued)

Table 9.5 Analysis of Electronic Loan Data (Key Fraud Signature Candidate Preparation) (Continued)

Warning Signs	Potential Problems	Ways to Detect	Journaling Criteria
			FinData_BorrowerNW
			FinData_PSOR
			Earnings
			Earn_ABUI
			Earn_Tot_LN
			Earn_Tot_Int&Fees_IL
			Earn_Tot_Int&Fees_RE
			Earn_Tot_Int&Fees_CI
			Loss (all KFIs)
			PD (30 to 60 days) (all KFIs)
			Nonaccrual (90+) (all KFIs)
			KFI candidate attributes (data and metadata)
			Admin/sum data
			Financial statements
			FinData_SSN
			FinData_MatDt
			FinData_LoanBal_IL
			FinData_LoanBla_RE
			FinData_LoanBal_C&I
			FinData_AppOfficer
			FinData_Ln_Officer
			FinData_PolicyExc
Delinquent loans to insiders are omitted from a past-due loan report	Loans may be omitted to conceal insiders' strained financial positions and avoid board scrutiny	Compare board reports to system-generated and departmental reports	

FinData_FICO
FinData_Collateral
FinData_Repay
FinData_BorrowerNW
FinData_PSOR

Earnings
Earn_ABUI
Earn_Tot_LN
Earn_Tot_Int&Fees_IL
Earn_Tot_Int&Fees_RE
Earn_Tot_Int&Fees_CI

Loss (all KFIs)

PD (30 to 60 days) (all KFIs)

Nonaccrual (90+) (all KFIs)

KFI candidate attributes
(data and metadata)

Admin/sum data

Financial statements
FinData_SSN
FinData_MatDt
FinData_LoanBal_IL
FinData_LoanBla_RE
FinData_LoanBal_C&I
FinData_AppOfficer
FinData_Ln_Officer
FinData_PolicyExc

Nonaccrual (90+) (all KFIs)

(continued)

Review board reports and request supporting detail or internal institution work papers

Insider attempting to conceal charged-off fraudulent loans

The board does not receive an itemized list of charged-off loans

Table 9.5   Analysis of Electronic Loan Data (Key Fraud Signature Candidate Preparation)   (Continued)

Warning Signs	Potential Problems	Ways to Detect	Journaling Criteria
New loan report provided to the board does not reconcile to that generated from the loan system	All new loans are not being reported to the board	Review board and system-generated reports for differences	Manual check
Report providing a list of loans made as exceptions to policy is not provided	Inadequate monitoring of policy exceptions	Review board reports and discuss the existence of policy exceptions with examiners reviewing loan file	KFI candidate attributes (data and metadata) *Admin/sum data* *Financial statements* FinData_SSN FinData_MatDt FinData_LoanBal_IL FinData_LoanBla_RE FinData_LoanBal_C&I FinData_AppOfficer FinData_Ln_Officer FinData_PolicyExc
An insider appears to receive special favors from borrowers or shows unusual favoritism toward certain customers	An insider may be involved in a kickback scheme where loans are granted in exchange for personal benefits or cash	Engage in discussions with employees. Observe employee and officer behavior	Manual check
An insider will not allow employees to talk to examiners about loans	Employees may have knowledge of irregular loan transactions	Insist on sufficient verifiable objective information to resolve discrepancies	Manual check

(continued)

		Engage in informal discussions with employees, if possible	Manual check
A dominant insider exerts influence or intimidates without restraint	An insider with this level of control can force alteration of institution records to his or her benefit	Engage in informal discussions with employees to the extent possible. Review board and committee minutes and comparative departmental records for inconsistencies	Manual check
High turnover of lending personnel	Might signify working conditions or ethical compromises that employees are unwilling to accept	Engage in discussions with employees. Review personnel records	Manual check
An insider's lifestyle is inconsistent with income	Insider may be booking fictitious loans or involved in a kickback scheme	Engage in discussions with employees. Review insider's financial statements, income tax returns, and credit reports	Manual check
Disregard for or significant disagreement with regulatory authorities	Insider may be trying to discourage or impede in-depth review of institution records	Review prior exam reports. Arrange discussions with management and examiners. Insist on corroborating information for management's views	Manual check

Table 9.5 Analysis of Electronic Loan Data (Key Fraud Signature Candidate Preparation) (Continued)

Warning Signs	Potential Problems	Ways to Detect	Journaling Criteria
An insider dictates that different loan departments are audited at different times	An insider attempting to control access to records, which gives him or her the ability to shift and manipulate data to cover loan fraud	Engage in discussions with internal audit staff. Review internal audit schedule. Review records of loan transfers or sales near the time an audit is scheduled to start	Manual check
Insider frequently takes loan papers out of the institution for customer signature, personally handles disbursements of loan proceeds, routinely cashes loan proceeds checks for borrower, and insists on personally handling certain past-due accounts	Indicates possible existence of fictitious loans and insider manipulation of loan status to hide irregularities	Engage in discussions with employees. Conduct an internal control review	Manual check
An insider involved in undisclosed silent trusts, partnerships, or shell corporations that borrow from the institution	Loan purpose or insider's involvement is concealed to circumvent institution's legal lending limits	Engage in discussions with employees. Search for undisclosed related interests in state incorporation records and investments listed on the insider's financial statement. Review the insider's financial statements and those of any	KFI candidate attributes (data and metadata) *Admin/sum data* *Financial statements* FinData_SSN FinData_MatDt FinData_LoanBal_IL FinData_LoanBla_RE

Scenario	Potential issue	Detection procedure	KFI candidate attributes
(continued from previous page)		undisclosed related interest for intercompany borrowings. Conduct a loan file review	FinData_LoanBal_C&I FinData_AppOfficer FinData_Ln_Officer FinData_PolicyExc FinData_BorrowerNW FinData_TAFinData_TL
An insider lending personal funds to or borrowing from customers, which may or may not be disclosed on insider's or borrower's financial statement	An insider may have violated a fiduciary duty by placing his or her own interest above that of the financial institution. An insider may be applying borrowed funds to conceal fraudulent loans	Engage in discussions with employees. Review customers' financial statements	KFI candidate attributes (data and metadata) *Admin/sum data* *Financial statements* FinData_SSN FinData_MatDt FinData_AppOfficer FinData_Ln_Officer FinData_PolicyExc FinData_TA FinData_TL FinData_Collateral FinData_BorrowerNW FinData_PSOR
An insider purchases assets from customers	An insider may extend preferential treatment to a customer in exchange for kickbacks or a reciprocal arrangement	Engage in discussions with employees. Review insider's financial statements and loan files	KFI candidate attributes (data and metadata) *Admin/sum data* *Financial statements* FinData_SSN FinData_MatDt FinData_LoanBal_IL

(continued)

Table 9.5   Analysis of Electronic Loan Data (Key Fraud Signature Candidate Preparation) (*Continued*)

Warning Signs	Potential Problems	Ways to Detect	Journaling Criteria
			FinData_LoanBla_RE
			FinData_LoanBal_C&I
			FinData_AppOfficer
			FinData_Ln_Officer
			FinData_PolicyExc
			FinData_FICO
			FinData_Collateral
			FinData_Repay
			FinData_BorrowerNW
			FinData_PSOR
An insider refuses to fully answer questions or provide relevant records	An insider could be concealing information relevant to uncovering lending irregularities	Conduct discussions with insider and examiners	Manual check
An insider making payments on a customer's loan	Nominee, straw borrower, or fictitious borrower	Engage in discussions with employees. Trace loan payments and original loan proceeds	Manual check
An insider is responsible for resolving loan confirmation exceptions	An insider can conceal exceptions and fraudulent loans	Engage in discussions with employees. Consider conducting loan confirmation as part of the examination	Manual check

			KFI candidate attributes (data and metadata)
Insider has access to both the loan system and the general ledger system. Insider has control over both loan receipts and disbursements and the recording of these transactions	Insider can divert loan payments/proceeds or post/alter institution records	Determine whether there is proper segregation of duties. Review user profiles for the various information systems to determine if insiders have access to system not needed to perform their daily function	Manual check

Insider and Borrower Financial Statement Analysis

An insider's financial statement discloses significant indebtedness in relation to disclosed income sources. There may also be a poor credit score	An insider may have motive to commit loan fraud	Review the insider's financial statements, credit reports, income tax returns. Obtain compensation information for human resources	*Admin/sum data* *Financial statements* FinData_SSN FinData_MatDt FinData_LoanBal_IL FinData_LoanBla_RE FinData_LoanBal_C&I FinData_AppOfficer FinData_Ln_Officer FinData_PolicyExc FinData_FICO FinData_Collateral FinData_Repay FinData_BorrowerNW FinData_PSOR *Balance sheet* BS_TotAllInsiders

(continued)

Table 9.5 Analysis of Electronic Loan Data (Key Fraud Signature Candidate Preparation) *(Continued)*

Warning Signs	Potential Problems	Ways to Detect	Journaling Criteria
			BS_TotIndRE
			BS_TotIndC&I
			BS_TotIndIL
			Earnings
			Earn_Tot_LN
			Earn_Tot_Int&Fees_IL
			Earn_Tot_Int&Fees_RE
			Earn_Tot_Int&Fees_CI
An insider's financial statements show large or unusual fluctuations. Net worth cannot be reconciled with disclosed sources	An insider may have financial difficulties and be motivated to engage in fraudulent lending activities	Review the insider's financial statements	KFI candidate attributes (data and metadata)
			Admin/sum data
			Financial statements
			FinData_SSN
			FinData_MatDt
			FinData_LoanBal_IL
			FinData_LoanBla_RE
			FinData_LoanBal_C&I
			FinData_AppOfficer
			FinData_Ln_Officer
			FinData_PolicyExc
			FinData_FICO
			FinData_Collateral
			FinData_Repay

Rapidly appreciating assets not supported with independent valuations

An insider knowingly accepting unreliable financial information in order to grant loan approval. There may be financial incentive or reciprocal favors

Review financial statements

FinData_BorrowerNW
FinData_TA
FinData_TL
FinData_PSOR

KFI candidate attributes (data and metadata)

Admin/sum data

Financial statements
FinData_SSN
FinData_MatDt
FinData_LoanBal_IL
FinData_LoanBla_RE
FinData_LoanBal_C&I
FinData_AppOfficer
FinData_Ln_Officer
FinData_PolicyExc
FinData_FICO
FinData_Collateral
FinData_Repay
FinData_BorrowerNW
FinData_PSOR
FinData_TA
FinData_TL
FinData_BorrowerNW
FinData_LTV
FinData_IntRate
FinData_Mat_Dt

(continued)

Table 9.5 Analysis of Electronic Loan Data (Key Fraud Signature Candidate Preparation) (Continued)

Warning Signs	Potential Problems	Ways to Detect	Journaling Criteria

Commingling of business assets on personal financial statement without disclosure of business liabilities	An insider knowingly accepting unreliable financial information in order to grant loan approval. Financial incentives or reciprocal favors may be involved	Review financial statements	KFI candidate attributes (data and metadata)
			
			Admin/sum data
			
			Financial statements
			  FinData_SSN
			  FinData_MatDt
			  FinData_LoanBal_IL
			  FinData_LoanBla_RE
			  FinData_LoanBal_C&I
			  FinData_AppOfficer
			  FinData_Ln_Officer
			  FinData_PolicyExc
			  FinData_FICO
			  FinData_Collateral
			  FinData_Repay
			  FinData_BorrowerNW
			  FinData_PSOR
			  FinData_TA
			  FinData_TL

A financial statement fails to disclose debts reported on credit bureau report	An insider knowingly accepting unreliable financial information in order to grant loan approval. Financial incentives or reciprocal favors may be involved	Review financial statements and compare to the credit report	KFI candidate attributes (data and metadata) *Admin/sum data* *Financial statements* FinData_SSN

Undisclosed contingent liabilities such as personal quarantine of debt to a related interest	Insider may be unable to service debt to the institution if required to repay related interest's debt	Review financial statements	FinData_MatDt FinData_LoanBal_IL FinData_LoanBla_RE FinData_LoanBal_C&I FinData_AppOfficer FinData_Ln_Officer FinData_PolicyExc FinData_FICO FinData_Collateral FinData_Repay FinData_BorrowerNW FinData_PSOR

KFI candidate attributes (data and metadata)

Admin/sum data

Financial statements

FinData_SSN
FinData_MatDt
FinData_LoanBal_IL
FinData_LoanBla_RE
FinData_LoanBal_C&I
FinData_AppOfficer
FinData_Ln_Officer
FinData_PolicyExc
FinData_FICO
FinData_Collateral
FinData_Repay

(continued)

Table 9.5 Analysis of Electronic Loan Data (Key Fraud Signature Candidate Preparation) (*Continued*)

Warning Signs	Potential Problems	Ways to Detect	Journaling Criteria
			FinData_BorrowerNW
			FinData_PSOR
			Loss (all KFIs)
			PD (30 to 60 days) (all KFIs)
			NA (90+) (all KFIs)
An insider's related interest is not disclosed or reported	Circumvention of an institution's legal lending limits. Masking of true financial condition	Review financial statements	KFI candidate attributes (data and metadata)
			Admin/sum data
			Financial statements
			FinData_SSN
			FinData_MatDt
			FinData_LoanBal_IL
			FinData_LoanBla_RE
			FinData_LoanBal_C&I
			FinData_AppOfficer
			FinData_Ln_Officer
			FinData_PolicyExc
			FinData_Collateral
			FinData_Repay
			FinData_BorrowerNW
			FinData_TAFinData_TL

Loan files are missing	Borrowers do not exist; loans are to fictitious borrowers or nominees	Employees are unable to provide loan file requested by examiners	Manual check
An insider conceals noncompliance with lending policies, guidelines from management and the board, regulatory policies, or violations of laws	An insider is involved in kickback or a fraudulent loan scheme. Blackmail may be involved	Loan file review	KFI candidate attributes (data and metadata) *Admin/sum data* *Financial statements* FinData_SSN FinData_MatDt FinData_AppOfficer FinData_Ln_Officer FinData_PolicyExc FinData_Collateral FinData_Repay FinData_BorrowerNW FinData_TAFinData_TL
The loan amount exceeds loan officer's lending authority	An insider attempting to conceal a questionable or fraudulent loan, policy exceptions, or legal lending limit violation	Review loan file, loan approval form, and lending authorities	KFI candidate attributes (data and metadata) *Admin/sum data* *Financial statements* FinData_SSN FinData_MatDt FinData_AppOfficer FinData_Ln_Officer FinData_PolicyExc FinData_Collateral

(continued)

Table 9.5 Analysis of Electronic Loan Data (Key Fraud Signature Candidate Preparation) (*Continued*)

Warning Signs	Potential Problems	Ways to Detect	Journaling Criteria
			FinData_Repay FinData_BorrowerNW FinData_TAFinData_TL
Loan terms are different from terms approved by loan committee or board of directors	Fraudulent transaction	Loan file review. Compare loan documents to loan approval form or board/loan committee minutes	Manual check
Collateral inspections or valuations are missing	Collateral is inadequate or does not exist	Employees unable to provide the required information at the examiner's request. Conduct a loan file review	Manual check
Documents used to verify borrower's identification are missing	Loan is to a nominee or straw borrower	Employees unable to provide the required information at the examiner's request. Conduct a loan file review	Manual check
An insider keeps "shadow" files or omits certain documents from loan files reviewed by examiners	An insider attempting to conceal documentation, underwriting, or collateral problems. Loan transaction may be fraudulent	Conduct a loan file review. Engage in discussions with employees	Manual check
Insider maintains signed, blank notes in personal or customer loan files	Documents may be used for fictitious loans	Conduct a loan file review. Engage in discussions with employees	Manual check

			KFI candidate attributes (data and metadata)
Insider's loans do not comply with lending policies and exceptions are not authorized	Insider circumvents controls to receive preferential treatment of prohibited transaction	Review loan file, loan approval form, and board and loan committee minutes	*Admin/sum data* *Financial statements* FinData_SSN FinData_MatDt FinData_LoanBal_IL FinData_LoanBla_RE FinData_LoanBal_C&I FinData_AppOfficer FinData_Ln_Officer FinData_PolicyExc FinData_FICO FinData_Collateral FinData_Repay FinData_BorrowerNW FinData_PSOR
Insider loans with unusual or preferential terms, interest rates, or collateral	Insider collusion involving possible kickbacks, bribes, or other fraudulent schemes	Review loan files, loan approval form, and board and loan committee minutes	*Admin/sum data* *Financial statements* FinData_SSN FinData_MatDt FinData_LoanBal_IL FinData_LoanBla_RE FinData_LoanBal_C&I FinData_AppOfficer

(continued)

Table 9.5 Analysis of Electronic Loan Data (Key Fraud Signature Candidate Preparation) (Continued)

Warning Signs	Potential Problems	Ways to Detect	Journaling Criteria
			FinData_Ln_Officer FinData_PolicyExc FinData_FICO FinData_Collateral FinData_Repay FinData_BorrowerNW FinData_PSOR
Appraisals for insiders' loans contain deficiencies or values appear overstated and are not adequately supported	An insider influencing an appraiser to conceal inadequate collateral position. This may involve a kickback scheme	Review appraisal report and appraisal regulations	KFI candidate attributes (data and metadata) *Admin/sum data* *Financial statements* FinData_SSN FinData_AppOfficer FinData_Ln_Officer FinData_PolicyExc FinData_Collateral FinData_LTV
Purpose of loan is not recorded or proceeds are not used for stated purpose	Purpose does not comply with lending policies or violates the law. True purpose may be to pay accrued interest on other loans to borrower	Review loan file, payment history, and paid loan disbursement checks. Trace loan proceeds	KFI candidate attributes (data and metadata) *Admin/sum data* *Financial statements* FinData_SSN FinData_AppOfficer

			FinData_Ln_Officer FinData_PolicyExc FinData_Collateral FinData_Purpose
Insider makes or approves loans to him- or herself, family members, or related interests	Self-dealing. Concealment of loans that do not meet policy guidelines. Violation of code of conduct	Review loan file and loan approval form	KFI candidate attributes (data and metadata) *Admin/sum data* *Financial statements* FinData_SSN FinData_AppOfficer FinData_Ln_Officer FinData_PolicyExc FinData_Collateral FinData_Purpose FinData_TA FinData_TL FinData_BorrowerNW
Insider loans not approved by the board or board committee	Self-dealing. Fraudulent loan transaction	Review loan file and loan approval form	Manual check
Loan funded prior to approval	Fraudulent loan transaction	Review loan file. Compare date of loan proceeds check to date loan was booked and loan approval date. Debit to loans in process or suspense account for amount of loan proceeds	Manual check

(continued)

Table 9.5 Analysis of Electronic Loan Data (Key Fraud Signature Candidate Preparation) (Continued)

Warning Signs	Potential Problems	Ways to Detect	Journaling Criteria
Loan documents appear altered or forged	An insider knowingly accepting or preparing forged or falsified documents	Compare loan documents to minutes	Manual check

Credit reports with no or very limited credit history and absence of letters from landlords, utility companies, etc., stating satisfactory payment record. Earnings statements appeared altered	Fraudulent transaction. Borrower's true credit history may be concealed by using fictitious social security number to generate credit report. Forged letters and forged earnings statements	Credit history is inconsistent with borrower's financial information. Various loan files contain similar documents	KFI candidate attributes (data and metadata)
			
			Admin/sum data
			
			Financial statements
			  FinData_SSN
			  FinData_AppOfficer
			  FinData_Ln_Officer
			  FinData_PolicyExc
			  FinData_Collateral
			  FinData_Purpose
			  FinData_FICO

Files without documentation to identify how loans were funded, such as official checks, deposit tickets, funding sheet, etc.	True beneficiary of funds may be hidden	Trace loan funds as described in Appendix D	Manual check
Borrower's financial statements are prepared by an insider	False information used as basis for loan decision	Verify with information provided by borrower/compare to credit reports	KFI candidate attributes (data and metadata) *Admin/sum data*

Internal Reports and Accounting Records

				Financial statements
Loan disbursement checks are presented for payment before loan is booked	Insider using loan proceeds for personal benefit, hiding problem loans, or lending limit violation	Review loan disbursement account reconcilements. Compare new loan report with loan check register	Manual check	FinData_SSN FinData_AppOfficer FinData_Ln_Officer FinData_PolicyExc FinData_Collateral FinData_Purpose FinData_FICO
Insiders or related interests have frequent overdrafts or appear in suspense account item listings	Insider having financial difficulties and motive to commit fraud	Review overdraft reports, suspense items, and suspense account reconcilements	Manual check	
Adversely classified loan paid off or paid down just prior to or during the examination	Insider attempting to conceal fraudulent loans	Compare previously classified or problem balance to current balance	Manual check	
An insider loan is paid off prior to or during the examination	Insider attempts to conceal lending limit violations, delinquency or fraudulent loans	Review recently paid off insider loans		KFI candidate attributes (data and metadata) *Admin/sum data* *Financial statements* FinData_SSN FinData_MatDt

(continued)

Table 9.5 Analysis of Electronic Loan Data (Key Fraud Signature Candidate Preparation) (Continued)

Warning Signs	Potential Problems	Ways to Detect	Journaling Criteria
			FinData_LoanBal_IL
			FinData_LoanBla_RE
			FinData_LoanBal_C&I
			FinData_AppOfficer
			FinData_Ln_Officer
			FinData_PolicyExc
			FinData_FICO
			FinData_Collateral
			FinData_Repay
			FinData_BorrowerNW
			FinData_PSOR
			Balance sheet
			BS_TotAllInsiders
			BS_TotIndRE
			BS_TotIndC&I
			BS_TotIndIL
			Earnings
			Earn_Tot_LN
			Earn_Tot_Int&Fees_IL
			Earn_Tot_Int&Fees_RE
			Earn_Tot_Int&Fees_CI
Customer loan proceeds disbursed by wire transfers to institution secrecy haven countries	Loan proceeds not used to stated purpose. Fraudulent transaction	Review wire transfer activity	Manual check

High level of loan losses	Charge-off of fraudulent loans. A loan officer directed by senior officer or director to grant loans that normally would be declined. There could be financial incentives or reciprocal benefits involved	Review charged-off loan files and payment histories. Be alert to an unusual level of charge-offs resulting from loans originated by a particular loan officer	KFI candidate attributes (data and metadata) *Admin/sum data* *Financial statements* FinData_SSN FinData_MatDt FinData_LoanBal_IL FinData_LoanBla_RE FinData_LoanBal_C&I FinData_AppOfficer FinData_Ln_Officer FinData_PolicyExc *Loss (all KFIs)*
No review of inactive or dormant accounts	Insider using dormant or inactive accounts for fraudulent lending activities. Possible use of customer information to generate fictitious loans could be involved	Review dormant and inactive account reports. Cross check with loan trials to determine if a large number of dormant account holders also have loans	Manual check
Cash disbursement of loan proceeds	Insider receiving kickbacks or bribes	Internal control review. Copies of transaction tickets in loan file should trigger further research. Trace loan proceeds, if appropriate	Manual check

(continued)

Table 9.5 Analysis of Electronic Loan Data (Key Fraud Signature Candidate Preparation) (Continued)

Warning Signs	Potential Problems	Ways to Detect	Journaling Criteria
Insider changes loan payment due dates, renews loans, or grants loan extensions	Conceal delinquent or fraudulent loans	Loan file system maintenance reports	KFI candidate attributes (data and metadata)
			Admin/sum data
			Financial statements
			FinData_SSN
			FinData_MatDt
			FinData_AppOfficer
			FinData_Ln_Officer
			FinData_PolicyExc
			FinData_Repay
			Earnings
			Earn_Tot_LN
			Earn_Tot_Int&Fees_IL
			Earn_Tot_Int&Fees_RE
			Earn_Tot_Int&Fees_CI
Internal debits/credits (noncash transactions) posted to insider or customer's loan/deposit accounts	Fraudulent transactions. Insider receiving kickbacks from loan customer or embezzling loan proceeds or funds from deposit accounts	Review deposit and loan account histories for noncash transaction codes. Trace transactions	Manual check
Rapid loan growth	May be partially attributable to fraudulent lending transactions	Comparative analysis of balance sheet accounts	KFI candidate attributes (data and metadata)
			Admin/sum data
			Financial statements

No reconciliation of loans-in-process and disbursement accounts	Fraudulent loan activity may be processed within these accounts	Perform reconciliations of these accounts	Manual check	FinData_SSN FinData_MatDt FinData_LoanBal_IL FinData_LoanBla_RE FinData_LoanBal_C&I FinData_AppOfficer FinData_Ln_Officer FinData_PolicyExc FinData_FICO FinData_Collateral FinData_Repay FinData_BorrowerNW FinData_PSOR *Balance sheet* BS_TotAllInsiders BS_TotIndRE BS_TotIndC&I BS_TotIndIL *Earnings* Earn_Tot_LN Earn_Tot_Int&Fees_IL Earn_Tot_Int&Fees_RE Earn_Tot_Int&Fees_CI

Source: From Federal Financial Institution Examination Council (FFIEC), Insider Detection, Investigation, and Prevention of Insider Loan Fraud: A White Paper, Produced for the FFIEC Fraud Investigations Symposium, October 20–November 1, 2002. (With permission.)

9.3   Conclusion

This chapter highlights the following points:

- The KFS selection process is initially more of an art rather than a science and will need the benefit of time and experience for users to more fully gain from the benefits of its use.
- KFIs are used within an application to detect suspicious insider misuse and fraudulent activity.
- KFMs are key ratios calculated from the KFIs to detect suspicious activity.
- KFSs are association rules for KFIs and KFMs and involve several key phases, which include the following:
  - Asset risk prioritization
  - Data criticality
  - Taxonomy (macro) of ICF
  - Taxonomy (micro) of ICF
  - KFSAR process
- Novelties detected from the neural network will change the significance of KFS.

Chapter 10

Application and System Journaling and the Software Engineering Process

10.1   Introduction

The goal of this chapter is to introduce the importance of application and system journaling within the software engineering process. A few of the most important highlights of this chapter are as follows:

- The Defense in Depth Framework
- Journaling and computer forensics
- The current state of software engineering industry, standards, and application journaling best practices
- The current research on logging and fraud detection

10.2 Selection Strategies for Application and System Journaling for the Software Engineering Process

10.2.1 Overview

Given the primary focus of this research being on insider computer fraud (ICF) activities, the focus of the attention on this topic should be at the application security level. However, network journaling and operating system journaling should also have equal time, particularly if the enterprise operates within a Web services environment. Reflected in Figure 10.1 in a macro perspective is how journaling can be integrated into the overall information technology (IT) infrastructure.

A Service Oriented Architecture that includes the application server and, more specifically, the log and audit management module is shown in Figure 10.1.

Now focusing in on the application server and the log and audit management module, displayed in Figure 10.1, we can now see at a macro level the interrelationships and the importance of maintaining sound journaling via the log and audit management module.

Again, we can see the importance of identifying valid key fraud indicators (KFIs), key fraud metrics (KFM), and key fraud signatures (KFSs) that will be journaled, and the importance of this activity in serving as both a preventive and detective deterrent within this Defense in Depth Framework.

To elaborate further on the Defense in Depth Framework, equally as important to ICF activities are data monitoring activities as compared to the previously discussed data journaling process. Each function adds another layer to our overall ICF controls framework, and together, both offer different levels of protection for the detection and prevention of suspicious ICF activities.

10.2.2 Data Monitoring

Monitoring involves observing data flows involving specific events, unlike the actual recording of those same events through the journaling process. Typically, the term "monitoring" is associated with the real-time analysis activity, customarily performed on the network, for example, conducting packet sniffing. Data monitoring is as close to ICF prevention as we will discuss in this research. The majority of the paper is primarily focused on ICF detection. This focus on ICF detection versus prevention was done by design given the current state of the industry in developing technical solutions in this space, as compared to network solutions, which are more mature and beginning to evolve from intrusion detection systems (IDS) versus intrusion prevention systems (IPS).

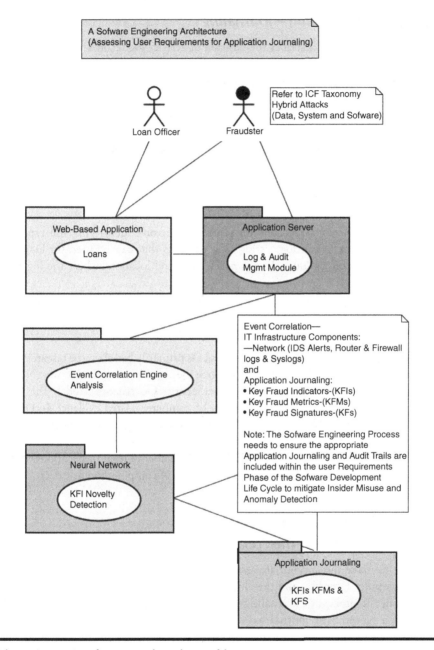

Figure 10.1   A software engineering architecture.

10.2.3 Introduction—Journaling

The term "journaling" describes the creation of activity log records and the capture of key information about all security-relevant information technology (IT) systems. Journaling is not considered a real-time activity, but rather an after-the-fact analysis of a transaction and data. Typically, such activities include the capture of the following information:

- Date and time of activity, actions taken, and users involved.
- Successful and unsuccessful log-on and log-off activity.
- Successful and unsuccessful accesses to security-related files and directories.
- Denial of access to excessive failed log-ons.

The important considerations for journaling involve identifying the types of information that you can log, various mechanisms that can be used for logging, locations where the log journaling is performed, and locations where the log files are stored.

10.2.4 Introduction—Computer Forensics

The following discussion of computer forensics is primarily based on the research and writing from this author's 2003 Master's degree thesis at New York University (NYU) entitled, The Computer Forensics and CyberSecurity Governance Model. The term "computer forensics" involves the discovery of computer-related evidence and data. Computer forensics is commonly used by law enforcement, the intelligence community, and the military. There are many technical implications involving the identification and collection of data, along with an equal number of legal implications in the identification, collection, preservation, and analysis of computer forensic data.

10.2.5 Journaling and Computer Forensics—Interrelationships

In order to make the appropriate associations, the parent process behind journaling is computer forensics, and the child of this process is computer journaling. By definition, the process of journaling (logging) is to record selected events as they occur in a system. The journal basically contains all of the transaction information, including the contents of the data elements that will be changed. Journaling also provides management the ability to restore the system in the event of failure, based on the last checkpoint. For our purposes, what is critical to the journaling process is the selection of which information is determined to be most important to a forensic examination in the event of a suspected unauthorized intrusion and perhaps criminal activity. The determination of evidentiary data to be collected and journaled should include, at minimum, the following functions: legal, law enforcement, regulatory personnel, senior management, and audit.

10.2.6 Computer Forensics/Journaling and Computer Incident Response (Interrelationships)

The concepts of computer forensics, journaling, and computer incident response team (CIRT) processes are all inextricably linked together. Specifically, computer forensics is the science behind the collection and analysis of computer journaling and other evidence, and journaling is the practice of capturing key data for security monitoring and during a computer forensics examination, if ICF activity arises. When a suspected problem does arise, then the CIRT processes are activated to ensure the survivability of the organization and to determine a root cause.

Journaling is the heart and soul of computer forensics and represents the evidentiary data that will aid those involved in the investigatory process in conducting a root cause analysis and investigation. Given the high level of importance of journaling and its direct relationship to computer forensics, there are obviously legal implications in the collection, handling, and analysis of this information that will only be briefly introduced in this section. The following legal discussion is not intended to capture all the legal implications of journaling and its role within computer forensics, but is rather an introduction to a few legal implications of journaling and where it fits in describing evidence. It is important to note that an organization develops comprehensive CIRT policies and procedures that map the connections between CIRT processes, computer forensics, and journaling. Specifically, the aforementioned policy and standards should address the journaling requirements and recommend journaling as part of the evidentiary data collection requirement for assessing the existence of hacking and other computer crime (for example, fraud, money laundering, embezzlement, or other misuse of the system).

Under the federal rules of evidence, computer output such as automated journals logging is admissible in both civil and criminal proceedings, provided the documentation is regularly kept on a timely basis, performed as a regularly conducted business activity, and the court determines the preparation is considered trustworthy. Management needs to ensure that journaling produced from information systems be recoverable in the event the contents are partially or totally lost in a system crash or through human error or by malicious intent (e.g., hacker).

Audit logs need to be stored in a secure place where attackers will not have access to the files. Following are a few ways to ensure protection of the logs:

- Setting the logical protection on the audit log so that only privileged users have write access.
- Storing the audit log to another computer dedicated to storing audit logs where no one has access to the machine.

The following discussion will not provide every aspect of all the legal aspects surrounding the collection of evidentiary data; however, it will introduce the topic and its objective from a high-level governance perspective. Legal involvement is critical at this phase of the process, supported by formal training for those individuals involved in the computer forensics process.

An individual's failure to understand the types of evidence, rules of evidence, the exclusionary rule, the hearsay rule, chain of evidence, admissibility of evidence, collection and identification, storage, preservation, and transportation may result in the evidence being inadmissible in a court of law and could result in civil law issues (e.g., defamation, threats or harassment, wrongful termination, etc.).

10.2.6.1 Types of Evidence

- *Direct*: This category of evidence is basically oral testimony given by an individual to either validate or dispute a given fact. The source of direct evidence is any of an individual's five senses (e.g., observing the physical location of computer equipment at the alleged crime).
- *Real*: This category of evidence is made up of tangible objects (e.g., the computer and storage media used during an alleged crime).
- *Documentary*: This category of evidence is tangible (e.g., computer printouts). It is important to note that the actual printout of data is considered hearsay evidence, because it is only evidence of the original evidence, which is the original data element stored within the computer. For additional details on documentation evidence, refer to the best evidence and hearsay rules noted below.
- *Demonstrative*: This category of evidence is created to illustrate or further support criminal activity (e.g., a flowchart that graphically illustrates how a computer fraud occurred).
- *Best Evidence Rule*: As previously described, documentary evidence, although admissible in a court of law, does not comply with the best evidence rule, which prefers the original evidence and not a copy.
- *The Exclusionary Rule*: Any violation of the search and seizure mandated by the courts and detailed within the "Searching and Seizing Computers and Obtaining Electronic Evidence in Criminal Investigations" dated January 2001 is a violation of the Fourth Amendment, and any evidence obtained is considered nonadmissible in a court of law. Individuals, investigators, and CIRT team members must be in compliance with the civil liberties granted under the Electronic Communications Privacy Act (ECPA), which is commonly referred to as the Privacy Act.
- *The Hearsay Rule*: Documentary evidence is considered secondhand evidence and therefore falls under the hearsay rule because there is no firsthand proof that the evidence is accurate, reliable, and trustworthy, and it is therefore not admissible as legally acceptable evidence in a court of law. An exception

to the hearsay rule would include audit logs, e-mails, system performance results, and other regularly conducted activity.

■ *Chain of Evidence*: Once evidence is obtained through search and seizure, there needs to be accountability and protection of the information. Specifically, under the chain of evidence rule, there must be documented evidence that shows who obtained the evidence, who secured the evidence, and who had control or possession of the evidence.

■ *Admissibility of Evidence*: Adequate precautions must be taken to ensure that computer-generated evidence has not been tampered with, erased, or added to, and that only relevant and reliable evidence will be entered into a court of law. Documentary evidence, such as computer-generated evidence (that is, journaling), if determined to meet the requirements of the business record exemption to the hearsay rule, and not be discounted due to a technicality and follow the chain of custody requirement, will be considered as admissible evidence. The admissibility of evidence in a court of law requires that the evidence be competent, relevant, and material.

■ *Collection and Identification*: Ensuring evidence integrity is a crucial part of the computer forensic and legal process. In brief, the process for marking evidence should include, at minimum, marking the actual piece of evidence without destroying the evidence or placing it in a container and then marking and sealing it with evidence tape. For further details on the collection and identification of evidence, it is recommended that further reading within the 2001 "Searching and Seizing Computer and Obtaining Electronic Evidence in Criminal Investigations" by the U.S. Department of Justice be considered. Additionally, further discussion on this topic can be found within the Incident Response (Seizing Electronic Evidence) section below, as noted within item number four.

■ *Storage, Preservation, and Transportation*: If evidence is not properly packed and preserved to prevent contamination against extreme environmental conditions, then the individual or entity could be held liable for damages.

There is currently no industry standard that can serve as a basis for evaluating what journaling criteria are needed in applications to ICF activities. There also is an absence of any universal logging format standard to capture the data to be used for other purposes, such as determining a root cause analysis from data ascertained from the application or through the use of event correlation software. Although this statement may appear quite alarming at first, the reality of the matter is that journaling within many home-grown applications and perhaps purchased commercial off-the-shelf (COTS) software packages have not undergone an initial application information security risk assessment. The initial application security risk assessment is the nucleus for all the other steps involved in the process of determining what journaling is necessary to evaluate suspected ICF activities, particularly involving hybrid ICF activities relating to system misuse and data manipulation to perpetrate ICF activities.

Unfortunately, most applications, once they have gone into production, are rarely risk assessed again from either a functionality evaluation or from an information systems security perspective, unless problems arise from those applications while in production. Despite the fact that most applications developed in-house in many organizations receive programmatic modifications, patches, and upgrades, over a period of time, they rarely ever are looked at again, particularly from a journaling assessment vantage point. There are many applications that are designed to have the front-end controls at the operating system level, then once a user gains legitimate access into the network, the user basically has the "keys to the kingdom" within an application. This situation becomes problematic given the fact that most organizations have probably not evaluated even their operating system's configuration settings to determine if they in fact have any access control vulnerabilities that could be maliciously exploited by an insider fraudster. The ICF journaling workflow diagram will provide a straightforward approach to steps needed to be taken to ensure that application journaling criteria to detect insider ICF are being initially considered and continually reevaluated through the risk assessment process.

10.2.6.2   Compliance Control

There are many organizations that require some level of compliance control within their software development processes and may include the following three areas: auditability, regulatory, compliance, etc.). Unfortunately, based on the research conducted for this book, there appeared no substantive discussion on best practices for the marketplace to consider for journaling standards and criteria that should be considered within the software development life cycle (SDLC). Furthermore, there is no single industry standard relative to a standardized journaling format that can be universally used within applications, which is also problematic, if management of organizations wishes to tackle the ICF problem.

10.2.7   Current Research on Logging and Fraud Detection

Based on research conducted by Emilie Lundin Barse from Chalmers University of Technology, School of Computer Science and Engineering, Sweden, the importance of logging for intrusion and fraud detection is discussed. Specifically, the research states the following:

> Logging or data collection is done for different reasons in computer systems or services. Many systems have logging for accounting purposes. In particular, services where fraud detection is needed have logging for billing purposes. Systems may also have some kind of logging to monitor

the status of the system, i.e., whether it is running normally or there are problems. Logging for intrusion and fraud detection can make use of all kinds of log sources, e.g., network traffic and system calls for intrusion detection and call data records in detection of telecom fraud. Those sources can provide signs of Logging for intrusion and fraud detection, suspicious user actions, give information that clarifies the nature of the user actions, the identity or location of the user, or any other useful information about the intrusion or fraud. A few working definitions used in this thesis that are related to logging are presented below.

Application-based logging: Application-based logging requires instrumentation of the source code of the application. Some applications have basic built-in log data generation, such as logging of http requests on web servers. Any application can be the target of an attack and may generate useful log data. Web servers are especially often attacked and have been the subject of application-based detection.

In addition, some applications can intercept events that are of importance in many other applications. For example, user commands logged by a command interpreter (shell) are useful for the detection of a large range of attacks. I look below at the advantages and disadvantages of application-based logging.

Application-based logging is high-level logging, which means that we get the application's interpretation of the event.

It is possible to adapt the logged information and get the pieces of information that are most important for detection.

It is difficult and costly to implement useful logging in all applications.[1]

10.2.8 The Federal Financial Institution Examination Council (FFIEC)

Based on FFIEC regulatory guidance, an institution's ongoing security risk assessment process should evaluate the adequacy of the system logging and the type of information collected. Security policies should address the proper handling and analysis of log files. Institutions have to make risk-based decisions on where and when to log activity. Although logging activity is important information for all IT infrastructure components, the discussion within this document will be primarily focused on application journaling.

Based on FFIEC guidance, the following data are typically logged to some extent, including the following:

■ Inbound and outbound Internet traffic
■ Internal network traffic
■ Firewall events
■ IDS events
■ Network and host performance
■ Operating system access (especially high-level administrative or root access)
■ Application access (especially users and objects with write-and-executive privileges)
■ Remote access

10.2.9   General Criteria for Journaling/Audit Trails

It is not practical or an efficient use of time for security personnel and audit to have every user activity logged from an InfoSec and computer forensic perspective. Listed below are a few criteria to evaluate when determining what should be included in an audit trail:

■ Does the audit trail provide for accountability by providing a trace of user actions?
■ Can the audit trail record information that would add value within an intrusion detection investigation (e.g., type of event, when the event occurred, the user identification [UID] associated with the event, and the program or command used to initiate the event)?

According to NIST 800-18 Guide for Developing Security Plans for Information Technology Systems, dated December 1998, keystroke monitoring is the process used to view or record both the keystrokes entered by a computer user and the computer's response during an interactive session. Keystroke monitoring is usually considered a special case of audit trails. The Department of Justice has advised that an ambiguity in U.S. law makes it unclear whether keystroke monitoring is considered equivalent to an unauthorized telephone wiretap. If keystroke monitoring is used in audit trails, organizations should have a written policy and notify users. The rules of behavior may be one vehicle for distributing the information. If keystroke monitoring is used, provide references to the policy and the means of notification. Also indicate whether the Department of Justice has reviewed the policy.[2]

For additional background information concerning journaling, refer to Federal Information Processing Standards (FIPS) 73, June 1980, "Guidelines for Security of Computer Applications." Also refer to NIST 800-18 Guide for Developing Security Plans for Information Technology Systems, December 1998.

10.2.10 The National Industrial Security Program Operating Manual (NISPOM)

NISPOM sets the standards for protection of classified information. Covered under NISPOM are all commercial contractors who have access to classified information. Within Chapter 8 of NISPOM, information system security requirements are spelled out, particularly as relates to audit capabilities.

Listed below are the highlights of Chapter 8, which has relevance to both the public sector for those who have access to classified information as well as to those in private sector organizations who have access to critical information, who could also stand to benefit from NISPOM processes and practices.

10.2.10.1 8-602, Audit Capability

Security auditing involves recognizing, recording, storing, and analyzing information related to security-relevant activities. The audit records can be used to determine which activities occurred and which user or process was responsible for them.

10.2.10.2 Audit 1 Requirements

1. *Automated Audit Trail Creation*: The system shall automatically create and maintain an audit trail or log. (On a PL-1 system only: In the event that the operating system cannot provide an automated audit capability, an alternative method of accountability for user activities on the system shall be developed and documented.) Audit records shall be created to record the following:
   a. Enough information to determine the date and time of action (e.g., common network time), the system locale of the action, the system entity that initiated or completed the action, the resources involved, and the action involved.
   b. Successful and unsuccessful log-ons and log-offs.
   c. Successful and unsuccessful accesses to security-relevant objects and directories, including creation, open, close, modification, and deletion.
   d. Changes in user authenticators.
   e. The blocking or blacklisting of a user ID, terminal, or access port and the reason for the action.
   f. Denial of access resulting from an excessive number of unsuccessful log-on attempts.
2. *Audit Trail Protection*: The contents of audit trails shall be protected against unauthorized access, modification, or deletion.
3. *Audit Trail Analysis*: Audit analysis and reporting shall be scheduled and performed. Security-relevant events shall be documented and reported. The frequency of the review shall be at least weekly and shall be documented in the SSP.

4. *Audit Record Retention*: Audit records shall be retained for at least one review cycle or as required by the CSA (Cognizant Security Agency).

10.2.10.3 Audit 2 Requirements

In addition to Audit 1,

Individual accountability (i.e., unique identification of each user and association of that identity with all auditable actions taken by that individual). Periodic testing by the ISSO or ISSM of the security posture of the IS.

10.2.10.4 Audit 3 Requirements

In addition to Audit 2,

Automated Audit Analysis: Audit analysis and reporting using automated tools shall be scheduled and performed.

10.2.10.5 Audit 4 Requirements

In addition to Audit 3,

An audit trail, created and maintained by the IS, that is capable of recording changes to mechanism's list of user formal access permissions.[3]

10.2.11 Journaling: Web Servers

Forensic data should include the following documentation. Request supporting documentation from corporate senior management or a security professional, which may include the following data relating to Web servers:

■ Server log and system audit files.
■ Access list for Web server log files: The Web application can write Web server log files, but log files cannot be read by the Web server application. Analyze the documentation provided to ensure that only root/system administrative-level processes can read Web server log files.
■ DoS attacks: Determine that Web content resides on a different hard drive or logical partition from the operating system and Web application.
■ Log files are stored in an appropriately sized storage location to protect against attackers seeking to fill the file system on the Web server host operating system with extraneous and incorrect information to cause the system to crash.

- Location of Web server log files and configuration files.
- Web server log files and configuration files should reside outside the specified file directory tree for public consumption.
- Web server file directory listings are disabled.
- The Web server host operating system access controls need to ensure that the Web application can write Web server log files, but log files cannot be read by the Web server application.
- Temporary files created by the Web server application are restricted to a specified and protected subdirectory.
- Ensure the public Web site does not contain sensitive and classified data (e.g., personal information about personnel of the corporation, financial records, copyright material, security policies, etc.).
- Encryption is used to protect data transmitted between a Web browser client and a public Web server.
- Ensure the Web server architecture has the Web server external to the firewall from a security standpoint to isolate and protect the internal network from DoS attacks.
- Ensure application layer firewalls (commonly referred to as application-proxy gateway firewalls) are used to ensure the firewall permits no traffic directly between the Internet and the internal network.
- IDS tools are used to detect port scanning probes, DoS, and to log events.
- Web server backups occur incrementally on a daily basis, with full backups weekly.
- Use of third-party software for auditing purposes: www.rsasecurity.com/products/securid/techspecs/apache.html.

Based on the CERT publication, "Securing Public Web Servers."[4] The following comments are noted:

- You may need Web server logs to:
  - Alert you to suspicious activity that requires further investigation.
  - Determine the extent of an intruder's activity.
  - Help you to recover your systems.
  - Help you to conduct an investigation.
  - Provide information required for legal proceedings.
- Identify the Web server software information to be logged.
- Four different logs may exist:
  - *Transfer Log*: Each transfer is represented as one entry showing the main information related to the transfer (see below).
  - *Error Log*: Each error is represented as one entry including some explanation of the reason for this error report.

- *Agent Log*: If this log is available, it contains information about the user client software used in accessing your Web content.
- *Referer Log*: If this log is available, it collects information relevant to Hypertext Transfer Protocol (HTTP) access. This includes the universal resource locator (URL) of the page that contained the link that the user client software followed to initiate the access to your Web page.

■ Several log formats are available for transfer log entries. Typically, the information is presented in plain ASCII without special delimiters to separate the different fields:

- *Common Log Format (CLF)*: This format stores the following information related to one transfer (Transfer Log) in the indicated order:
  - ■ Remote host
  - ■ Remote user identity in accordance with RFC 1413
  - ■ Authenticated user in accordance with the basic authentication scheme
  - ■ Date
  - ■ URL requested
  - ■ Status of the request
  - ■ Number of bytes actually transferred

10.2.12   Journaling: Network Security

There is no single source which provides a roadmap for determining network security journaling requirements. The primary determinants for what should or should not be the primary factors for establishing a journaling criteria for each component of the IT infrastructure should be from the risk assessment, the threat assessment, the Privacy Impact Assessment (PIA), and the regulatory landscape.

10.2.13   Firewalls

Journaling for firewalls may include the following:

- ■ Hardware and disk media errors
- ■ Log-in/log-out activity
- ■ Connect time
- ■ Use of systems administrator (SA) privileges
- ■ Inbound and outbound e-mail traffic
- ■ Transmission Control Protocol (TCP) network connect attempts
- ■ Inbound and outbound proxy traffic type

10.2.14 *Journaling: Operating Systems (UNIX)*

The purpose of this section is not to cover every flavor of UNIX and for the auditing and InfoSec professional and law enforcement official to have intimate knowledge of the UNIX operating system as does a SA, but rather focus on the key logging tools that may be of value in a computer forensics examination.

Forensic data should include the following documentation. Request supporting documentation from corporate senior management or a security professional, which may include the following data relating to the UNIX operating system:

- *Log Root*: Direct log-in as "root" should be restricted and controlled. Logging of all root access should be turned on. Where feasible, root access shold be secured via cryptographic techniques or authentication toke (e.g., SecurID).
- *Modify Field*: Uncomment and modify the "CONSOLE=/dev/console" entry in /etc/default/login to be "CONSOLE=" (Solaris). By having a null field, direct root access is not allowed from any device, including the console.
- *Log Console Message*: Standard logging for console messages should be enabled. Unsuccessful log-in attempts should be logged and reviewed.
- *Solaris—Log-In Attempts*: On Solaris, the file /var/adm/loginlog needs to be created to enable logging of all log-in attempts.
- *Solaris—Su Attempts*: On Solaris, for *su* logging, verify that the SULOG entry in /etc/default/su is uncommented to enable logging of all *su* attempts in /var/adm/sulog. Uncomment the CONSOLE entry to display the detailed *su* attempts to the console in addition to the logging to the sulog.
- *Inspect Log*: Inspect system log and console message files for activity of note (/var/adm/messages*).
- *UNIX*: UNIX-based routers should log to a security system via Syslog.
- *Fingerd*: Display information about users (e.g., UID, home directory and log-in shell, time last logged in, last received, etc.).

10.2.15 *System Logs*

- Use of a TCP wrapper daemon that logs all requests for selected network services (Syslog)
- /usr/adm/lastlog (records last log-in by each user)

Can list for any user using *finger* command:

- /etc/utmp (records who is currently logged in)
- Can list with the *who* command
- /usr/adm/wtmp (records log-ins, log-outs, shutdown, boot)
- /usr/adm/sulog (records *su* attempts)

10.2.16 Journaling: Operating Systems (NT)

The native auditing features within Windows NT are limited, and third-party software is necessary (e.g., http://somarsoft.com). SomarSoft's DumpSec is a security auditing program for MS NT, which dumps the permissions and audit settings for the file systems, registry, and printers, and shares the information in a listbox format.

The purpose of this section is not to cover the entire security governing Windows NT, but rather to focus on the key logging tools that may be of value in a computer forensics examination:

- Forensic data should include certain documentation. Request supporting documentation from corporate senior management or a security professional.
  - Listed below is a recap of the Audit Event Table as prescribed by the National Security Agency (NSA), within their "NSA Windows NT Security Guidelines" as found at www.trustedsystems.com.

10.2.17 Journaling: Mainframe (ACF2)

Access Control Facility 2 (ACF2) is a Computer Associates International software product that provides centralized discretionary access control while allowing distribution of control to individual users or groups of users. CA-ACF2 provides security for the OS/390 and virtual machine (VM) business transaction environments, including UNIX system services.

Forensic data should include supporting documentation from corporate senior management or security professionals, which may include the following data relating to ACF2. The list of various logs produced by ACF2 as noted below does not represent every viewable log within ACF2, and consultation with the systems administrator and security professional is recommended. Log descriptions are as follows:

- ACFRPTXR: The ACF2 Cross Reference Report was created for auditors, security administrators, and management to identify which users could access which datasets and resources.
- ACFRPTIX: The ACF2 Dataset Index Report identifies all changes to the access rules affecting any specified high-level index (or pattern) over any period of time, assuming the input SMF records are available. This report is usually produced by request only, and is potentially very useful to auditors.
- ACFRPTDS: This report shows the following information about all violation attempts:
  - Dataset that received the violation
  - Task the user was trying to accomplish

- The Log-inID and UserID
- Name of the user
■ ACFRPTRV: This report shows the following information about all violation attempts:
  - Resource that received the violation
  - Task the user was trying to accomplish
  - The Log-inID and UserID
  - Name of the user
■ ACFRPTPW: The ACF2 Invalid Password/Authority Log contains an entry for each denial, for any reason, of an attempt to access the system, and the reason for each denial.
■ ACFRPTLL: The ACF2 LogonID Modification Log contains an entry for each occurrence of an update to the ACF2 LogonID database. Updates include changed, inserted, or deleted records.
■ ACFRPTRL: The ACF2 Rule-ID Modification Log has an entry for each change, addition, or deletion of any access rule record.
■ ACFRPTSL: The ACF2 selected LogonID List allows you to select almost any combination of users and display their LogonID information.

10.2.18 ICF Journaling Workflow Diagram and Descriptions

Based on the prior background describing the journaling process as related to various components of an enterprise's IT infrastructure, we can now focus on the journaling process specifically related to ICF activities. In the following paragraphs, an attempt is made to provide a framework that will allow IT professionals to design an application or system that will incorporate the steps outlined in this chapter within their software engineering process. Attribute selection for journaling for most applications is inadequate and excludes key criteria or consideration for evaluating risks involved in the detection of either internal or external fraud.

Although there may be variations to this framework in terms of the means by which the journaling attributes are selected, the final goal of selecting effective and risk-based data and metadata attributes to detect ICF activities should be the same. As a note of caution, any journaling activity within an application needs to be selected very judiciously because of the potential performance impact on the application.

Specifically, let us now focus on the ICF journaling workflow diagram (Figure 10.2), along with the corresponding descriptions:

1. *Risk Assessment*: The application/system risk assessment process is discussed in Chapter 7. However, suffice it to state at this point that it represents the nucleus of the ICF journaling workflow and decision-making process relative to what attributes should be considered for journaling. For details on the application risk assessment criteria, refer to the spreadsheets found in Chapter 7.

2. *Macro Taxonomy*: The macro taxonomy has already been prepared and reflects the ICF general categories of data, system, and software (Table 10.1).

3. *Micro Taxonomy*: The micro taxonomy (Table 10.2) should take one component of the macro taxonomy to decompose to its functional primitive state for selecting KFIs and KFMs to journal and for training and testing the neural network. Using the insider loan sample, the micro taxonomy would be isolated to data manipulation, which was the primary focus of this research and writing.

4. *KFI Taxonomy*: This is the next step involved in the decomposition process. Basically, a particular area (i.e., insider loan fraud) is considered and the risk is isolated down to specific KFIs that will, in effect, be used for monitoring and data capture journaling and other purposes (Figure 8.3)

5. *KFI Selection*: Based on Figure 8.3, a risk analysis will have to be performed to determine the relative importance of each of these categories in relation to each other to determine which KFIs represent the best "early warning" of suspected ICF activities.

6. *KFM Selection*: Based on Figure 8.3, after selecting the KFIs, which are denoted in red, a decision should also be made relative to which KFMs would be considered the best "early warning" of suspected ICF activities. The KFMs selected should ideally correspond to or have some relationship to the KFIs selected. For example, if the KFIs pertain to earnings generated from loans, then the KFMs selected should also have some relationship to earnings generated from loans. The marriage between attributes (KFI and KFM) will make a stronger association, when using these attributes to make up the dataset used for training and testing the neural network and for evaluation by the event correlation software for assessing the root cause of a suspected misuse or network breach.

7. *KFS Selection*: As noted within the Pinnacle ICF Fraud diagram (Figure 9.1), selecting the KFS is the last step in the KFI and KFM selection process. (Refer to Chapter 9 for more details.)

8. *Neural Network Dataset Selection*: The dataset used for training and testing the neural network should closely resemble the KFI and KFM data and metadata attributes used for journaling purposes. The consistency between the journaling and the neural network training criteria will facilitate better communication and adjustment of testing and journaling results between all layers of the Defense in Depth Model. For example, if the neural network does not produce KFIs and KFMs that are also being journaled individually

or included as a KFS, then adjustments will need to be made to reflect this new reality.

9. *Event Correlation Dataset*: As noted in the Figure 1.1, the Defense in Depth Layer 3 involves the integration and use of an event correlation software. There should also be a close alignment between the attributes (KFI, KFM, and KFS) data flow that is being collected and analyzed between each layer of the Defense in Depth framework.

Finally, as illustrated in Figure 1.1, the last leg of the journey from the event correlation dataset selection is an arrow pointing back to the risk assessment process, where the ICF journaling workflow process began. The inclusion of the risk assessment component of this process to serve double duty was done intentionally to ensure pre- and post-ICF journaling workflow risks are identified, captured, and adjusted where appropriate to continually evolve the risk assessment process.

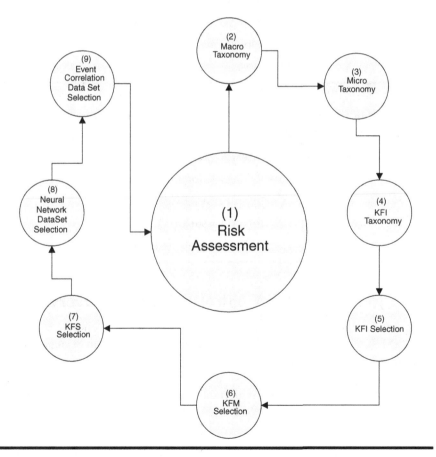

Figure 10.2 Insider computer fraud journaling workflow diagram.

Table 10.1   Insider Computer Fraud Taxonomy

	Ontological Category (parent)	Ontological Category (child)	
Genesis	Data	Data input manipulation	*Hybrid ICF*
		Data destruction	
	System	Misuse of system capabilities (authorized users)	
		Hardware destruction or damage	
		Access control misuse	
		Hacking (unauthorized user)	
		Unauthorized system access through the fraudulent use of ex-employees	
	Software	Code manipulation	
		Logic bomb	
		Malcode injection	
		Trojan horse	

Table 10.2   Micro Taxonomy of Insider Computer Fraud— Bank Insider Loan Fraud

Data Manipulation	Insert	Falsified data
		Nominee loan name
		Improper use of loan proceeds
		Integrity issues
		Preferential rate and term for loan

10.3   Journaling Risk/Controls Matrix (An Overview)

As a practical illustration of a few of the previously discussed concepts contained within this section, the insider loan fraud example will continue to be used to illustrate how to apply these concepts.

Before we go through the process for creating and analyzing the journaling risk/controls matrix (JRCM), it is important to first review the metadata taxonomy and extraction process that was used to develop the numerous variations of KFI contained within this matrix. Developing a taxonomy of metadata was a challenging process given the absence of clear guidelines over its creation. Based on my research and what I felt were key areas that should be journaled, I developed my own metadata taxonomy that covers the basics of what I feel are important attributes to journal and to use in developing the dataset for training and testing the novelty neural network.

10.4 Metadata

Based on the premise of modeling the behavior of data involved in a particular transaction, over time an organization will quickly establish a profile of a particular individual ("know your customer"), and will also be able to establish a profile of that individual's transactions, including the data and metadata associated with a representative transaction. Using the framework of this ICF Model, the ability to profile the normal behavioral characteristics of transactions and their values will become quickly apparent through the capture of key data and metadata values for training and testing the novelty neural network. Based on the associative memory of a novelty neural network, anomalies in data and metadata values will be flagged. For example, under regulation "O" for bank loans to senior executive officers and members of the board of directors, the insider at a bank cannot receive a loan under preferential rates and terms.

10.5 A Taxonomy of Metadata

There are approximately 10 different sources of metadata that can be selected as potential KFI candidates. The type of metadata selection should relate directly to the prior completion of a detailed taxonomy and data flow diagram as previously discussed. The taxonomy of metadata below includes a brief description and criteria for what could be included within this category and is not intended to provide an unabridged list of every possible element for each of these categories.

Based on the metadata taxonomy noted below (Figure 10.3—"The Metadata Element Description"), I then performed a metadata extraction that basically established a standardized logging criteria for Forensic Foto Frames. (Refer to the "ICF Service Oriented Diagram"—Figure 4.1).

Dictionaries **XBRL Schemas**	• Standard Naming Convention • Standard Customer Information • Version Control

Reporting **Instructions**	• Unique Data Name • Line Number • Line Description • Version Control • General Instructions • Schedule Instructions • Line-by-Line Instructions (i.e. include and exclude) • Version Control • Technical (Format) • Accuracy (Mathematical) • Business (Comparisons & Relationships) • Provides Standard Error Messages & Exceptions, Classifications, and Remarks • Built-in Properties (Title, Author, Company) • Document Statistics (Creation Date, Last Save Time, Time Last Printed, Last Saved By, Revision Number, Total Edit Time) • Custom Document Properties • Last 10 Authors • Version • Track Changes • Fast Saves • Hidden Text • Comments • Graphics • Hyperlinks • Document Variables • Smart Tags

• Hardware and Software Documentation
• Tracking of System Response Times
• Authentication and Security Data (e.g., Encryption keys, passwords)

Data Access Rules	• Defining who can use an object • An access list of who can view the object • A condition of use statement that might be displayed before access to the object is allowed • Definition of permitted uses of an object

Business Rules	• Linkage or relationship between data
	• Reporting Basis
	• Averaging Techniques
	• Growth Rates
	• Annualization rates
	• Income derivation
	• Merger adjustments
	• Tax-equivalency adjustment
	• Data parsing, ensuring controls exists to mitigate the risks associated with:
	  ▪ Ensuring the information in a field matches its MetaData profile
	  ▪ "Misfielded" data – Data that are placed in the wrong field, such as name data in an address field

Figure 10.3 The metadata element description.

- Floating data—Customer data that may be contained in different fields from record to record, resulting in data "floating" between fields
- Extraneous information—Data that may contain irrelevant or blank fields
- Atypical words—Records that may include multicultural and hyphenated names, unusual titles, abbreviated business names, industry specific acronyms
- Inconsistent structures and formats—Operation, purchased, and exchanged data sources that may be formatted differently from each other or from the data warehouse

Provenance	• Data defining sources of origin of some content object, for example the location of some physical artifact from which the content was scanned. • Summary of algorithmic transformations that have been applied to the object (filtering, decimation, etc.)
Graphics	• The number of embedded objects within a file or document (This excludes any files created from the MS Office Suite)
Preservation	• Metadata related to the preservation management of information resources • Documentation of physical condition of resources • Documentation of actions taken to preserve physical and digital versions of resources (e.g., data refreshing and migration)
Descriptive	• Metadata used to describe or identify information resources • Cataloging records • Finding aids • Specialized indexes • Hyperlinked relationships between resources • Annotations by users
Administration	• Recordkeeping systems generated by records creators • Audit trails created by recordkeeping systems • Version control and differentiation between similar information objects • Documentation of legal access requirements • Rights and reproduction tracking
Web Services	• Description of what other endpoints need to know to interact with them • WS-Policy describes the capabilities, requirements, and general characteristics of Web service • WSDL describes abstract message operations, concrete network protocols • Endpoint addresses used by Web services • XML Schema describes the structure and contents of XML-based messages received by and sent by Web services

Figure 10.3   The metadata element description (continued)

10.5.1   Metadata Extraction (Standardized Logging Criteria for Forensic Foto Frames)

1. Administration/summary data:
   a. The number of metadata elements in each Forensic Foto Frame
   b. Author
   c. Author e-mail

    d. Data owner/maintainer

    e. Description

    f. Name of approving officer

    g. Attribute name, author, date, time, and frequency of TOTAL data object CREATIONS

    h. Attribute name, author, date, time, and frequency of TOTAL data object ACCESSES

    i. Attribute name, author, date, time, and frequency of TOTAL data object DELETIONS

    j. Attribute name, author, date, time, and frequency of TOTAL data object ADDITIONS

    k. Attribute name, author, date, time, and frequency of TOTAL data object MODIFICATIONS

    l. Attribute name, author, date, time, and frequency and TOTAL VIOLATIONS OF DATA ACCESS RULES

    m. Attribute name, author, date, time, and frequency and TOTAL number of embedded graphics (objects) creation, additions, and deletions

    n. TOTAL of algorithmic transformations (i.e., calculations)

2. Frame statistics:

    a. Creation date

    b. Creation time

    c. Last save time

    d. Revision number

    e. Total edit time (minutes)

3. Data access rules violations (access Level 1: read only—loan officer; access Level 2: write only—data entry personnel only; access Level 3: read/write—supervisory loan officer):

    a. Social security number

    b. Name of borrower

    c. Total portfolio value by loan officer

    d. P.O. box address

    e. Policy exceptions

    f. Loan purpose

    g. Name of approving officer

    h. Total assets

    i. Total liabilities

    j. Borrower net worth

    k. Collateral value

    l. Loan to value (LTV)

    m. FICO score

    n. Years employed

    o. Loan officer name

    p. Interest rate

    q. Maturity date

    r. Repayment terms

    s. Primary source of repayment

    t. Total dollar amount of earnings (individual "insider loan")

    u. Total interest and fee income on individual "insider" installment loan

    v. Total interest and fee income on individual "insider" RE loan

    w. Total interest and fee income on individual "insider" C&I loan

    x. Total loan amount of all individual "insider" loan(s)

    y. Total loan amount of all individual "insider" I/L

    z. Total loan amount of all individual "insider" RE loan(s)

  aa. Total loan amount of all individual "insider" C&I loan(s)

4. Graphics/objects:

    a. Number of embedded objects:

    b. Date of embedded object creation, deletion, addition, modification

    c. Time of embedded object creation, deletion, addition, modification

    d. Frequency of embedded object creation, deletion, addition, modification

    e. Source of embedded object

5. Algorithmic transformations (i.e., calculations)

    a. Number of algorithmic transformations:

    b. Date of algorithmic transformations creation, deletion, addition, modification

    c. Time of algorithmic transformations creation, deletion, addition, modification

    d. Frequency of algorithmic transformations creation, deletion, addition, modification

    e. Source of algorithmic transformation

10.6 Journaling Risk/Controls Matrix

The following matrix details all the KFI and KFM attributes, which incorporates all the metadata previously discussed. The maturity date KFI (MATDT) was selected because of its pervasiveness in use by insider loan fraudsters at financial institutions, according to the FFIEC Insider Detection, Investigation and Prevention of Insider Loan Fraud: A White Paper Produced for the FFIEC Fraud Investigation Symposium, October 20–November 1, 2002.

It is noteworthy to mention that selecting the appropriate KFI and KFM will take time and careful planning. Establishing a well-conceived journaling risk/controls matrix, such as that shown in Table 10.3, is an important first step in determining how many KFIs and KFMs will be selected and what attributes will actually be logged. As you can see from the example below, there are numerous logging possibilities for the MATDT KFI; however, only a few were selected in comparison to

Table 10.3　Journaling Risk/Controls Matrix (Key Fraud Indicator and Key Fraud Metric)

Controls	Risks									
Attributes[a] (Data and Metadata) Key Fraud Indicators (KFIs)	Direct[b] Fraud Scenario[c]						Indirect[b] Fraud Scenario[c]			
	2	3	4	6	7	75	25	56	57	70
AL_MATDT	X	X	X	X	X	X	X	X	X	X
FinDat_MATDT	X	X	X	X	X	X	X	X	X	X
FinData_MATDT_Create_Date_Meta	X									
FinData_MATDT_Time_Meta	X									
FinData_MATDT_Create_LastSaveTime_Meta										
FinData_MATDT_Create_Rev#_Meta										
FinData_MATDT_Create_TotalEditMin_Meta										
FinData_MATDT_Create_Tot_MetaData										
FinData_MATDT_Create_GPF_Date_Meta	X	X	X	X	X	X	X	X		X
FinData_MATDT_Create_GPF_LastSaveTime_Meta	X									
FinData_MATDT_Create_GPF_RevNum_Meta										
FinData_MATDT_Create_GPF_TotEditTime_Meta				X						
FinData_MATDT_Create_GPF_TotGraphics_Meta										

Row					
FinData_MATDT_Create_Alg_Date_Meta					
FinData_MATDT_Create_Alg_LastSaveTime_Meta					
FinData_MATDT_Create_Alg_RevNum_Meta	X				
FinData_MATDT_Create_Alg_TotalEditTime_Meta					
FinData_YRSEMP_TotAlg_Meta			X		X
FinData_MATDT_Acc_Date_Meta					X
FinData_MATDT_Acc_Time_Meta	X				
FinData_MATDT_Acc_LastSaveTime_Meta					
FinData_MATDT_Acc_Rev#Access_Meta	X				
FinData_MATDT_Acc_TotEditTime_Meta				X	
FinData_MATDT_MetaData				X	
FinData_MATDT_Acc_Gpf_Date_Meta					
FinData_MATDT_Acc_Gpf_LastSaveTime_Meta					X
FinData_MATDT_Acc_Gpf_RevNum_Meta				X	
FinData_MATDT_Acc_Gpf_TotEditTime_Meta					
FinData_MATDT_Acc_Gpf_TotGraphics_Meta		X			
FinData_MATDT_Acc_Alg_Date_Meta					
FinData_MATDT_Acc_Alg_LastSaveTime_Meta					

(continued)

Table 10.3 Journaling Risk/Controls Matrix (Key Fraud Indicator and Key Fraud Metric) (*Continued*)

	Risks									
	Direct[b]						Indirect[b]			
	Fraud Scenario[c]						Fraud Scenario[c]			
Controls / Attributes[a] (Data and Metadata) Key Fraud Indicators (KFIs)	2	3	4	6	7	75	25	56	57	70
FinData_MATDT_Acc_Alg_RevNum_Meta					X					
FinData_MATDT_Acc_Alg_TotalEditTime_Meta		X								
FinData_MATDT_Acc_Alg_TotAlg_Meta	X									
FinData_MATDT_Del_Del_Date_Meta										
FinData_MATDT_Del_Del_Time_Meta			X							
FinData_MATDT_Del_LastSaveTime_Meta				X						
FinData_MATDT_Del_Rev#_Meta										
FinData_MATDT_Del_TotalEditMin_Meta							X			
FinData_MATDT_Del_Tot_MetaData										
FinData_MATDT_Del_Gpf_Date_Meta					X					
FinData_MATDT_Del_Gpf_LastSaveTime_Meta										
FinData_MATDT_Del_Gpf_RevNum_Meta								X		
FinData_MATDT_Del_Gpf_TotEditTime_Meta										

FinData_MATDT_Del_Gpf_TotGraphics_Meta	
FinData_MATDT_Del_Alg_Date_Meta	
FinData_MATDT_Del_Alg_LastSaveTime_Meta	
FinData_MATDT_Del_Alg_RevNum_Meta	X
FinData_MATDT_Del_Alg_TotalEditTime_Meta	X
FinData_MATDT_Del_Alg_TotAlg_Meta	
FinData_MATDT_Mod_Date_Meta	
FinData_MATDT_Mod_Time_Meta	
FinData_MATDT_Mod_LastSaveTime_Meta	
FinData_MATDT_Mod_Rev#Access_Meta	
FinData_MATDT_Mod_TotEditTime_Meta	
FinData_MATDT_Mod_TotMetaData	
FinData_MATDT_Mod_Gpf_Date_Meta	
FinData_MATDT_Mod_Gpf_LastSaveTime_Meta	
FinData_MATDT_Mod_Gpf_RevNum_Meta	
FinData_MATDT_Mod_Gpf_TotEditTime_Meta	
FinData_MATDT_Mod_Gpf_TotGraphics_Meta	
FinData_MATDT_Mod_Alg_Date_Meta	

(continued)

Table 10.3 Journaling Risk/Controls Matrix (Key Fraud Indicator and Key Fraud Metric) (Continued)

Controls	Risks									
	Direct[b]						Indirect[b]			
	Fraud Scenario[c]						Fraud Scenario[c]			
Attributes[a] (Data and Metadata) Key Fraud Indicators (KFIs)	2	3	4	6	7	75	25	56	57	70
FinData_MATDT_Mod_Alg_LastSaveTime_Meta										
FinData_MATDT_Mod_Alg_RevNum_Meta										
FinData_MATDT_Mod_Alg_TotalEditTime_Meta										
FinData_MATDT_Mod_Alg_TotAlg_Meta										
Key Fraud Metrics (KFMs) (Optional)										
Loan Portfolio Metrics										
KFM_LPM_AvgTot_Ln&Lse										
KFM_LPM_Tot_Ln&Lse										
Earnings Metrics										
KFM_Earn_AvgEarnLns										
KFM_Earn_%AvgLn_IncIntInc										
Loss Metrics										
KFM_Loss_AvgLns&Lse										

(continued)

KFM_Loss_TotLns&Lse

KFM_Loss_%Avg

KFM_Loss_IL

KFM_Loss_RE

KFM_Loss_C&I

KFM_BS_TotAvgLns

KFM_BS_AvgGrowthRateLns

Past Due/Noncurrent (30 to 60 Days)

KFM_PD_AvgPDGrowthRate

KFM_PD_TotPDAmtLns

KFM_PD_%AvgPDLns

KFM_PD_Tot_RE

KFM_PD_Tot_CI

KFM_PD_Tot_IL

KFM_NA_AvgTotNALns

Nonaccrual Loans (90+ Days Past Due)

KFM_NA_TotNA_IL

KFM_NA_%NA_Lns

Table 10.3 Journaling Risk/Controls Matrix (Key Fraud Indicator and Key Fraud Metric) (*Continued*)

Controls	Risks							
			Direct[b]				Indirect[b]	
			Fraud Scenario[c]				Fraud Scenario[c]	
Attributes[a] (Data and Metadata) Key Fraud Indicators (KFIs)	2	3	4	6	7	75	25	56	57	70
KFM_NA_Tot_IL										
KFM_NA_Tot_Re										
KFM_NA_Tot_CI										

Note: Definitions for each of these attributes can be found in the Total Attribute List. Refer to the metadata extraction list for details on criteria.

[a] Attributes: Source documents (data definition table and the Total Attribute List).

[b] Direct risk: Reflects fraud scenarios that are *directly* impacted by a KFI or KFM value change (positive or negative value change). Indirect risk: Reflects fraud scenarios that are *indirectly* impacted by a KFI or KFM value change (positive or negative value change).

[c] Fraud scenario: Source document (analysis of electronic KFS candidate preparation report).

the entire population. For a complete listing of all the KFIs and KFMs, refer to the *Total Attribute List* for details.

The software engineering process for developing a new application or system needs to be designed in such a way to allow flexibility in creating, adding, modifying, and deleting new or existing KFIs and KFMs for being journaled.

Finally, the total novelty score coming from the output of the novelty neural network (see Chapter 11), should also play an important role in management's decision as to what attributes should or should not be journaled. Based on my experimental testing of using a novelty neural network, I found that the network was good at detecting associations between various KFIs and KFMs; however, changes in absolute values for individual data elements were problematic for the neural network. Consequently, to complement or offset this shortcoming, absolute value changes need to be captured primarily from the journaling perspective and not from the neural network.

For each of the KFI values, there needs to be a "clipping level" or threshold to ensure you are not logging every minor change in value. Percentage thresholds should be established for each KFI so that only the appropriate level of logging occurs and to exclude noise that has no or minimal relevance for assessing normalcy of activity.

10.7   Conclusion

- The Defense in Depth concept maintains numerous interrelationships between policies, asset risk prioritization, data criticality, macro taxonomy, micro taxonomy, neural network, and event correlation software.
- The topic of computer forensics involves the discovery of computer-related evidence and data and represents an integral part of application and system journaling.
- Data monitoring involves observing data flows involving specific events.
- Journaling involves the creation of activity log records and the capture of key information about all security-relevant IT systems.
- It is not practical or an efficient use of time for security personnel and audit to have every user activity logged from the InfoSec and computer forensic perspectives.
- Metadata extraction represents the standardized logging criteria for Forensic Foto Frames, which includes administration/summary data, frame statistics, data access rule violations, graphics/objects and algorithmic transformations (i.e., calculations).

References

1. Barse, Emilie Lundin. Logging for Fraud and Intrusion Detection, Ph.D. thesis, Chalmers University of Technology, School of Computer Science and Engineering, Sweden, 2004.

2. NIST 800-18. *Guide for Developing Security Plans for Information Technology Systems.* 1998.
3. U.S. Department of Defense, *National Industrial Security Program Operating Manual* (NISPOM), 2006, Chapter 8, "Automated Information System Security" (http://nsi. org/Library/Govt/Nispom.html).
4. Kossakowski, Klaus-Peter and Allen, Julia. Security Improvement Module, "Securing Public Web Servers," CMU/SEI-SIM-011, Copyright 2000 by Carnegie Mellon University.

Chapter 11

The Role of Neural Networks in the Insider Computer Fraud Framework

11.1 Introduction

One of the primary objectives of this research is to introduce the concepts surrounding neural nets, while also giving equal time to the more contemporary approach to the neural networks, using association memory and anomalistic or novelty pattern recognition, which I leveraged in developing my proof of concept for this book. There are many dimensions to this paragraph on neural networks, and to provide the illusion that I adequately covered each of them completely would be misleading. However, with that caveat in mind, the greatest contribution I can make in this chapter is to provide a survey of the past, present, and perhaps the future of neural networks. This chapter will attempt to introduce the traditional concepts surrounding neural nets and then leverage off this conceptual foundation by introducing a more revolutionary neural network concept involving the use of associative memory to identify anomalistic patterns of activity based on the concept of associative memory which parallels how the human brain functions. Particular attention will be paid to associative memory given its crucial role in compressing data so that novelty detection may be utilized. Finally, in closing this chapter, I will introduce a few examples of where neural networks are actively being used for intrusion and misuse detection.

11.2 The Concept of Artificial Intelligence and Neural Network

Artificial intelligence (AI), in its most basic form as a component of computer science, is primarily concerned with making computers behave in a similar fashion as humans. One of the primary goals of AI is to generate heuristics, to guide a search for solutions to problems of control, recognition, and object manipulation.

11.2.1 Neural Networks

One of the primary objectives of this research will be to understand the basic concepts of neural networks and how they impact the detection of insider computer fraud (ICF) activities. The primary goal of this chapter is not to provide a mathematical evaluation of all the calculations involved in neural network computing, but rather to introduce the topic at a level that will facilitate the ability of the reader to quickly understand the foundational concepts of neural nets, which will foster a clearer understanding of the more traditional statistical models, and to extend this discussion to the use of associative memory neural nets that are not statistical based and do not require the use of classifiers. The emphasis of this research is to explore the use of neural networks, which apply the use of associative memory to detect patterns of behavior that are considered normal and then to perform anomaly detection, by flagging transactions that possess anomalies, or no prior associations. The topic of associative memory will be discussed in greater length within this chapter, after providing a high-level introduction to the concept of neural networks to set the foundation on this topic.

11.2.1.1 Statistical Models

The traditional neural networks use statistical models, and these models are constructed based on a set of parameters, and these parameters are commonly referred to as weights. Through the use of these parameters or weights, a mapping is formed based on a given set of values known as inputs to an associated set of values, which are the outputs. Basically, under the statistical model, the neural network performs a mapping from one set of variables onto another set of variables that have different size. The input space represents the total set of combinations of possible values of a set of variables, which are located in a point in space. To that end, the role of the

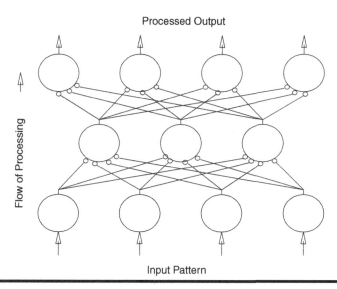

Figure 11.1 Neural network learning laws. (From Dr. Charles Butler.)

neural network in this regard is its knowledge of the route from each point in the input space to the correct point in the output space. Refer to Figure 11.1 for details on distributed processing.

11.2.2 Artificial Neural Network (ANN) (Software Computing Techniques and Components)

Neural network techniques and components are briefly discussed below.

11.2.2.1 Perceptrons

A perceptron is a connected network that simulates an associative memory. The most basic perceptron is composed of an input layer and output layer of nodes, each of which are fully connected to the other. Assigned to each connection is a weight that can be adjusted so that, given a set of inputs to the network, the associated connections will produce a desired output. The adjusting of weights to produce a particular output is called the "training" of the network, which is the mechanism that allows the network to learn.

11.2.2.2 Competitive Layers

Although the definition of a competitive layer is not clearly described, the concept of competitive layer fundamentally discusses the fact that neurons of competitive networks learn to recognize groups of similar input vectors. A competitive layer automatically learns to classify input vectors. Neurons in a competitive layer simply excite themselves and inhibit all other neurons.

11.2.2.3 Self-Organizing Maps (SOMs)

Although the definition of SOMs is not clearly described, Kohonen's SOM is in contrast to the typical training of neural nets, where the teacher determines what output he or she desires for each of many possible input values. Specifically, the SOM automatically categorizes the varieties of input presented during training and can then express how well new inputs fit the patterns it discerned.

11.2.2.4 Differences between Artificial Intelligence (AI) and Neural Nets

The primary difference between AI and neural nets is that AI attempts to capture intelligent behavior without regard to the underlying mechanism producing the behavior. With AI, behaviors are described with rules and symbols, versus the neural net that does not describe behaviors but rather imitates them. AI systems are closely aligned to expert systems, which typically involve the input from a subject matter expert in a particular area who has input into the establishing of the rules involved with AI systems.

11.2.3 A Graphical Illustration—Distributed Processing

The human brain is made up of several components; however, the component graphically illustrated in Figure 11.1 is the distributed processing capability, which should reinforce the previously described statistical model concept. Shown in Figure 11.1, this neural network has two inputs, a three-layered network and two hidden neurons. The number of hidden neurons determines the complexity of the network; the more hidden neurons that exist, the more complex the network will be, given the increased number of connections that exist between neurons and, consequently, more parameters that have to be determined and a larger data training set required.

As discussed in Section 11.2.1.1, an associated (synapse) "weight" and each triangle (see Figure 11.1) represent a numerical operation on all its inputs, which are called activation functions. (See Section 11.3.1 for additional detail.) Both memory and processing instructions reside in an interconnected pattern (synapse).

Processing takes place as a pattern of node activation, initiated by the input pattern, which flows from the input to the output node.

11.3   Designing the Neural Network

There are many challenges facing the designer of a neural network system, including the following issues: the number of hidden neurons in the hidden layer, which impacts training time; overfitting that occurs when the ANN recognizes too many characteristics of the data; underfitting that occurs when significant characteristics of the data are not noticed by the ANN; and training through the use of supervised training when the desired outputs are known and unsupervised training when the desired outputs are unavailable and a need exists for the development of applications used for pattern discovery.

The activity of a node is determined by the input from many other nodes. Each node sends a copy of its output to many other nodes. The connection strengths increase or decrease slightly as each training pattern is processed. Learning can be supervised, unsupervised, or graded.

11.3.1   Learning Laws

Prior to our discussion on training, it is important to introduce the concept of learning law, which impacts how the neural network learns. An important component of most neural networks is learning laws or rules. A learning rule allows the network to adjust its connection weights in order to associate given input vectors with corresponding output vectors. During training periods, the input vectors are repeatedly presented, and the weights are adjusted according to the learning rule, until the network learns the desired associations.

As previously introduced, the concept of activation function was discussed. In brief, the activation function is one component of the learning laws which governs how the synapse weights change to make the network learn from the training dataset. Basically, the activation function determines the activation level resulting from the net input. This is in contrast to the other internal transfer functions of neural network learning laws involving the input function and the output function (Figure 11.2). The input function determines how a node combines the input from all other nodes, and the output function determines how the activation affects the node's output.

11.3.2   Supervised Training

In supervised training, the training set is many paired input/output examples. For each example, the desired output is impressed on the output nodes as the input is presented. The training set is repeated many times in random order.

Supervised learning involves reliance on the previously compiled and sanitized data "training set." The neural network (NN) is told that if it sees this pattern it should report the following conclusion. The NN then tweaks its internal "weights"

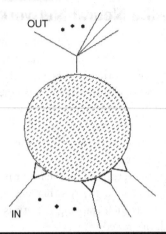

OUT

IN

Figure 11.2 Neural network—(input and output function). (From Dr. Charles Butler.)

such that it will try to accurately classify the largest majority of training vectors. The aforementioned method looks for a pattern match, versus the search for a specific match currently in use for intrusion detection systems (IDSs) and anomaly detection systems (ADSs).

Each layer of a NN (Figure 11.3) has a unique purpose and includes the following:

■ *Input Layer*: Usually distributes the input pattern unchanged to every node of the hidden layer
■ *Hidden Layer*: Constructs feature detectors that encode specific features of the training data
■ *Output Layer*: Synthesizes the proper response pattern from the outputs of the hidden-layer nodes

11.3.3 Unsupervised Training

In unsupervised training, the training set consists of many random examples that are repeatedly given to the input nodes, with no desired output pattern given to the network. Using unsupervised learning, instead of being told what they should be looking for or what to report, the NN model attempts to find patterns within a dataset and then seeks to group them according to the most relevant features. This technique is useful when dealing with large volumes of raw data and only little or no knowledge of the interrelation between the various fields in a vector.

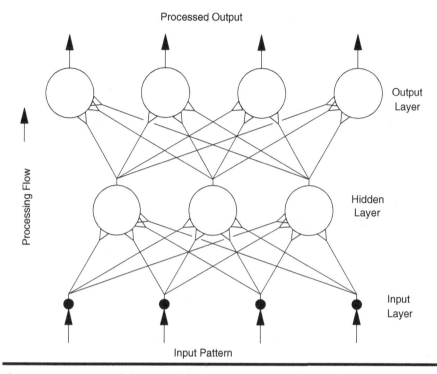

Figure 11.3 Layers of the neural network. (From Dr. Charles Butler.)

11.3.4 Lazy Learning

The concept of lazy learning is introduced in this chapter given its significant relevance to novelty neural network software used within the experimental section of this book.

In brief, lazy learning is a memory-based technique that postpones all the computation until an explicit request for a prediction is received. This process involves a local modeling procedure, which in simple terms involves leveraging previous experiences, combining them through a weighted average (which weights similar experiences higher), and through that combination makes a prediction. One reason for the growing popularity of lazy learning or just-in-time learning is that they defer the processing of data until an explicit request for information is received. There are distinct advantages in using the lazy learning technique, which include the reduced computational and storage expense associated with the training phase of a NN.

11.4 Neural Associative Memory (NAM)

11.4.1 Overview

The concept of neural associative memory (NAM) is introduced in this chapter given its significant relevance to its use in novelty neural network software used within the experimental section of this book. Conceptually, an associative memory is a memory system that stores information through association and correlation. This NAM concept closely parallels the way in which an event correlation software operates, which is one of the reasons for my selection of this software type for integration into my ICF framework.

11.4.2 NAM Characteristics

NAM are NN models consisting of neuron-like and synapse-like elements. At any given point in time, the NN is given a vector of neural activities called the activity pattern. The neurons will update their activity value based on the inputs they receive over the synapses. The synapses in a NN are the links between neurons or between neurons and fibers carrying external input.

Associative memories are represented by patterns of activation of the active elements, or nodes, in the network. These patterns are determined by the magnitudes of the weighted connections between the nodes. The learning process, the formation of memories, is represented by the manipulation of these weighted connections in response to the presentation to the network of selected relevant training examples.

Unlike a computer, one of the primary distinguishing features of a NAM characteristic which is unique to NNs is its ability to recall information based on either incomplete or garbled inputs; along with NAM's distributed memory capabilities. Therefore, there is no single location within the memory that contains each item of information. This is in contrast to a computer, which houses data within "addresses" in memory.

11.4.3 A NAM Example

An example presented in *Naturally Intelligent Systems*, by Maureen Caudill and Charles Butler, provides the simplest example of illustrating this concept.

Imagine the following conversation between two friends:

"Do you remember the guy at work?" asks Sue.
"Which one?" George responds.
"You know, the one with the black hair," she replies.
"Do you mean the man with the funny purple glasses?"

"No, I mean the guy who always wore green and orange plaid pants."

"Oh, you mean Joe Flamespitter! Didn't he have the very worst temper of anyone you ever met?"

In this conversation George recalls Joe Flamespitter based on the combination of facts that the person in question (1) worked with Sue and George, (2) had black hair, (3) did not have funny purple glasses, and (4) consistently wore green and orange plaid pants.[1]

11.4.4 Advantages of Associative Memories

First, NAM is considered very robust, as exampled by the memory's ability to provide the correct response to incorrect stimuli as well as its ability to become insensitive to any errors within small sections of the memory.

Second, any inputs to the NN's associative memory can be categorized as an activity pattern, which is a positive feature when taken in context of the fact that associative memory is not exclusively reliant upon only one part of the input pattern, but rather the entire input pattern. Consequently, NAM is not disturbed by minor differences, but rather is impacted only when major changes to the overall input activity pattern occur.

11.4.5 Types of Associative Memories

There are several types of memories that can be classified, including the following:

- *Autoassociative Memory*: This occurs when each data item is associated with itself.
- *Heteroassociative Memory*: This occurs when two different data items are associated with each other.

Neural network models that use associative memories include crossbar networks, adaptive filter networks, and competitive filter networks. Butler describes these networks as follows:

- *Crossbar Networks*: A crossbar network has one or two layers of neurodes arranged so that each input line can connect to any output line through a variable-weight interconnect.
- *Adaptive Filter Network*: An adaptive filter network can be thought of as a collection of neurodes, each of which tests the input pattern to see if it is in one specific category assigned to that neurode.

■ *Competitive Filter Networks*: Use competition among the neurodes in order to sort patterns. In this type of network, an input pattern is sorted into one of many categories in a manner similar to that of an adaptive filter network.

11.5 Memory Creation—Similarities between the Human Brain versus the Neural Network

Presented in Figure 11.4 and Figure 11.5 are the human brain and the neural network.

11.6 The Human Brain—The Cerebrum or Neocortex

The neocortex or isocortex is the largest part of the brain and constitutes about 85 percent of the human brain's total mass. The neocortex is thought to be responsible for high-level cognitive functions, such as language, learning, memory, and complex thought. It is divided into four or five arbitrary divisions or lobes. The four lobes on the surface are the frontal, parietal, occipital, and temporal. The fifth lobe is underneath the surface lobes and is called the limbic lobe or limbic system. The frontal lobe, at its rearmost portion, includes areas that control motor functions or movements. The parietal lobe, at its frontmost portion, monitors sensory information. The occipital lobe receives sensory input from the eyes and analyzes and interprets visual stimuli. The temporal lobe receives sensory input from the ears, and sounds are analyzed and interpreted as language.

The area of the neocortex we are most interested in, in terms of memory, is the roof of the cerebral cortex (the wrinkled outer layer of the front part of the brain—

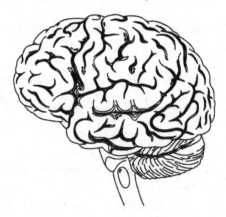

Figure 11.4 The human brain. (From Dr. Charles Butler.)

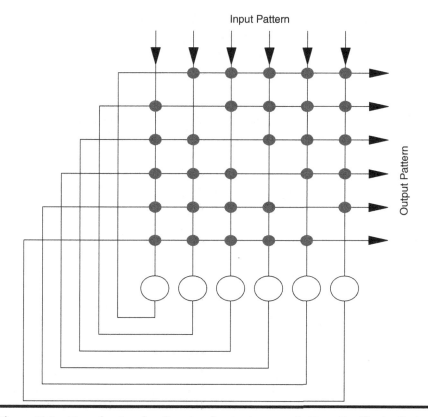

Figure 11.5 Neural network—(input and output patterns). (From Dr. Charles Butler.)

the cerebral hemispheres). It is within the cerebral hemisphere of the neocortex where functions include the perception of sensations, learning, reasoning, and memory.

The chief technology officer of Palm Computing and Handspring, Jeff Hawkins (also the author of *On Intelligence*), also makes the distinction between the human brain and computers relative to the neocortex and states the following four characteristics:

- The neocortex stores sequences of patterns.
- The neocortex recalls patterns autoassociatively.
- The neocortex stores patterns in an invariant form.
- The neocortex stores patterns in a hierarchy.[2]

11.7 Neurons

The functionality of the brain is due to neurons being connected in different ways to form functional circuits. A neuron accumulates its inputs over time and produces an output that is some (nonlinear) function of its input. The functionality comes from the interaction between neurons. The output of a network of neurons is the pattern of activity of the individual neurons. All neurons have a wire-like structure made up of axons and dendrites. When the axon from one neuron touches the dendrite of another, they form small connections called synapses. Synapses are where the nerve impulse from one cell influences the behavior of another cell. A neural signal, or spike, at the neurons will increase the likelihood that a recipient cell will also spike. The primary class of neurons within the neocortex are the pyramidal neurons that connect to other neurons and send out lengthy axons to other areas of the cortex. With each pyramidal cell containing thousands of synapses, the neocortex is roughly estimated to have 30 trillion synapses altogether, which translates into an unprecedented memory capacity of the human brain.

The large memory capacity of the human brain coupled with the ability of neurons to extend their axons to make new connections thus allows the remaining neurons to cover for the several thousand of the brain's neurons that die every day. Although the brain's neurons do not reproduce, human mental capacity is not diminished based upon the axons' new connections.

The human brain's mental capacities to store memories in the neocortex are based upon events happening in a sequential manner. All memories are like this, and your brain needs to walk through the temporal sequence of how you do things. For an example of this sequential process, one pattern may be (approach the door), which then evokes the next pattern (either go down the hall or ascend the stairs), and so on. This is the process for memory creation in the neocortical memory system, which has some similarities to the manner in which the NN is trained.

11.8 The Novelty Neural Network—Linkage between the Human Brain and the Experimental Portion of This Research

In this section, we can now leverage off the discussion on how the brain functions relative to memory creation and recall and now apply these same concepts to the experimental section of this research involving training and testing a novelty NN for ICF detection.

An example of how memory works in a NN can probably be best described in the most simple manner, by stating that memory is created in sequential patterns, again a process that closely parallels the way the human mind works. As you will recall within the previously discussed paragraph on associative memory, there are two primary types of associative memory used within the human mind. The easiest way to illustrate the similarities between the learning process of the NN and how the human brain learns would be to review the steps taken during the experimental phase of this research, which were also applied during the training and testing phase of the novelty neural network. A process walk-through will be conducted in the next few paragraphs; however, at this point in the discussion, it would be appropriate and timely to introduce the concept of novelty detection in neural networks, prior to proceeding with the process walk-through.

11.9   Novelty Detection (Saffron Technologies)

By definition, novelty detection identifies abnormal or nonrandom behavior that demonstrates a process is under some influence of special causes of variation, without impeding the normal learning process that is so vital to creating associative memory. (See Section 11.10 for a description of the Saffron Technologies use of associative memory.) The detection of novelty is an important concept, particularly when dealing with ICF activities, because it provides a feedback mechanism to the user and validates the effectiveness and accuracy of the training and testing dataset or perhaps flaws within the initial underlying logic of the software. Substantive user acceptance and quality assurance testing would have to be conducted prior to any conclusions in either scenario.

Using Saffron's didactic tool, LabAgent and companion documentation, the properties of this software and the underlying concept behind novelty NNs in general involve the following fundamental characteristics or properties:

- *Incremental*: Start from zero, learn case-by-case.
- *Nonparametric*: No knob-tweaking to build.
- *Malleable*: Adapt on the fly to new features.
- *Unified Representation*: Various inferences can be computed at query time.
- *No Overtraining*: Do not get worse as more data is seen.

11.10   The SaffronOne Associative Memory

Based on an excerpt of the associative learning concept as described in Saffron Technologies' Technical White Paper (January 2004), the following description of associative memory is provided:

> The associative learning concept lies at the heart of the theory that people learn from the relationships between things, over time. From the computing point of view, associative memories techniques are a mechanism to capture associative learning, and trace their conceptual roots to just after World War II. The use of associative lookup instead of index-based lookup lies at the heart of understanding the application of associative memories. Associative memories are a form of content addressable memories (CAMs), in which the object (content) forms the

address used to read and write. The most familiar analog in computer science is the hash table, in which a hash key is used to compute the bucket where the object is stored. CAMs work in a similar fashion. However, instead of a simple value (such as a hash code), associative memories construct indexes based on attribute vectors. At its most basic level, an associative memory employs a mechanism similar to a cooccurrence matrix in that it stores counts of how items and their respective attributes occur together. Unlike traditional cooccurrence matrix techniques, SaffronOne's memories solved the geometric scaling problem that historically prevented associative memories from being used in production settings. Known as the crossbar problem, this was by far the most limiting aspect of associative memories and prevented their commercial viability in the past. By definition, an associative network represented by a matrix must intersect all inputs with one another, which causes a geometric explosion of connections between inputs: $[N*(-1)/2]$ where N is the number of inputs.[3]

11.11   Confidence Level

The use of novelty detection can also be a double-edged sword in its effectiveness in detecting ICF activities. For example, if the confidence level or measure is determined to be low, the novelty detected may not in fact raise an increased level of concern, because the NN could still be in a training mode. Conversely, if the confidence level or measure is determined to be high and there exists a high degree of novelty, then the findings triggered by the novelty may be a cause for concern.

11.12   Use of Neural Networks for Monitoring Anomaly Detection

Normally, NNs are most commonly used for monitoring and hopefully preventing external attacks into a network's perimeter; however, my contention is that the concept of capturing network forensic journaling for monitoring the external threat can also be applied toward the identification and, hopefully, the prevention of future insider threats.

Currently, NNs are used for monitoring and analyzing anomalistic external user behavior for external users, through the collection of all commands and audit logs for each user. The data captured and used by the neural network to monitor anomalistic external user behavior can also be used to monitor the insider threat. This may be accomplished by identifying the appropriate internal application and system data forensic journaling data feeds, not necessarily from the operating system alone, but through application and system audit logs as well.

11.13   Neural Networks and ICF

Based on this ICF framework that I developed and incorporated within my research, NNs that use associative memory were chosen given their ability to be trained on exclusively normal data behavior and the smaller dataset needed for training and testing a novelty NN. This is in contrast to the more traditional statistically based NNs that are more "data hungry" and require training and testing for both normal and suspicious transactional data.

The absence of any credible data on known ICF cases makes having to train a NN a challenge. Furthermore, training a NN on suspicious activity would be problematic under any circumstances, by virtue of the fact that you are dealing with an unknown variable, which is trying to predict human behavior or the behavior of data, which makes the modeling effort for such an undertaking extremely difficult.

11.14   Computer Forensic Benefits of Neural Networks

The forensic journaling that will be built into the software engineering process for new application development will also assist in the development of NNs to detect unknown or anomalistic insider user behavior. The use of NNs for ICF detection has many advantages and is well suited to the elusive nature of ICF activities:

- Has the ability to handle nonlinear problems.
- Needs no processing algorithm.
- Has the ability to model chaotic time series.

11.14.1   The Neural Network Development Process

Prior to understanding the nexus between the use of digital forensics data and the development of neural nets for capturing key journaling criteria, there is a need to establish a fundamental understanding of the NN development process. Specifically, anomaly detection in NNs is created by having systems learn to predict the next user command based on a sequence of previous commands by a specific user. Basically, the building of a NN for use within intrusion detection systems consists of three phases:

1. Collect training data by obtaining the audit logs for each user for a certain period. A vector is formed by each day and each user, which shows how often the user executed each command.
2. Train the NN to identify the user based on the command distribution vectors.
3. Command the NN to identify the user based on the command distribution vector. If the network's suggestion is different from the actual user, an anomaly is signaled.

To address this increasing information security threat, there has been a growth in the industry in the use of ADSs and IDSs. There are many cited issues involving the use of anomaly/intrusion detection, which include the following:

■ Problems with scalability
■ False positives
■ An inability to determine what is really important information
■ A lack of a complete, comprehensive database of attack signatures

11.15 Research Efforts in Intrusion Detection Systems-Based Neural Networks

Fundamentally, an ANN is built up from a large number of artificial neurons (known as processing elements), and each processing element performs a simple task. NNs are built from several layers of processing elements (PEs), with the most common being the multilayer perceptron. Within a multilayer perceptron, the input is connected to an input layer and is again connected to a hidden layer. Although there may be a number of hidden layers, the last one is connected to the output layer. On each layer, all the neurons are independent of each other, and the knowledge of the ANN is represented by the weights between the neurons of the different layers. These weights may be randomly initialized and are updated as a result of inputting data to the network, which means that an ANN must be trained before it contains useful knowledge. A typical multilayer perceptron has one or two hidden layers.

11.16 Anomaly Detection Using Neural Networks (Fuzzy Clustering)

Technologies that include fuzzy clustering are beginning to be used. Fuzzy clustering is being chosen instead of relying on the use of classifiers, which may not deal as effectively with detecting events that do not neatly fall into any predefined cluster. Basically, the term *fuzzy clustering* works by ostensibly training itself, through the creation of a baseline profile of the network in various states, to determine what happens under normal conditions. It then determines what different users do and the resources they normally request, and what types of files they transfer and other activity. Then those routine events are grouped into clusters that represent normal activity. Various models can then be developed for different user categories, such as administrators, marketing employees, and others, and then what events are considered normal can be determined and grouped into a cluster.

11.17   Misuse Detection Using Neural Networks

As previously noted, the use of attack signatures alone is not as effective as if they were combined with other forms of prevention and detection when it comes to network or ICF attacks involving Web-based or traditional applications accessed only in-house. The signature-based attack detection process can be effective if tuned and continually baselined against known networks or can be compared against application attacks.

11.18   Preprocessing Activities

Production applications typically go through some level of preprocessing, involving data normalization, grouping of data, and then data conversion into a NN-readable format. The experiment conducted for this dissertation had the novelty NN ingest raw data versus preprocessed data by design. The primary reason for using raw data was to not filter any data without knowing how the NN would first react to the data, patterns, and association capabilities. The only attempt that I made that would probably indicate some attempt toward data preprocessing activities was in my initial effort to identify those baseline cases of normal activity to be grouped as normal insider versus general public transactions. Obviously, if this was a production application, I would probably want some level of preprocessing, even at the preproduction level, for my training, testing, and validation data. Data preprocessing can be of value to ensure all variables receive equal attention during the training process.

Transforming the input data into some known forms, such as linear, log, exponential, and so forth, may be helpful to improve the performance of the NN.

Related indirectly to the preprocessing activities that the NN Model may want to consider are the following questions:

- What information do you want from the NN's output?
- What variables can be used to access the designed information?
- Can other variables or relationships capture the same information indirectly?
- Is a particular variable significant in a static context, where only the current value of that variable is of interest, or is it important within a dynamic context, where perhaps historical trends are important?

These are a few of the important considerations that factor indirectly in the decision of what preprocessing activities should occur.

After testing of the novelty NN is complete, if there were plans to conduct further testing, it would probably be necessary to conduct some level of preprocessing of the data activity that may include data normalization to ensure improved data integrity and reduce the potential of duplicative data and overfeeding of the neural network.

11.19 Conducting Edit and Validation Activities to Ensure Data Integrity

Testing key fraud indicators (KFIs) and key fraud metrics (KFMs) based on pre-established categories of data by increasing the clustering and correlation of the datasets based on similar data characteristics could increase the understanding of the behavior of data. For example, leveraging the Service Oriented Architecture (SOA) and Forensic Foto Frame design concept and establishing only a small training and testing dataset involving ICF for one or two KFIs or KFMs might reduce the "noise" by increasing the likelihood that the NN would be detecting negative or positive patterns in regard to the behavior of data with greater accuracy and speed.

The potential for increased accuracy in the output of the novelty NN might occur just by virtue of the reduced volume of interrelated data the neural network is being trained and tested on and with fewer associations that would have to be initially made. Logically, it would stand to reason that you would want to start out with the fewest number of data attributes for training and testing purposes and then layer additional attributes. Although this concept of having fewer initial attributes that could be associated with attributes, is slightly paradoxical to having associative memory within a NN, it could be an approach that would generate fewer false negatives and false positives and increase the number of bona fide accurate novelties detected.

11.20 Data Postprocessing

Similar to IDSs, NNs have their fair share of false negatives and false positives in the output. These are not desirable results from a cost and efficiency perspective, given the added overhead of following up on such flagged "suspicious activity" and the retraining activity of the NN, through the process of backing out what was the conventional wisdom at the time of data normalcy, which may now be considered as being incorrect, based on new information.

11.21 Increasing the Sensitivity of the Neural Network to Absolute Value Change

The NN was largely effective in detecting new associations in data attributes (KFIs and KFMs); however, it did not pick up absolute value changes as effectively as new associations. The novelty detection would have greatly benefited from a greater sensitivity to absolute value changes that are equally as important as new attribute associations, particularly in the financial services sector where financial value changes are closely monitored.

11.22 Postprocessing

Equally as important to data preprocessing is data postprocessing. Just as the input data should ideally be normalized during the preprocessing process, data output should also have some level of normalization to ensure preservation of the confidentiality, integrity, and availability of the data. Specifically, a filtering process should be in place to screen through and eliminate "false negatives" and "false positives." The specifics of other postprocessing activities will be contingent upon the goals and objectives of the NN and the reporting desires and capabilities of management.

11.23 Benford's Law

By definition, Benford's law is used to determine the normal level of number duplication in datasets, which makes it possible to identify abnormal digit and number occurrence. An analysis of the frequency distribution of the first or second digits can detect abnormal patterns in the data and may identify possible fraud. Historically, some organizations, such as the public accounting firms, may use computer-assisted audit techniques as a tool for fraud detection, which includes the use of digital analysis, ostensibly the digits checked based on Benford's law (i.e., digit 1, first two digits, last two digits, and digit 2), as graphically illustrated in Figure 11.6. The significance of using Benford's law is that it integrates best into the third layer of defense where data is being collected for a number of purposes, particularly as it relates to training and testing the NN. The same dataset used for training and testing the NN can also be evaluated as part of a digit analysis to determine if there exists any abnormal frequency distribution of the first or second digits.

Perhaps as a component of the data pre- and postprocessing, the finessed numbers could be imported into a third-party Excel spreadsheet as a .CSV file format and fed into either a home-grown application or a third-party software tool similar to that illustrated in Figure 11.6 (www.sherry.uk.net) and then compared against the values as determined under Benford's law. The software can determine the

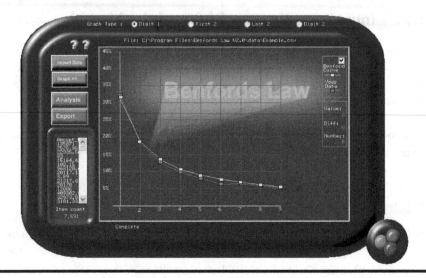

Figure 11.6   Benford's law software.

frequency distribution for the first digit (Figure 11.6), first two digits, and second digits. (Refer to Figure 11.6, Benford's law software, for details.) One of the primary benefits of integrating Benford's law into the data pre- and postprocessing steps is the benefit of continually reviewing data on a routine basis versus conducting this type of analysis only on an annual basis when the data integrity is being evaluated prior to an audit of the books and records of the organization.

Consider an example of how Bedford's law could be used in potentially detecting suspicious insider loan fraud. Using a software application or perhaps logic incorporated within a NN, data input manipulation might be detected to "flag" suspicious insider loan originations where a loan officer books fraudulent loans at quarter-end or annually just prior to bonus time or through some means of compensation. For example, a self-dealing loan officer could create a bogus loan number for a loan he or she is extending to a member of his or her family at favorable rates and terms. The loan officer could be using the same loan number for a loan that was recently paid off by another borrower. Using Benford's law could potentially pick up the reuse of an existing loan number, based on a digital analysis, and perhaps through the use of a software package. (Refer to Figure 11.6 for details.) Figure 11.6 reflects the importing of 7,591 values contained within an Excel spreadsheet into the Benford's law software. The software generates two curves, with one curve representing Benford's law in terms of what is considered to be a normal frequency distribution of the first digit, while the second curve is generated from the 7,591 imported values. Based on the close alignment of the two curves, it can be interpreted that there is little noticeable variance between Benford's curve and the data imported into the software. For example, if the 7,591 values imported into the software represented new loan originations at a bank, then based on the output of the software it can be inferred by the output results that there is no abnormal digit and number occurrence, given the close alignment of the Benford's law curve and the loan data curve.

Mark J. Nigrini, in "Fraud Detection—I've Got Your Number,"[4] published May 1999, offered the following comments (refer to Tables 11.1 and 11.2: Benford's Law—"Expected Digital Frequencies"):

■ Accountants and auditors have begun to apply Benford's law to corporate data to discover number–pattern anomalies. For large datasets, CPAs use highly focused tests that concentrate on finding deviations in subsets.

■ Frank Benford made a simple observation while working as a physicist at the GE Research Labs in Schenectady, New York, in the 1920s. He noticed that the first few pages of his logarithm tables books were more worn than the last few, and from this he surmised that he was consulting the first pages, which gave the logs of numbers with low digits, more often. The first digit of a number is leftmost—for example, the first digit of 45,000 is 4. (Zero cannot be a first digit.) Benford extrapolated that he was looking up the logs of numbers with low first digits more frequently because there were more numbers with low first digits in the world.

Table 11.1 Benford's Law—Expected Digital Frequencies

| Digit | Position of Digit in Number | | | |
	First	Second	Third	Fourth
0		0.11968	0.10178	0.10018
1	0.30103	0.11389	0.10138	0.10014
2	0.17609	0.10882	0.10097	0.10010
3	0.12494	0.10433	0.10057	0.10006
4	0.09691	0.10031	0.10018	0.10002
5	0.07918	0.09668	0.09979	0.09998
6	0.06695	0.09337	0.09940	0.09994
7	0.05799	0.09035	0.09902	0.09990
8	0.05115	0.08757	0.09884	0.09986
9	0.04576	0.08500	0.09827	0.09982

Example: The number 147 has three digits, with 1 as the first digit, 4 as the second digit, and 7 as the third digit. By analyzing the table, see that under Benford's law, the expected proportion of numbers with a first digit 1 is 30.103 percent, and the expected proportion of numbers with a third digit 7 is 9.902 percent.

Table 11.2   Benford's Law—Expected Digital Frequencies

Not all datasets follow Benford's law. Those data phenomena (for example, market values of corporations) sets most likely will have the following characteristics:

The numbers describe the sizes of similar phenomena

The numbers do not contain a built-in maximum or minimum value (such as deductible IRA contributions or hourly wage rates)

Assigned numbers, such as SSN, zip codes, or bank account numbers will not conform to Benford's law

Benford's Law Formula: P(D1 = d1) = log10(1 + 1/d1) for d1 {1, 2, . . . 9}

Source: Mark Nigrini. Fraud Detection—I've Got Your Number, *Journal of Accountancy*, 79–83, May 1999.

11.24   Future Neural Network Trends

The use of neural nets will continue to evolve in its use at the network level for external intrusions, and will continue to grow as a potential avenue for detecting and perhaps one day preventing ICF. The evolution of the use of neural nets will be somewhat slow until its use becomes more standardized and requires less up-front and continual administrative overhead to maintain its relevance within an enterprise.

Although it is unlikely over the next few years that a *plug and play* ICF application or system will be uniformly designed to identify all the many ICF categories based on the taxonomy, there is, however, an important role served by having a system designed that can add some level of AI to an extremely complex and misunderstood topic.

11.25   Conclusion

In the final analysis, fraud prevention of any kind has significant relevance and grounding within the culture of the enterprise, which embraces leadership in establishing a clear mission of the organization and demonstrates the support and nurturing of the greatest asset of the enterprise, which of course is the human capital.

All the technology in the world cannot substitute for the hiring and retention of honest and law-abiding employees, who share similar values of the organization in terms of goals, virtues, and sound ethics of their senior management and members of the board, as applicable. To that end, all the preventive and detective technology will not prevent ICF activity. However, if management creates the right working environment for its employees, maintains a culture that embraces the importance of information security governance and all employees simply *doing the right thing* for the company and themselves, the elusive topic of ICF merely becomes an afterthought in the risk assessment process of that enterprise.

Based on my experimental results, there is a sufficient number of positive test results to be cautiously optimistic that NNs can play a vital role in detecting ICF; however, further research would be needed into how best to develop new or refine existing NN software to detect changes in the behavior of data, along with the need for not using raw data but conducting preprocessing on that data before use within the NN.

References

1. Caudill, Maureen and Butler, Charles, *Naturally Intelligent Systems,* MIT Press, Cambridge, MA, 1992.
2. Hawkins, Jeff, *On Intelligence,* Times Books, Henry Holt, New York, 2004.
3. Saffron Technologies, Technical White Paper, Morrisville, NC, 2004 (www.saffrontech.com).
4. Nigrini, Mark, Fraud Detection—I've Got Your Number. *Journal of Accountancy,* May, 79–83, 1999.

Appendix A

Application Access
Controls

Controls Testing Residual Risk Form (CTRRF) Access Controls

Risk Reference Number	Key Risks Access Controls	Key Controls for Reducing Insider Computer Fraud	Risk-Mitigating Actions
1	Inadequate logical security controls could present an opportunity for unauthorized modification, destruction, or disclosure of information assets.	1. Written policies and standards governing logical access controls should exist within the firm, be approved by senior management, and be disseminated to the business lines for implementation. The business line should adhere to firmwide access control policies and procedures and substantiate deviations based on the relative risk of the business.	1. (a) Determine that the organization has appropriate policies and procedures in place to ensure that effective security standards are consistent across the businesses. (b) Determine if roles and responsibilities have been clearly defined and whether procedures are established to ensure the enforcement of security policies and controls. (c) Ascertain whether there is an information classification methodology used either at the business line or the firm-wide level to clearly define the types of information deemed to be sensitive. (d) Determine whether incident response plans are in place and identify the steps to be taken in the event of a security breach.
		2. An effective organizational structure should be in place to allow for the development of firm-wide information security policies and standards and ensure compliance with those policies and standards by the business lines. The security	2. (a) Interview business line management to determine how the business line security function interacts with the corporate information security function and how both ensure compliance with security policies and procedures. (b) Ensure that individuals responsible for

Risk Reference Number	Key Risks Access Controls	Key Controls for Reducing Insider Computer Fraud	Risk-Mitigating Actions
		officer should have sufficient authority and independence to enforce compliance with security policies and procedures.	information security at the business line level do not have conflicting responsibilities (i.e., users, programmers, etc.).
2	Weak physical access controls could permit unauthorized access to business systems.	1. Policies governing access to business line operational areas and computer facilities by employees, visitors, and vendors should be established.	1. (a) Determine whether security checks and screening processes are as stringent for visitors, vendors, and consultants as they are for employees. (b) Ascertain whether contractual commitments (such as background checks and other security precautions related to the vendor's hiring practices) exist with third-party vendors working on business line systems and whether vendor staff is bonded.
		2. Where appropriate, physical barriers should be used to segment and prevent unauthorized access to computer equipment.	2. Interview management to ensure that paths of physical entry are evaluated for proper security (entry doors, glass windows and walls, modular partitions, etc.).
3	Improper procedures for granting, changing, and revoking access rights to business line systems could result in inadequate	1. Requests for access to business line systems should be approved by business line management. Controls should be in place to ensure that individuals' access rights are limited	1. (a) Review the procedures and documentation required to request access to business line systems. (b) Ensure that proper approvals are obtained and that an individual's access rights are

separation of duties and unauthorized access by individuals using inactive user IDs and passwords.

2. A process should be in place to ensure that access rights are revoked for individuals who leave the business line or change functions.

3. A quarterly recertification process should be in place whereby the security administrator sends out the list of users and their access rights to business line managers and receives a confirmation that access privileges for all users are appropriate and commensurate with their responsibilities.

1. Well-designed business line systems should not have recurring errors or a high number of access violations. Business line systems

Information integrity problems, often related to a breech in access, can seriously erode

to those necessary for their job function and do not conflict (i.e., an individual should not be able to input and confirm a transaction).

limited to the function he or she performs.
(c) Validate that effective separation of duties exists by comparing functional assignments within business line systems to responsibilities usually known to be in conflict (i.e., inquiry only function should not have input ability and input access should not exist with approval authority, etc.).

2. (a) Review security administration procedures to ensure that a process is in place to revoke an individual's access upon his or her departure from the business line.
(b) Request a list of individuals who have left the business line and ensure that their access to business line systems is not active.

3. Determine whether a recertification process is in place within the business line and the action taken if the forms are not returned in a timely manner.

1. (a) Determine if the business line systems highlight transaction problems in process queues and alert users of unusual or troublesome activity.

4

Risk Reference Number	Key Risks Access Controls	Key Controls for Reducing Insider Computer Fraud	Risk-Mitigating Actions
	confidence in the business line systems and information.	note exceptions as they occur throughout the business day and capture problem items in end-of-day reports.	(b) Ensure that historical data cannot be changed and that changes to information can only be made through transactions in the business system. Changes to information made by directly accessing files, program code, or by manipulating fields in the business system may cause the integrity of the business line systems to come into question.
		2. Business line managers and system administrators should keep logs of errors and system anomalies impacting daily operations.	2. Review a sample of error logs and reports showing system anomalies. Evaluate the process in place to investigate and correct items on the reports.
5	Ineffective access controls over both internal and external networks could make business line systems vulnerable to attack.	1. If the business line is responsible for its own systems, a process should be in place to aggressively monitor system activity and ensure that network security risks have been evaluated.	1. Determine who is responsible for monitoring network activity passing through business line systems and evaluate the services and protections rendered.
		2. User managers should be knowledgeable about the networks linked to their business systems and workstations and the protective measures in use. A central dial-in	2. (a) Determine if the business system is a stand-alone application or has internal or external connectivity (i.e., LAN, local area network; WAN, wide area network; Internet capability). (b) Determine if user managers allow direct dial-in connections to their workstations.

and dial-out modem pool should provide remote access from networked desktop systems. Analog phone lines should not permit direct connection to a desktop or workstation. Virus-scanning software should be provided at entry points into the network, such as remote-access servers and on each desktop system on the network.

Confirm the controls that are in place to prevent unauthorized access (i.e., segregating PCs with dial-in connections from PCs with access to internal networks and limiting the type of information that is stored on PCs with dial-in connections to nonsensitive information).

(c) Interview user managers to determine the security controls over external links to their system (i.e., firewalls and intrusion detection systems).

(d) Ascertain what networks (both internal and external) are linked to the workstations by simply looking at the desktop icons and questioning their function. Access to public file-sharing networks such as Napster should be prohibited.

(e) Determine if virus protection software is active on desktops. Confirm that a process is in place to update virus protection on a periodic basis.

3. Strong authentication methods should be required for access to critical systems/business processes and highly sensitive data.

6

Data is not classified according to criticality and sensitivity and in accordance with internal policy.

Classifications and criteria have been established and communicated to resource owners.

Review policies and procedures.

Risk Reference Number	Key Risks Access Controls	Key Controls for Reducing Insider Computer Fraud	Risk-Mitigating Actions
7	Data is not classified, documented, and approved by an appropriate senior official and does not receive periodic review.	Data classifications are documented and approved by an appropriate manager and are periodically reviewed.	Review resource classification documentation and compare to risk assessments. Discuss any discrepancies with management.
8	Management does not maintain a current list of authorized users and their access authorized. Resource owners have not identified authorized users and their access authorized.	Access authorizations are documented on standard forms and maintained on file, approved by senior managers, and securely transferred to security managers.	Review pertinent written policies and procedures. For a selection of users (both application user and IS personnel), review access authorization documentation.
9		Owners periodically review access authorization listings and determine whether they remain appropriate.	Interview owners and review supporting documentation. Determine whether inappropriate access is removed in a timely manner.
10		The number of users who can dial into the system from remote locations is limited and justification for such access is documented and approved by owners.	For a selection of users with dial-up access, review authorization and justification.

11		Security managers review access authorizations and discuss any questionable authorizations with resource owners.	Interview security managers and review documentation provided to them.
12	Data resource owners have not identified authorized users and their access authorized.	All changes to security profiles by security managers are automatically logged and periodically reviewed by management independent of the security function. Unusual activity is investigated.	Review a selection of recent profile changes and activity logs.
13		Security is notified immediately when system users are terminated or transferred.	Obtain a list of recently terminated employees from Personnel and, for a selection, determine whether system access was promptly terminated.
14	Emergency and temporary access authorization is not adequately controlled.	Emergency and temporary access authorizations are documented on standard forms and maintained on file, approved by appropriate managers, securely communicated to the security function, and automatically terminated after a predetermined period.	Review pertinent policies and procedures. Compare a selection of both expired and active temporary and emergency authorizations (obtained from the authorizing parties) with a system-generated list of authorized users. Determine the appropriateness of access documentation and approvals and the timeliness of terminating access authorization when no longer needed.
15	Owners do not determine disposition and sharing of data.	Standard forms are used to document approval for archiving, deleting, or sharing data files.	Examine standard approval forms. Interview data owners.

Risk Reference Number	Key Risks Access Controls	Key Controls for Reducing Insider Computer Fraud	Risk-Mitigating Actions
16		Prior to sharing data or programs with other entities, agreements are documented regarding how those files are to be protected.	Examine documents authorizing file sharing and file-sharing agreements.
17	Both physical and logical controls do not exist to prevent or detect unauthorized access.	Physical safeguards have been established that are commensurate with the risks of physical damage or access. Facilities housing sensitive and critical resources have been identified. All significant threats to the physical well-being of sensitive and critical resources have been identified and related risks determined.	Review a diagram of the physical layout of the computer, telecommunications, and cooling system facilities. Walk through facilities. Review risk analysis.
18		Access is limited to those individuals who routinely need access through the use of guards, identification badges, or entry devices, such as key cards. Management regularly reviews the list of persons with physical access to sensitive facilities.	Review lists of individuals authorized access to sensitive areas and determine the appropriateness for access. Before becoming recognized as the auditor, attempt to access sensitive areas without escort or identification badges. Observe entries to and exits from facilities during and after normal business hours. Observe utilities access paths. Interview management.

#	Condition	Control	Audit Procedures
19		Keys or other access are needed to enter the computer room and tape/media library.	Observe entries to and exits from sensitive areas during and after normal business hours. Interview employees.
20	Physical safeguards have not been established that are commensurate with the risks of physical damage or access.	All deposits and withdrawals of tapes and other storage media from the library are authorized and logged.	Review procedures for the removal and return of storage media from and to the library. Select from the log some returns and withdrawals, verify the physical existence of the tape or other media, and determine whether proper authorization was obtained for the movement.
21		Unissued keys or other entry devices are secured.	Observe practices for safeguarding keys and other devices.
22		Emergency exit and reentry procedures ensure that only authorized personnel are allowed to reenter after fire drills, etc.	Review written emergency procedures. Examine documentation supporting prior fire drills. Observe a fire drill.
23	Visitors are controlled.	Visitors to sensitive areas, such as the main computer room and tape/media library, are formally signed in and escorted.	Review visitor entry logs. Observe entries to and exits from sensitive areas during and after normal business hours. Interview guards at facility entry.
24		Entry codes are changed periodically.	Review documentation on and logs of entry code changes.
25		Visitors, contractors, and maintenance personnel are authenticated	Observe appointment and verification procedures for visitors.

Risk Reference Number	Key Risks Access Controls	Key Controls for Reducing Insider Computer Fraud	Risk-Mitigating Actions
		through the use of preplanned appointments and identification checks.	
26	Adequate logical access controls have not been implemented.	Passwords, tokens, or other devices are used to identify and authenticate users. Passwords are unique for specific individuals, not groups; controlled by the assigned user and not subject to disclosure; changed periodically—every 30 to 90 days; not displayed when entered; at least six alphanumeric characters in length; and prohibited from reuse for at least six generations, limited by time of day.	Review pertinent policies and procedures. Interview users. Review security software password parameters. Observe users keying in passwords. Attempt to log on without a valid password; make repeated attempts to guess passwords. Assess procedures for generating and communicating passwords to users.
27		Use of names or words is prohibited.	Review a system-generated list of current passwords. Search password file using audit software.
28		Vendor-supplied passwords are replaced immediately.	Attempt to log on using common vendor-supplied passwords. Search password file using audit software.
29		Generic user IDs and passwords are not used.	Interview users and security managers. Review a list of IDs and passwords.

30		Attempts to log on with invalid passwords are limited to three to four attempts.	Repeatedly attempt to log on using invalid passwords. Review security logs.
31		Personnel files are automatically matched with actual system users to remove terminated or transferred employees from the system.	Review pertinent policies and procedures. Review documentation of such comparisons. Interview security managers. Make comparison using audit software.
32		Password files are encrypted.	View dump of password files (e.g., hexadecimal printout).
33		For other devices, such as tokens or key cards, users maintain possession of their individual tokens, cards, etc, and understand that they must not loan or share these with others and must report lost items immediately.	Interview users. To evaluate biometrics or other technically sophisticated authentication techniques, the auditor should obtain the assistance of a specialist.
34	There is no identification of access paths which may result in security vulnerabilities.	An analysis of the logical access paths is performed whenever system changes are made.	Review access path diagram.
35	The absence of logical controls over data files and software programs may lead to unauthorized user access to data.	Security software is used to restrict access. Access to security software is restricted to security administrators only.	Interview security administrators and system users. Review security software parameters.
36		Computer terminals are automatically logged off after a period of inactivity.	Observe terminals in use. Review security software parameters.

Risk Reference Number	Key Risks Access Controls	Key Controls for Reducing Insider Computer Fraud	Risk-Mitigating Actions
37		Inactive users' accounts are monitored and removed when not needed.	Review security software parameters. Review a system-generated list of inactive log-on IDs, and determine why access for these users has not been terminated.
38		Logical controls over data files and software programs. Security administration personnel set parameters of security software to provide access as authorized and restrict access that has not been authorized. This includes access to data files, load libraries, batch operational procedures, source code libraries, security files, and operating system files. Naming conventions are used for resources.	Determine library names for sensitive or critical files and libraries, and obtain security reports of related access rules. Using these reports, determine who has access to critical files and libraries and whether the access matches the level and type of access authorized. Perform penetration testing by attempting to access and browse computer resources including critical data files, production load libraries, batch operational procedures (e.g., JCL libraries), source code libraries, security software, and the operating system. These tests should be performed as (1) an "outsider" with no information about the entity's computer systems; and (2) an "outsider" with prior knowledge about the systems (e.g., an ex-insider), and (3) an "insider" with and without specific information about the entity's computer systems, and with access to the entity's facilities.

	Risk	Controls	Audit Procedures
39	The absence of logical controls over a database may leave the bank vulnerable for unauthorized access and use of confidential and proprietary data	Database management systems (DBMS) and data dictionary (DD) controls have been implemented that restrict access to data files at the logical data view, field, or field-value level; control access to the DD using security profiles and passwords; maintain audit trails that allow monitoring of changes to the DD; and provide inquiry and update capabilities from application program functions, interfacing DBMS or DD facilities.	When performing insider tests, use an ID with no special privileges to attempt to gain access to computer resources beyond those available to the account. Also, try to access the entity's computer resources using default/generic IDs with easily guessed passwords. Determine whether naming conventions are used.
		Use of DBMS utilities is limited.	Review pertinent policies and procedures. Interview database administrator. Review DBMS and DD security parameters. Test controls by attempting access to restricted files.
		Access and changes to DBMS software are controlled.	
		Access to security profiles in the DD and security tables in the DBMS is limited.	Review security system parameters.

Risk Reference Number	Key Risks Access Controls	Key Controls for Reducing Insider Computer Fraud	Risk-Mitigating Actions
40	The absence of logical controls over telecommunications may lead to hacking attempts, spread of viruses, and unauthorized entry into a bank's information systems.	Communication software has been implemented to verify terminal identifications in order to restrict access through specific terminals; verify IDs and passwords for access to specific applications; control access through connections between systems and terminals; restrict an application's use of network facilities; protect sensitive data during transmission; automatically disconnect at the end of a session; maintain network activity logs; restrict access to tables that define network options, resources, and operator profiles.	Review pertinent policies and procedures. Review parameters set by communications software or teleprocessing monitors. Test telecommunications controls by attempting to access various files through communications networks. Identify all dial-up lines through automatic dialer software routines and compare with known dial-up access. Discuss discrepancies with management. Interview telecommunications management staff and users.
41		Allow only authorized users to shut down network components; monitor dial-in access by monitoring the source of calls or by disconnecting and then dialing back at preauthorized phone numbers; restrict in-house access to telecommunications software; control changes to telecommunications software.	

42	Ensure that data is not accessed or modified by an unauthorized user during transmission or while in temporary storage, and restrict and monitor access to telecommunications hardware or facilities.		
43	In addition to logical controls: The opening screen viewed by a user provides a warning and states that the system is for authorized use only and that activity will be monitored. Dial-in phone numbers are not published and are periodically changed.		Review pertinent policies and procedures. View the opening screen seen by telecommunication system users. Review documentation showing changes to dial-in numbers. Review entity's telephone directory to verify that the numbers are not listed.
44	Cryptographic tools have been implemented to protect the integrity and confidentiality of sensitive and critical data and software programs.	The absence of encryption may result in loss of data confidentiality for the bank and its customers.	To evaluate cryptographic tools, the auditor should obtain the assistance of a specialist.
45	Procedures are implemented to clear sensitive data and software from discarded and transferred equipment and media.	The absence of sound InfoSec policies and practices governing the sanitation of equipment and media prior to disposal or reuse could result in releasing sensitive data to the public.	Review written procedures. Interview personnel responsible for clearing equipment and media. For a selection of recently discarded or transferred items, examine documentation related to clearing of data and software. For selected items still in the entity's possession, test that they have been appropriately sanitized.

Risk Reference Number	Key Risks Access Controls	Key Controls for Reducing Insider Computer Fraud	Risk-Mitigating Actions
46	Failure to monitor and report unauthorized user access, investigating apparent security violations, and taking appropriate remedial action may result in undetected security violations and release of that information to unauthorized personnel.	Audit trails are maintained. All activity involving access to and modifications of sensitive or critical files is logged.	Review security software settings to identify types of activity logged.
47	Failure to monitor and report actual or attempted unauthorized, unusual, or attempts to gain access to sensitive/classified data may result in the release of that information to unauthorized personnel.	Security violations and activities, including failed log-on attempts, other failed access attempts, and sensitive activity, are reported to management and investigated.	Review pertinent policies and procedures. Review security violation reports. Examine documentation showing reviews of questionable activities.

48	Suspicious access activity is not investigated and the inaction leads to the release of that information to unauthorized personnel.	Security managers investigate security violations and report results to appropriate supervisory and management personnel. Appropriate disciplinary actions are taken.	Test a selection of security violations to verify that follow-up investigations were performed and to determine what actions were taken against the perpetrator.
49		Violations are summarized and reported to senior management.	Interview senior management and personnel responsible for summarizing violations. Review any supporting documentation.
50		Access control policies and techniques are modified when violations and related risk assessments indicate that such changes are appropriate.	Review policies and procedures and interview appropriate personnel. Review any supporting documentation.

Appendix B

Application Data Origination/Input

Risk Reference Number	Key Risks: Data Origination and Input	Key Controls for Reducing Insider Computer Fraud	Risk-Mitigating Actions
Controls Testing Residual Risk Form (CTRRF)			
Data Origination			
1	Inappropriate segregation of duties.	All stages of information systems processing are segregated.	Ensure that duties are separated so that no individual performs more than one of the following operations: data origination, data input, data processing, output distribution.
2	Source documents are inadequately destroyed.	Source documents capture all relevant data.	Determine if source documents are used to minimize errors and omissions. Specifically, are special-purpose forms used to guide the initial recording of data in a consistent format? Are preprinted sequential numbers used to establish controls? Does each type of transaction have a unique identifier? Does each transaction have a cross-reference number that can be used to trace information to and from the source document?
3	All users have access to source documents.	Source documents are satisfactorily safeguarded.	Verify that access to source documents and blank input forms is restricted to authorized personnel.
4	Lack of management approval for release of source documents.	Management release is required prior to the release of blank source documents.	Ascertain whether authorization is required from two or more accountable individuals required before source documents and blank input forms are released from storage.

Risk Reference Number	Key Risks: Data Origination and Input	Key Controls for Reducing Insider Computer Fraud	Risk-Mitigating Actions
5	The absence of a control or quality assurance (QA) function increases the potential for inaccuracies within source documentation.	To maintain a control or quality assurance function within a business.	(a) Determine if the user department has a control group responsible for collecting and completing source documents; (b) determine if the control group identifies errors to facilitate the correction of erroneous information; (c) determine if the control group produces error logs used to ensure timely follow-up and correction of unresolved errors; (d) determine if the control group ensures that source document originators are immediately notified by the control group of all errors.
6	The absence of a control or quality assurance (QA) function increases the potential for inaccuracies within source documentation.	To maintain a control or quality assurance function within a business.	Determine if the control group verifies that source documents are accounted for, are complete and accurate, are appropriately authorized, and are transmitted in a timely manner.
7	The absence of a control or quality assurance (QA) function increases the potential for inaccuracies within source documentation.	To maintain a control or quality assurance function within a business.	Determine if the control group independently controls data submitted for transmittal to the DP department for conversion or entry by using the following: turnaround transmittal documents; batching techniques; record counts; predetermined control totals; logging techniques; other?

8	The absence of a control or quality assurance (QA) function increases the potential for inaccuracies within source documentation.	To maintain a control or quality assurance function within a business.	Ascertain that if the user department is responsible for its own data entry, there is a separate group within that department to perform this input function.

Input

1	Source documents are not controlled and do not require authorizing signatures.	1. Access to blank source documents is restricted to authorized personnel. 2. Source documents are prenumbered to help maintain control over the documents. 3. Key source documents require authorizing signatures. 4. For batch application systems, a batch control sheet is prepared for a group of source documents and includes date, control number, number of documents, a control total for a key field, and identification of the user submitting the batch.	1. Review written procedures. (a) Interview user management and personnel. (b) Observe source document preparation and blank document storage area. (c) Inspect prepared source documents, and batches if batch application. (d) Determine procedures for recording and tracking of numbers if prenumbered documents are used. 2. Determine if documented procedures explain the methods for data conversion and entry. 3. Ensure that the DP department has a control group responsible for data conversion and entry of all source documents received from user departments.

Risk Reference Number	Key Risks: Data Origination and Input	Key Controls for Reducing Insider Computer Fraud	Risk-Mitigating Actions
2	Supervisory or independent reviews of data do not occur before entering the application system.	1. Data control unit personnel verify that source documents are properly prepared and authorized. 2. Data control unit personnel monitor data entry and processing of source documents.	(a) Review written procedures. (b) Interview management and data control unit personnel. (c) Observe the process.
3	Master files are not used to identify unauthorized transactions.	1. Before transactions are processed, they are verified using master files of approved vendors, employees, and so forth, as appropriate for the application. 2. Master files and program code that does the verification are protected from unauthorized modifications.	1. Review application documentation and interview application programmers. (a) Interview user management and personnel. (b) Review reports of transactions rejected by this technique. (c) Process test transactions and evaluate results. 2. Evaluate general controls that protect the master files and program code from unauthorized modifications.
4	Exceptions are not reported to management for their review and approval.	Exceptions, based on parameters established by management, are reported	(a) Review application documentation and interview application programmers. (b) Interview user management and personnel.

	Exposure	Control	Audit Procedures
			for their review and approval.
			(c) Determine criteria for exceptions reported. (d) Review exception reports of transactions listed by this technique. (e) Process test transactions and evaluate results.
5	Source documents are not designed to minimize errors.	1. The source document is well-designed to aid the preparer and facilitate data entry. 2. Transaction type and data field codes are preprinted on the source document.	1. (a) Obtain and review key source documents. (b) Observe data entry activities. (c) Interview user management and personnel. (d) Obtain and evaluate any analysis by entity of causes for data entry errors. 2. Determine if turnaround transmittal documents returned to the DP control group are accounted for to ensure that no documents were added or lost during conversion.
6	Preformatted computer terminal screens are not used to guide data entry.	Preformatted computer terminal screens are utilized and allow prompting for data to be entered, and editing of data as it is entered.	
7	Key verification increases the accuracy of significant data fields.	1. Significant fields are rekeyed to verify the accuracy of data entry. 2. The person assigned to rekey the data is sufficiently separated and independent from the	1. Determine if key verification is used to check the accuracy of all keying operations. 2. Determine if keying and verifying of a document are done by different individuals. 3. Determine if preprogrammed keying formats are used to ensure that data is recorded in the proper field, format, and so forth.

Risk Reference Number	Key Risks: Data Origination and Input	Key Controls for Reducing Insider Computer Fraud	Risk-Mitigating Actions
7		original data entry person, so as to not negate the effectiveness of this process.	
8	Automated entry devices are not used to increase data accuracy.	Effective use is made of automated entry devices to reduce the potential for data entry errors.	
9	Programmed validation and edit checks identify erroneous data.	1. Programmed validation and edits include checks for reasonableness, dependency, existence, mathematical accuracy, range, check digit, document reconciliation, relationship or prior data matching, authorization or approval codes, relationship or prior data matching, field format controls, required field controls.	1. (a) Review application documentation. (b) Interview application programmer and user personnel. (c) Review validation and edit reports. (d) Process test transactions and evaluate results. (e) Using audit software, search key application files for erroneous data. 2. Evaluate general controls that protect data validation and editing resources from unauthorized modifications.

10	Tests are not made of critical calculations.	Programs perform limit and reasonableness checks on critical calculations.	Review application documentation. Interview application programmer and user personnel. Review reports of data resulting from tests. Process test transactions and evaluate results.
11	Tests are not made of critical calculations.	Program code and criteria for tests of critical calculations are protected from unauthorized modifications.	Evaluate general controls that protect program code and criteria from unauthorized modification.
12	Overriding or bypassing data validation and editing is not restricted.	1. Overriding or bypassing data validation and editing is restricted to supervisors and then only in a limited number of acceptable circumstances. 2. Every override is automatically logged by the application so that the action can be analyzed for appropriateness and correctness.	1. (a) Review application documentation. (b) Interview application programmer and user management personnel. (c) Review logs and determine analysis by management to assess appropriateness and correctness of overrides. 2. Determine if all personnel are prevented from overriding or bypassing data validation and editing problems.
13	Rejected transactions are not controlled with an automated error suspense file.	1. Rejected data is automatically written on an automated error suspense file and held until corrected. Each erroneous transaction is annotated with codes indicating the	1. Review application documentation and interview application programmers. (a) Interview user management and personnel. (b) Is data rejected automatically written to an automated cumulative suspense file or log? (c) If yes, is a printed error listing delivered to the user on a timely basis which includes sufficient

Risk Reference Number	Key Risks: Data Origination and Input	Key Controls for Reducing Insider Computer Fraud	Risk-Mitigating Actions
		type of data error, date and time the transaction was processed and the error identified, and the identity of the user who originated the transaction.	information about the reason(s) for rejection to allow correction—date of original entry (used to produce reports in aged sequence).
		2. Record counts and control totals are established over the suspense file and used in reconciling transactions processed.	(d) Are corrected transactions reentered through error correction processing functions that provide hard-copy reports of original and corrected transactions and remove invalid transaction records? If Yes, are these reports reviewed to ensure that the resubmitted transaction was accepted by the system, the correcting entries were accurately made, and no unauthorized additions or deletions were made?
		3. A control group is responsible for controlling and monitoring rejected transactions.	
		4. The suspense file is purged of transactions as they are corrected. Review application documentation and interview application programmers.	

| 14 | Erroneous data is not reported back to the user department for investigation and correction. | 5. This file is used to produce, on a regular basis and for management review, an analysis of the level and type of transaction errors and the age of uncorrected transactions.

1. Error reports or error files accessible by computer terminal show rejected transactions with error messages that have clearly understandable corrective actions for each type of error.
2. Errors are corrected by the user originating the transaction.
3. All corrections are reviewed and approved by supervisors before the corrections are reentered. | 1. (a) Review application documentation and interview application programmers.
(b) Interview user management and personnel.
(c) Determine criteria for exceptions reported.
(d) Review exception reports of transactions listed by this technique.
(e) Process test transactions and evaluate results. |

Appendix C

Application Data Processing

Controls Testing Residual Risk Form (CTRRF): Data Processing

Risk Reference Number	Key Risks: Data Processing	Key Controls for Reducing Insider Computer Fraud	Risk-Mitigating Actions
1	Record counts and control totals are not accurate.	1. User-prepared record count and control totals established over source documents are used to help determine the completeness of data entry and processing. 2. For online or real-time systems, record count and control totals are accumulated progressively for a specific time period (daily or more frequently) and are used to help determine the completeness of data entry and processing.	1. (a) Review application documentation and interview application programmer. (b) Interview user management and personnel. (c) Observe activity for developing record counts and control totals. (d) Review supporting documentation generated by system.
2	Computer sequence checking does not exist.	1. Preassigned serial numbers on source documents are entered into the computer and used for sequence checking. 2. Transactions without preassigned serial numbers are automatically assigned a unique sequence number, which is used by the computer to monitor that all transactions are processed. 3. Sequence checking is used to identify missing or duplicate transactions. 4. Reports of missing or duplicate	1. (a) Review application documentation and interview application programmer. (b) Interview user management and personnel. (c) Review reports of missing and duplicate transactions. (d) Observe activity to investigate items reported as missing or duplicate.

Risk Reference Number	Key Risks: Data Processing	Key Controls for Reducing Insider Computer Fraud	Risk-Mitigating Actions
		transactions are produced, and items are investigated and resolved in a timely manner.	
3	Computer matching of transaction data is inaccurate or incomplete.	1. Computer matching of transaction data with data in master or suspense files occurs to identify missing or duplicate transactions. 2. Reports of missing or duplicate transactions are produced and items are investigated and resolved in a timely manner.	1. (a) Review application documentation and interview application programmer. (b) Interview user management and personnel. (c) Review reports of missing and duplicate transactions. (d) Observe activity to investigate items reported as missing or duplicate.
4	Checking reports for transaction data does not exist.	Individual transactions or source documents are compared with a detailed listing of items processed by the computer, particularly to control important low-volume, high-value transactions.	1. (a) Interview user management and personnel. (b) Observe activity. (c) Review listings for notations showing checking was performed.
5	Reconciliations do not show the completeness of data processed at points in the processing cycle.	1. Record courts and control totals are established and entered with transaction data and reconciled to determine the completeness of data entry. 2. Trailer labels or control records containing record counts and control totals are generated for all computer	1. (a) Review application documentation and interview application programmer. (b) Interview user management and personnel. (c) Interview data control personnel. (d) Observe reconciliation activities. (e) Review control reports.

6

files and tested by application programs to determine that all records have been processed.

3. Computer-generated control totals (run-to-run totals) are automatically reconciled between jobs to check for completeness of processing.

4. System interfaces require that the sending system's output control counts equal the receiving system's determined input counts.

5. A data processing control group receives and reviews control total reports and determines the completeness of processing.

Reconciliations are performed to determine the completeness of transactions processed, master files updated, and outputs generated.

Reconciliations do not show the completeness of data processed for the total cycle.

1. Does the control group independently control data processing through the following:

Ensuring that application schedules are met?

Balancing batch counts of data submitted for processing?

Balancing record counts of data submitted for processing?

Balancing predetermined control totals of data submitted for processing?

Maintaining accurate logs of input/output files used in computer processing?

Risk Reference Number	Key Risks: Data Processing	Key Controls for Reducing Insider Computer Fraud	Risk-Mitigating Actions
			Ensuring that input/work/output files used in computer processing? Ensuring that restarts are performed properly? Other? 2. Do data processing controls ensure the following: Output counts from the system equal input counts to the system? Program interfaces require that the sending program output counts equal the receiving program input counts?
	Processing log records are nonexistent.	Adequate audit trails exist which evidences UID and other indications from the application that processing was successful.	1. Are there processing log records for this application? If yes, what information is logged (UID)? Is the log compared to source documents?
	The application does not generate control totals and reconciliations.	Control totals and reconciliations are performed.	1. Does the program generate control totals and perform reconciliations to check for completeness of processing? (a) Do output counts from system equal input counts? (b) System interface reconciliation controls.

Application Output/ Management Information System (MIS)

Controls Testing Residual Risk Form (CTRRF) MIS

Risk Reference Number	Key Risks, Output/MIS	Key Controls for Reducing Insider Computer Fraud	Risk-Mitigating Actions
1	MIS report disposition is not properly controlled.	Ensure adequate policies, practices, and procedures govern MIS distribution and use.	Select and review samples of ongoing transaction processing systems/operational reports for the targeted MIS area(s). Determine whether: (a) The source of the information collected originates from the expected business area. (b) Users of the information are the appropriate employees or managers within that area of activity. (c) The reports are distributed ultimately to the appropriate users. (d) The flow of these MIS information/reports is consistent with the responsibilities reflected on the area's official organization chart. (e) MIS is timely, accurate, consistent, complete, and relevant.
2	MIS is ineffective to adequately support a business operation (example, timeliness, accuracy, consistency, completeness, and relevance).	Management has performed an assessment of the adequacy over MIS.	Determine the degree to which management and the staff in an area under review use MIS adequately and can support that its use is appropriate and effective. Perform the following steps: (a) Discuss the five MIS elements with a senior manager of the respective business unit. (b) Repeat this step with an employee of the business unit who has experience with the MIS system. (Note: This task is designed to determine if significant

Risk Reference Number	Key Risks, Output/MIS	Key Controls for Reducing Insider Computer Fraud	Risk-Mitigating Actions
			differences about the adequacy of the MIS exist among management or staff.)
			(c) Based on management's self-assessment of the usability of its MIS, identify any planned activities to enhance, modify, or expand these systems.
3	MIS is ineffective to adequately support a business operation (example, timeliness, accuracy, consistency, completeness, and relevance).	Management has performed an assessment of the adequacy over MIS.	AUDIT Determine if the MIS target area was internally or externally audited in the past two years: (a) If it has, review the scope of the audit, the findings, and management's response to that report. (b) If it has not, coordinate with the MIS EIC in interviewing audit management to determine what their plans are regarding an audit review of the MIS system
4	Management lacks a clear understanding of risks and controls over transaction flows through an application or system.	Management has clearly identified application risks by conducting risk assessments for information technology (IT) critical applications that support key business processes.	Obtain from the user manuals or the appropriate manager a workflow showing data from the point-of-entry, through user processes, to the final product. This task is designed to review how information is identified, gathered, merged, manipulated, and presented and: (Depending on the organization's sophistication and system size, examiners may have to develop this workflow themselves.) (a) Discuss the area's MIS process with a representative sample of users and determine if they know where the data is coming from, where it is going, and how it

4b	Management lacks a clear understanding of risks and controls over transaction flows through an application or system.	Management has clearly identified application risks by conducting risk assessments for IT critical applications that support key business processes.	gets there. A complete understanding would suggest the interviewees both use and understand the MIS system(s) supporting them. (b) Identify and note the points where adjustments to data occur. (c) Identify the department staff responsible for MIS-related input data and reports—that is, obtain a list of users, ad hoc software report writers, and the programmers involved. Compare this information with the material acquired in the immediately preceding item. (d) Determine if preparation and reconciliation processes are sufficient to reasonably ensure integrity of information. (e) Determine if data adjustments are documented adequately. (f) Determine the effectiveness of ad hoc report writing capabilities by reviewing the software vendor's user manual for data presentations.
5	End-user computing can introduce significant technology risks, which include inaccurate MIS reporting.	A developed end-user computing policy that identifies, measures, monitors, and controls technology risk over end-user computing. The policy needs to ensure the confidentiality, integrity, and availability of data generated from end-user	End-user policy and practices should include management's development and adherence to the following policy and practices to ensure accurate MIS. Primary examiner reliance for evaluating the criteria listed below should be centered on the audit function of the bank: (a) Assurance that information (audit trails), controls, and security features are generated and stored within an end-user-developed application system. (b) Data storage, file retention, backup, purging,

Risk Reference Number	Key Risks, Output/MIS	Key Controls for Reducing Insider Computer Fraud	Risk-Mitigating Actions
		computing. The usability of adequate end-user-generated MIS can be partly attributed to the assurance given by management during their risk assessment over end-user computing.	archiving, and rotating procedures are available and adequate. (c) Supporting documentation used to develop the end-user system or application is adequate and correct. (d) Program change controls are available and effective.
6			(a) End-user downloads from a micro to a host computer are satisfactorily restricted and controlled. Downloaded data may be manipulated and reported inaccurately. (b) Algorithms used within end-user systems or applications are validated for accuracy and integrity. (c) Data downloaded and processed through the end-user system and then uploaded to the host computer (mainframe, midrange, or microcomputer) needs to be validated for accuracy and relevance prior to data transmission. (d) Programming standards exist over end-user computing. (e) Software testing exists to ensure accurate MIS reporting.

7			(a) Documentation standards for the system or application exist to enhance MIS reporting. (b) Testing standards exist to ensure data integrity and accuracy of MIS reporting. (c) Limitations on in-house software development. (d) Confidentiality of data (ensuring compliance with the consumer financial privacy provisions of the Gramm–Leach–Bliley Act). (e) Service bureau processing and MIS are accurate.
8	Commercial off-the-shelf (COTS) software fails to generate accurate MIS, and customizations are required.	The modifications made to the software package are thoroughly tested and meet or exceed all testing expectations, including user acceptance tests (UATs).	Review all COTS packages for customizations and evaluate the existence of algorithm changes and new soft code development. Review the findings of all test results (unit, system, regression, point to point, end to end, and UAT) to determine if there were any unresolved development testing issues prior to use in production. Validate the accuracy of the MIS generated from the use of the COTS package.

Appendix E

Key Fraud Signature (KFS) Worksheet

Reference ID	INSIDER LOAN Problem Description Source: FFIEC Insider Loan Fraud Report, 2002	Forensic Foto Frames																				
		1	2	3	4	5	6	7	8	9	10	11	12	13	14	15	16	17	18	19	20	21
1	Reconcile download data to board reports, call report data, and institution's systems generated reports.																						
2	Analyze fields containing past-due loan counters by using search criteria to identify loans with chronic past-due loan histories.																						
3	Establish criteria to identify loans with multiple payment extensions.																						
4	Establish criteria to identify loans with multiple renewals and an outstanding loan balance that exceeds the original loan amount.																						

Forensic Foto Frames

Reference ID	INSIDER LOAN Problem Description Source: FFIEC Insider Loan Fraud Report, 2002	1	2	3	4	5	6	7	8	9	10	11	12	13	14	15	16	17	18	19	20	21
5	Identify loans with partial charge-offs.																					
6	Determine reasonableness of accrued interest in relation to loan type, repayment terms, and payment status.																					
7	Establish criteria to identify loans significantly paid ahead.																					
8	Identify loans to different borrowers with the same mailing address but different customer identification numbers.																					
9	Identify loans to different borrowers with the same social security number or taxpayer identification number and different customer identification numbers.																					

10	Identify loans with similar names or forms of the same name. Also identify addresses that are similar or the same.
11	Generate a list of loans, by loan officer, with a post office box mailing address or hold mail notation.
12	Identify loans by loan officers who may have been terminated or left the institution.
13	Identify loans that are associated with a loan officer who has a substantial portfolio or whose portfolio has experienced rapid growth.
14	If the institution recently raised additional capital, determine if insider loans or total loans increased substantially around the same time.

Reference ID	INSIDER LOAN Problem Description Source: FFIEC Insider Loan Fraud Report, 2002	Forensic Foto Frames																				
		1	2	3	4	5	6	7	8	9	10	11	12	13	14	15	16	17	18	19	20	21
15	Identify loans with comparably low interest rates.																						
16	An institution changes loan review personnel or firm without apparent valid reasons.																						
17	An insider inappropriately suggests or resists changes in appraisers.																						
18	Insider receives compensation incentives of bonuses based on new loan volumes without compensating controls.																						
19	The insider is a defendant in a lawsuit alleging improper handling of a transaction.																						

Appendix F

Cyber-Security HealthCheck

Cyber-Security HealthCheck (A Diagnostic Scorecard for Evaluating Enterprise Cyber-Related Information Technology Risks and Controls)— The Risk Assessment Scorecard Criteria

Section #	Controls Scoring Criteria — Green: Fully Implemented—(Low Risk) / Yellow: Partially Implemented—(Moderate Risk) / Red: Not Implemented—(High Risk)	Rating and Comments
1	**Roles and Responsibilities** Evaluate the organization's information security risk assessment process based on the following criteria:	
1.1	Does the institution have a written information security risk assessment program that includes safeguards to address the risks associated with insider computer fraud, which has been approved by the board of directors or subcommittee?	RED Comments:
1.2	Does the board of directors, or appropriate subcommittee, oversee the development, implementation, and maintenance of the institution's information security program, including assigning specific responsibility for its implementation and reviewing reports from management at least annually?	YELLOW Comments:

	Controls Scoring Criteria	
Section #	*Green: Fully Implemented—(Low Risk)* *Yellow: Partially Implemented—(Moderate Risk)* *Red: Not Implemented—(High Risk)*	*Rating* *and* *Comments*
1.3	Has the institution conducted a comprehensive information security risk assessment? a. Has the information security risk assessment been documented in writing? b. Does the board of directors receive reports on the information security risk assessment at least annually?	YELLOW Comments:
1.4	Do reports to the board of directors provide adequate information concerning: a. Matters such as material security breaches or violations? b. Results of institution's information security risk assessment, such as changes in security risk ratings by business line, results of testing, and management's responses? c. Material changes in new business activities or initiatives that may impact the security profile of the institution and require changes in the information security program? d. Specific recommendations for changes to the information security program as well as time frames for implementation?	YELLOW Comments:
1.5	Does business line management understand and participate in the information security risk assessment process? a. Are managers involved in the process to identify the business impact of security failures? b. Do they participate in the development of control enhancements to mitigate risks? c. Are they sufficiently involved in implementing board-approved security strategies and action plans? d. Do they have an adequate understanding of security issues impacting their business lines and processes?	GREEN Comments:
1.6	Does the institution's information security risk assessment reflect appropriate participation from specialists from technology, compliance, audit, and other support functions?	YELLOW Comments:

1.7	Do technology specialists have sufficient knowledge, training, and expertise in information systems and security?	RED
		Comments:

      a. Do they understand the connectivity between systems, applications, and business parties (internal and external) and assess the associated risks?

      b. Can they effectively communicate to business line managers the information security risks posed by these relationships?

Overall Risk Level: YELLOW

2   **Characterization of Systems and Data Flows**
Evaluate the organization's systems and data flows based on the following criteria:

2.1	Does the risk assessment appropriately identify, inventory, and characterize the information assets and systems to be protected?	Comments:

      a. Does the process include a review of the institution's networks, computer systems, and connections to business partners and the Internet, and interconnections between internal and external systems? Are points of data entry, processing, transfer, storage, and destruction identified as well as critical information systems and databases?

      b. Does the process reflect a sufficient understanding of information flows and identify potential vulnerabilities/gaps in existing controls?

      c. Does the process adequately identify and characterize the risks associated with customer information assets and systems?

2.2	Does the institution have an appropriate information data classification program in place to identify and rank data, systems, and applications in order of importance?	Comments:

      a. Have policies and procedures been established for the protection of information based on classification? Are they applied consistently across the organization?

      b. Does the program appropriately identify categories of nonpublic personal information that the institution collects and discloses?

      c. Has the institution developed strategies and implemented controls to protect information classified as sensitive or highly sensitive (for example, use of encryption, VPNs, or utilizing secure protocols for data transmission such as IPSec, Secure Socket Layer [SSL], and S-HTTP, etc.)?

Overall Risk Level:

	Controls Scoring Criteria	
Section #	*Green: Fully Implemented—(Low Risk)* *Yellow: Partially Implemented—(Moderate Risk)* *Red: Not Implemented—(High Risk)*	*Rating* *and* *Comments*
3	**Threat and Vulnerability Risk Assessment** Evaluate the organization's threats and vulnerabilities based on the following criteria:	
3.1	Has the institution appropriately identified potential threat scenarios, including: 　a. Internal threat scenarios (e.g., malicious or incompetent employees, contractors, service providers, and former insiders)? 　b. External threat scenarios (e.g., malicious hackers, recreational hackers, competitors, terrorists)? Common types of threats that could be launched internally or externally include: 　a. Denial of service: Large volume of attacks designed to overload the network to prevent authorized users from accessing its services. 　b. Malicious code: Malicious software code designed to cause damage to a target computer (e.g., virus, worm, Trojan horse, or embedded code). 　c. Unauthorized access: System access that circumvents identification and authentication processes. 　d. Inappropriate usage: May violate the bank's acceptable use policy and potentially create backdoors, permitting unauthorized access to confidential data and files.	Comments:
3.2	Have the different capabilities, motivations, and likelihood of occurrence for each of the threat sources been evaluated?	Comments:
3.3	Has the institution conducted a vulnerability assessment to determine sufficiency of the institution's policies, procedures, and internal controls, including: 　a. Administrative controls (e.g., segregation of duties, system logs, and access controls)? 　b. Technical controls (e.g., vulnerability assessments, penetration testing, security audits)? 　c. Physical controls (e.g., access to records, equipment, bank, and data center facilities, protection against physical attack)? 　d. Service provider and vendor management programs (e.g., independent reviews of service provider internal controls)?	Comments:

3.4   Have security controls been reviewed against critical   Comments:
links, data entry, and exit points?
a. Are controls commensurate with the information
assets and systems they protect?
b. Do controls adequately address risks to customer
information assets and systems?

3.5   To the extent that the institution uses vulnerability   Comments:
assessment tools, are these tools sufficiently robust
to identify vulnerabilities within the network and
operating systems? For example, does the vulnerability assessment software:
    a. Receive updates on vulnerabilities from the
    vendor or other databases on an ongoing basis?
    b. Have the ability to scan for select vulnerabilities
    as well as conduct full vulnerability scans of the
    network?[a]
    c. Have the ability to apply the new software,
    operating system upgrades, or the most recent
    patches to eliminate vulnerabilities?
    d. Have packet-sniffing capabilities to identify
    anomalies in network traffic?[b]

3.6   Does management conduct vulnerability scanning of   Comments:
all active devices and open ports on the network?[c]
Network components and open ports that may have
active devices include:
    a. Operating systems (Microsoft Windows, Unix,
    and Linux)
    b. Novell Netware servers
    c. Network switches, routers, hubs, modems
    d. Wireless access points
    e. Web servers and Web-based applications
    f. Lotus Notes applications
    g. Remote access systems (e.g., Telnet, pcAnywhere,
    etc.)
    h. Telephone systems
    i. Public information Web site

3.7   Is the frequency of vulnerability scans adequate? For   Comments:
example, does management conduct vulnerability scans:
    a. After any changes to the network infrastructure
    (e.g., adding/deleting firewalls, routers, or
    switches) or configuration (e.g., rule-based
    changes required as a result of changes in policy)?
    b. As a matter of routine practice to identify if any
    new vulnerabilities have been introduced as a

Section #	*Controls Scoring Criteria* *Green: Fully Implemented—(Low Risk)* *Yellow: Partially Implemented—(Moderate Risk)* *Red: Not Implemented—(High Risk)*	*Rating and Comments*
	result of implementing software patches or version updates?	
	c. Based on frequency of exploits (e.g., higher incidents of malicious code events may warrant more proactive scanning practices)?	
	Overall Risk Level	
4	**Independent Diagnostic Tests (Penetration Testing)** Evaluate the organization's penetration testing based on the following criteria:	

4.1	Assess the adequacy of any independent diagnostic tests (e.g., penetration tests) performed of the network.[d] For example, are penetration tests conducted:
	a. Of all high-risk system components on the network, including contingency plans, at least annually?
	b. By persons independent of the design, installation, maintenance, and operation of the tested system?
	c. Under various scenarios involving different degrees of access? For example, does penetration testing emulate situations involving an:
	  • Internal employee with low-level access to the network?
	  • Internal consultant with technical skills and only physical access rights?
	  • External party equivalent to a total outsider with limited knowledge about the system?[e]
	d. Utilizing different methods or approaches, such as:
	  • Remote network: Simulating an attack launched across the Internet with the goal of defeating various components of the network infrastructure (e.g., firewalls, filtering routers, and Web servers).
	  • Local network: Simulating an employee or other authorized person who may have legal connections to the institution's network.
		Comments:

> - Stolen laptop computer: examining the computer for passwords that may be stored in dial-up software thereby allowing an ethical hacker to dial-in an institution's intranet.
> - Physical access attempts to facilities and systems such as office spaces and document or information disposal or destruction locations

e. Utilizing social engineering, which involves manipulation of human trust by an attacker to obtain access to computer systems?

f. By all high-risk service providers that transmit, process, or store customer data on behalf of the institution?

4.2	Is the frequency of penetration testing adequate? For example, is frequency based on: a. The value and sensitivity of data and systems? b. Changes to systems, policies and procedures, personnel, and contractors? c. Results of vulnerability assessments, prior penetration tests, and audit findings?	Comments:
4.3	Are penetration test results effective? Test results should: a. Provide metrics and recommendations that are logical, objective, and directly related to threat scenarios. b. Provide feedback to the risk profile and risk rating for the business. c. Serve as input to the scope of the ongoing vulnerability assessment process.	Comments:
4.4	In instances where the institution has outsourced the penetration testing function, assess the adequacy of the institution's service provider selection criteria. Consider the extent to which: a. Background checks are performed on members of the service provider's ethical hacking team. b. Documentation is available to support test results and completion of the terms of the engagement.	Comments:

Overall Risk Level

	Controls Scoring Criteria	
Section #	*Green: Fully Implemented—(Low Risk)* *Yellow: Partially Implemented—(Moderate Risk)* *Red: Not Implemented—(High Risk)*	*Rating* *and* *Comments*
5	**Assessment of Probability and Impact** Evaluate the organization's assessment processes for probability and impact for threats:	
5.1	Has the likelihood that identified threats may materialize been determined, taking into consideration the sensitivity of information and known vulnerabilities in existing controls? a. Have probabilities been assigned to threats (e.g., probable, highly possible, unlikely)? b. Have threats deserving priority attention been identified? c. Is the institution's threat assessment process dynamic, taking into consideration customer service areas or the potential for new threats that may be introduced as a result of new operating systems, software applications, or delivery channels? d. Are there effective processes in place to update systems and controls when new software or operating system upgrades or patches are released?	Comments:
5.2	Is an impact analysis of all threats and vulnerabilities performed for the business lines? a. Does the impact analysis take into consideration loss of data integrity, confidentiality, and availability of customer information? b. Do business line managers and technical specialists work together to properly assess the potential impact of a threat or vulnerability?	Comments:
	Overall Risk Level	
6	**Assignment of Information Security Risk Ratings** Evaluate the organization's assignment of information security risk ratings:	
6.1	Are security risk ratings assigned? Do they appropriately take into consideration the: a. Likelihood that threats will materialize? b. Magnitude of potential impact? c. Adequacy of existing controls?	Comments:

6.2   Are policies in place that require the documentation   Comments:
        supporting risk ratings?

6.3   Is there a clear and consistent application of the risk   Comments:
        ratings across business lines?

Overall Risk Level

7   **Evaluate the organization's development of effective
         strategies and action plans based upon the results of
         the risk assessment process:**

7.1   Has management developed effective strategies and   Comments:
        action plans to address risks identified through the
        information security risk assessment?
        a. Have specific time frames for implementation of
        strategies and action plans been developed?

Overall Risk Level

8   **Intrusion Detection**
        Evaluate the organization's development of effective
        intrusion detection systems (IDSs) relating to internal
        and external attacks:

8.1   Are policies in place governing the: Comments:
        a. Strategic architecture of IDS?
        b. Functionality of IDS systems and software?
        c. Monitoring of IDS performance?
        d. Management, monitoring, and archival of activity
        logs (firewall, OS, IDS, etc.)?
        e. Intrusion risk assessment, analysis, and reporting?

8.2   Has the institution implemented an appropriate IDS   Comments:
        architecture based on the results of its information
        security risk assessment (including the results of
        vulnerability assessment and penetration testing)?
        For example, has the institution:
        a. Established a network-based IDS (NIDS)[f] to
           identify and analyze attack events utilizing either
           attack signatures (known exploits) or unusual
           behavior on a host or network?
        b. Established a host-based IDS (HIDS) to identify
           and analyze attack events based on changes to files
           or other unusual activity (e.g., excessive log-in
           attempts, modifications to system privileges,
           unapproved access to applications or data, or
           restricted ports)?
        c. Placed sensors inside the demilitarized zone

Section #	Controls Scoring Criteria Green: Fully Implemented—(Low Risk) Yellow: Partially Implemented—(Moderate Risk) Red: Not Implemented—(High Risk)	Rating and Comments
	(DMZ), inside and outside the firewalls, on the local area network (LAN) or subnet, or in other areas of the network that may be exposed to increased risk of wireless hacks, war-dialing, or other intrusions? d. Set up rogue networks that may include Honey-Pots or HoneyNets[g] to support intelligence gathering and strengthen information security defenses?	
8.3	Has management consulted legal counsel and law enforcement on the requirements and restrictions associated with setting up a rogue network?	Comments:
8.4	Do the institution's intrusion detection systems have sufficient functionality to identify and report on common hacker attack methods and strategies, such as: a. Denial of service (e.g., buffer overruns, large packet ping attacks, Internet Protocol (IP) spoofing, remote and local DOS strategies, etc.)? b. Penetration attacks (e.g., remote and local penetration, network vulnerability scanners, password crackers, sniffers, etc.)? c. Unauthorized insider attempts? d. Unauthorized attempts to gain access to administrator rights and privileges? e. Unauthorized host-based data modifications? f. Other unusual activity such as volume, type of activity, or time spent on the network?	Comments:
8.5	Does management appropriately monitor its IDS? For example: a. Is someone reviewing IDS alerts and reports on an ongoing basis? b. Is there an effective process in place to refer high-risk intrusions to the computer incident response team (CIRT)?	Comments:

8.6 Is the performance of the institution's IDS effective? Comments:
a. Do IDSs evaluate the type, extent, magnitude, and severity of intrusions identified?
b. Are intrusion risks assessed (e.g., evaluated in terms of high, moderate, or low risk) to determine appropriate action?
c. Is there an undue volume of false positive and false negative alerts?
d. Does the institution adjust the thresholds and configuration settings appropriately to increase the accuracy of alerts?

8.7 Is intrusion detection management information system (MIS) timely, accurate, and complete? Comments:
a. Are intrusion reports generated on a real-time basis?
b. Are false negatives and false positives eliminated from MIS before they are referred for action?
c. Does the MIS produce sufficient information to appropriately analyze symptoms of attack (e.g., source of attack, target of attack, and location of attack occurrence)?

8.8 To the extent the institution utilizes event correlation (EC) software to gather and analyze intrusion information to support root cause analysis and vulnerability assessment, is the software being utilized effectively? For example: Comments:
a. Are there a sufficient number of data feeds being correlated (e.g., IDS alerts, router and firewall logs, operating system Syslog messages, application audit trails, etc.) to effectively determine root cause analysis?
b. Does management have a sufficient understanding of the information being correlated (e.g., type and timing of events, rules governing activity over firewalls, routers, etc.) to rely on the effectiveness of the software to perform root cause analysis?
c. Does the EC software provide sufficient MIS to determine the appropriate actions necessary to address the vulnerability and mitigate the risk?

8.9 Are control processes over intrusion detection periodically reviewed by internal or external audit? Comments:

Overall Risk Level

<table>
<tr><td></td><td colspan="2" align="center">*Controls Scoring Criteria*</td><td></td></tr>
<tr><td>*Section #*</td><td colspan="2" align="center">*Green: Fully Implemented—(Low Risk)*
Yellow: Partially Implemented—(Moderate Risk)
Red: Not Implemented—(High Risk)</td><td align="center">*Rating*
and
Comments</td></tr>
</table>

Section #		
9	**Incident Response Management**	
	Evaluate the organization's development of an effective incident response management process:	
9.1	Has the institution established an effective incident response program to protect against reasonably foreseeable internal and external threats to the security of information systems and assets? Consider the following:	Comments:

a. The existence of policies that call for the delineation of roles, responsibilities, levels of authority, escalation, and incident reporting procedures.
   • Are responsibilities for identifying security incidents versus remediating actions clearly defined?[h]
   • Are responsibilities for determining whether a system or application should be removed from production clearly defined?

b. Incident handling processes to support the detection, analysis, and eradication of attacks. Are incident handling processes comprehensive? For example, do they include procedures for remediating incidents involving:
   • Remote users?
   • Subsidiaries and affiliates?
   • Service providers?
   • Turnkey solutions (e.g., Bloomberg, Reuters, etc.)?

c. Procedures to address security breaches involving customer information maintained by the bank or its service provider(s).

d. Processes to support the collection, analysis, and preservation of evidentiary data for postmortem reviews and potential prosecution.

e. Processes for filing appropriate internal and external reports.

| 9.2 | Do intrusion detection processes effectively identify incident type, frequency, magnitude, and severity of the problem? | Comments: |

a. Are incidents risk assessed to determine the

degree of urgency associated with the remedial action?

b. Are response priorities established in instances involving multiple security incidents?

9.3   In regards to security breaches involving customer information maintained by the bank or its service provider(s), as a matter of practice, does the institution:

    a. Identify the type of customer information affected?

    b. Notify its primary regulator regarding security breaches involving sensitive customer information?

    c. File suspicious activity reports (SARs) for incidents involving sensitive customer information?

    d. Take measures to contain and control the incident to prevent further unauthorized access to or use of customer information?

    e. Address and mitigate harm to individual customers? Steps taken should include:

- Flagging accounts: The institution should identify accounts of customers whose information has been compromised, monitor the accounts for unusual activity, and initiate appropriate controls to prevent unauthorized withdrawal or transfer of funds from customer accounts.

- Securing accounts: The institution should secure all accounts associated with the customer information that has been the subject of unauthorized access or use.

- Customer notice and assistance: The institution should notify each affected customer when it becomes aware of unauthorized access to customer information, unless the institution, after an appropriate investigation, reasonably concludes that misuse of the information is unlikely to occur.

Comments:

9.4   Are remedial actions to address the root causes of security problems timely and appropriate:

- Release and implementation of software patches?
- Reconfiguration of systems, firewalls, routers, etc.?
- Systems maintenance?
- Elimination of unnecessary services?

Comments:

Section #	Controls Scoring Criteria	Rating and Comments
	Green: Fully Implemented — (Low Risk) Yellow: Partially Implemented — (Moderate Risk) Red: Not Implemented — (High Risk)	

9.5	Are evidentiary data collection, analyses, and preservation processes comprehensive? For example, do they include: 　　a. Policies and procedures governing the collection of data, to protect its integrity and support root cause analysis? 　　b. Interviews of key personnel involved in the incident (e.g., systems administrators and users, service providers, etc.)? 　　c. Evaluation and analysis of trust relationships (e.g., between networks, operating systems, applications, and databases)? 　　d. Review, analysis, and documentation of all evidentiary data (e.g., systems hardware, software, storage media, journals, logs, and reports) to determine: 　　　　• How the incident (malicious or nonmalicious) occurred. 　　　　• When (e.g., time) the incident occurred. 　　　　• The specific networks, operating systems, applications, and databases affected by the incident. 　　e. Reports identifying the root cause of the incident and outlining strategies for containment, eradication, and restoration of service and remediation: 　　　　• Containment strategies may include isolation of compromised systems, or enhanced monitoring of intruder activities, search for additional compromised systems, collection and preservation of evidence, and communication with affected parties, primary regulator, and law enforcement. 　　　　• Eradication strategies may include installation of software patches, disabling certain services or ports to prevent reoccurrence or reinstallation of entire operating systems. 　　　　• Restoration strategies may include restoration of systems, programs, and data as well as coordination with the institution's disaster recovery plan. 　　　　• Recommendations for remediation.	Comments:

Overall Risk Level

10   **Patch Management**
                Evaluate the patch management process by consider-
                ing the following criteria:

10.1   Does the institution maintain an accurate and up-to-   Comments:
                date inventory of its information systems hardware
                and software, including specific applications and their
                location? At a minimum, does the inventory include:
                    a. A description of the systems hardware, main-
                    frame and midrange computers, operating
                    systems, and applications software (versions and
                    all patches installed) and storage devices?
                    b. All production servers, firewalls, network appli-
                    ances, routers, and other network infrastructure?

10.2   Are responsibilities for patch management clearly   Comments:
                defined? For example, has clear accountability been
                established for:
                    a. Prompt identification of software vulnerabilities
                    and relevant patches?
                    b. Timely implementation of patches?
                    c. Removing applications and systems from the
                    production environment?
                    d. Tracking of both implemented and rejected
                    patches?
                    e. Documentation of decisions to install or reject
                    specific patches?
                    f. Evaluation and testing of patches?
                    g. Independent reviews (e.g., audit, other) to
                    ensure that vulnerabilities have been appropri-
                    ately identified and patches installed?

10.3   Does the institution have an effective process in place   Comments:
                to monitor the availability of relevant software
                patches? Sources of patch information include:
                    a. Vendor Web sites;
                    b. Vendor patch alert e-mail list subscriptions;
                    c. Third-party security vendor Web sites and e-mail
                    alert services;
                    d. Third-party subscription or periodic vulnerability
                    scanning and reporting services;
                    e. Third-party public service security Web sites and
                    e-mail alert services (e.g.,
                    http://icat.nist.gov/icat.cfm, www.mitre.org, www.
                    cert.org); and
                    f. Internet discussion newsgroups related to patch
                    management.

Section #	*Controls Scoring Criteria* *Green: Fully Implemented—(Low Risk)* *Yellow: Partially Implemented—(Moderate Risk)* *Red: Not Implemented—(High Risk)*	*Rating and Comments*

10.4	Has a comprehensive impact analysis of the application of the patch been performed on the institution's information systems and business environment? For example, does the impact analysis include the following:
	  a. Technical evaluation: Assesses whether the patch will correct the problem affecting all the application services and features used by the institution.
	  b. Business impact assessment: Determines if applying the patch (or not applying the patch) will impact business processes, and the appropriate time for patch installation (i.e., immediately, after hours, or over the weekend).
	  c. Security evaluation: Determines whether there are security implications that were not identified during the technical evaluation.[i]
		Comments:

10.5	Are patches and other forms of remediation tested in a quality assurance environment before they are introduced into production to ensure that they will function as expected and be compatible with other applications and systems?	Comments:
10.6	In instances where multiple patches are required, are controls in place to ensure that patches are installed in the proper order and do not cause additional problems?	Comments:
10.7	Does management maintain the original software (e.g., CD-ROM, tape, floppy disk) and all subsequent patches to the production environment to minimize any additional vulnerabilities or disruption in service that may result from the reinstallation process?	Comments:
10.8	Are systems and software comprehensively tested after being patched or reconfigured to ensure that new vulnerabilities are not being introduced (including vulnerabilities previously corrected)?	Comments:

---

[a] For example, institutions should have the ability to selectively scan their networks for specific new viruses or malicious code versus having to scan the entire network every time for all potential vulnerabilities, which would be costly and inefficient.

b   Software with "packet-sniffing" functionality can analyze the characteristics of data packets transmitted via the Internet (e.g., size of the data packet, protocols, destination of IP addresses, etc.) to determine unauthorized access to the network or malicious executables that may infect the network. Although often found within intrusion detection software, institutions that use vulnerability assessment software with packet-sniffing functionality can be more proactive in analyzing the data to restrict traffic on the network and prevent these incidents from occurring in the future.

c   Note that stand-alone PCs are not considered active devices on the network.

d   Independent diagnostic testing of a proxy system is generally not effective. By its nature, proxy testing does not test the operational systems policies and procedures or its integration with other systems.

e   This is the preferred method because it simulates the profile of a real hacker.

f   Network-based versus host-based systems: In a network-based intrusion detection system (NIDS), the individual packets flowing through a network are analyzed. The NIDS can detect malicious packets overlooked by a firewall's simplistic filtering rules. In a host-based system, the intrusion detection system (IDS) examines the activity on each individual computer or host.

g   An emerging business practice at some sophisticated institutions may include the use of HoneyPots and HoneyNets. A HoneyPot is an Internet-attached server that acts as a decoy, luring in potential hackers in order to study their activities and monitor how they are able to break into a system. HoneyPots are designed to mimic systems that an intruder would like to break into but limit the intruder from having access to an entire network. HoneyNets are essentially a network of HoneyPots.

h   An emerging business practice among large, complex institutions involves identification of security incidents by a centralized security function, with responsibility for remediating incidents left within the business lines.

i   As an example, even though there may be no performance benefit to applying a patch, there may be security benefits.

Appendix G

Acronym List

ACF	Access control facility
ADS	Anomaly detection system
AI	Artificial intelligence
AICPA	American Institute of Certified Public Accountants
AIS	Artificial immune system
ANN	Artificial neural network
ASP	Application service provider
AUP	Acceptable use policy
AXML	Annotated eXtensible Markup Language
B2B	Business to business
B2C	Business to consumer
BIA	Business impact assessment
CAM	Content addressable memories
CEO	Chief executive officer
CERIAS	The Center for Education and Research in Information Assurance and Security
CERT	Computer emergency response team
CERT/CC	The CERT® Coordination Center of Carnegie Mellon University's Software Engineering Institute
CIFD	Computational immunology for fraud detection
CIP	Critical infrastructure plan

CIRT	Computer incident response team
CLF	Common log format
COTS	Commercial off-the-shelf software
CPU	Central processing unit
CSI	Computer Security Institute
CTRRF	Controls testing residual risk form
DBMS	Database management system
DCID	The Director of Central Intelligence Directive
DDos	Distributed denial-of-service
DTD	Document type definition
ECPA	Electronic Commerce Protection Act
FBI	The Federal Bureau of Investigation
FFIEC	Federal Financial Institution Examination Counsel
FISMA	The Federal Information Security Management Act
FOIA	Freedom of Information Act
FSTC	Financial Services Technology Consortium
FTP	File Transfer Protocol
HIDS	Host-based intrusion detection systems
HTML	Hypertext Markup Language
HTTP	Hypertext Transfer Protocol
ICF	Insider computer fraud
ICFTA	Insider computer fraud threat assessment
IDS	Intrusion detection system
IM	Instant messaging
INTEL	Intelligence
IPF	Intellectual property rights
IPS	Intrusion prevention system
IRC	Internet Relay Chat
ISO	International Organization for Standardization
JRCM	Journaling risk/controls matrix
KFI	Key fraud indicator
KFM	Key fraud metric
KFS	Key fraud signature
KFSAR	Key fraud signature association rules

LAN	Local area network
MIS	Management information system
NAM	Neural associative memory
NIDS	Network intrusion detection system
NISPOM	National Industrial Security Program Operating Manual
NRR	Net residual risk
NSA	National Security Agency
NTAC	The Secret Service National Threat Assessment Center
OASIS	Organization for the Advancement of Structured Information Standards
OSI	Open system interconnection
PBX	Private branch eXchange
PC	Personal computer
PCAOB	The Public Company Accounting Oversight Board
Pen	Penetration
RFC	Request for comments
SA	System administrator
SAML	Security Assertion Markup Language
SGML	Standard Generalized Markup Language
SMTP	Simple Mail Transfer Protocol
SOA	Service Oriented Architecture
SOAP	Simple Object Access Protocol
SOM	Self-organizing map
SOX	The Sarbanes–Oxley Act
SQL	Software Query Language injection
SSL	Secure Sockets Layer
SSO	Single sign-on
TCP	Transmission Control Protocol
TDND	Total degree of novelty detected
TLS	Transport Layer Security
UDP	User Datagram Protocol
UID	User identification
USSS	The United States Secret Service
UUP	Unacceptable use policy

VA	Vulnerability assessment
W3C	World Wide Web Consortium
WSDL	Web Services Description Language
WS-I	Web Services Interoperability Organization
XACL	eXtensible Access Control Language
XKMS	eXtensible Markup Language Key Management Specifications
XML	eXtensible Markup Language

Appendix H

Glossary

Anomaly

A rule or practice that is different from what is normal or usual, and which is therefore unsatisfactory.

Artificial intelligence

A discipline that attempts to mimic the cognitive and symbolic skills of humans using digital computers.

Artificial neural system

Another term for neural network, which distinguishes between biological and nonbiological neural systems.

Associative memory

A memory system that stores information by associating or correlating it with other stored information.

Attack

An attempt to bypass security controls on a computer. The attack may alter, release, or deny data. Whether an attack will succeed depends on the vulnerability of the computer system and the effectiveness of existing countermeasures.

Authorization controls

Ensuring all data is authorized before entering the application system. Restricts data entry terminals to authorized users for authorized purposes. Master files and exception reporting help ensure all data processed are authorized.

Autoassociative memory

An associative memory in which a stored data item is associated or correlated with itself.

Autoassociative neural network A network that aims to reproduce, at the output layer, the pattern given as input. This must be done through a hidden layer that contains fewer units than the input layer. Autoassociative neural networks are often used to compress data or characterize data so that novelty detection may be carried out.

Availability The system contains information or provides services that must be available on a timely basis to meet mission requirements or to avoid substantial losses.

Batch totals How many records are being processed.

Behavior of data The changes in the data or metadata values or characteristics of key fraud indicators (KFIs).

Benford's law Developed by Frank Benford in the 1920s. It predicts the occurrence of digits in data. Benford's law concludes that the first digit in a large population of transactions (10,000 plus) will most often be a 1. Less frequently will the first digit be a 2, even less frequently a 3. Benford calculated the occurrence of each numeral appearing as the first digit and found that it decreased inversely with its value.

Computer fraud Any defalcation or embezzlement accomplished by tampering with computer programs, data files, operations, equipment, or media, and resulting in losses sustained by the organization whose computer system was manipulated.

The following circumstances involve computer fraud:

- Unauthorized input or alteration of input
- Destruction or suppression or misappropriation of output from a computer process
- Alteration of computerized data
- Alteration or misuse of programs

Confidentiality The system contains information that requires protection from unauthorized disclosure.

Content addressable memory One that has the trait of content addressability.

Control totals A manually calculated figure, such as the number of hours worked.

Data compression
A process by which data of a certain size (number of bits) is reduced to a fewer number of bits. Ideally, the important information encoded by the original data will still be recoverable from the compressed version.

Data validation
Ensuring that training data contains the information required to perform a certain task.

Defense in Depth
Is a twofold approach to securing an information technology (IT) system: layering security controls within a given IT asset and among assets, and ensuring appropriate robustness of the solution as determined by the relative strength of the security controls and the confidence that the controls are implemented correctly, are effective in their application, and will perform as intended. This combination produces layers of technical and nontechnical controls that ensure the confidentiality, integrity, and availability of the information and IT system resources.

Director of Central Intelligence Directive (DCID) 6/3
The DCID 6/3 applies to all organizations, including U.S. government and commercial contractors, that process, store, or communicate intelligence information. All information systems in organizations with access to intelligence information must be classified a High Confidentiality Level-of-Concern. The DCID 6/3 guidelines mandate monitoring capabilities for all information systems, with specific auditing and reporting requirements. The level of auditing depends on the protection level for a given site or project.

Distributed memory
A memory system that stores information throughout the system rather than in a single identifiable address.

Distributed processing
A term often used to refer to processing with neural networks, may also be used to reference standard parallel computer systems.

DMZ
Abbreviation for "demilitarized zone." A computer or small subnetwork that sits between a trusted internal network, such as a corporate private local

	area network (LAN), and an untrusted external network, such as the public Internet.
Edit and validation checks	Reasonableness: Contents of a data element fall within predetermined limits. Dependency: Contents of two or more data fields are logically related. Existence: Only valid codes are entered into the system. Mathematical accuracy: Verifies calculations, such as on an invoice. Range check: Verifies whether a number falls within a predefined set of numbers. Check digit: Controls accuracy of input of reference numbers. Document reconciliation: Verifies the accuracy of transaction's numeric data entry. Relationship or prior data matching: Determines whether incorrect but valid reference number has been entered into system for master record update, or whether a data field update is possibly in error.
Encryption	(1) A data security technique used to protect information from unauthorized inspection or alteration. Information is encoded so that it appears as a meaningless string of letters and symbols during delivery or transmission. Upon receipt, the information is decoded using an encryption key. (2) The conversion of information into a code or cipher.
Excitatory (synapse)	A synapse that, when stimulated by an input signal, causes an increased activation in its attached neurode.
Expert system	A system specifically designed to display a high degree of knowledge about a specific, limited subject. Usually these are capable of making inferences or decisions based on that knowledge and are normally implemented as a collection of if–then or production rules.
Exploit	A technique or code that uses a vulnerability to provide system access to the attacker.
False negative	Occurs when an actual intrusive action has occurred but the system allows it to pass as nonintrusive behavior.

False positive	Occurs when the system classifies an action as anomalous (a possible intrusion) when it is legitimate.
Firewall	A hardware or software link in a network that relays only data packets clearly intended and authorized to reach the other side.
Hacker	An individual who attempts to break into a computer without authorization.
Heteroassociative memory	An associative memory in that stored data items are associated or correlated with other, different data items.
HoneyPots/HoneyNets	A HoneyPot is an Internet-attached server that acts as a decoy, luring in potential hackers in order to study their activities and monitor how they are able to break into a system. HoneyPots are designed to mimic systems that an intruder would like to break into but limit the intruder from having access to an entire network. HoneyNets are essentially a network of HoneyPots.
Input fraud	Someone who is able to enter misleading information into a computer system without being detected, and the system carries out transactions which are fraudulent.
Input vector	The pattern presented to the input neurodes of a network.
Insider	From a financial institution definition, an insider is intended to mean an institution-affiliated party, such as an officer, director, employee, agent, consultant, or any other person who participates in the affairs of a financial institution.
Insider computer fraud (ICF)	A current or former employee or contractor who intentionally exceeded or misused an authorized level of access to networks, systems, or data in a manner that targeted a specific individual or affected the security of the organization's data, systems, or operations.
Integrity	The system contains information that must be protected from unauthorized, unanticipated, or unintentional modification.

Internal fraud

Losses due to acts of a type intended to defraud, misappropriate property, or circumvent regulations, the law, or company policy.

Intrusion detection system (IDS), also host-based IDS (HIDS) and network IDS (NIDS)

Software/hardware that detects and logs inappropriate, incorrect, or anomalous activity. IDSs are typically characterized based on the source of the data they monitor: host or network. A host-based IDS (HIDS) uses system log files and other electronic audit data to identify suspicious activity. A network IDS (NIDS) uses a sensor to monitor packets on the network to which it is attached.

Intrusion prevention system (IPS)

These are systems that provide a proactive defense mechanism that is designed to detect malicious packets within normal network traffic and block the offending traffic automatically before creating any damage. Uses of IPS include Host IPS (HIPS), which relies on agents installed directly on the system being protected. It binds closely with the operating system kernel and services, monitoring and intercepting system calls to the kernel or application programming interfaces (APIs) in order to prevent attacks as well as log them. Another use of IPS includes the network IPS (NIPS) that combines the features of a standard intrusion detection system (IDS), an IPS, and a firewall, and is sometimes known as an inline IDS or gateway IDS (GIDS).

Journaling

The recording of selected events as they occur within a system, referred to as journaling or logging, provides a basis for identifying and tracing events involved in the processing of data and in the use of computer resources.

Key fraud indicator (KFI)

The data or metadata attributes or critical data used within an application or system to detect suspicious insider misuse and computer fraud.

Key fraud metric (KFM)

Financial ratios used to detect potential suspicious or fraudulent activities based on the financial statements or an organization.

Key fraud signature (KFS)	The association rules for key fraud indicator (KFI) and key fraud metric (KFM) for the detection of insider computer fraud (ICF).
Learning	Learning, in a statistical sense, refers to any process requiring the use of data for tuning a set of parameters which describe a statistical model of that data. It does not imply any human qualities such as understanding, consciousness, or intelligence associated with our learning abilities.
Learning law	A rule for updating the synaptic weights of a neural network during training.
Malicious code, malicious logic, malware	Hardware, software, or firmware that is intentionally included or inserted in a system for a harmful purpose.
Multilayer perceptron (MLP)	A neural network with distinct input, hidden, and output layers.
Neural network	A type of data processing system whose physical architecture is inspired by the structure of biological neural systems. One of many networks composed of neurons, dendrites, axons, synapses, and other biological structures making up the neural systems of living beings.
Neurode	The element of an artificial neural network that corresponds to the neuron of biological networks; also known as processing element.
Neuron	A biological neural cell.
Node	An individual processor and associated computing and memory chips in a parallel computer. A functional grouping of neurodes that act as a single unit within one layer of a network.
Novelty detection	Deciding whether a given input pattern is representative of the single category of data with which the neural network was trained. Useful in condition monitoring applications where the only available data describes the correct operation of the system and any deviation from that behavior should be detected.
Operational risk	According to the Basel Accord, operational risk is the risk of direct or indirect loss resulting

from inadequate or failed internal processes, people, and systems or from external events.

Output fraud   The last stages of a system are compromised so that misleading printouts (transaction records, vouchers, printed checks, etc.) are created.

Pattern   Any combination of a set of variables.

Penetration test   The process of using approved, qualified personnel to conduct real-world attacks against a system so as to identify and correct security weaknesses before they are discovered and exploited by others.

Preprocessing   The process of preparing new data for presentation to a neural network.

Protected computer   A protected computer under this section includes the following: A computer that is used exclusively by a financial institution or the U.S. government; any computer the use of which affects a computer used by a financial institution or the federal government; a computer that is used in interstate or foreign commerce or communication.

Protocol   A format for transmitting data between devices.

Regulation "O"   Preferential lending by a bank to executive officers, directors, and principal shareholders of another bank when there is a correspondent account relationship between the banks, and the opening of a correspondent account relationship between banks when there is a preferential extension of credit by one of the banks to an executive officer, director, or principal shareholder of the other bank.

Risk assessment   A process used to identify and evaluate risks and their potential effect.

Router   A hardware device that connects two or more networks and routes incoming data packets to the appropriate network.

Security event   An event that compromises the confidentiality, integrity, availability, or accountability of an information system.

Server A computer or other device that manages a network service. An example is a print server, a device that manages network printing.

Service Oriented Architecture (SOA) A collection of services that communicate with each other and can involve either simple data passing or it could involve two or more services coordinating some activity.

Sniffing The passive interception of data transmissions.

SOAP SOAP is an eXtensible Markup Language (XML)-based protocol for document-based messaging and remote procedure calls across distributing computing environments. SOAP-based messages are transport independent: designed for use over Hypertext Transfer Protocol (HTTP), SOAP also can be used with other transport mechanisms, such as the Simple Mail Transfer Protocol (SMTP), that may be required when traversing corporate firewalls.

Social engineering Obtaining information from individuals by trickery.

Suspicious activity report (SAR) Reports required by the Bank Secrecy Act to be filed when a financial institution identifies or suspects fraudulent activity.

Synapse In biology, the junction between an axon collateral and a dendrite. In neural networks, the junction at an interconnect's end that joins the output of one neurode (or a signal from the environment) to the input of another neurode.

SYSLOG A comprehensive logging system used to manage information generated by the kernel and system utilities. Allows messages to be sorted by their sources and importance, and then to be routed to a variety of destinations.

Taxonomy A division into order groups or categories.

Topology A description of any kind of locality in terms of its physical layout. In the context of communication networks, a topology describes pictorially the configuration or arrangement of a network, including its nodes and connecting communication lines.

Training   The process of allowing a neural network to learn.

Training set   A collection of data typical of that which a neural network will see in operation, and that is used to train the network.

Trojan horse   Malicious code that is hidden in software that has an apparently beneficial or harmless use.

Unsupervised learning   Learning that occurs without the system being provided with the correct answers. Also called "unsupervised training."

Vector   A quantity that consists of a magnitude and a direction. A vector is usually represented by an arrow with its tail at the origin of the coordinate system. The length of the arrow represents the magnitude of the vector's direction. Vectors are often broken down into their component magnitudes along each of the coordinate system axes. This is commonly expressed as a column or row matrix where each matrix element is the magnitude along one of these axes.

Virus   Malicious code that replicates itself within a computer.

Vulnerability   A flaw that allows someone to operate a computer system with authorization in excess of that which the system owner specifically granted him or her.

Weights   Connections of varying strength which carry activation information between network units.

Worm   Malicious code that infects computers across a network without user intervention. Typically, a worm is a program that scans a system or an entire network for available, unused space in which to run. Worms tend to tie up all computing resources in a system or on a network and effectively shut it down.

XML   EXtensible Markup Language (XML) provides a context by which applications can send and receive messages and documents that describe the nature of their own content in machine-readable form.

Contributors

Jim Nelms, CISSP
   THE WORLD BANK TREASURY
   WASHINGTON, DC

Tom Kellermann, MA, CISM
   CORE SECURITY TECHNOLOGIES
   BOSTON, MASSACHUSETTS

Index

Italicized page numbers indicate tables and figures.

A

"A Framework for Understanding and Predicting Insider Attacks," 12–14, 22
Acceptable use policy (AUP), 10, 21, 182
Access; *see also* Penetration (Pen) testing
  to applications, 104
  controls, 55, 100, 186
  log-on and log-off activity, 316
  restriction, 56
  roles pattern (RBAC) for, 98
Access Control Facility 2 (ACF2), 328–329
Access Controls Testing Residual Risk Form, 49
Accountability, 29, 98, 324
Accounting forensics, 247–248
Adaptive filter networks, 355
Address screening routers, 120
AI, *see* Artificial intelligence (AI)
American Institute of Certified Public Accountants (AICPA), 181
Annotated eXtensible Markup Language (AXML), 129
Anomaly detection, 100
  false positives, 115
  using neural networks, 360–361, 362–363
Anomaly detection system (ADS), 352
  problems with, 362
Application and Code Review
  penetration test, 82, 98
Application and Information Access Controls, 56

Application control optimizers, *see* Optimizers
Application Control Point Ratings Matrix, 63
  for Defense in Depth Security Efficiency Calculation, 64–65
Application Criticality Matrix, 37, 39
Application defect taxonomy, 188, 199
Application gateway, 104
Application security, 182–183
  continuous monitoring, 178
  control types, 55
  controls, 37, 54–57
  and insider computer fraud (ICF), 186–187, 188
  net residual risk, 139–140
  optimizer, 65, 68, 71
  overview, 136
  policy, 37–40
  risk assessment process, 138–140
  software engineering considerations, 140, 176–178
  source code analyzers, 136
  standardization of control processes, 243
  standards, 136–137
Application service provider (ASP), 179
Applications; *see also* Application security
  access, 104
  criticality factors, 41, 43
  development, 95–96
  journaling, 245
  misuse of features, 233
  risk weightings, 41, 43, *44*
Applications residual risk, 63
  forms, 49, 50, 51

457

Printed in the United States
by Baker & Taylor Publisher Services